Old Bill's tales of the Railw

Forty Nine Years Of

Working for the British Transport Police

1971 – 2020

By

Bill Rogerson MBE

First published in 2021

By

Bostin Books
www.bostinbooks.co.uk

DEDICATIONS

Dedicated to Shirley my wife, for her patience, understanding and proofreading the book for me.

Also, to all my police colleagues both serving and retired in the British Transport police and the provincial forces whom I worked alongside.

Finally, not forgetting my colleagues in the railway industry, whom I worked alongside and gave me valuable assistance in dealing with incidents.

CONTENTS

3

INTRODUCTION

A different book to the others

Hello there. I know what you must be thinking, *'Not another book of old Copper's tales'*. Well yes you are right, but you must have had a good reason to pick up the book and I thank you for doing that. This is, hopefully, one that is a little bit different from the others.

I never intended to write a book about my police career. A few years ago, whilst I was working in the Magistrates' Court at Holyhead, during a break of the proceedings, I spoke of my activities in the police and a defendant described me as the, *'Fred Dibnah of the courts'*. I have delivered after dinner speeches and one or two people have asked if I have written down my memoirs. One lady in her summing up stated that, *'I was a great and enthusiastic raconteur'*.

However, it wasn't until 2015 that I thought seriously about putting pen to paper. Early in 2015 I was approached by Michael Layton QPM a former police officer himself, with the British Transport Police and the West Midlands Police, to co-write a book with him on the History of the British Transport Police Dog Section, *'Police Dog Heroes'*, and twelve months later, *'The Hooligans are Still Among us'*, a book regarding football hooliganism both on and off the railways. It was after co-writing these two books and critically proof-reading others that I actually got the writing bug to compile my memoirs.

Having been stationed at Birmingham, Coventry, Leicester, Heysham Harbour, Crewe, Holyhead and Bangor I have accumulated a lot of material.

I am one of the few officers who have actually worked in a majority of the jurisdictions that were policed by the British Transport Police - The British Railways, The British Transport Docks Board, The Harbours and Shipping Division, The British Waterways (Canals), the London Underground and Southern Ireland.

I was born into a railway family at the Victoria Hospital, Morecambe, due to the fact that my mother was there at the time. At the time of my birth my father was a fire-fighter with the Lancashire Fire Brigade based in Morecambe. My paternal grandfather was an engine driver at Carnforth and my paternal grandmother worked in the refreshment room on Carnforth railway station *('Brief Encounter' fame)*. I had several other relatives working on the railway in the area, none of whom were in the British Transport Police.

My father nearly joined the British Transport Commission Police at Carnforth, after his National Service, in which he served in the Military Police in Germany. On returning he secured a position as a clerk in the railway telegraph office, which was next to the police office on Carnforth station. At this time the police post was supervised from Barrow in Furness and the District Inspector was a gentleman by the name of Harold Wickens.

He tried to persuade my father to join the British Transport Commission Police, as he was toying with the idea of continuing his police career or looking for one in the fire service. He was torn between the two.

Mr. Wickens tossed a coin, heads, father would join the Police and tails he would join the Fire Brigade. It landed on tails, so my father enjoyed a career in the Fire Brigade. During his career with the Fire Brigade he got to know quite a number of British Transport Police Officers in the locality.

If the coin had landed on heads my father would have in all probability joined the British Transport Commission Police and I might have pursued another career path.

Like most boys of my time, I wanted to be an engine driver, just like Granddad, but the writing was on the wall and a few years later I joined the British Transport Police in Birmingham.

Upon leaving school I took employment at a Builders Merchants in Morecambe. It was at this time that I became a volunteer at 'STEAMTOWN', Carnforth, a private railway museum. My career with the British Transport Police nearly didn't get off the ground. Whilst working at the Builders Merchants, one of my fellow volunteers, and a very great friend of mine, the late Graeme Brocken, who worked in the British Railways, London Midland Region, train planning office at Eversholt Street, London, managed to establish a sub-branch of the British Railways owned Collectors Corner, London, at 'STEAMTOWN'. Supplies of old railway relics were sent up to Carnforth. Around this time the old railway station at Heysham Harbour closed and everything apart from the old signs were transferred to the new station.

Graeme purchased all the remaining signs from the old station for the princely sum of £2.50 to sell them in the Collectors Corner sub–branch. A receipt and letter of authority were duly obtained. I was asked if I could purchase a hacksaw, screwdrivers and some cans of WD40 from where I worked, which I did at cost price. Off we went to remove the signs. At this time the British Transport Police office was still operational on the old station, due to the fact their new accommodation was not ready.

Armed with our documents of authority and hardware, Graeme went to the police office and showed the officer on duty the appropriate paperwork and we set to removing the signs. Graeme, not thinking, removed the two British Transport Police signs from the doors. As we were driving off the station a couple of BTP CID officers who Graeme knew very well, having previously worked in the Booking Office at Heysham Harbour, were walking up the ramp and he offered them in gest, the two BTP signs for five pounds, looking to double his money. They just laughed at him.

A few days later I received a telephone call from Graeme stating that Inspector George Smith-Leach at Heysham Harbour, wanted to see him, and to bring the signs back. I went up to the police office with him but was told to stay outside. I could see the shadow of Inspector Smith-Leach, in his office shaking his finger at Graeme who at this time had his head bowed. He came out all red faced and said that we should not have taken the signs as the office was still operational. We spent the next few minutes putting them back.

CHAPTER 1

KEEPING IT IN THE FAMILY

A senior police officer in the family and a murder in the family

During my years of growing up in Hest Bank, near Morecambe, I got to know a couple of the British Transport Police officers from the area, through my train spotting activities, so, I did know quite a lot about the force, unlike a lot of other people who thought they were part of the local police or a security organisation.

I came from a virtually law-abiding family. However, records show that a family member, in 1665, along with three others was tried at Appleby, Westmorland, before four of His Majesty's Justices of the Peace for the County, *'for killing one deare within the forest of Mallerstang belonging to the Right Honourable Ann Countess Dowager of Dorsett, Pembroke and Montgomerye'.* Upon their confession, *'Every one of them to forfeit for the said offence the sume of twenty pounds to be levied by way of distraint upon the goods and chattels of every one of the said persons'.* (The spellings are correct and have been taken from the court records).

On a date, not given, in the records in 1670, another family member was presented to the Quarter Sessions at Kirkby Stephen along with another person for driving sheep on the Lord's Day, an offence, Contrary to the Act of Charles 1 which provided *'that no carrier with any horse or horses, nor wain-man with any wain or wains, nor drovers with any cattle or sheep shall travel upon the Lord's Day, commonly called Sunday under a penalty of 20s for every such offence'.* I presume he was fined the 20s.

My father found himself in trouble with Her Majesty's Customs and Excise when he came back from Jersey with a few extra duty-free cigars. A few years later he was seen by police motor cyclist to go through a red traffic light at a set of road works.

A few years ago, whilst I was in Vancouver, Canada, I met up with a cousin of mine. Whilst we were having dinner, just as I was enjoying a pint, he admitted to being involved in the Great Train Robbery. He quickly clarified the statement in that that he was a young bank clerk working in Leicester and that he had bundled up a quantity of disused notes for destruction, signing the wrappers. These notes were part of the haul from the train. He subsequently had to give a statement to the police as part of the investigation.

Having relatives working on the railway I was told in no uncertain terms not to get into trouble with the British Transport Police or else!! It didn't matter if I committed a murder in the street, as long as it was not on the railway.

Ironically, my first real encounter with a police officer was with Detective Sergeant George Hart of the British Transport Commission Police based at Carnforth. When I was attending the Secondary Modern School in Carnforth, I used to travel on a double-decker bus, which was usually provided by the Morecambe and Heysham Corporation Transport or Ribble Motor Services.

The Corporation bus was usually an old half - cab one with an open rear entrance. As you boarded the bus there were two, three-seater side seats opposite each other. Myself and my mates used to sit on these.

Most days a smartly dressed gentleman would join the bus about five stops after us, for the five-minute journey to Carnforth. We thought that he was a top manager at Carnforth railway station or the manager of a local bank. One day I discovered who he really was. Just after this gentleman joined the bus, he sat in front of us, and I hit the middle seat of where I was sitting with the flat of my hand and an almighty cloud of dust erupted from the seat and rose up into the air just like a nuclear cloud and came down again, just and so missing the gentleman. At this point he rose from his seat and produced his warrant card and introduced himself as Detective Sergeant Hart of the British Transport Police, from Carnforth. I went white and froze with fear. Certain words that young boys should not really know suddenly came into my mind. I lived in fear for the next few weeks just in case he told my father, whom I discovered he knew. Luckily, he gave me a break.

I did have a Great Aunt, Daisy Mason, on my maternal Grandmother's side, who served in the Metropolitan Police and a fourth Cousin Mary Jane Rogerson, who was brutally murdered by a Doctor.

AUNT DAISY

Daisy Birkett Mason was my Great, Great Aunt. Her father was JAMES WILLIAM MASON (who was the brother of my maternal Grandmother's father, THOMAS MASON). She was born on the 24 July 1916, in Strickland Roger, 3 miles, North West of Kendal Westmorland.

My maternal Grandmother, spoke of her cousin DAISY BIRKETT MASON, as serving in the Metropolitan Police as a senior officer, but did not elaborate. The only known facts about the early life of DAISY BIRKETT MASON is that she received an elementary education and was a clerk.

Wanting to find out a bit more about her I contacted the Metropolitan Police in January 2012 and was furnished with the following details from her Record Card.

On the 17, November 1941 she joined the Metropolitan Police and was posted to 'A' Division as a Woman Police Constable. Her warrant number was 14/499. Her height was 5'.4 ½". She received £2 per week wages.

On the 13 October 1944 she received a Commendation for 'Ability and devotion to duty in case of false particulars'.

On the 21 October 1946 she was posted to 'H' Division.

On the 15 March 1948 she became a Temporary Detective Constable still in 'H' Division.

On the 22 April 1949 she was confirmed as a Detective Constable still in 'H' Division.

On the 05 April 1951 she was on a Class 3 driving course 227, which she passed. Being 5'4 ½" she had to have two cushions on the driving seat to see over the steering wheel.

On the 13, August 1951 she was promoted to Woman Police Sergeant (CID) and posted to 'J' Division.

On the 6 July 1959 she was promoted to Detective Inspector 'C' Division (This promotion was shown in General Orders 03 July 1959.)

She attended a Junior Course at the Police College between 06 July and 11 December 1959 (Shown in General Orders 23 June 1959).

On the 20 March 1963 she received the Police Long Service and Good Conduct Medal.

On the 23 November 1964 she was promoted to Detective Chief Inspector (shown on General Orders 20 November 1964) and posted to COC1 at the Old Scotland Yard. In 1968 she transferred to the New Scotland Yard. She was the first ever female Detective Chief Inspector in the Metropolitan Police.

On the 20 September 1971 she was still in COC1 working on the Department of Health and Social Security cases.

She finally retired from the Metropolitan Police on the 16 November 1971, aged 55, with 30 years' service.

During her time with the Metropolitan Police she was part of a squad that dealt with the notorious Richardson's, the nude murders and she also conducted enquiries into the Moors Murders.

Her certificate of conduct was Exemplary.

I wanted to find out a bit more information about Aunt Daisy, so I wrote to the Metropolitan Police's Pensioner Magazine '**London Police Pensioner**' and following publication of my letter in the March 2012 edition I was contacted by a number of retired officers, who all had one thing in common to say about her, that she was a lovely lady, was nobody's fool and could stand her ground in what was predominantly an all-male environment in the CID.

One officer knew her as a Detective Constable at Hackney 'JD' which later became 'GH' Division. He stated that she was very quiet and lived in Ede Section House.

A former Metropolitan Police Officer and who subsequently became a senior officer in a number of provincial forces wrote to me as follows:

'I joined the Metropolitan Police in 1949, and on being posted to 'E' Division (Bow Street), was provided with accommodation in MacNaughton House, Tavistock Street, London. At that time Daisy Mason, then a Detective Sergeant, was also a resident. In 1953 another lady (who became my wife) joined the police and became a resident at MacNaughton House.

When my wife joined in early 1953, Chief Superintendent Elizabeth Bather, who had been a senior officer in the WAAF during the war, was responsible for the women's police department and she had just commenced the transition of the role of women officers from being solely involved in problems involving women and children into the much wider involvement in general policing that we know today.

It was from talking to Daisy Mason that my wife realised that there were increasing opportunities for women to become members of the CID and in fact your great aunt was extremely helpful in giving advice and encouragement to her. Despite the age and rank difference, they became friends and to this day my wife has very fond memories of the time she spent at MacNaughton House.

In her view, Daisy Mason was a role model for very many young policewomen in showing what women could aspire to, in what at that time, was a very male-orientated organisation.

After we married and started our family, my wife left the police, but I continued my career in the CID and although I did not have the privilege of working directly with your great aunt I do remember her well. I know that she was a talented and professional detective who worked on many high-profile cases and earned the respect of both male and female officers.

As a Detective Chief Inspector, she played a major part in the complex investigation and subsequent conviction of the Messina brothers who were running a huge prostitution empire in the West End of London.

I cannot be sure about this, but I believe she worked with Chief Superintendent John Du Rose in a lengthy enquiry which involved the murder of several prostitutes in the Shepherds Bush area. This was a case which generated a lot of publicity at the time, but which unfortunately did not result in an arrest.

I agree with what my wife has said about Daisy Mason – in her day she achieved a great deal and laid the foundations for the opportunities enjoyed by women officers today'.

Another retired officer wrote as follows: -

'Daisy Mason was a lovely lady and she was two offices down the corridor from me in COC1 department at New Scotland Yard.

Her birthday was the day after mine and for four consecutive years we had a drink to celebrate with our respective squads. I served with her in COC1 from 1967 until she retired in 1971.

She was a Detective Chief Inspector and shared a department with some great women detectives such as Mary Wedlake, Barbara Kelly, Shelia Acton, Morag McGibbon, Winnie Taylor and others.

After her retirement she was involved in a security company in partnership with her old friend Mary Wedlake. She was a great lady and I am pleased to be able to shed some information about her'

A retired Metropolitan Police senior officer wrote to me as follows:

'I was posted to West End Central police station in 1963 as a Detective Sergeant and one day was told that they were forming a Cheque Squad as they were having problems with cheques bouncing all-round the West End Clubs and I was to report with a couple of DCs to Detective Inspector Mason and work on the problem.

I had my leg pulled by some of the others who informed me that I was to work with 'Aunty Daisy', I didn't realise they were referring to a female as in those days nicknames were sometimes attached to male officers.

Duly reporting to her office on the third floor I was very surprised to find a very small and gentle looking lady, (everybody's Aunty) confronting us (that was a front, she was nobody's fool and no way soft) and she outlined our duties of going around the various clubs where these cheques had been bounced. Mostly good class Mayfair type clubs with their hostesses and covert gambling rooms.

She then gave us a lecture about the dangers of these types of premises and the temptations that befell young men, as she thought we might be open to these vices.

Mike, my companion and I tried to keep a straight face during this lecture because what she did not know then, was that we had both served in the West End for six years, Jerry was an ex Royal Marine and I had served in the army. So, we said nothing and left to sort out our first case.

I found her to be a pleasant person, and a competent Detective Officer who as I have said was nobody's fool, who could talk straight when needed, but who did have what we called a motherly streak for the young aides and used to worry about the wicked old world that they were working in.

I worked with her for 6 months before moving to Tottenham Court Road. I enjoyed that short time, but she never stopped being concerned about our exposure to the wicked, wicked ways of the West End.

A very nice lady and a good Detective officer who held her own in a strong male environment of those days.

That is how I remember your great aunt and I hope that it gives you some idea of what she was like in the job'.

Another retired Metropolitan Police officer wrote to me as follows.

'I did indeed know Daisy Mason but was unaware of her unusual middle name i.e. Birkett. This was when I was a young Aide to CID flitting from Tottenham Court Road police station to West End Central for duty.

I first met Daisy when she was a DI and was for a while at Tottenham Court Road police station. For what reason I cannot recall. I will not use police language but will say that a woman DI was very rare indeed at that time which was in 1959 or 1960. Although we obviously didn't share duties, we did have a friendship.

I thought she was a very nice person in fact after some celebration or other in the CID office I took her to the Blarney Club in Tottenham Court Road for a chat with friends, Irish people who frequented that club. I knew the alleged owner and somehow had managed to gain useful bits of info from time to time. I think Daisy and I listened to the band music for a while but didn't dance together.

On another occasion as we were very late leaving the station, she wanted to travel by Underground train home. I wouldn't have it and popped her on the rear seat of my Triumph motorcycle, no safety helmet for her and took her home, it seemed a long way somewhere in the west of London, I think. Anyway, after seeing her OK at the front door of her house I then went back to my quarters at Trenchard House, a Police Section House in Broadwick Street, Soho, and a single Policeman's accommodation building.

That's about all I can tell you. Daisy was eventually promoted to DCI and transferred to NSY; department unknown. I served for 30 years in the job, 19 of them at NSY but never saw Daisy again, she may have retired early. We were quite an age difference. I was born in 1935. Daisy was respected by all who knew her'.

Another officer who did not know her, kindly did some research and found that in 2002 she was residing in W13 8HN, (the Ealing area), and resided there until 2004.

An ex Detective Inspector has been very helpful with obtaining information for me.

He established that in 1980 she was a Senior Investigator with the Department of Health and Social Security and was awarded the MBE.

No doubt at some point in her career she would have come across officers from the British Transport Police and the London Underground Police.

MARY JANE ROGERSON

The other connection the family had with the police, was that a fourth cousin of mine, Mary Jane Rogerson on my father's side, was brutally murdered in Lancaster in September 1935. A murder which involved at least three police forces including two in Scotland.

The story is of the 'Savage Surgeon' Dr. Buck Ruxton, who murdered his common law wife Isabella and their Nursemaid Mary Jane Rogerson. This was one of the United Kingdom's most publicised murder cases of the 1930s, which gripped the nation at the time. The case is remembered now for the innovative forensic techniques employed in solving it. It was the first time that the two forensic departments of Glasgow and Edinburgh Universities had worked together. The murders were named the '*Jigsaw Killings*' by the world's media.

The police knew he was guilty: their problem was to prove that the skillfully dismembered remains they found were those of the two women. The result was one of the most sensational murder trials of the 20 century.

Ruxton's tragedy is mirrored in the Shakespearean story of Othello, the Moor of Venice, who in a jealous frenzy suffocates his wife Desdemona to death as she lies asleep, in the mistaken belief that she was unfaithful to him.

Bukhtyar Rustomji Hakim was born into a Parsee family of Indian French origin, in Bombay, on 21 March 1899. He had a respectable, middle class upbringing and received a thorough education. An apparently thoughtful and sensitive youth, he studied at Bombay University where, in 1922 he qualified as a Bachelor of Medicine and later as a Bachelor of Surgery. Great achievements were expected of the young doctor. He changed his name to Buck Ruxton by deed pole.

Isabella, who was born in Falkirk and legitimately married to a Dutchman, met Ruxton in Edinburgh whilst he was practising there. They both moved to Lancaster. Isabella was an outgoing lady who enjoyed socialising with Lancaster's elite and was a popular guest at functions. Emotionally unstable and obsessively jealous, Dr Ruxton became convinced that she was having an affair behind his back, though no evidence of infidelity was ever found.

In Isabella, he found a woman whom he believed to be a formidable catch – intelligent, charming, independent and British. To cap it all, she was sexually emancipated. From the outset, there was a sadomasochistic streak to their love. Violent quarrels, invariably initiated by Ruxton accusing Isabella of infidelity, would be followed by passionate lovemaking. There is no evidence that Isabella was unfaithful. Ruxton became increasingly jealous of Isabella's popularity.

Eventually, his jealousy overwhelmed him, and on Sunday 15 September 1935, he strangled Isabella with his bare hands. In order to prevent the housemaid, Mary Jane Rogerson, from discovering his crime before he could dispose of the body, he suffocated her too. Ruxton, then proceeded to use his medical knowledge and training to skillfully dismember and mutilate both bodies, in his bath, by removing all features that he thought would identify them. He then wrapped the seventy different pieces of the bodies up in a national Sunday newspaper, which had a local supplement advertising the Morecambe Carnival, and a carpet.

He then took the bodies to Moffat and Johnstonebridge in the Scottish Borders. He dumped a majority of the body parts in Gardenholm Linn, a ravine in Moffat. The other parts were dumped in Johnstonebridge. They were discovered on 29 September 1935 by a lady who was out walking. Enquiries were commenced by the Dumfriesshire Constabulary who brought in the Glasgow City Police to assist.

Enquiries eventually led them to Lancaster and the Lancaster Borough Police took over the investigation. Ruxton was arrested and denied the offences.

His trial, which started on 2 March 1936, lasted for eleven days and was marked by overwhelming forensic evidence against Ruxton. He was defended by Norman Birkett K.C. and Philip Kershaw K.C., who were instructed by Edwin Slinger, a solicitor in Lancaster; the prosecution counsel were Joseph Cooksey Jackson K.C., David Maxwell Fyfe K.C. and Hartley Shawcross.

The trial ended on 13 March 1936. The Judge in part of his summing up said 'There is too much to damn him, if there is an avenue, let him walk down it to freedom. But if there is not, he cannot'.

In little over an hour the jury had reached their verdict - 'Guilty' and Mr. Justice Singleton sentenced him to death.

A petition urging clemency for Ruxton, collected over ten thousand signatures. However, three judges at the Court of Criminal Appeal dismissed Ruxton's appeal on 27 April 1936 and he was hanged at Strangeways prison, Manchester, on the morning of 12 May 1936, by Albert Pierrepoint.

Following Ruxton's execution, a Sunday newspaper published his confession to the murders, recorded initially a day after his arrest. The newspaper was reported to have paid £3.000 (worth around £167.670.00 today) for the confession, from which parts of the costs of his defence were paid. This kind of deal between newspapers and people who had been accused of sensational crimes was fairly common at the time. And the name of the newspaper.... you've guessed it...... 'The News of the World'.

It is unclear why Ruxton chose the area around Moffat in Scotland to dispose of the victims, but he lived and had studied in Edinburgh, so he might well have visited the area and remembered it as a wild and lonely place.

The bathtub is still in use as a drinking trough for the horses of the Lancashire Constabulary's mounted division.

CHAPTER TWO

THE ORIGINS OF THE BRITISH TRANSPORT POLICE

On duty before the Metropolitan Police

The railway police have an immensely proud history and were actually on duty three years before the formation of the Metropolitan Police, on the 29 September 1829.

British Transport Police's policing of Britain's railways is considered to be one of the most sophisticated and successful railway policing models in the world. Working closely with the rail industry and community partners, they provide a specialist dedicated service protecting passengers, staff and the rail network from disruption and crime.

The history of policing goes back to the Roman times. Methods of combating crime have varied in success throughout the ages. In Tudor times the ineffectiveness of the hard-pressed magistrates and constables at that time meant that methods of combating crime were not always successful. In Tudor times Magistrates sat four times a year in courts of law called Quarter Sessions to deal with criminal business. At other times, they were constantly dealing with less serious offences. In addition to seeing that proclamations and laws were carried out, they were responsible for a wide range of things, from repair of bridges to licensing of alehouses. They were not paid; they were chosen from the gentry and as Justices of the Peace, they had great social status.

The origins of modern police forces came with the establishment of the Bow Street Runners the original 'thief takers' – and the Thames Marine Police in 1797, to combat piracy which was rife on the Thames. The Bow Street Runners were successful at combating crime as they covered only a small part of London. Even with the Metropolitan Police, success was slow in coming, as the public were against an organised form of policing. However, the Metropolitan Police proved themselves.

In 1825 the Stockton and Darlington Railway made its inaugural run and just a few months later, on the 30 June 1826, came the first recorded mention of a police establishment of one Superintendent, four Officers and a number of Constables or 'gate-keepers'. One of the Constables was PC Metcalfe and a crude oil painting of him in his red tunic can be seen at the National Railway Museum in York. The railway police were therefore on duty three years before the formation of the Metropolitan Police on the 29 September 1829.

Over the next fifty years the railway network expanded at an extraordinary rate using a huge workforce of men previously used to dig canals, or navigations – hence the word 'navvy'. People used to think of these navvies as being Irish, but the majority came from the English agricultural classes, while others came from Germany and France to gain work.

In the days before county constabulary, large gangs of navvies brought fear to genteel Victorian Britain, provoking Parliament to pass an Act on the 10 August 1838 requiring all railway companies to provide constables to patrol and protect the railway. Some railway police forces were quite large and had several hundred staff, although the Ffestiniog Railway in Wales employed just one officer.

The navvies kept the early railway policeman very busy. In 1839 a fight broke out during the construction of the Chester and Birkenhead Railway. It took four days and the threat of the military intervention to restore order. Across the country, gangs of navvies fought each other and there are many tales of murder and mayhem.

Early railway police also had a role in running the railways with a policeman based along every mile of the line to regulate the trains and operate each set of points. It has been suggested that the term 'point duty' for an officer on duty at a road junction, comes from the railway police. As does the railway term 'Bobby' for the Signaller. The word 'Bobby' is believed to come from Sir Robert Peel who founded the Metropolitan Police, whose first name was shortened to Bob and the policemen were known as 'Bobbies'.

When the trains first started running, people were extremely nervous of this new 'Iron Horse' and some nervous travellers travelling from London to York even made out their wills on Kings Cross Station.

Another first for the railways came in 1845 when John Tawell became the first person to be arrested with the help of Information Technology (IT). Mr. Tawell had murdered a former servant at Slough and escaped aboard a London bound train. A message was sent to Paddington on the newly installed telegraph and Sergeant William Williams of the Great Western Railway Police met and arrested him off the train.

In the early 1900s many railway forces were reorganised. The North Eastern Railway Police were the first police force in the United Kingdom to use police dogs in 1909. Their Chief Constable, Captain Horwood went on to be the Commissioner of the Metropolitan Police.

With the outbreak of the First World War many railway policemen responded to the call to arms. The Midland Railway Police lost fifty six per cent of its staff to the military. To replace them, paid Special Constables and women were taken on, making railway police one of the first forces to recruit women.

After the war, returning officers to all forces found their wages cut and conditions worsened, leading to the creation of the Police Federation and Britain's only police strike in 1919. Railway Police also went on strike in support of their colleagues from other forces.

In 1921 the Railways Act amalgamated hundreds of railway, dock, and harbour companies' police into four large organisations: The Great Western, The London and North Eastern, The London, Midland and Scottish and The Southern. Each had a Police Force led by a Chief of Police.

The Second World War brought more challenges for the railway police who temporarily amalgamated into one police force, making it the second largest force in the United Kingdom, with around 4,000 officers.

Over 500 railway stations were permanently staffed by railway policemen and women, supplemented by hundreds of paid special constables.

Hitler's Luftwaffe targeted the railways and in 1940, sixty-eight people were drowned when a bomb fractured an underground river near Balham station in which people were sheltering. It took the railway police three months to remove and identify the dead.

In 1943 panic at Bethnal Green Underground Station left one hundred and seventy-three people crushed to death. It was during the war that the decision was made to open a railway police training school on a site in Tadworth in Surrey, which eventually closed in 2010.

The wartime amalgamation of the railway police worked well, and, on the 1 January 1949, the British Transport Commission Police was established, formed from the four old railway forces, the canal police, and several dock forces. The London Transport Police with just 100 officers was not to amalgamate for another ten years.

In 1957 an arbitrator granted parity in pay and conditions with the home department forces, but the railways established an inquiry to decide if there needed to be a separate police force at all. The Maxwell Johnson enquiry not only found that there should be parity but recommended that the force should have a Chief Constable and a Headquarters, and this was duly established at Park Royal in north London. The first Chief Constable, Arthur West, is noted as the last ever police officer to arrest a witch under the Witchcraft Act of 1735.

This was certainly not the last review that railway policing was to undergo. In 1961, Lord Beeching made savage cuts in the mileage of the rail network and as a result the strength of the British Transport Commission Police was nearly halved. The following year the word 'Commission' was dropped from the name.

The force also covered the Ports of Dun Laoghaire and Dublin North Wall in Southern Ireland until 1965, and Belfast Donegal Quay until the early 1980s, with a full-time establishment of Officers.

Having pioneered the use of the telegraph in crime detection, in 1979 British Transport Police became one of the first forces in Europe to computerise crime recording.

Despite losing the buses, docks and harbours in the 1980s, British Transport Police pioneered contingency planning and the use of live and tabletop exercises and, as it did earlier in the 20 century, was in the front line of combating terrorism in its last decades with Provisional IRA bombs exploding on stations, trains and tracks across Britain.

Bringing the story up to date, in 2001 an Act of Parliament resolved the historic jurisdiction problems, and in 2004 an Independent Police Authority replaced the former Police Committee.

The establishment of a Special Constabulary and the recruitment of Police Community Support Officers (PCSOs) has enhanced the way the force can provide a uniformed presence of around 2914 warranted officers, 322 Police Community Support officers, 190 Special constables and 1,316 support staff, to protect and reassure those 6 million people travelling and working on Britain's railways every day on 10,000 miles of track, over 2,500 stations, and numerous trains.

The London Underground has nearly 5 million people using its system and 270 stations every day. Today the force is responsible for the railways of Great Britain including London Underground, The Glasgow Subway, The Docklands Light Railway in London, Eurostar. The force also cover the trams in Croydon and Wimbledon, the West Midlands between Birmingham and Wolverhampton and between Sunderland and Newcastle. They also provide a police service for the Arab Emirates Airlines cable car link across the River Thames.

CHAPTER 3

JOINING THE FORCE AND THE BIRMINGHAM YEARS

JANUARY 1971 – APRIL 1971

Leaving home to join the force and being suspected of theft

The year before I left school, 1966, I had an interview with the Careers Officer from the local Labour Exchange. I informed him that I would like to join the railway as an engine cleaner and later become an engine driver. He told me that there was no future in the railways, especially on the footplate. This was backed up by my Grandfather who had recently retired as an engine driver. I was therefore persuaded to apply for a job as a Postman.

I attended the main Post Office in Fenton Street, Lancaster to sit the Civil Service entrance exam, which I failed. I felt extremely disappointed and dejected at the failure. My father, who was still serving as a Sub-Officer with the Lancashire Fire Brigade in Morecambe, managed to find me a job as a counter assistant at a Builders Merchants showroom in Morecambe.

Whilst working at the showroom, I became a volunteer at Carnforth Motive Power Depot. At that time a local doctor, Dr. Peter Beet, had bought a steam locomotive from British Railways and was restoring it. As the shed was an operational steam shed, all the volunteers needed permission from British Rail to work there. This was obtained and we continued with our restoration work on the locomotive. Every so often members of the British Transport Police would come down to the Carnforth shed because railway enthusiasts would regularly come in to record the end of the steam era and they were clearly trespassing.

Later, Dr. Beet took a lease out on the shed after the British Railways closed it down and it became known as 'STEAMTOWN'. In February 1970 I became a full-time member of the staff there. Also employed were ex railway employees, Jack Cherry, himself a Special Constable with the Lancashire Constabulary and Ken Cottam, an ex-steam fitter at the shed.

By January 1971 I was getting fed up with the work, as Dr. Beet was finding a whole range of other tasks for us to carry out e.g. opposite the shed there was a haulage contractor *'Boddy and Co',* who operated tractor units with forty-foot trailers. Dr. Beet obtained the contract for us to paint them. This was something I hated.

Jack Cherry, seeing that I was disgruntled, suggested that I apply for the Prison Service at Lancaster Castle or the Lancashire Constabulary. My maternal grandmother mentioned Aunt Daisy who was serving in the Metropolitan Police and suggested that I try for the Police Force.

One Saturday night I was at home and as my father and I were watching *'Match of the Day'*, I just happened to comment that there were not many policemen on duty. By some strange leap of thought he suggested that I apply for the British Transport Police; and it so happened that about this time two friends of mine, John Simpson and John Leyland joined the force as Cadets.

The following Monday morning I rang Inspector George Smith-Leach who was in charge of the British Transport Police at Heysham Harbour railway station and asked if there were any vacancies. He advised me that he had a couple of vacancies, and within two hours he came to 'STEAMTOWN' to have a chat with me. A couple of weeks later I was invited to his office to sit the Civil Service exam - a much more difficult version of the one I had tried to enter the Post Office.

As a safeguard just in case the British Transport Police (BTP) did not accept me, I applied to the Lancashire Constabulary as well. But the good old BTP came up trumps.

Because of the postal strike in 1971, the letter informing me of my success in passing the entrance exam had to be hand delivered by no less a person than Sergeant Bob Kirk of BTP Heysham Harbour. I was both thrilled and proud of overcoming this important hurdle. I had to face a medical by the railway doctor followed by a chest x-ray at St Joseph's Hospital, Preston and, a few days later, I received another hand-delivered letter stating that my medical was successful and that I was to report to Assistant Chief Constable (Area Commander), Charlie Steed at Manchester for a formal interview.

I attended the interview and was told that there were no vacancies at Heysham. I was a little dejected at this and returned home. I spoke to PC Vince Seddon, a family friend, he told me to apply for the Metropolitan Police. I rang Inspector Smith-Leach to inform him of the outcome of the interview, who assured me that there were vacancies, but it appeared they were not being filled. Having served in the Midlands Division himself, he advised me to apply for Birmingham New Street, which I did.

I later received a letter informing me that I had been accepted as a Constable on probation at Birmingham New Street and that I was to report to the Divisional Commander, Chief Superintendent W.E. Brunskill on the 5 April 1971.

I duly reported to Mr. Brunskill as a Police Constable on a two-year probation period, and there began a career of over forty years, serving at Coventry, Leicester, Heysham Harbour, Crewe, Holyhead and finally, Bangor. During that time and in all the different places I certainly saw life, sometimes it was comic, sometimes it was tragic and sometimes it was in between.

The first person I met when I started working in Birmingham was Michael Layton, who was a Cadet at the time. A few years later, being appointed as a Police Constable, Mike left and went to the Birmingham City Police. It was not until 2008 that I met up with Mike again and by this time, he had returned to the BTP when he became Operations Superintendent at Birmingham. We re-acquainted our friendship and he persuaded me to co-write a couple of books with him and supply material for others.

Like most other people, prior to joining the police force, I had no real idea of what police work was like. I had only seen the work through the eyes of television and film – *The Blue Lamp; Z Cars; No Hiding Place, Dixon of Dock Green* and many others created images in my mind which were now to be tested against the reality.

There could have been no greater contrast than the city atmosphere of Britain's second city and the fresh coastal air of Morecambe, and the Inspector who I first met, on discovering where I came from said "The sparrows chirp and sing in Morecambe, here they cough and splutter". Yes, Birmingham and the Midlands were quite a contrast to Lancaster, Morecambe and Heysham where I grew up. But I quickly settled to my new surroundings and I took to 'big city life' like the proverbial 'duck to water'. Policing the railways in Birmingham was varied and certainly never dull. No two days were ever the same.

At Birmingham New Street we had three fixed beats – the station forecourt (which included the short-stay car park), the platforms, and the Birmingham Shopping Centre. Our usual tours of duty were 06.30 hours to 14.30 hours; 14.30 hours to 22.30 hours and 22.30 hours to 06.30 hours. On some night shifts, two PCs were rostered to commence duty at 21.30 hours to cover the Travelling Post Office (TPO) trains that called at the Station. 12-hour shifts were usually worked at the weekends.

There were around sixty officers stationed at Birmingham, ranging from clerical support, Cadets, Constables, Sergeants, Dog Handlers, CID officers up to and including Inspectors. A Chief Inspector was appointed sometime later.

At Birmingham not only did we police Birmingham New Street station, but we had a Police Office at Curzon Street Parcels Concentration Depot, (The original site of the Birmingham Terminus of the London to Birmingham Railway and the proposed site for the new HS2 line), and Lawley Street Freight Depot. Lawley Street had a permanent establishment of one Detective Sergeant and three Detective Constables. A uniform presence was provided from Birmingham New Street. We used to work a three-month roster at Birmingham New Street, then one month at Lawley Street and one month at Curzon Street and then back to New Street.

There were two unmarked Vauxhall Viva Estate cars registration numbers *TOA 919H* and *TOA 920H (TOA 921H* was out based at Coventry), two fawn coloured Austin Cambridge cars used by the CID, *FRO 520G and FUR ???*. The dog section also had a blue Vauxhall Van. In 1972 we took delivery of a Commer Karrier Minibus, call sign Bravo 54, which was used by the dog section and uniform section.

On joining the force, I joined the British Transport Police Federation. I also joined the Birmingham branch of the International Police Association (IPA), which was founded in 1950 by Arthur Troop, a Lincolnshire Police Sergeant. The motto of the organisation is *Servo Per Amikeco* (Service Through Friendship). It was formed to create friendly links and encourage cooperation between individual police officers around the world.

My home for the next few weeks was to be the Y.M.C.A. Hostel, in the Erdington district of the city. The hostel was within walking distance of Erdington railway station, so I was able to use the train each day.

It was six weeks before I went to a Home Office District Police Training Centre. I did not know which one I was going to go to. During my six weeks, I quickly learned that any similarity between fictional police work and the real thing was purely coincidental. I learned that a police officer must be able to converse on equal terms with everyone he came into contact with be they rich or poor. He must take insult and praise with equal humility and never be surprised at the heights or depths to which human nature can reach.

I had the honour of being 'sworn in' at the City Magistrates' Court and I also remember having to travel to a tailor's shop in Bethnal Green, East London for my new uniform. Early in my career, I was entrusted with the correspondence, which included the highly confidential Police Gazettes from New Scotland Yard and the local crime information bulletins. During this six-weeks, except for a couple of days when I worked 14.30 hours – 22.30 hours, I worked a regular 09.00 hours - 17.00 hours shift with every weekend off.

Figure 1 Bill and his father (Who was a Firefighter with the Lancashire Fire Brigade) Taken a couple of days before Bill went to the District Training Centre at Bruche.

On the Wednesday of my second week, I was asked to play football for the Birmingham BTP team, which at the time was in the Birmingham City Police league. although I had not played football for about six years, I readily accepted the challenge. In the dressing room, I was quickly introduced to the ten other officers in the team who were strangers to me. I was nervous and it was not easy to remember not only their names but also their ranks.

During the game, I remember running up the wing and I could see that one of our team members, who was in possession of the ball, was about to be tackled by a City Police player. I shouted, "Joe (not his real name) pass the ball to me". He stopped dead in his tracks and said, "It's Sergeant to you", pointing with his hand to his left arm. He was tackled, the ball taken from him and a goal scored. I will not repeat here what my fellow team players said to him. I believe we lost the game 14 -1.

Every Tuesday, the dog section from the Midlands Division trained at a farm in Sutton Coldfield on the outskirts of the city. Myself and some of the cadets, under the regular instruction of Sergeant Fred Taylor, who was the General-Purpose Sergeant and looked after everything from the Administration, uniform, radios, dogs, vehicles etc. would go to the farm and act as a stooge for the dog section. On arrival, I was given a *'dog-proof' coat and a leather 'arm-sleeve'*; I would then run away from 'the scene of the crime', carrying a large stick – Normally, the 'criminal' was armed in order to create a sense of realism but they would not trust me with a starting pistol!

My task was to hide in some nearby bushes, trees, hedgerows, hay bales, or any other suitable location. The dog would come and find me and try to tear off my arm while growling and foaming at the mouth. Whilst I worked at 'STEAMTOWN', we had a German Shepherd dog there which acted as a guard dog for the site, and I was used to him. Fortunately, because of my experience with this guard dog, I escaped unscathed from the BTP dogs.

One of the dogs I tried to befriend, by talking to it, was 'Pip' that was handled by PC Don Hughes of Wolverhampton. I was talking to 'Pip' in my broad north Lancashire accent and Don said, "He doesn't understand you. He can only understand the Black Country dialect," – one of the most distinctive of all the regional accents, which of course Don spoke very fluently.

Another day saw me working with Detective Constable Roy Timms from Coventry, to prepare for a Royal Visit, when Her Majesty, the Queen and His Royal Highness, the Duke of Edinburgh were to visit Birmingham and the Inspector felt that I could go out in order to gain some experience. He also added that if an incident happened, he would rather see me being blown up than the Royal couple.

At that time, there were two Constables (PC Brian Preece and PC Bob Freeman) who had joined the force in February 1971 and were on their initial training at Ryton-on-Dunsmore, District Police Training Centre, near Coventry. Some officers received their wages directly into bank accounts, many others like myself preferred to be paid weekly in cash.

Brian and Bob were in this category of officers being paid weekly and someone would go out to Ryton with the pay envelopes, and one Thursday, which was pay day, the job fell to me.

I left on a train at about 12.00 hours and went to the Coventry police office where I met up with PC Keith Groves who took me to Ryton. Signatures in my pocketbook from the two officers were duly obtained for the wages and Keith and I returned to Coventry. I was having a cup of tea before returning to Birmingham, when a call came in to say that there were six children trespassing on the Coventry to Leamington Spa railway line at Kenilworth. Detective Sergeant Norman Oakes (a fellow Lancastrian as it happens), instructed Keith to go to the scene and to take me for the experience.

On arrival, we caught the six juveniles who were on their way home from school. I thought this was a great job because, although I was still a probationer and waiting to go to training school, I was being allowed to do some real policing.

However, time went by very quickly whilst we were dealing with them. We had to take them home and interview them in the presence of their parents.

Meanwhile, I was missed at Birmingham. The afternoon duty Sergeant thought that I had run off with the wages. He tried to ring the office at Coventry but there was no reply and although we had a Coventry and Warwickshire Police radio, we were out of range from Little Park Street police station at Coventry.

I returned to Birmingham at about 19.00 hours oblivious to the fact that my presence had been missed and that they thought I had absconded with the two sets of wages around £13 each. (At this time, the police force was not really an attractive career as the income and unsocial hours were less favourable than work offered by other employers such as the car factories, I believe that some forces were drastically understaffed). An examination of my pocketbook by the Duty Sergeant revealed that I had not run off with the money but that I had been '*second jockey*' to a trespass job.

At the end of April 1971, I began to prepare for my initial recruit training in Warrington.

CHAPTER 4

THE BIRMINGHAM YEARS MAY 1971 – DECEMBER 1971

Learning a valuable lesson and preventing the Mafia

On the 10 May 1971 I attended the Home Office Training Centre at Bruche, Warrington, for a thirteen weeks Initial Training Course, Intake 417.

There were three other BTP Officers on the intake. PC Mike Morris from Manchester, PC Mike Rhodes from Holyhead, and PC Paul Kenyon from Liverpool.

On the first day, I was placed in 'R' class, under instruction from Inspector John Colledge of the Liverpool and Bootle Police.

He started by telling the other students that I was an *'experienced officer'*, having joined the force some six weeks earlier. The others were totally inexperienced as they had only joined their respective forces a week ago and had no idea of where they would be stationed.

About halfway through the course Mike Morris broke his leg and for obvious reasons he was excused several duties including the morning parade. However, he was gainfully employed by playing the recorded music for us to march to at the morning parade, when given the signal by Sergeant Jack Nicholls, the 'Drill Pig' from the Cheshire Constabulary.

However, unknown to us on the parade ground, and to Jack, a couple of female officers from another intake had gone to Mike's *'studio'* and tied him to his chair.

When Jack came to give the signal to play the Military Band record for us to march to, the first few notes of martial music were heard and then, very unexpectedly, the opening bars of the Beatles song 'She Loves You' were played.

Jack's face was as red as a beetroot and he was absolutely fuming with rage. He then burst out into a stream of unrepeatable expletives which shocked even the most worldly-wise of us. I still wonder what conclusions were reached by any subsequent inquiry.

But Bruche was not all parades and intensive training – I came across a Lancashire Constabulary recruit there who, it transpired, was a distant cousin of mine.

The police world can be a small one at times.

Figure 2 Bill's Home Office recruit course at Bruche. Bill is 3rd from left on the back row.

My Initial training at Bruche was completed on the 6 August 1971. I then had a week's holiday to recover and prepare myself for the return to Birmingham. On returning to Birmingham the force found me accommodation in the Y.M.C.A. Hostel in the Snow Hill district of the city. This was about fifteen minutes' walk from New Street station. I re-started working at Birmingham New Street in mid-August and I was assigned to accompany more experienced officers to learn my new 'trade'. In those days, we were not accompanied by individual, dedicated officers – it was, rather a case of joining up with whoever was available at the time (including, occasionally, fellow probationers). I clearly remember my first arrest – a male person was found to be Drunk and Disorderly on railway premises and I was allowed to be recorded as the arresting officer.

I finished one tour of night duty, went to the Magistrates' Court with a prisoner and returned to the Hostel at around 11.00 hours. I put the 'Do Not Disturb' sign on the door. Whilst I was in a deep sleep, I was awoken by the cleaning lady entering the room with a very noisy vacuum cleaner. She was very apologetic and left.

But my training was not at an end. In September 1971 I was sent to the BTP training school at Tadworth for my initial two-week course on the complex railway legislation. Then, I had a one-week, Phase Training every three months for the next eighteen months at Birmingham New Street station. There were around twelve of us on these courses. We came in very handy for searching the station during bomb hoaxes etc, which were a daily occurrence at that time.

Figure 3 Bill's British Transport Police recruit course at Tadworth. Bill is on the 3rd row, 4th from the left

On returning from Tadworth, the first football train I worked was in September 1971, from Birmingham New Street to Bristol Stapleton Road. It was the match between Bristol Rovers and Birmingham City. The outward journey to Bristol was without incident. The return was much livelier. The Bristol fans charged the Birmingham fans outside the station. Being young and keen, I was about to jump over a wall to apprehend some fans, but unknown to me at that point, I was on the platform, where there was a sheer drop on the other side of the wall, and it was only the Bristol Inspector, who saved me, by pointing out the drop, By the time I got further along the platform the fans on the other side of the wall had run away.

In those early days, after leaving the Y.M.C.A, I lived in a guest house, then I shared a flat with another PC, a fellow probationer, in one of the suburbs. One night I was rostered night turn at New Street and my flatmate was rostered night turn at Lawley Street Freight Depot. He dropped me off at New Street, collected his radio batteries and went off to Lawley Street.

Around 02.00 hours I received a call to go back to the office to see Duty Inspector Ray Rixon, who asked if this PC had reported for duty. No contact had been received from him even though all officers were under orders to report in every two hours. I confirmed that this PC had definitely started his tour of duty. A search of the freight depot was undertaken, and he was found fast asleep in the first aid room. Shortly after this he resigned.

I accompanied one Constable who had a few years' service under his belt and, could be described as 'colourful' and a cross between the PC Alf Ventress and Claude Jeremiah Greengrass, the characters in the TV series 'Heartbeat'.

He was a chain smoker and constantly had a cigarette on the go, which he hid in the palm of his hands, under his fingers. His professional actions were not always strictly in line with the BTP Code of Conduct, e.g. he was a bit of a 'ladies' man' and one incident I recall involved a couple of ladies.

One day we were on the concourse at New Street station, outside the Left Luggage Office, when a lady in company with a particularly extrovert friend approached us. The friend clutched her side - not in pain, but in concern because a vital piece of elastic had given way.

Nothing daunted this friend, who walked up to my colleague, (obviously looking for a more experienced man and not the young handsome one!), and said, "What do you do in the middle of Birmingham when your panties are falling down?" My colleague did not even blink, but said, "Come with me my dear" and took her into the Left Luggage Office. He said to the attendant, "Excuse me, this lady would like to go behind your counter for a minute to remove her knickers". He smiled rather cheekily at the lady and left. The look on the attendant's face was an absolute picture. The offending garment was removed and put into her handbag, to the total astonishment of the attendant.

Another day we were working together in the taxi rank on the forecourt of the station. The rank held about fifty or so taxis and stretched around the corner along Stephenson Place towards Hill Street. Trains used to come into Birmingham every few minutes from all over the country, and the Inter City trains from London arrived every half an hour and these were the busiest ones. Most of the commuters would rush up and take a taxi. Both the passengers and the taxis would not queue, so we usually ended up with taxis spilling into Hill Street thus blocking that street and causing complaints from our colleagues in the City of Birmingham Police. So, we had to ensure that the taxis took their proper place at the head of the queue. My elderly colleague on this day shouted to the taxi drivers. "Pull 'em down". A woman looked at him and quick as a flash he said to her "Not you dear".

Another party trick of his, during the morning rush hour, was to stop the ascending escalators without warning, when they were full of commuters. They were not amused.

One evening, I was selected to go in plain clothes with PC Lorna Lewis who was somewhat older than me, to go to the bar area of the main Refreshment Room on Crewe railway station, as the staff there were suspected of fiddling the till and pocketing money for themselves. Our brief was to pose as mother and son and to observe the actions on the till. We sat in a strategic place, using a newspaper to hide our notebooks.

So not to draw attention to ourselves, I purchased for myself an Aberdeen Angus steak sandwich and an ordinary ham sandwich for Lorna along with two coffees.

The bill came to over £4, a lot of money in those days considering I was only on £13 a week and that the standard police expense was 47 pence when away from your home station. I duly put my claim in for my extra expenses. Rumour has it that Division were asked to send someone else with less expensive tastes the next time.

The emergency exit from New Street station led from the concourse on to Stephenson Place. The exit doors were in darkness and it was not unusual for male persons to go and urinate against the door. We would approach them whilst they were in full flow and surprise them by tapping them on the shoulder. On turning round, they would put their 'tackle' away whilst still in action. They would be prosecuted under the railway byelaws.

The entrance to the National Car Park, multi-story car park was from Stephenson Place. Sadly, the car park was the target of car thieves and vandals, but we had a reasonable success rate of arresting the culprits.

One evening, a Sergeant and I were called to the top level of the seven-storey car park, as a young black girl was acting strangely. We approached her and it was apparent that she had a mental problem. The next thing, she produced a large broken bottle and starting lunging at me with it. I was walking backwards towards the ledge of the car park, over which was a sheer drop onto the 25.000-volt overhead live wires. With some quick thinking, we managed to arrest her. She had come from a home somewhere in the Lickey Hills, Worcestershire. We took her back and as I was making sure that she reached her room safely, she turned around catching me completely off guard and kicked me in the groin. I learned a very valuable lesson that night. Due to her mental state no further action was taken, but I was sore for a few days.

One of the areas we had to patrol regularly were the carriage sidings at Vauxhall on the outskirts of the city. At night, the empty coaching stock especially the buffet cars were the target of thieves mainly trying to steal the alcohol which had been left on board. They were also the habitat of the local homeless people and courting couples. We ejected quite a few of the latter over the years.

One suburb of Birmingham is called Edgbaston, which at the time contained a mix of affluent housing and what can only be described as 'less desirable dwellings'. It was to one of these dwellings that a colleague and I went to serve a set of summonses on a female who lived in a flat in a three-story terraced house. It was my colleague's case. He said that I might as well stay in the car as he was going to serve the summonses on the doorstep. I saw him ring the doorbell of the flat. A few moments later the window of the top upstairs flat opened and a female popped her head out of the open window. My colleague established that the female was the one whom he wanted and requested her to come to the front door. She said, "Just a moment". A few seconds later she re-appeared at the window and poured a bucket of water over him. She was arrested for assault.

One of the 'Sergeants' at New Street had a heart complaint and had to stay home to recover and recuperate. After a few months he returned to light duties. One day I was walking down to the Mess Room and I saw him coming out of the 'gents' toilet, panting, obviously short of breath.

I asked him if he was alright and he assured me that he was. I watched him walk down the corridor to make sure he was okay, only to notice a girlie magazine sticking out of his back pocket.

On one-night shift we received a telephone call from the BTP at Holyhead, to say that they had detained a young boy from Birmingham who was trying to get to Ireland. We were asked to make enquiries at the address. A Sergeant and I went to a terraced house in the Small Heath district. I knocked on the door of the house, which was in darkness, which we expected, as it was around 02.30 hours. The door was opened, but no light was switched on. Instinctively we shone our torches only to find that the door opened straight off the pavement, into the front room, and that there were hardly any floorboards. We had to walk on the joists over to an old leather, two-seater settee, which was occupied by an old Irish lady smoking a clay pipe. We established that it was where the boy lived and that he ran away after having an argument with his Granny.

On another occasion I was halfway through a late turn tour of duty at Birmingham New Street, when I was called into see Norman Plover, one of the Duty Sergeants. He informed me that a group of officers, led by himself, and consisting of another PC, PC Street, 'Rebel', the police dog and myself were going to Stourport, Worcestershire, to remove some travellers who had illegally camped on some railway land. West Mercia Police had no luck in moving them on and stated that there may be trouble from them.

We went in 'Bravo 54 the 'Commer Karrier' with 'Rebel' enjoying his brand-new mobile kennel in the rear. On arrival at Stourport, a contingent of West Mercia Police were waiting as back up, to assist us. Norman and I saw that there were about six or seven caravans all occupied. We approached the traveller in charge of the camp, and he was informed that we were from the British Transport Police and that they were illegally camped and that they should remove themselves forthwith. The traveller took one look at our helmet plates and said "Yes, sir, we are going no problem, you are the British Transport Police". The West Mercia police officers just stood there in amazement. Within a few hours the travellers had left.

A memorable incident was my journey as a front-seat passenger in the CID car. I felt the mat in the well give way as I put my feet on it and when I lifted it, I was amazed to see daylight and the road surface. The floor had rusted through completely and I was pleased to hear that the car was condemned very soon afterwards.

Finally, in this section, I'd like to relate one more of my 'adventures' from that time. On Sunday 12 December 1971 at 21.15 hours, I was on duty at Birmingham New Street Station when I received a report from a young person aged 17 who gave an address in New York, USA, to the effect that his Trans World Airlines shoulder bag had been stolen from Platform Three, whilst he was waiting for his train to London. Because of his age and his accent, which had a strange twang – a mixture of American and Black Country,

I became suspicious of him and I involved the duty CID officer. We further interviewed him, and it turned out that he was a young man from West Bromwich in the Black Country, who was wanted by the original West Midlands Constabulary, (Prior to the 1974 force amalgamations this force covered the cities and towns of the Black Country, such as Wolverhampton, Dudley and Walsall), for breaking into a gas meter at his home. I arrested him on behalf of the West Midlands Constabulary.

TRAVELLING POST OFFICE DUTIES

Travelling Post Office (TPO) duty was a regular duty in my days at Birmingham New Street. The basic purpose of a TPO was to sort mail for onward distribution during the time that would otherwise be wasted in transit. As previously mentioned, two officers would book on duty at 21.30 hours for a nine-hour tour of duty, Monday to Friday to cover the Travelling Post Office trains that served Birmingham New Street. Unlike some of our colleagues we did not travel on the trains but patrolled the platforms. Since the Great Train Robbery in 1964, British Transport Police Officers would travel on the TPO trains, sometimes working a fourteen hour shift each night. At Birmingham New Street, the *'Down Special'* consisting entirely of postal carriages, from London Euston to Glasgow, would arrive in Platform Eight at around 22.00 hours and the Bristol to Newcastle postal train with postal carriages and ordinary passenger carriages would arrive on Platform Nine. Mail of all descriptions would be exchanged between the two trains. We would contact the officers on each of the trains. At around 01.30 hours the reverse procedure would take place, when the *'Up Special'* from Glasgow to London Euston would arrive and the Newcastle to Bristol postal train would arrive at Platforms Eight and Nine respectively.

The Royal Mail staff would have their own security staff on the platform to oversee the transfers. Sometimes the Post Office Investigation Branch would turn out in plain clothes to observe the operation. The person in charge of the portable alarm box was identified by wearing a brown smock coat. He carried this cumbersome box in one hand. The purpose of this alarm was, if any attempt was made to steal anything from the train i.e. the mail bags which contained high value cash and jewellery, the person in charge of the alarm would set it off to alert the staff on the platform.

One night he left it on the wall of the subway leading down to the Royal Mail sorting office whilst he went to speak to someone. My elderly colleague whom I was on duty with saw his chance and hid it out of sight. When the security man returned there was a sheer look of panic on his face. He was about to implement the station lock down procedure, (should an attempt be made to attack one of the trains) when my colleague came clean and reunited him with his box.

ATTENDING THE COURTS

As part of my probationary training, I had to attend the various courts in the area to learn all about the procedures there. We used to arrest people, charge them, and be responsible for prosecuting them in the Magistrates' Courts.

It was all exciting stuff, but it was good grounding for us. All that has changed now with the Crown Prosecution Service (CPS).

There were two regular Birmingham City Police officers who worked in the main Court – Court Number One at the City of Birmingham Law Courts, Steelhouse Lane. Sergeant 'R1' Watts and PC Paddy Hewitt.

The night-time at Birmingham attracted a lot of homeless people to the benches and the waiting rooms on the station as they were warm and dry. There was a law which we could use, called 'Trespass and Refuse to Quit'. The offender if not on railway business, would be asked, on three clear occasions, to leave the station and if they refused, they could be arrested and detained in custody to appear before the Magistrates' the next day. A lot would do this because they would be guaranteed a half decent bed for the night and a good breakfast the next morning.

These cases were good grounding for probationers to gain experience of arrests and subsequent procedures. If you made any type of arrest on a Monday night shift and took them to Court on the Tuesday morning, you would get what was called a 'Guaranteed Day'. After a tour of duty on a Monday night you would normally finish at 06.30 hours and come back at 14.30 hours until 22.30 hours on the Tuesday. The two days following, Wednesday and Thursday would be our Rest Days. So, having a 'Guaranteed Day' meant that you had three days off.

Sergeant Watts was very sympathetic to you and would try and get your case on as quickly as possible so you could enjoy more of your extra day at home. PC Hewitt was a different kettle of fish he would try and keep you there as long as he could.

One Monday night, I came across a woman who was bedding down for the night. I established that she was not travelling by train nor had she any lawful business with the railway. I asked her to leave on three separate occasions and on each request, she refused to leave. I told her that she was under arrest for Trespass and Refuse to Quit, to which she invited me round the back of the station for a '*quickie*' instead of taking her to court. It turned out she was a local prostitute. She was conveyed to Digbeth Police Station and subsequently charged. I prosecuted her at the Court the next morning and got my 'Guaranteed Day'.

I remember being in the Magistrates' Court at Birmingham one day when a defendant had been fined £10 for an offence of theft. To someone who was unemployed or on a low income, this was a lot of money. The defendant asked to pay in instalments of 50 pence a week. The Chairman of the bench, a rather stern looking character, turned to him and said, "This is a court of law not a mail order catalogue. You will pay the amount in full or face a jail sentence." The offender offered to pay at £1 a week, which was accepted.

Birmingham City Magistrates' Court had a Stipendiary Magistrate, a Mr. Millward. He always appeared to be asleep, but one wrong word from the Prosecution or the Defence, he was there to issue a telling off. We had to be on our toes when presenting the facts of our case to him.

Very early on in my career I went to Dudley Magistrates' Court to prosecute a trespass offence that I had dealt with in the area. The person was duly fined. As was the normal way of things at that time, the case was reported in the local newspaper.

There was nothing different about this particular case, but the reporter did state that the prosecuting officer was **Inspector** William Rogerson of the British Transport Police in Birmingham. I was ribbed over this for a few weeks.

Another court I attended was Hagley Juvenile Court, in Worcestershire. One particular case I was prosecuting involved three juveniles who I had caught trespassing on the railway. The bench consisted of six female magistrates all wearing big hats. (It was bit like Ladies Day at Ascot Races!). When prosecuting cases in Birmingham it was customary to give the brief facts as there could be up to twenty-six courts sitting each day, except at the weekend, when there was one. I opened my case with the words "May it please your worships, I am PC William Rogerson of the British Transport Police from Birmingham and I prosecute this case. The brief facts are". Before I could continue, the chair of the bench slammed her hand on the bench, looked down her glasses and said to me "Officer we want the full facts, none of your big city talk here, we want to know what is going on in our area, do I make myself clear?" "Yes Ma'am", said I rather sheepishly.

And finally, in this section I remember prosecuting at Birmingham City Magistrates' Court when the Chairman, a fellow Lancastrian, leaned over and whispered to me "Ah, someone I can understand".

THE BIRMINGHAM SHOPPING CENTRE

One Sunday afternoon in September 1971, shortly after returning from the training school at Tadworth, I was placed on late turn – 14.30 hours to 22.30 hours. During the early evening, I was patrolling the Birmingham Shopping Centre, above New Street Station, with a PC who was nearing the end of his Probation. The Shopping Centre had its own security organisation, but the force had the contract to provide a policing service to the centre and to the shops.

It was while we were walking round that I met my wife to be. We saw three young ladies walking towards us and we stopped to talk to them. We went on our way, but decided they were worth another look. We caught up with them again and asked them out. On the date we found another PC for the third one.

Whilst we were on Shopping Centre duty one of our regular calls was the ASDA supermarket to deal with the numerous shoplifters that ranged from the little old lady to a City Police Officer. It is there that I encountered my first professional shoplifter. He wore a long overcoat and false hands. He used his real hands to take goods from the shelves and place them in specially designed pockets within the coat.

One of our Inspectors was *'seeing another lady'* and he used to meet her for coffee and cake in a bakers cafe on the Centre. He would sit facing the window whilst his lady friend would sit with her back to the window. Everyone in the office knew that this was going on. Those days we did not have mobile phones or pagers, so whenever he was meeting his *'lady friend'* he would inform the PC in the Information Room that he was going for a coffee. If he was required for anything, the duty PC on the Shopping Centre would get a message to attract his attention.

One day this fell to me. I received a message to say that he was required. I went to the Bakers and stood in front of the window, beckoning him by shaking my head repeatedly to one side. Goodness knows what the shoppers thought.

It was around this time that the Shopping Centre was in the process of being completed and there were still several empty units. In the middle of the Piazza of one of the Shopping Centre aisles there was an open-air cafe known as *'GINO's'* run by an Italian gentleman. Early in the morning, he was getting a lot of verbal abuse from youths. He wrote to Mr. Brunskill our Chief Superintendent, regarding the problem. In turn Mr. Brunskill instructed the Inspectors at New Street to give immediate attention by putting two of their best men on the case, as he didn't want the Mafia dealing with the problem which was the threat used by the proprietor of 'Gino's' when writing to the Chief Superintendent. So, PC Ian Mabbett and I were assigned to the case. We hid in an empty unit opposite the cafe and soon had our culprits under lock and key. We never went short of coffee after that and the Mafia were stood down.

During the early 1970s Birmingham sadly was the target of IRA bombs, and incendiary devices were placed all over the city including the Birmingham Shopping Centre and the adjacent Bull Ring Shopping Centre. Hoax calls were all too frequent, sometimes we received several in a day. Each one had to be treated seriously. We had a set procedure for searching the centre and shops. One evening we received a hoax call, and the Sergeant and a Constable set off, on their set procedure. When they got to the Combined Services recruiting office, (Army Navy and RAF) which overlooked Stephenson Street, they turned left instead of turning right as they should have done. As they were walking their new route a bomb exploded in the recruiting office, blowing out the plate glass window. To say that they had a lucky escape would be an understatement.

To conclude this section, on Stephenson Street underneath the Shopping Centre there was a *'Berni Inn'* which was on our patch. One night at around 02.00 hours I was walking past the *'Berni Inn'* and could see smoke in the premises, which was closed for the night. I immediately arranged for the Fire Brigade to be called to the premises. It transpired that someone locking up the premises for the night forgot to turn off the Chicken Rotisserie. Consequently, the chickens overheated. Chicken was definitely off the menu the next day.

CHAPTER 5

THE BIRMINGHAM YEARS 1972

Catching fire and in the shit for the first time

Whenever you were on duty on the Forecourt/Station Concourse of Birmingham New Street station, you were expected to pay attention to the 20-minute waiting area. As there was only room for around thirty or so vehicles, it could get very congested with drivers overstaying the allotted 20 minutes. Every so often we would have 'a blitz' on the motorists. I remember one Saturday evening going into the early hours of Sunday morning, in early 1972, there were around 25 cars that had been there for over four hours. So, I ticketed every one of them under the railway Byelaws. The drivers all came back together, I wished I had not booked them, for they were all Greek Fish and Chip shop owners from around the Birmingham area, with typical long Greek names. They had been to a Greek Fish Fryers convention at a nearby Banqueting Suite. I really struggled with their names. Lesson learned.

I remember one occasion, when in early 1972 I was part of a football train escort to Brighton from Birmingham. It was not usual, but not unheard of, to take a dog handler and dog on a football train escort. On this occasion Ron Woollaston and his dog 'Brutus' came with us. After dispersing the fans at Brighton, we travelled with the empty stock to the sidings at Preston Park. Bearing in mind my recent training at our training school, Tadworth, in relation to the 750 volt - third electrified rail line, being all around the area that we were travelling on, south of London, I was mindful of the fatal consequences if I stepped on them. So naturally I took extra care when alighting from the train in the sidings. Ron took his dog for a walk in the sidings and could not understand why it kept yelping. He had not realised we were in third rail territory and the dog kept touching the live rail. He was incredibly lucky.

I was on a night shift at the Curzon Street Parcels Concentration Depot at about 03.00 hours in January 1972. Having patrolled the depot, I went to the main gate to liaise with the security man there. As we were talking, a wagon drew up with the words '*Boddy's of Carnforth*' emblazoned on the side and the driver asked for directions to a merchant's yard. I consulted my trusty A to Z of Birmingham, gave the driver the directions. I then said to him, "How is Jack Cherry?" The look on the driver's face was a picture. Here he was, in the middle of Birmingham and he came across someone who knew Jack Cherry from *Boddy's*. As previously alluded to, just prior to joining the force I worked with Jack at 'STEAMTOWN', Carnforth before he went to work for *Boddy's*.

Another coincidence from the area as previously mentioned, I worked for a Builders Merchants in Morecambe. One of the places I lived at in Birmingham was Acocks Green, which was served by the Number 44 West Midlands bus.

I regularly travelled on the 44 bus service, which had regular drivers and conductors. I got to know one of the Conductors and he informed me that he was from Morecambe and that he used to work for a builder who used the Builders Merchants that I worked for.

Another night shift in January 1972 at Curzon Street, saw me going with the night duty Detective Constable to Willenhall in the Black Country to make enquiries into the theft of metal from some nearby sidings. It was a particularly cold and very frosty night and I was wearing my regulation 'Staffordshire' model mackintosh, which was very heavy, but warm and really useless in a fight. The epaulettes were not stitched down and could be grabbed by an attacker. Likewise, we had a belt and buckle this could also be grabbed by any would be attacker.

We entered the Signalbox and the Signalman had a roaring fire in the stove. I stood with my back to it and shortly afterwards could smell burning, yes, my mackintosh had caught fire, I was on fire. The signalman threw some water onto it to douse the flames. I had some explaining to do when I got back.

In those early days of the 1970's Manchester United supporters were regarded as the worse troublemakers in the football world. It was not uncommon for us to be sent to Crewe on a Saturday, for a four-hour rest day working to escort the Midlands based United fans back to Birmingham. One of my duties in early 1972, on this half rest day working was to travel to Crewe and escort an ordinary service train from Manchester back to Birmingham New Street, dressed as a United supporter.

I was on the train complete with a red and white bobble hat and scarf, with a wooden rattle, this was under duress as I am not a fan of Manchester United. A couple of CID from New Street were on the train as well. As the train was approaching Birmingham, I was in a compartment with a so-called genuine supporter, when one of the CID officers walked past us. He stuck out like sore thumb, trilby hat, open-coat and collar and tie. The 'supporter' said "He's a copper you can tell em anywhere". He then proceeded to smash the light bulbs and light shades. At which point I identified myself and arrested him for Criminal Damage. His reply to the caution is unprintable!!!

One Saturday in March 1972 I was part of a serial of four officers escorting Birmingham City football club supporters (Known as the *'blues'*) back from Bristol to Birmingham on a football special train. Most of the fans were drunk, shouting and swearing, so we arrested as many as we could. I had fourteen to my credit. They were all taken to Digbeth police station and charged with being Drunk and Disorderly. I think we had about forty in all. They all appeared at court on Monday morning and were all dealt with by being fined.

The following week I was off duty and out for a drink with my fiancé Shirley and her sister, Eileen, a fanatical *'Blues'* supporter. She was with a crowd of her friends. One of them came up to me and stated that he knew me. I told him that I did not think so, with that he went away. It turned out he was one of the fans I had arrested the week before.

A few months later, I equalled this record for arrests on one-night shift, what a shift! I just could not go wrong, Trespass and Refuse to Quit, Drunks, Ticket Frauds, Disorderly Conduct, and a Theft. I had writer's cramp. I think I had the court to myself the next day.

One evening in March 1972 I went out on mobile patrol with one of the sergeants who had a wicked sense of humour. We ended up at Kings Norton station on the south side of Birmingham. Those days Kings Norton only had about four trains a day therefore was very quiet; nowadays it has trains every 15 minutes in each direction.

In the bushes was an abandoned Morris Minor car, and on our arrival, we could see that a courting couple were frequenting it. It was obvious as to what they were doing. The sergeant went up to them and enquired as to what they were doing. "Just necking" came the reply from the male. "Put your neck away and go home," or words to that effect, replied the sergeant very dryly.

In April 1972, I got married at St Margaret's Church, Olton, Solihull, Warwickshire, as Shirley was living in Olton at the time. Being on a limited budget we had our wedding reception at the Boundary Club, so called because it was on the boundary of Warwickshire and the City of Birmingham near to where Shirley lived. A week or so later it was bombed by the IRA.

We spent our Honeymoon in Morecambe, the Lake District and Southampton. We got to know each other a lot more. I decided that if marriage is a lottery, I held the jackpot ticket.

In 1972, I became secretary of the British Transport Police Sports and Social Club, which was affiliated to the British Railways Staff Association Club (BRSA) at Monument Lane, Birmingham.

Each Christmas, we would hold a Christmas party for the younger children of the Officers, and we would invite some children from a children's home in Worcestershire. At one party all hell was let loose when the children of the police officers started fighting with the children from the home.

One of the Detective Sergeants, because of his build would play the part of Father Christmas, he looked the part once dressed up. Prior to playing this role he would go and have a couple of pints of beer to get the courage to face the children. One lad sat on his knee and on being asked what he would like for Christmas the lad replied "Blooming eck, Father Christmas, you reek of beer".

As part of the party festivities, I would hire a black and white, 16 mm film featuring the antics of the silent screen stars. Charlie Chaplin, Laurel and Hardy, Abbot and Costello etc. I was always instructed by the duty Inspector to let him know when it was being screened so that he could come and watch.

The older children were treated to the pantomime at one of the two theatres in Birmingham. I would book the tickets in June, when they went on sale, along with the interval ice-cream and drinks. At one performance, I was distributing the ice-cream and drinks to the children when I was aware of two old ladies behind me. One of them said "Two tubs when you are ready duck". They thought I was the ice cream seller.

Birmingham has more miles of canals than Venice, and when the Transport Act of 1949 came into being, thus creating the British Waterways Board, jurisdiction for the canals in Britain was included for the British Transport Police and we had dedicated officers to patrol the canals. Although we still have jurisdiction to this day under the Act, the canals are now policed by the local force due to costs etc.

The Houseboats on the Bridgewater Canal, on the outskirts of the city, were mainly occupied by students from Birmingham University. The boats had coal fired stoves in them. Some of the students used to steal coal from the nearby coal merchants. A complaint was made to the Birmingham City Police and they felt that it was not serious enough to warrant an investigation. The management of the British Waterways Board asked for assistance from the BTP. A Sergeant and I spent a whole week dressed as students patrolling the canal during the spring of 1972. We managed to detect a couple of offenders.

Incidentally, a few years ago as a force, we used to police the Regents Canal in London and we had an office at Bow Locks. Can you imagine answering the telephone there? *"Good afternoon, British Transport Police, Bow Locks..."*

Late one afternoon, in the summer of 1972, whilst on late turn on the Concourse at New Street Station, I came across a young man who looked as if he was on drugs. I searched him and found that he was in possession of a lump of Cannabis. I arrested him and took him to the police office. When he was seen by the Duty Sergeant, he tried to claim that I had planted the drugs on him. The elderly Sergeant went white. In the finish, the man admitted possession of the drug and was duly dealt with through the court system.

The start of the 1972 football season saw me travelling to Cardiff with Aston Villa fans, on a football special train. For the return, we were on Platforms One and Two, which are situated on an island platform, with our fans, awaiting the arrival of our train. The local Cardiff fans were on Platforms Three and Four, again another island platform, when suddenly, the Cardiff fans managed to get hold of some shunting poles (These poles are about six foot in length and have a hook on the end of them and are used to couple rolling stock together) and they were throwing them across the tracks at the Villa supporters. It was like a scene from the film 'Zulu'. All we needed was Ivor Emmanuel to come along the platform singing *'Men of Harlech'*.

On Monday 4 September 1972 at 20.15 hours I was on duty at Birmingham New Street Station, with a Cadet, when we were called to the off-licence on the station concourse. The Manageress had come across six boys all aged around 12 years from Cradley Heath in the Black Country, with a rather large amount of money and was suspicious about them. I located three of boys and questioned them. One of them stated that he got the money from his uncle. I then located the other three on a Hereford bound train. I took all six to the police office where I questioned them further. One of the boys admitted stealing the money from a house in Old Hill and the others admitted handling the money. I recovered £9.86 from them. I contacted the original West Midlands Constabulary at Old Hill and learned that they had received a report of a house being broken into in their force area and £286 had been stolen.

The boys were further questioned, and they admitted hiding the rest of the money in the disused Old Hill, High Street Halt, railway station. Officers from the West Midlands Constabulary attended the scene and recovered £100. The boys were then handed over to the West Midlands Constabulary and prosecuted by them.

It was a Saturday in November 1972 when Nuneaton Borough were drawn to play Torquay United in the first round of the FA Cup at Torquay. I believe that there were seven special trains from Nuneaton, each escorted by British Transport Police officers from the Midlands Division. The contingent from Birmingham of which I was a part, booked on duty at 06.30 hours and travelled to Nuneaton in a Ford Transit minibus. We duly escorted our train to Torquay. On arrival at Torquay, we waited until all the trains had arrived and the fans had left the station. The Devon and Cornwall Constabulary took us in their Black Marias to a Chinese restaurant in the town centre for a pre-booked meal. The sight of all these bobbies jumping out of the Marias was certainly a sight for the early Christmas shoppers to behold. It was like something out of a Keystone Cops movie. They must have thought the Chinese restaurant was being raided.

I had friends in Torquay who ran a guest house, just off the town centre, so a group of us went there for a cup of tea and a piece of cake after the Chinese meal.

The return journey was quiet apart from the fact that when we left Bristol Temple Meads station it was discovered that we had no guard and the train had to stop at Swindon, whilst the guard caught us up by taxi.

On arrival at Nuneaton, we were the last train to arrive and went over to the minibus only to find that the diesel had been siphoned out of it. Fortunately, the Warwickshire Police came to our rescue with a can of diesel, which was enough until we found a fuel station. It was unstaffed and only accepted pound or five-pound notes, after a hunt round we managed to find a couple of pound notes to purchase some fuel.

We eventually arrived back at New Street at around 04.15 hours and booked off at 04.30 hours. A total of 22 hours on duty. I was back on duty at 12.30 to cover Lawley Street Freight depot. I really should have had a Guaranteed Day after working nearly three shifts in a row.

In late November 1972 I was part of an escort to Blackpool North on a special train conveying Aston Villa supporters for a Blackpool v Aston Villa mid-week match, kick off 19.30 hours. On the return journey I was in a carriage with a centre aisle, when in the Preston area, the lights went out and I was jumped on by some fans and pushed underneath some seats and some of the fans repeatedly kicked me. Fortunately, one of the fans came to my rescue. We arrested a couple for assault. But my helmet was missing. A few days later a cardboard box arrived at Birmingham addressed to me, containing my helmet. A note inside was from British Transport Police at Preston which read, 'One helmet, Constable, for the use of' - it was a write-off.

At New Street, we had an elderly PC who acted as the Office Clerk. He went out on the beat very rarely; I think he had been made redundant from Walsall. He used to go to the markets at Birmingham and obtain, at cost price, fresh fruit, veg and meat for the officers.

Just before Christmas in 1972 he brought back a load of sprouts, cauliflowers, and cabbages. There were quite a number left over. He went on leave for the Christmas period leaving the vegetables, which rotted in the heat of his office. The stench became unbearable. No one had a key to get in. Someone managed to get in and remove the offending vegetables.

TRESPASS AND VANDALISM

The word 'vandalism' means an act or behaviour of a vandal. There is no actual crime of vandalism. It is one of those words, like 'hooliganism', 'shoplifting', 'graffiti' and 'mugging' which go some way towards obscuring what are straightforward criminal offences such as criminal damage, obstruction of the railway, endangering the safety of persons on the railway, trespass and stone throwing etc.

'Vandalism' in some shape or form has been with us ever since the 15 September 1830, when the Duke of Wellington formally opened the Liverpool and Manchester Railway. The events of that day are now very much part of railway history. Documents reveal that attempts were made to obstruct the train and stones were thrown.

The special position of railways as regards trespass has been recognised throughout their history. In 1840 an Act of Parliament was passed which empowered a constable or for that matter, any railway official, to arrest any person trespassing on railway premises and refusing to quit when asked to do so. These powers were found necessary for ensuring the safety, both of staff and travelling public.

The Special Acts for the construction of a railway contained many provisions, including those concerning fences, and Section 1 of the 1842 Railway Regulation Act stipulated that all railway companies must erect, maintain, and repair sufficient fences along their respective lines. These provisions were consolidated in the 1845 Railway Clauses Consolidation Act, requiring a railway company to make and at all times thereafter maintain 'Sufficient posts, rails, hedges, ditches, mounds or other fences for separating the land taken for the use of the railway from the adjoining lands not taken, and protecting such lands from trespass, or the cattle of the owners or occupiers thereof from straying thereout, by reason of the railway....' (Section 68). Thus, it was imposed upon the railway companies a legal and burdensome duty to fence both sides of the line throughout its length, but it was only for the convenience of the owners or occupiers of land adjoining the railway. It had nothing to do with the safety of the public and was not intended to prevent them from straying onto the railway. Rather, it was to stop those on the railway from trespassing on private land.

In 1861, the Malicious Damage Act was introduced. The Act was later repealed in 1971, apart from four sections which related to the obstruction of railways, which are still in use today. (A couple of other sections were retained, appertaining to interfering with buoys at sea).

Despite intensive efforts at blackspots, talks in schools and numerous other projects, the police have never been able to stamp out this extremely dangerous practice. We have had a certain measure of success with our tactics.

The cost to the community, taxpayers for damage caused by vandals, cannot be reckoned in terms of pounds and pence alone, inconvenience and even death must be taken into consideration when endeavouring to assess the total cost to the rail companies and subsequently to the travelling public.

Protecting the railways against persons such as trespassers was indeed one of the earliest duties of our predecessors, and it remains an important part of our work. A considerable amount of British Transport Police time is taken up with cases of trespass and vandalism.

In preventing trespass, we are not only safeguarding the lives of the travelling public and staff, but we are also saving the train operating companies, many millions of pounds a year, as well as on claims for compensation to parents of children maimed or killed on the line.

Children have always been attracted to the trackside, once on the 'wrong side of the fence' they are in immediate danger and get up to all sorts of mischief, looking for suitable objects to put on the line. Young people are not always to blame. One example, wire fencing, erected along one side of a route to prevent children wandering onto the track was damaged by adults. They are oblivious to the dangers that face them.

It was the thing, glamour, and publicity for the vandal, which caused other members of his gang to try and emulate him. So, we had a whole sequence of malicious damage. Trains now much frequented by young persons are places of sanctioned confinements. This also can be said for darkened cinemas. Both places, despite modern 'open plan' carriages on the railway are difficult areas of social control, vandals can release the tension and frustration in aggression.

In the past, vandals liked to be notorious, but now prefer to be anonymous. Anonymous vandalism has been increasing for years. The vandal is fighting the public and authority. In our personal society, it is possible to be anonymous and a vandal, but still to be conspicuously on public view.

Their attitudes reveal the nature of society to which they belong, from time immemorial to the present day, there has been hooliganism and vandalism from school children to young people milling about the streets of big cities, towns and villages, and on all forms of public transport. The railway for some reason seems to attract them like 'wasps to a jam pot' or 'moths around a light bulb'.

Youthful violence and vandalism and the inconvenience of the general public provide vandals both with relief and frustration, and the occasion for stabbing back at society which has bored and frustrated them.

Some officials regard vandalism against the railway as principally crimes of opportunity, crimes not committed, just because the chance is there and not because of any ill feeling borne towards the railway, or with premeditation involved.

Vandalism without doubt is surely the work of young people whose aggressive spirit must find an outlet and the appearance of many forms of non-participation. Amusements and sports do not help the situation. They offer the youth no opportunity to work off surplus energy.

The Midlands Division of the force certainly received more than its fair share of attention from offenders in the above offences during my time at Birmingham.

Immediately after my Honeymoon in April 1972, I was one of four officers to join the newly formed Mobile Patrol, which had been set up to combat trespass and vandalism in the Birmingham area. This was a two-shift system, 10.00 hours to 18.00 hours and 18.00 hours to 02.00 hours. We had a remit to work in plain clothes and to catch as many trespassers and vandals as possible. We were also given an unmarked car. I was teamed up with PC George Bellamy. We worked in uniform as required.

The week after returning to work after my Honeymoon, I was rostered on the 18.00 hours to 02.00 hours shift, much to the amusement of one of the Inspector's. George and I worked well as a team and were phenomenally successful in catching offenders.

One summer's evening in 1972, as George was on annual leave, I was covering a beat at New Street Station in uniform, when myself and a colleague were called to the railway line which runs through the Sutton Park area of the city. There had been a report of a youth shooting at trains with an air rifle. This is a freight line, it used to be used for regular passenger traffic many years ago and was still used as a diversion for passenger trains mainly on a Sunday.

On arrival we saw this youth up a tree. My colleague pointing to a route, told me to go one way, whilst he went in another direction to head him off. In my excitement, I jumped over this fence thinking I was jumping into a field. However, how mistaken I was. It was a sewerage farm and the green I mistook, as grass was actually slime on top of the sewerage. I manage to pull myself out and go over to the offender who was still in the tree unable to move as he was doubled up with laughter. He was taken home and I had to throw my uniform and other clothing away.

One incident that stands out in my mind was one Sunday afternoon in the late Summer of 1972 whilst George and I were on the mobile patrol, in plain clothes and with the unmarked car. We were directed to the Stechford area of Birmingham, where the main Birmingham to London Euston line passes through and is joined by the line from Walsall and Aston. The area was notorious for trespass and George and I had a lot of success here. The report we received was that there were in excess of ten children on the land between the two sets of lines. We arrived there and found fourteen juveniles, some of whom ran off. The ones we detained gave the names and addresses of the ones that got away. We then told the ones who we had detained that we would be coming to see them in the presence of their parents shortly.

As George and myself, were driving along a road of the nearby council estate, we could see a Birmingham City Police car behind us with its blue light flashing. It then overtook us and pulled in front of us. The Officer got out of the car and before we could say anything, he asked us to get out of our vehicle. We then explained who we were and produced our warrant cards. He informed us that one of the children, a young girl, we had detained, had run home and told her mother that we were a couple of rapists.

The mother immediately rung 999. Matter sorted out with the city officer, we continued with our task of interviewing the juveniles. We went to the home of the girl whose mum had made the complaint, and the girl answered the door. She was shocked to see us there. We quickly explained who we were.

After this incident, we had to work in uniform for a majority of the time and our detections went down and the unit was disbanded shortly afterwards. However, just before it was disbanded a complaint came in of early morning trespassers at Henley in Arden on the North Warwick line that runs from Tyseley to Stratford Upon Avon. Workmen were coming from a housing estate, walking through a field, and taking a short cut to a factory by crossing the line and walking through another field. George and I booked on at 05.00 hours and went in plain clothes to the scene and weighed it up. We decided to keep watch from a hut in a field from where we could see the trespassers coming over the brow of a hillock in the field and report them after they had crossed the railway line. No one came. Had we been rumbled? We soon discovered why no one took a short cut, the farmer had put a bull in our field, and it was out of sight when we went in. Apparently, it had been there for a couple of days and the would-be trespassers gave it a wide berth. George and I gingerly left the field, as we didn't fancy being trampled on by a couple of tons or so, of prime British beef. Our journey was not in vain as we had to go to the local Motor Vehicle Taxation Office in Warwick to obtain the details of a couple of motorists. No PNC (Police National Computer) in those days. We also had other enquiries in the area.

One early evening, I was out in the Winson Green area of the city, opposite the Soho Electric Train Depot chasing some lads who had been throwing stones at trains. As I went down the embankment, the bottom of my trousers caught on a nail in an abandoned wooden sleeper and ripped my trouser leg all the way up to the top exposing my underwear to the amusement of the local residents. Good job it was a Monday!

WALSALL

The town of Walsall, a few miles from Birmingham, had lost its establishment of uniformed staff but a Detective Sergeant and a Detective Constable remained there. Every so often a Uniformed Constable from Birmingham would go and patrol the area. This duty fell to me on a couple of occasions and I managed to catch a few trespassers there and take them to court once proceedings had been authorised.

I had relatives who were related to my Aunt Daisy of the Metropolitan Police fame, living in Walsall. One of my uncles, my grandmother's brother, had been an engine driver at Bescot locomotive depot, sadly his son, who was a locomotive fireman at Bescot, was knocked over and killed by a steam locomotive in the 1960s.

One evening, I was sat in the police office eating my sandwiches when a rat the size of a cat suddenly appeared from behind the skirting board. I drew my truncheon and threw it at the rat, missing it by a mile. I should have known there were rats there because of the rat poison in the dishes on the floor.

Just on the outskirts of Walsall, there were some freight sidings and they were the targets of thieves stealing the brass wagon bearings. One-night shift I was part of a team keeping observations on the wagons. The previous night we had a briefing from Detective Sergeant Cyril Ball instructing us not to wrap our sandwiches in greaseproof paper (Cling film had not been invented) and under no circumstances to bring any potato crisps for our snap. We sat underneath a couple of wagons. For communication, we had two Pye Bantam radios. These were strapped to your back, had an aerial of about two foot and had a range of about two yards. They were pretty useless. As an afterthought we were informed that the gang might be armed with guns. The gang never turned up.

One Friday in the early 1970s a coal train from Saltley, Birmingham, collided with the rear of a Kings Norton to Bathgate, Scotland, car train at Ryecroft Junction, Walsall. Several of the carflats along with the cars on them were completely destroyed.

I was dispatched on the following day to provide a police presence at the scene. It was a thoroughly wet day. The crew of the diesel hauling the breakdown train took pity on me and invited me into the cab from where I had a perfect view of the site and did not get wet. I also enjoyed a fully cooked breakfast courtesy of the train crew.

CHAPTER 6

THE BIRMINGHAM YEARS 1973 – 1974

Arresting a member of the Gentry

I arrested a male for Trespass and Refuse to Quit and Disorderly Conduct on Saturday 13 January 1973. He was lodged in the cells at Digbeth police station. During the night, he made a self-inflicted wound to his head by banging it on the wall of the cell and was treated at the Birmingham Accident Hospital. On the following Monday, he appeared before the Magistrates and refused to enter a plea to the charges. He was remanded in custody until Wednesday 17 January during which time he was assessed by the Mental Health Authorities who committed him under a 72-hour order under the Mental Health Act.

February of 1973 saw me at Tadworth for four weeks attending a Final Recruit Continuation Course, which I passed.

After successfully completing my probationary period I was permanently appointed to the force with effect from the 5 April 1973.

We used to arrange our retirement functions and other social functions at the British Railways Staff Association Social Club at Monument Lane, Birmingham, and would book some semi-professional bands and comedians. At this time, there was a popular soap opera called 'Crossroads' on the television about a Motel in the Midlands. It was screened on Monday to Friday nights. It seemed that everyone watched it, as the crime rate dipped when it was on. Two of the stars of the show, were a married couple, who played two old age pensioners 'Wilf and Madge'. In real life their son was an entertainer. On Thursday 19 April 1973, we held a social evening at the club. We booked their son as our cabaret. Word got round that 'Wilf and Madge' would be attending as well. The evening was a sell-out for us, tickets were only 40p for entertainment, raffle, bingo, and a buffet. Good value in those days.

One Sunday afternoon in the spring of 1973, due to the theft of components from brand new road vehicles, which were on freight wagons ready to go to various destinations in Britain, I was asked to go on observations with a dog handler to Washwood Heath freight sidings which were adjacent to the main Birmingham to Derby railway line.

We found a brake van where we took up residence keeping an eye on the wagons in the sidings. After a few hours, our patience was rewarded, a youth suddenly appeared on a wagon a few hundred yards away from us. We went towards him. On seeing us he started to run away from us. The dog handler shouted, "Stop or I'll let the dog go". He took no notice of this command and continued running. The dog handler let his dog loose with the instructions to 'fetch', and for me to remain where I was for a few minutes and then follow. The dog ran off like a greyhound out of a trap followed by the handler in pursuit of the youth.

A matter of seconds later the dog stopped, turned around and started chasing his handler. Needless to say, the youth made his getaway, whilst the handler had to fight his dog off. It was embarrassing to say the least. Inwardly I was laughing my socks off.

On Saturday 5 May 1973 at about 14.40 hours a young girl from Lichfield was on the Birmingham Shopping Centre with some friends when she was approached by three 'Skinhead' type girls demanding money and a ring she was wearing, or she would 'get her head knocked in'. One of the assailants forcibly searched the victim and stole 15 pence from her and forcibly removed her ring from her finger. I made extensive enquiries with a negative result.

In late May of 1973 one of the jobs I had was to report a local motorist for parking longer than 20 minutes in the 20 minutes waiting zone. The powers that be at Divisional Headquarters gave the offending motorist a written caution. He replied thanking the force for the leniency. However, he added a Postscript to the letter.

'I found your junior officer a very serious young man. He obviously is a reader of thrillers, and he warned me on four occasions in a few minutes, that anything I said might be used as evidence. No mean effort of self-control was needed to resist the desire to play out an equally melodramatic role'.

Ever since I started school, I excelled in geography and had a fascination with Russia and its people. During a week of the spring in 1973 a trade delegation came over from a town in Russia, the former USSR, (the name of which escapes me) to Birmingham and set up various stalls on the Birmingham Shopping Centre. I was on duty on the Shopping Centre one morning and I thought here is my chance to find out a little bit more about Russia and its people. I went to the stalls as 'the friendly British Bobby' to speak to them. All were very reluctant to divulge information to me. I think they thought that I was part of MI5 and that my radio was transmitting back to the MI5 headquarters. I think in Russia, they were not used to speaking to a police officer so openly. No doubt Ivan and Boris from the KGB (Komitet Gosudarstvennoy Bezopasnosti – Committee for State Security) were lurking in the background.

One evening in June 1973 the Birmingham City Police CID organised what was known as a 'Smoking Concert' at a public house in the Perry Bar district of Birmingham. BTP officers were extended an invite. The main attraction of the concert was a female stripper. I was sat on the front tables with some other BTP officers and civilian staff.

The stripper came on the stage and began her act for which there was rapturous appreciation from the assembled audience. She then came down to our tables and began to strip further down. She went to one of our civilian staff who had a bald head, removed one of her breasts and bounced it on his head. To which there were shouts of "more" from the audience. She then removed his pipe from his mouth, stuck it in a part of the anatomy that shall remain anonymous and put it back in his mouth. I could see that he was enjoying the experience as his spectacles steamed up. He was completely mesmerised by these actions. I had always thought of this person as being prim and proper.

I believe it was in the summer of 1973 when there was an arsonist on the loose in the town centre of Sutton Coldfield and neighbouring villages. It was feared that he would strike at railway stations in the area. So, one night I found myself on night turn at Blake Street railway station along with PC Don Evans and his dog from Wolverhampton. Don's dog was the biggest and hairiest German Shepherd I have ever seen. It was a fearsome brute and would have probably given the 'Hound of the Baskerville's' a run for its money. Don and I along with his dog duly settled down for the night in the glass waiting shelter on the Lichfield bound platform. This shelter was similar to the bus shelters that are in use on our streets. Don and I sat upright all night, but the dog laid down at Don's feet, snoring very loudly, dreaming about what dogs dream about, and only surfacing when he smelt our sandwiches, needless to say he didn't get anything. Fortunately, the arsonist did not strike on the railway.

The Rolling Stones pop group rolled into the Odeon on New Street Birmingham, on Wednesday 19 September 1973 for a sell-out concert. After the concert, their fans were in abundance outside the front entrance. However, for reasons unknown, the 'Stones' wanted to make a quick getaway, therefore they left the premises via the fire exit and onto the roof of the Birmingham Shopping Centre, where I and a couple of other officers were on duty to make sure that they got into their vehicle and left the area uninterrupted.

Another football train escort on 3 November 1973, saw me as part of a serial escorting a returning Cardiff to Wolverhampton football special train. As the train was entering Birmingham New Street station, at 19.45 hours, I discovered that a table in a compartment had been pulled away from the window fittings. The table was intact at 19.30 hours when I checked the compartment. Enquiries with the six hundred or so fans were made with a negative result.

Whilst on duty at New Street on Saturday 24 November 1973, I dealt with a male Civil Servant who travelled from Wylde Green Station to Birmingham New Street, using a female's season ticket. He was interviewed and reported for travelling on the railway without having previously paid his fare and with intent to avoid payment and also for receiving a female's season ticket. On the 10 January 1974 I interviewed the female, also a Civil Servant and reported her for transferring the ticket and aiding and abetting the male person to travel on the railway without having previously paid his fare. Both appeared at Birmingham City Magistrates Court on Wednesday 3 April 1974 and were each fined £5 on the offences against them. This case caused me extra paperwork as Civil Servants who were convicted of an offence had to be reported to the Home Office.

In 1973, I along with other officers went to an officer's stag night. We finished duty at 14.30 hours and went to the Railway Club at Monument Lane. At 23.00 hours after the club closed, we then went to the Peter Rabbit Night Club in Broad Street. We left there at about 04.00 hours the following morning. DC Brian Jones dropped me off at the mother-in-law's where Shirley and I were staying. She heard me open the door and asked what I was doing. I told her that I was just going out on rest day working. I went back to the city centre, had some breakfast, and returned home stating that my duty had been cancelled.

I think it was in 1973 that we received diced black and white bands to wear on our caps. This dicing is known by the nickname. *'The Sillitoe Tartan'*. This was before the Birmingham City Police had them and after they were issued to the Warwickshire Police. Needless to say, that we all wanted to pose in them. The Birmingham City Police got wind of this and assumed that we had been taken over by the Warwickshire Police. An order soon went out that we could only wear them whilst in the car and we had to revert to our helmets.

Friday 10 August 1973 at 23.50 hours saw me on a night turn of duty at Birmingham New Street, I came across a youth who was shouting and swearing, he was not drunk, but was arrested. Upon searching him, I discovered that he had a large lock knife in his possession. He was charged with both offences and appeared at Birmingham Magistrates' Court the following day, where he was fined.

Towards the end of a late turn of duty in Mid-August 1973 I was on the Concourse of New Street Station, when the 'Midland-Scot' Inter-City train from Glasgow Central arrived at 22.10 hours. A small, but smartly dressed gentleman came up to me, carrying a suitcase, which he could hardly hold, and demanded that I get his car for him from the car park. I could smell alcohol on his breath, and I suggested that he take a taxi. He insisted that I get his car and he became more vocal. He then started shouting and swearing and knocked my helmet off. So, I arrested him for being Drunk and Disorderly. With the assistance of the late PC Tony Richards, we conveyed him to our police office and the Sergeant took one look at him and told us to take him immediately to Digbeth police station. He struggled all the way to the police vehicle, a minibus, banging his head on the step of the side entrance to the vehicle as we tried to put him in.

At Digbeth he was placed straight in a cell. The Duty Sergeant asked if I knew who he was. I told him that he was too drunk to get any sense out of him. I found a business card in his possession that stated that he was 'Sir so and so' from the East Midlands. The Sergeant said that probably he was a con man going around conning old ladies out of their money. He went onto say that the CID would be extremely interested in him once he had sobered up.

I searched his suitcase and found a photograph of him with a prominent member of the Royal Family. I showed this to the Sergeant whose attitude changed completely and sheer panic set in. I could see that he was worried about his pension as he was about due for retirement. The man was in fact a member of the gentry and had been to a family funeral in Scotland.

To be fair, he was not given any preferential treatment. He was detained in custody along with the other drunks from the city streets. When he had sobered up, he was charged and taken to court the following morning. I came back after about three hours rest for the court proceedings, where he pleaded 'Not Guilty'. He was bailed.

A prosecution file was prepared and handed to Stan Short, the Prosecuting Solicitor for the force in not guilty pleas and more complex cases in Birmingham. On the day of the trial, he changed his plea to 'Guilty' and was fined £10.

Every Christmas time, British Railways used to erect a Christmas tree on the forecourt of New Street station and decorate it with coloured lights. A collecting box was placed adjacent to it with the proceeds going to the Railway Children's Home in Derby.

A few days before Christmas 1973, I was on duty on night turn on the forecourt, when a male person went by me and remarked how nice the tree looked. I replied to him. The next thing, in full view of me and much to my amazement, he started to remove about eight or nine of the bulbs from the tree and put them in his pocket. He then walked away. I arrested him for theft as it was now obvious he was not going to return them. I charged him and refused him bail. I then prepared the prosecution file. He appeared at court the next morning. I gave the facts, stating that due to the fact that the proceeds of the collection box would be going to the Railway Children's Home and that people might be deterred from donating money if the tree was not properly lit owing to the defendant's actions in stealing the lights. I went onto to say the children at the home would be denied much needed money. The Magistrates' Clerk leaned over to me and asked where my violin was. The man received one week in prison due to his previous record.

A couple of days after this arrest I was on duty on late turn on the station forecourt as it was fast approaching Christmas. We were told if possible, to move the drunks on and concentrate on more serious offences. I came across one man, an Irish Labourer, about 6'6" and built like the proverbial brick shed, from Sparkhill, a suburb of Birmingham. He was worse the wear for drink. I moved him on, but he came back to shake my hand for not arresting him. I then told him to be on his way. He walked away, came back, and started shouting and swearing at the top of his voice, so I had no option, but to arrest him. As I took hold of him, he pulled me up in the air and threw me down like a rag doll onto the fabric of the forecourt. As I hit the concrete floor, I could see the stars before me. I was momentarily knocked out, I came to, to find a woman screaming "He's killed the officer". I established which way he went and called for assistance. It took nine of us to hold him down. He was taken to Digbeth police station where he was charged with Drunk and Disorderly and Assault on Police. I attended the Birmingham Accident Hospital, where I received a brain scan. I pleased to say that contrary to popular belief, the Doctor found one. I was later discharged. I had received severe facial bruising.

Following the assault, I did not book sick, but was put on light duties in the Information Room, but more importantly didn't want to let my colleagues down as I had been rostered to work late turn on Christmas Day. Had I gone sick I would have been very unpopular with whoever had to cover my shift.

I was on duty at the counter in the Information Room one evening and an elderly lady came to enquire if her purse had been found which had been stolen some weeks previously. I was very sympathetic towards her and told her that it had not been found and that it was highly unlikely that it would ever be found. The lady looked extremely disappointed saying. "I can't understand it, if it had been Dixon of Dock Green, and that nice Mr. Crawford they would have had it solved in half an hour". Some people really believe in television.

Having recovered from my injuries just before Christmas 1973, on 5 January 1974 at 16.55 hours, I was on duty on Platform Ten of Birmingham New Street station when I was approached by a female who stated that she had just travelled on an Edinburgh to Plymouth train and that she believed a male person had stolen £27 from her handbag whilst she had inadvertently left it unattended in a toilet. I made a search of the ten-coach train with the complainant and she identified the suspect who denied all knowledge of the theft. I arrested him on suspicion of theft. As I was taking him to the police office, he became very violent and had to be restrained, fortunately PC Keith Fleetwood was on hand to assist me. During the struggle, he bit Keith's right thumb.

He was questioned and admitted stealing the money and throwing it out of the train. He was charged with Assault Occasioning Actual Bodily Harm and Theft.

During an early turn tour of duty in January of 1974 whilst I was on the concourse of New Street station, I met up with Detective Sergeant Oakes who was the Officer in Charge at Coventry. He asked if I would consider transferring to Coventry as he was short staffed. I said I would give it some thought. I discussed the transfer with Chief Inspector Maurice Woodman at Divisional Headquarters and asked if I could have a temporary transfer just in case I did not settle down there. My request was refused.

I had just commenced a night turn on Friday 18 January 1974 when at around 21.30 hours, I and two other officers received a call to go to the 'Taurus Bar' on the main concourse as there was a dispute over the payment of drinks and food. A male person was claiming to have paid for his drinks, and some food, but the bar staff were refuting this. I took the lead in the case. Although he smelt strongly of alcohol, he was asked to accompany us to the police office whilst further enquires were made. Outside on the concourse he started to swear, so I arrested him for being Drunk and Disorderly. He struggled violently and the three of us tried to calm him down, but he became unmanageable putting up a formidable struggle. He was eventually handcuffed and taken to the police office with the assistance of another three officers. In the interview room, he continued to struggle violently and in doing so, damaged a wall ventilation grill, two wall mounted coat hangers and damaged the plaster on the wall. He was taken to Digbeth police station where was placed in a cell. Whilst in the cell he damaged a toilet pan and a windowpane. In the end, he was charged with Criminal Deception, two counts of Criminal Damage and being Drunk and Disorderly.

I had a lucky escape on Sunday 20 January 1974. At 01.20 hours I was on duty in the short wait car park on the station concourse of New Street station when I saw a 7 cwt Bedford van parked there. The registration plates were unreadable and there was no Road Fund Licence visible. At around 02.05 hours the driver of the van approached and started up the engine and began to drive off. I went over to the van and signalled him to stop. He failed to do so. I ran after the van and tried to open the driver's door. The van accelerated and dragged me along the road for about, thirty-five yards, when I lost my grip. Subsequent enquiries failed to locate the driver. Fortunately, I was uninjured.

A young lady on Friday 1 March 1974, was the unfortunate victim of a Robbery on the Birmingham Shopping Centre, by two black youths who stole her handbag and contents. Unfortunately, she did not report the incident until Tuesday 5 March when she saw me on patrol on the Birmingham Shopping Centre. Subsequent enquiries failed to trace the two offenders.

I will always be eternally grateful to Mr. Brunskill. After Shirley and I were married we were unable to afford a house, even though we had a decent deposit for a mortgage and were both in full time employment. The big building societies were only giving out around twelve mortgages a month and it seemed that we did not qualify. Therefore, we lived in flats and with Shirley's family. In early 1974 when Shirley was expecting our son, Stephen, I was speaking to Mr. Brunskill, who was asking how I was getting on in the force. I informed him that I was enjoying my career but was unable to get a mortgage and with a baby due in May things looked difficult re housing. A few days later a letter arrived at the police office for me, from the City of Birmingham Treasurer's office inviting me for an interview in connection with a mortgage. I attended the interview and was accepted for a mortgage. I discovered that Mr. Brunskill had written to them regarding my plight.

Early in March 1974 I moved into a small terraced house in South Yardley, Birmingham. I also went on to the four-weekly pay system, whereby my salary was paid direct into the bank.

I was within sight of completing a late turn tour of duty on Sunday 24 March 1974. It was around 21.00 hours when I received a report that a man had broken one of the booking office windows which was situated on the concourse. The man, who turned out to be a Royal Marine from Plymouth, had an argument with the booking clerk over his ticket. He lost his temper and grabbed hold of the part of the window where you speak through and pulled it with such force that it cracked from one corner to the other. These windows were supposed to be made of toughened glass, which was supposedly bullet proof and shatter proof! However, this was not the case. I arrested him, as I was taking him in an approved hold, he started to struggle violently with me. It took six police officers and three members of the rail staff to take him to the police office. He was charged with Criminal Damage and Disorderly Conduct and detained in custody to appear at court the next day. After being sentenced he was handed over to the Royal Navy Police from Devonport and went with them like a lamb.

At the end of March 1974, I came off my long weekend to commence a night shift of seven days commencing with a twelve-hour night shift at Birmingham New Street, 18.30 hours to 06.30 hours. I arrived in the office at about 18.00 hours and there in my basket was a hand-written note from the day Duty Inspector, instructing me to take the first available train after 18.30 hours to Coventry, as I had been selected to go there for a few weeks to cover, on the understanding that I performed duty at New Street as and when required. I obtained a duty pass, collected the files from my basket, along with my uniform and went off to Coventry.

CHAPTER 7

THE COVENTRY YEARS 1974

Upsetting the Detective Constable and meeting the 'Von Trapp family' of Coventry

I caught the 18.40 hours train to Coventry arriving there at just after 19.00 hours on that March evening in 1974, to meet up with PC Maurice King who was just completing his tour of duty. He gave a whistle stop tour of the office accommodation and booked off duty. I had barely settled in when Reg Gould the duty Station Supervisor came to the office, he stated that there were children playing on the Nuneaton line, near to the Warwick Road goods yard. I told him that I was the new Sheriff in town. He advised me to go to the end of Platform One, walk along the track to the right, take a deep breath after about 200 yards and I would be at the scene of the trespass. I asked him why the deep breath. He informed me that there was a pig farm adjacent to the railway. Area searched, negative result. Back to the office to get my bearings and have a cup of coffee, having inhaled 'Eau de pig'.

The police office at Coventry was on the first floor of the railway administrative block and consisted of two offices, a general office, which had a couple of desks for report writing, a table for the messing facilities and our clothing lockers. Next door was the communal toilets and next door to them was the Sergeant's office. The rear of the stage of the British Railways Staff Association Club was next to the Sergeant's office. To a club full of members, enjoying their drinks, the singer on a Saturday night sounded like Al Martino or Max Bygraves, but to a stone-cold sober copper, under pressure, trying to complete his paperwork he sounded like a cat being strangled.

During my stay at Coventry, I worked alone most of the time, again this was good grounding, there was a Detective Sergeant, who usually worked days, after he went home you were the Chief Constable. I believe the official establishment at Coventry was one Detective Sergeant, a Detective Constable and seven Police Constables who worked in plain clothes and received a regular plain clothes allowance. Uniform was worn as and when required, usually on nights and at the weekend. A Uniform Sergeant and a second Detective Constable were appointed as additional resources in late 1974. There was no clerk at Coventry, so you had to type all your own files and reports, in at the deep end. At Birmingham, we had a very efficient Clerical Officer, Hilary Foulds. The Sergeant would check your draft written copy then it would go to Hilary, once ready for typing. At Coventry the Sergeant usually prosecuted, but sometimes the officer in the case would. We also covered the police post at Northampton from Coventry and one PC and DC were based there. The Police Post at Rugby had been closed a few years earlier, but we still retained an office there for the purpose of interviews etc.

We had an unmarked Vauxhall estate car, dark blue in colour, registration number TOA 921H which was shared between the CID and uniformed officers. There were two parking spaces allocated to the BTP at the station. One was used by the official car and the other was used by the Detective Sergeant.

I soon realised that there were only four uniform Constables to cover Coventry at this time. I and three others including the Constable from Northampton. To say that we were stretched was an understatement. I regularly worked a twelve-hour day and twelve-hour nights. In late 1974 one of the Constable's went to Holyhead as part of a serial to deal with the farmer's dispute, so we really struggled for manpower.

Roy Timms the Detective Constable, sadly was not a well man, he suffered from a chest complaint and other ailments, but to his great credit he would not go sick but performed his duties to the best of his abilities. He was one of the 'old school'. He nicknamed me 'Chequebook Charlie' as I had gone onto four-weekly pay. Roy was still paid weekly and drew his wages on a Thursday from the booking office.

Chris Cooper was a fellow Constable at Coventry with me and like me was a great joker. We were on the same wavelength and shared the same sense of humour. The police service at that time was well known for playing jokes on colleagues.

Roy Timms was very anti-Japanese. He served in the Second World War, but never spoke about his service. I suspect that he might have been a Prisoner of War by the Japanese. At this time, I had some old Japanese Yen, which I kept at home. Chris and I hatched a plot to play a joke on poor old Roy. I brought it in to the office and kept it in my locker until I saw my chance.

One Thursday morning Chris and I were on duty together. I said that I was going out for a patrol of the station. Roy who at this time was typing up a prosecution file asked me if I could get his wages. I took his card and drew his wages. I then obtained a blank wage slip and an empty wages envelope and went to the clerk's office on the station, where I typed up the wage slip and wrapped it round the Japanese Yen and placed it in the envelope. I returned to the office and Roy stopped what he was doing. He always insisted on counting his money. It did not matter if he was interviewing a triple murderer he would stop. He opened the envelope and Chris and I retreated from him. On seeing the Yen, he came out with several expletives and was coughing and sputtering. Norman Oakes came out of his office to see what was going on. When Roy had calmed down, we got a bollocking from Norman.

Another trick we played on Roy was cutting two eye holes in a newspaper. Roy was a reader of the Daily Express, which in those days was a broadsheet. He would usually dispose of it in the litter bin before he went home.

We retrieved one and kept it back, so as not to damage his current one. Chris and I cut two 'eye holes' in this paper, folded it over and awaited our chance. It came along one morning when Roy announced that he was going to go on the concourse to carry out some observations. We knew that he would take his newspaper with him. We swapped the papers over without Roy knowing. When he came back there were a few expletives. He took it all in good part and saw the funny side.

On the first of April 1974 when the new forces came into being and the new West Midlands Police force was established, I had to return to Birmingham to go to Sutton Coldfield Magistrates' Court with a couple of cases. On arrival at the police station which was adjacent to the court I introduced myself to the PC on duty at the counter and before I could ask him where the canteen was, to partake of a bacon sandwich and a cup of tea, he told me that he didn't know where my office was. He thought that the BTP had been amalgamated and that I was reporting for duty. I managed to get to the canteen for a cup of tea and a bacon sandwich before attending court.

Monday 15 April 1974 between 04.15 hours and 04.20 hours saw the theft of a Ronson gas lighter and seventeen cigarettes belonging to a Railway Clerk, from the central signing on point at Rugby railway station. He suspected that a couple of employees were responsible. Enquiries were made by DS Oakes and myself with a negative result.

Situated on the outskirts south of Coventry, on the main railway line to London there were two notorious trespass and vandalism locations, namely the suburb of Willenhall, where there was a large housing estate and Humber Road.

Monday 22 April 1974 at 18.15 hours due to regular trespass reports between Coventry, Willenhall and Stoke Aldermoor, I carried out a lineside patrol and saw a youth in the distance walking along the railway embankment carrying a ·22 air rifle. The offender left the railway. I made enquiries in the locality and went to a nearby farmyard. On arrival I saw the youth who initially denied being the person responsible, but he later confessed to being the person who was on the railway embankment for the purpose of shooting rabbits. I had to recover the rifle; the only snag was that he had thrown it in a pile of pig dung. A very unpleasant experience trying to recover it as I was slipping and sliding in the dung. My boots and the bottom of my trousers were covered in the stuff. The youth was reported for trespass with a firearm.

A Permanent Way Inspector from Rugby on the 19 May 1974 at 11.30 hours reported the theft of two telephone handsets from a signal post near to Brandon ballast pit near Coventry on the main line between Coventry and Rugby. So, it was out to the remote location to make enquiries, which proved negative.

I think it was in May 1974 when I received a report of a Flasher on a train between Birmingham New Street and Coventry. I teamed up with PC Maurice King, to investigate the matter. A statement was duly obtained from the victim. We established that the offender was a regular traveller on an all-stations Birmingham to Coventry train. Maurice and I travelled in plain clothes and, 'bingo', he flashed to a female just as we were approaching Hampton-in-Arden station. He was removed from the train. It transpired that he lived in Hampton-in-Arden. He pleaded with us not to tell his wife. It was quite easy to verify his address as he resided in a local shop which was run by his wife. He went into the shop and I followed him into the shop and purchased a bar of chocolate and from the conversation he had with the lady behind the counter it was obvious that it was his wife and that he lived there. He was summoned to appear at Solihull Magistrates' Court. He came to the office at Birmingham New Street to collect his summons. I believe that his wife did find out because the case was highlighted in the local papers.

At around 01.45 hours on 16 May 1974, an unidentified member of the public saw a guard's brake van on fire in Holbrook Colliery sidings, Coventry. The local Fire Brigade and Police attended the scene. The BTP were not informed until 09.52 hours that day. I commenced enquiries with the CID, but with a negative result.

In May of 1974, my son was born in Solihull Hospital. Before I went to see him, I purchased the biggest toy panda that I could from Mothercare. On the way to the hospital, I went to Barclays Bank in Birmingham city centre to draw out some money and one of the clerk's there admired my panda. I told her what it was for. A few weeks later I was prosecuting a case at Birmingham City Magistrates' Court and the Chair of the bench leaned over to me and asked how my son and panda were doing. She was the clerk in Barclays Bank who admired the panda.

Most of us have seen the film *'The Sound of Music'*. I wonder if many of you have ever had a 'Sound of Music moment', you know, when Captain Von Trapp lines up his children to meet Maria. Something similar happened to me at Coventry when I had only been there for about two months. One Sunday afternoon I was called to the freight sidings at Humber Road (where the cars from the Chrysler factory were despatched from) to an 8-year-old trespasser. I took him home and met his mother. After initial introductions and suitable words of guidance to her and her son, she realised that we had not met before, as the British Transport Police officers were regular visitors to her home. She informed me that her off-spring were regular visitors to the railway and that I best meet them, so I knew who they were for future reference. She called them in and lined all nine of them up one by one, just like the scene from the *'Sound of Music'*. I did meet some of them again.

A detonator was placed on the up fast West Coast Railway Line at Shilton near Nuneaton on 21 May 1974 prior to 20.43 hours. The locomotive of the 19.04 hours Liverpool Lime Street to London Euston Inter-City passenger train exploded the detonator and the driver brought the train to a halt. Other trains in the area were 'cautioned'. This type of detonator contained gunpowder and is used by railway staff for warning trains of dangers on the track. Extensive enquiries were made but with a negative result.

A pile of scrap iron was placed on the railway line at Stockingford, Nuneaton prior to 18.05 hours on 24 May 1974. The 'lifeguard' of the Diesel Multiple Unit pushed the obstruction clear of the track. A passenger on the train asked the driver if he was going to report the incident. The driver stated that it was too late. The passenger himself reported it some thirty minutes later. Enquiries were made in the area, but the trail was cold.

Persons unknown threw hessian sacking on to the overhead live wires at Willenhall Coventry, on the 31 May 1974, causing a delay to the 18.40 hours London Euston to Wolverhampton passenger train. Other trains were delayed as a result. The incident was not reported to the BTP until 10.00 hours on 2 June 1974. After extensive enquiries no one was detected for this offence.

Three boys aged nine years of age from the Tile Hill area of Coventry, were detected by the Railman from Tile Hill railway station for Trespass and Stone Throwing in Tile Hill goods yard. I took them to their homes and warned them as to their actions in the presence of their parents.

I was officially transferred to Coventry as from the 2 June 1974. I had no need to move to a new house as I lived on the south side of Birmingham and was able to use the train service from Lea Hall, about two miles from where I lived in South Yardley.

One of my duties at the beginning of June was on the Coventry to Nuneaton railway line to prevent trespassers using the railway as a short cut to the Nuneaton Carnival / Summer Fair in Pringles Field recreation ground. An easy duty. As far as I am aware it was a request from the Nuneaton Carnival committee to the force to have a police presence. I am not aware of any invoices being raised for our services. Our presence was useful, as much needed gate money for the local community would have been lost. I remained on duty there until the close of play to ensure members of the public did not return home via the railway, which incidentally in those days only saw a couple of freight trains a day and the odd diversion of a passenger train. Nowadays there is a regular passenger train service on the line.

From the top of the railway line, you actually looked down on to the field and could see for miles around. Only an idiot would try and trespass whilst a Policeman was in attendance. One female from one of the stalls, feeling sorry for me, came to the bottom of the embankment and brought me a cup of tea and a piece of homemade cake. I went down for it, returning almost immediately only to find a chap walking through a field and no doubt trying to climb the embankment from the opposite side. On seeing me he turned round and doubted my parentage.

In June of 1974 I spent two weeks at Tadworth on a pre-Home Office Detective Training Course, which I had been selected to attend.

Figure 4 Bill's pre Home Office Detective Training Course at Tadworth. Bill is in the middle row 3rd from the left

A wooden sleeper and several bricks were placed on the railway line on Wednesday 3 July 1974, at the scene of the old Bedworth railway station on the Coventry to Nuneaton railway line and these were struck by the Nuneaton to Banbury ballast train. I went to the scene with DS Oakes and we saw two juveniles on a bridge. They were questioned and admitted obstructing the railway. They were duly dealt with at court.

I dealt with a report of Criminal Damage to a large sidelight window of a 'local' passenger train from London Euston to Birmingham New Street which had been broken by a group of children, who were on the railway embankment at Humber Road on Friday 5 July 1974 at 2015 hours. Notwithstanding extensive enquiries the miscreants were never caught.

Sunday 7 July 1974 proved busy for me. At 15.00 hours I was on duty on the station concourse at Coventry when I saw a man leaning against the ticket barrier. He was unable to stand without assistance. I formed the opinion that he was drunk. He, like most drunks, doubted my parentage, and threatened me with the IRA. He was arrested and taken to Little Park Street police station where he was later charged and dealt with the following morning at court.

At around 19.45 hours that evening, as the 18.59 hours Wolverhampton to London Euston passenger train was passing through Willenhall, the driver from Wolverhampton noticed a ten-foot length of rope hanging from the overhead line equipment. Whoever threw it was very lucky indeed, they could have been electrocuted. The driver brought the train to a halt. The electric current was switched off in order to have the rope removed. I was called to the area, but the culprits had made good their escape. I made enquiries with several people in the area, but with a negative result. Train services were delayed for around two hours.

Prior to 20.15 hours on that Sunday evening, small concrete slabs and wooden sleepers were placed on the railway line at Foss Road, Leamington Spa. The driver of the 17.05 hours London Paddington to Birmingham New Street managed to stop without hitting the sleepers but was delayed for fifty minutes. I made enquiries, but they proved negative.

They always say that things come in threes, but for me they came in fours. That evening as the 20.29 hours Wolverhampton to London Euston passenger train was between Coventry and Rugby, a female from Belfast, who was a passenger on the train, locked herself in one of the toilets and pulled the communication cord. The train came to a halt and the guard went to the toilet and found that the female was in a hysterical condition. The guard was unable to calm her down. He took the decision to take the train to Rugby where it was met by officers of the Warwickshire Constabulary. The woman was removed from the train and taken to a nearby hospital where she was sedated. I then liaised with the local police. She was later certified under the Mental Health Act and taken to a hospital in Hatton where she received treatment. She was later discharged and returned to Belfast.

Saturday, 13 July 1974 saw me on a late turn tour of duty at Coventry. At around 20.17 hours I was in the police office at Coventry typing up a prosecution file, when I received a call from the BTP at London Euston to the effect that an off duty railway employee from London Kings Cross, was a passenger on the 16.36 hours Coventry to London Euston passenger train, when he thought he saw what appeared to be the body of a woman lying on the trackside approximately two minutes train ride from Coventry. This would have placed the train in the notorious area of Willenhall.

I, Sergeant Maurice Hyslop, and a couple of members of the railway staff made a search of the area, using an electric multiple unit. We found the body of a black and tan German Shepherd dog lying in between the railway tracks of the adjacent line in the Willenhall area. Apparently, whilst the dog was crossing over the line it was hit by a train, but this was not reported to us. A search of the line was made as far as Rugby and no body of a human being was found. So, we assumed that the dog was the 'body' that the person had seen.

In July 1974 I went on a four day long weekend after duty on a Thursday, and unusually I was not working a rest day on the Saturday. Prior to completing my tour of duty, I noticed that there was a non-police motor car parked in one of our dedicated parking spaces. I put a ticket on the windscreen requesting the driver to come to the police office so that they could be interviewed.

Just before I went off duty the driver, a Mr. Singh, came to the office, he was a Railman from the station. He was very apologetic and stated that he had been delayed in traffic and would have been late for duty if he had gone to the staff car park. I gave him a verbal warning and he was most appreciative for this. He asked me if I liked curry, not to offend him, I stated that I did (I am not a lover of curries). I went home and on returning on Tuesday night there was a strange smell coming from my desk drawer. It was a plate of curry in a brown envelope, which had gone off in the heat. All the grease had soaked into the brown envelope as well. There was a note affixed to my drawer stating that I should get rid of it ASAP. I later thanked Mr. Singh for his truly kind gesture.

Willenhall came to our attention again on 17 July 1974, as between 18.10 hours and 18.30 hours a signal telephone handset was stolen from a box adjacent to a signal. Enquiries in the area proved negative. People in this area were very uncooperative towards the police.

The same evening at 20.53 hours a large window of a passenger coach on the 19.40 hours London Euston to Wolverhampton passenger train was broken by children who were throwing stones at the train as it passed through Willenhall. Again, due to the uncooperative residents I was unable to trace the offenders.

At 00.40 hours on Wednesday 24 July 1974 whilst I was on a night tour of duty at Coventry, I arrested a male person at Coventry for Ticket Fraud, and for being Drunk and Disorderly whilst travelling on a train from London Euston to Coventry. He was later dealt with at court.

The following night, Thursday 25 July 1974, I was on a night shift again and dealt with a small theft of tins of Guinness which had been stolen from a carton in transit on a parcels train from Worcester to Coventry. Enquiries were made with a negative result. This was typical of the small thefts that were experienced from cartons and parcels in transit. The rail staff would usually be responsible helping themselves to a cheap drink. As I was returning from my enquiries, I found a male person urinating against a wall of a station building. I couldn't prove that it was the Guinness. He was reported under the byelaws.

The wooden level crossing gates on the main line at Canley, near Coventry were the focus of attention on Friday 26 July 1974 at about 02.25 hours, a blue Mini Minor motor car was being driven along Canley Road, when it crashed into the level crossing gates, which were closed to road traffic at the time. I later reported the driver for road traffic offences.

Like every large industrial town and city, Coventry had its annual fortnight holiday, when all the factories in the area closed down. The workers would go off on their annual holidays to wherever they fancied. One man in particular and his family from Coventry went to the sea-side resort of Weymouth in Dorset. Weymouth was the port for the ships to the Channel Islands. There was a railway line, from the main line that ran along the Weymouth Quay known as the Weymouth Tramway. And boat trains from London would run along this line to Weymouth Quay railway station. The Quay was also a main road. This was about one of the only railway lines that you could lawfully walk along.

However, motorists would park their cars indiscriminatory on the road in such as manner as to obstruct the train. The locomotive of which, carried a bell and was escorted by railway officials and members of the British Transport Police from Weymouth either on foot or in a vehicle. The vehicle would have to be 'bounced' out of the way by the staff.

On the 28 July 1974, a motorist on holiday from Coventry parked his car in such a manner that it obstructed the train. A request was sent to me asking if I would interview and report him for the offence.

Now, no one likes 'Not Guilty' pleas in court. But the gentleman concerned refuted the allegation during the interview and I advised him that the best course of action would be to challenge the evidence and attend court. A 'Not Guilty' plea would find that yours truly would have three days in beautiful Weymouth to give evidence of interview in court. A day to travel there, a day in court, and a day to travel back. Well, it backfired on me. He pleaded 'Guilty' in the end.

I thought I had a parcel thief in my sights on Sunday 28 July 1974 at 18.15 hours. I was on duty on Platform Two of Rugby railway station when I saw a male person standing near to a row of parcel cages. I kept him under observation for a while. Nothing happened so, I approached him, and he stated that he had travelled by train and gave me the names of several stations during the course of the interview. It transpired that he had travelled from London Euston with a ticket valid as far as Watford. He was arrested and conveyed to Rugby police station where he was detained in custody to appear at a special Magistrates' Court sitting the following day. The cost of his ticket fraud was £1.80p. He was duly fined and ordered to pay compensation.

Saturday 3 August 1974 saw me in Stratford upon Avon interviewing a local woman who had made several fraudulent train journeys between Solihull and Stratford upon Avon, whereby she offered to pay her fare from Bearley, a less distant station. She was reported for the offences and appeared at the local Magistrates' Court.

Between 13.40 hours and 14.15 hours on 9 August 1974 a Ford Cortina motor car was taken without consent of the owner from the car park at Hampton-in-Arden railway station whilst he was seeing someone off on a train. The vehicle was found the following day in Lea Hall a suburb of Birmingham. Sadly no one was ever detected for the offence. Those days there was no CCTV around.

Sometime towards the middle of August 1974, I had to take a witness statement from a lady in Leamington Spa re the theft of her luggage. I went over with Detective Sergeant Oakes as he had another enquiry in the area. He dropped me off on this lady's drive, which was made out of loose gravel. As he drove off, the rear wheels of the car skidded on the gravel, which at this time was wet after a heavy downpour. I got covered in mud and gravel bits. The lady's dog a standard Poodle came out to greet me, followed by the lady herself. She saw the state of me and enquired if 'Doggie-kins' had jumped up me. I told her very dryly that it was 'Sarge-ikins'.

At 10.30 hours Friday 16 August 1974 an overhead maintenance engineer from Rugby was working on the overhead wires at Canley, near Coventry when he found a General Post Office first-class mail bag lying by the trackside. Enquiries revealed that it was in transit from Bournemouth to Southern Ireland and had commenced its journey on the 10 August 1974. Mail bag thefts from trains on the West Coast Main Line and other locations were all too common in those days. We had a special squad of detectives at Force Headquarters who specialised in mail bag thefts. I handed the enquiry over to them.

A young lady from Leicester was the victim of a mindless act whilst she was standing on Hatton railway station, waiting for a local train to Birmingham when an unknown person threw a beer bottle from the 17.31 hours London Paddington to Birmingham New Street passenger train which was travelling through the station at speed, at 19.35 hours on 17 August 1974. The bottle struck the complainant on the legs causing three cuts to her right leg and one to her left leg. She was taken to the hospital in Birmingham. We never did find her assailant.

At about 16.30 hours on 19 August 1974 a large sidelight window in the Buffet Car of the 15.10 hours London Euston to Birmingham New Street passenger train was broken by a group of children who were throwing stones at the train as it was passing through the relatively rural area of Berkswell. The incident was not reported until 17.55 hours. By the time I arrived at the scene the trail was well and truly cold.

Sadly, on Thursday 22 August 1974 a passenger aged 39 years of age from London, travelling on the 13.22 hours Holyhead to London Euston passenger train, died in a toilet in one of the coaches. He joined the train at Crewe at around 16.00 hours with some work colleagues. Just before the train departed from Crewe, he remarked to his fellow passengers that he was not feeling too well. Shortly after leaving Crewe he went to a toilet, and when he did not return after some time, one of his colleagues went to the toilet to find him in a collapsed condition. On arrival at Nuneaton the Ambulance service along with a Doctor attended. The Doctor certified him as being dead. The following day Friday, 23 August a post-mortem examination was held at Nuneaton Hospital and the cause of death was found to be from a 'Coronary Insufficiency'. It transpired that he had been under medical supervision for the previous five years with a high cholesterol level, but it was being controlled. I then had to prepare a file for the local Coroner.

A resident of Coventry had his bicycle stolen from the multi storey car park at Coventry railway station between 07.20 hours and 18.15 hours on 28 August 1974. Again, no CCTV in those days.

At 10.08 hours on 28 August 1974 a large window on the 09.33 hours Wolverhampton to London Euston passenger train was broken by a group of children who were throwing stones at it whilst it passed through Hampton-in-Arden. Despite enquiries and observations no one was ever caught.

The placing of three metal fishplates at 19.30 hours on the Coventry to Leamington Spa line saw me visit Kenilworth Junction on 28 August 1974. As a Freightliner train from Liverpool Garston Dock to Southampton was running at a slow speed the driver was able to stop and remove the offending items. Unfortunately, enquiries proved negative.

Two concrete sleepers were placed on the railway line at Humber Road, Coventry prior to 18.30 hours on Thursday 5 September 1974 and these were struck by the 17.51 hours Birmingham New Street to Rugby passenger train, which was delayed for ten minutes. Again, these sleepers had the potential to derail the train.

A potentially serious incident took place on Friday 6 September 1974 when three 5' x ½" steel rods were placed on the railway line at Willenhall, prior to 19.15 hours and were struck by the 18.10 hours London Euston to Wolverhampton passenger train. The rods had the potential to derail the train.

Between 09.00 hours and 19.15 hours on Friday 6 September 1974 a Triumph Tiger motor scooter belonging to a gentleman from Leamington Spa was stolen from the ground floor of the multi-story car park at Coventry station. The motor scooter was later recovered in a nearby street. Despite making enquiries into the above-mentioned incident and others, no one was ever detected for the theft.

The flagship train of the newly electrified West Coast Main Line between Crewe and Glasgow Central, 'THE CLANSMAN' 10.30 hours Inverness to London Euston via Birmingham New Street, was delayed due to stones and bricks which had been placed on the railway line at Willenhall, prior to 20.08 hours on Friday 6 September 1974. Fortunately, I was in the cab of the locomotive en-route to Willenhall to investigate five earlier incidents, including one where the cab window of a locomotive hauling the 17.29 hours Wolverhampton to London Euston passenger train was broken by children throwing stones. The train was delayed for ten minutes. The driver of 'THE CLANSMAN' stopped the train before it hit the obstruction. Enquiries commenced and after observations two youths were detected and they cleared up several offences for us. As a result of the two detections, I arranged a visit to the local Juvenile Court for them and their parents.

I was part of an escort on a returning football special train from Stoke on Trent to Coventry on the 14 September 1974, when twelve small light bulbs were stolen from compartments on the train between 17.20 hours and 18.55 hours. With so many football supporters on the train it was impossible to detect an offender.

Foss Road Signalbox, between Leamington Spa and Banbury was the scene of a Burglary between 10.00 hours on Saturday 21 September 1974 and 06.00 hours on 23 September 1974 when three brass name plates were stolen from the block instruments. It was assumed that the Burglars entered the Signalbox by means of a duplicate key as there was no sign of forced entry. The enquiry was taken over from me by the CID.

Over the same period another Signalbox at Greaves Sidings about three miles away was broken into and similar items were stolen. Eventually a couple of people were detected for this and the above offence.

In September 1974, a local Councillor from Nuneaton made allegations in a local newspaper to the effect that persons were jumping from passenger trains as they passed through the Stockingford and Galley Common, areas of Nuneaton. The trains would pass through these locations at speeds of up to fifty miles per hour It was only when the signals were at caution they would slow down. Sergeant Hyslop and I went to the scene and over several days, maintained observations, which proved negative. It transpired that on Saturday 14 April 1973 five young football supporters had been detected in the locality whilst a train was stationary at signals, and it is believed that the instigator of the allegations was referring to this incident.

At 00.50 hours on Sunday 22 September 1974, a motorist travelling along Lavender Hall Road, Balsall Heath, Coventry, in an Austin 1100 motor car, failed to negotiate a left-hand bend and collided with a railway bridge, damaging a section of wall approximately 12' x 8'. The offending driver after being released from Hospital was reported by me for Criminal Damage.

At 18.40 hours on 26 September 1974, I received a report that a large sidelight window of a passenger coach on the 17.20 hours London Euston to Birmingham New Street passenger train had been broken by a group of children who were standing on the railway embankment at Willenhall as the train passed through at 18.15 hours. Obviously, the message had not got to the culprits about the earlier detections.

Several Leeds football supporters on Saturday 9 November 1974 at 17.28 hours went into the refreshment room of Coventry station. The Manageress heard the bell of the cash till ring. She saw a Leeds United football supporter taking money, a total of £1.49 from the till in loose change. She reported the matter to two British Transport Police officers who were part of a serial escorting a football special to back to Leeds. She was unable to identify the culprit.

Humber Road, Coventry was the scene of an obstruction on Monday 11 November 1974 at around 12.40 hours when a car tyre was placed on the up-railway line there. The locomotive of the 12.18 hours Birmingham New Street to London Euston train knocked the tyre from the line. Detective Sergeant Norman Oakes and I went to the scene. We searched the area and found two boys from the nearby housing estate hiding in a disused car body on the railway embankment. They admitted placing the tyre on the track and they admitted rolling a car tyre down the embankment at 12.03 hours in front of the 10.40 hours London Euston to Wolverhampton passenger train, the same day. They were duly dealt with at Coventry Juvenile Court. The car body along with other debris was later removed. The area suffered from serious fly tipping from the nearby residents.

In late November I took two weeks annual leave with the family up at my parents' home in Morecambe. On the night of the 21 November 1974, I heard on the radio about the terrible pub bombings in Birmingham. The bombs exploded in two public houses killing twenty-one persons and injuring one hundred and eighty-two others. Shortly afterwards I learned that my sister-in-law had been very severely injured whilst she was on a night out in one of the pubs. Later she was sent to Spain to recover for three months. Today she still has nightmares about the incidents and is reluctant to go into a crowded pub.

On returning to work after my annual leave, I did a short spell of duty back at Birmingham to cover for the extra patrols that were being carried out.

A gentleman from Handsworth, Birmingham, who was returning from an antiques sale in Banbury on Tuesday 17 December 1974 and who had purchased several antique items in the sale was the victim of a theft. He joined the 19.57 hours London Paddington to Birmingham New Street train at Banbury. He had to leave two clocks and two bottles of wine and sherry in a carrier bag in the corridor of the coach he was travelling in. During the journey he fell asleep. After the train left Leamington Spa at 21.49 hours, he noticed that the items had been stolen from the corridor. The guard informed him that he believed a group of youths who alighted at Leamington Spa were responsible. He did not report the offence until he arrived at Birmingham New Street at 22.30 hours. The enquiry was adopted by the CID after my initial enquiries.

Again, at Coventry there was a PC who had the reputation of being somewhat of a ladies' man. He had several years' service under his belt. I got on well with him as he was a fellow Lancastrian. I remember one winter's day in December 1974; he was going over to patrol the Warwick Road goods yard. The quickest way to the yard was to walk through the station car park up some steps and across Warwick Road itself, which went over the railway station on an incline.

This particular day the pavement was very slippery after a fall of snow. My colleague saw a lady walking precariously down the road, carrying two full cans of paraffin, one in each hand. He went up to her and offered to carry the cans for her, an offer which was gladly accepted. He went a few yards slipped and went sliding down the pavement with much embarrassment, on his backside. He quickly reunited the lady with her paraffin cans and made a hasty retreat to the goods yard to nurse his bruises and wait for the humiliation to die down.

As the year was rapidly drawing to an end, I began to prepare to join a ten-week Home Office Detective Training course with the Merseyside Police in Liverpool, in January.

CHAPTER 8

THE COVENTRY YEARS 1975

Getting a thrill going over the points at Rugby. Being offered a quickie on the A45

Between 6 January 1975 and 14 March 1975, I attended the Home Office Detective Training course J.32/75 at the Merseyside Police Training School, Mather Avenue, Liverpool.

During the course our Detective Chief Superintendent Basil Nicholls came to give the class, a talk on the work of the British Transport Police. All the students were extremely impressed indeed with what Mr. Nicholls had to say. Needless to say, following his talk, I was given the customary pep talk from him.

I did well on the course and the Chief Inspector back at Division stated that I was 'Deserving of commendation'. But with all the socialising, I gained two stone in weight. The senior officers at Division were not impressed when I applied for a new uniform.

Settling back into active police work at Coventry, found me dealing with the same type of offences I had dealt with the previous year. Willenhall was still there and just as busy with the problems of trespass and vandalism.

The level crossing at Blackhorse Road, Exhall, on the Coventry to Nuneaton line, kept me busy with road traffic offences, whereby motorists would disobey the red flashing lights at the crossing and driving across the crossing as the barriers were descending. An extremely dangerous practice. The offending motorists were dealt with under the Road Traffic Act 1972 with the more serious cases being dealt with under the Malicious Damage Act 1861 - Obstructing a Railway.

The Bank of England would send bags of coins for banks up and down the country via train in sealed containers to a goods yard where they would be loaded onto a road lorry. One of our duties at Coventry was to ride with the railway motor lorry to the bank and stand on the pavement outside the bank in full uniform and witness the bank staff unload the coins. One day outside one of the banks in Coventry city centre, the bank clerk, in the container threw a bag of pennies from the container towards the trolley, but it fell on the pavement and split open. There were pennies everywhere. I have never seen as many bank officials on their hands and knees picking them up. It was like a scramble at a Scottish wedding.

The last two inter-city trains out of London to Wolverhampton were fairly busy with businessmen who had stayed in the capital for a variety of reasons. Also, people who had been to the theatre shows in London would travel on these trains. They would arrive in Coventry at 00.40 hours and 02.10 hours. On selected nights I used to travel to Rugby and travel back with one of them. The latter train was frequented by prostitutes who would pick up a client, usually a businessman returning late from the office. They would perform their sexual acts in the toilets as all the carriages were 'open plan' with a central aisle.

On one occasion I travelled on the latter train and shortly after leaving Rugby and going over the complex point work at the junction I could hear grunting and groaning coming from a toilet. When the businessman and the lady of horizontal virtue came out, I spoke to them. The lady of the night explained to me that she got a real thrill going over the points at Rugby when engrossed in her favours. I'm sure that the Magistrates had a good laugh privately after hearing the facts

On Friday 28 March 1975, a gentleman joined the 19.30 hours Inverness to London Euston Sleeping Car train at Aviemore and placed his travelling wardrobe in the brake van. He went and sat in a passenger compartment. On arrival at Rugby at 05.55 hours the following morning he discovered that his wardrobe had been stolen. Enquiries along the line proved negative. These types of crimes were hard to detect, as they could have occurred anywhere during the four hundred plus miles journey.

I arrested two British Rail Permanent Way employees, who were built like brick sheds, for being Drunk and Disorderly whilst on Platform One of Coventry station. I requested assistance from the West Midlands Police to convey them to Little Park Street police station. After lodging them in the cells, the Duty Sergeant gave me an almighty telling off. "Never, never do that again. Whenever an officer of mine makes an arrest involving two people like you have done, they call for assistance first. You are one of my officers. Do I make myself clear?" "Yes Sarge". I said. "Go and get a cup of tea". He replied.

Late one evening, I believe it was in early April of 1975 when we received a report of a man trying to swim the River Avon at Stratford upon Avon. I will not mention which country he came from, but you can imagine. He had stolen some copper telephone wire from the Stratford upon Avon to Honeybourne and Cheltenham Line. He was trying to swim across the river, but the roll of wire was far too heavy for him and the roll of wire sunk, and he had to be rescued himself. He was suitably dealt with at court. We never did recover the wire.

It was back to Willenhall, on Wednesday 30 April 1975 at 18.30 hours for observations with DC Roy Timms on the railway embankment, when we saw two local boys come from the housing estate and place scrap metal, which had been thrown onto the embankment by local residents, onto the railway line. The boys were detained and reported for Obstructing the Railway.

I was still living in Birmingham and commuting daily from my house in South Yardley to Coventry. The nearest railway station to me was Lea Hall. On Thursday 1 May 1975 at 10.25 hours, I was on the platform waiting for my train to Coventry to commence an 11.00 hours to 23.00 hours shift, when I saw two boys cross over the railway lines. They remained by the lines. I went to them and identified myself. They stated that they were looking for Slowworms. (Good job they were not Adders). They were interviewed in the presence of their parents.

Stratford upon Avon is a beautiful town and is visited by people from all over the world, mainly, with people wanting to pay homage to the Bard himself, William Shakespeare and his good lady wife Anne Hathaway. We used to perform duty at the railway station, particularly when the Goose Fair was on and at Bank Holidays.

The Americans in particular would arrive in town by coach and be dropped off at the railway station. On seeing a police officer, the cameras would come out and several photographs would be taken. We would get asked questions such as, "Say officer, where is Bill Shakespeare's abode?" and "Gee there officer, where is Miss Hathaway's cottage?" Reports came in of a so-called enterprising chap, a real conman, who was selling what purported to be genuine William Shakespeare manuscripts typed on his own typewriter, to the Americans for £5. He was arrested for deception and he appeared at the local Magistrates' Court. The opening lines of the prosecution case were, "May it please your worships, as you are aware, William Shakespeare was born in this town on the 23 April 1564 and died, also in this town on the 23 April 1661. What your worships may not be familiar with is that the first commercial typewriter was not patented until 1868. Therefore......" As the facts of the case unfolded, he lowered his head further and further. That put paid to his little business.

It was customary for the early turn PC to wash the police vehicle on a Sunday morning. On one Saturday just before the end of the football season we had a group of supporters arrive at Coventry from London. One lad was a bit vocal, but border line on being reported. I took him to one side to warn him about his conduct and he pleaded with me not to book him as he wanted to go to the match. In return for me allowing him to go free with a verbal warning, he washed the police vehicle for me.

One Sunday in the spring of 1975 I was on late turn 15.00 hours to 23.00 hours when I received a radio call from the West Midlands Police at Little Park Street to the effect that a Llama was on the loose in Warwick Road goods yard. I checked the date in my pocketbook, it was definitely not 1 April. I asked them to repeat the message and yes there was a Llama on the loose. It transpired that the circus was in town and the Grand Parade was starting off from the goods yard, but nobody had informed us. I went to the yard only to find the circus staff along with the clowns frantically trying to capture the errant Llama. It was eventually caught, and the circus went on its way. The railway staff on duty there were in their element as there was plenty of assorted animal manure for their gardens.

Working in plain clothes had its advantages. In uniform you could be spotted a mile away. One particular evening following reports of trespass on the Coventry to Nuneaton line just on the outskirts of Coventry, I was on duty in plain clothes and I saw a youth on the railway embankment. If I had approached him in uniform he would have probably run away. I asked him where the nearest Fish and Chip shop was. He came down and showed me. He was reported for trespass.

In the early hours of the 6 June 1975 Nuneaton experienced a serious railway crash involving a night-time London to Glasgow train that derailed on the southern approach to Nuneaton Station. The train had undergone problems in the London area which had resulted in a replacement locomotive being added to the original faulty locomotive in order to continue its journey. The train was now running as a double headed train and proceeded northwards. On the approach to the station there was a temporary speed restriction, but the driver took the line at full speed. Sadly, six people were killed and thirty-eight were injured.

At the time of the crash I was on a long weekend and was rostered to work my rest day on Saturday 7 June 1975 for duty in connection with the Nuneaton Carnival. Due to the train crash, this duty was cancelled. I was called out on Friday 6 June for a fourteen-hour night Rest Day Working duty. I was working with Sergeant Norman Plover from Birmingham New Street, to look after the recovered property. We took over a waiting room on a platform. We took it in turns to have a little sleep in an old three-wheeled wooden bath chair which the railway used for less able people.

One morning in June 1975, DS Oakes and myself, in plain clothes, went to Northampton to investigate the theft of parcels from the depot there. We drove there stopping off at a transport café, a real 'greasy spoon', on the main A45 road, for a cup of tea and doorstep toast. After an early breakfast at home, the delicious aroma of the hot food being cooked made me salivate. We duly ordered our tea and toast and went and sat down taking our pint pot of builder's tea with us to await the toast. Whilst we were deep in conversation, a young waitress came over and started to wipe the table. She then said, with a wink of the eye. "Once you've finished your breakfast, you can come upstairs, and I'll look after you". It transpired that she had a room upstairs where she carried out sexual favours mainly for the lorry drivers, for a fee. We quickly consumed our tea and toast and left.

In the middle of June 1975, I was on a night shift at Coventry. After the last London to Wolverhampton passenger train had departed at around 02.10 hours I returned to the office for a cup of tea and made a contact call to Birmingham New Street Information Room. In those days we did not have direct communication with Birmingham, only the local police force, so we had to make two-hourly contact calls.

I settled down to enjoy my cup of tea, I had the door of the police office fully open. The ground floor entrance door to the office block was also open. I heard someone coming up the stairs and saw a shadow of a large person against the wall of the staircase. It was like something from the beginning of an Alfred Hitchcock movie.

The person walked in; it was none other than Chief Superintendent Brunskill. I stood up. He said to me "Surprised to see me Rogerson?" I said, "Yes sir". He informed me that he had been to a retirement function in Leicester and prior to setting off he found that I was on night turn so he thought he would pay me a visit and discuss my annual report with me. After giving me a satisfactory report, he signed the books and left.

I rang the Information Room at Birmingham and informed the duty Constable that Mr. Brunskill had just paid me a visit. He did not believe me and accused me of being fast asleep, waking up suddenly from a dream and told me to go back to sleep. I made my 04.00 hours point call and was told that Mr. Brunskill had in fact paid them a visit. Told you so!

Whilst stationed at Coventry one of our duties was to escort football trains conveying Coventry City Supporters. I escorted a train with the Sky-Blue fans to London. I forget which team they were playing.

On arrival at Euston we were left to our own devices and I along with the other escorting officers in 'half blues' ended up in Soho. One of the doormen of a strip joint realised who we were and invited us in to watch a show, we stood at the back. The club was full of the dirty mackintosh brigade and it transpired that once the strippers had performed at a club, they moved on to another followed by some of their 'fans'. Soon after our arrival the strippers had finished their act and moved on. Some of their 'fans' followed them and came past us. I stepped back to let them go by, only to fall through a curtain and down a laundry chute and ended up in a laundry basket, to be covered in dirty washing. We all had a good laugh.

At Coventry, as previously mentioned we worked alone quite a lot of the time, therefore we had a good working relationship with the local police. I remember one Saturday afternoon working by myself and was relying on the escorting officers of an incoming special train to assist, when the local Superintendent came up to me and asked where my senior officer was. I looked around and said, "I am he sir". To which he replied, "Where do you want my men to assist you?". I put the officers into position.

The Northampton football fans, which was the other league team on our patch would have nothing to do with the local police and considered the British Transport Police to be 'their police' and we did not have any problems from them.

If at all possible, we would patrol the concourse area of Coventry station when the last trains came in from London as there was always potential for a job. One evening a gentleman alighted from the train and did not have a ticket. He paid for his journey from London Euston and the Ticket Collector wrote out an excess fare ticket but did not give it to the man. This was a usual practice, so I thought no more about it. A few weeks later the Ticket Collector came under suspicion for pocketing excess fares. Tests were carried out on him and he took the bait and was arrested. I mentioned the night I was on duty at the ticket barrier. And a check of the excess book revealed that he had shown the man who had travelled from London, as only travelling from Rugby. He had pocketed the fare from London to Rugby right under my nose. Cheeky so and so. He was convicted at court on all counts.

One late turn in the summer of 1975 I was called to a collapsed male at the ticket barrier. I gave him artificial resuscitation, until I was relieved by a member of his entourage. He was none other than Joe Gormley, a prominent Trade Unionist from the TUC.

Following my success on the CID course it was around this time that I started applying for Detective Constable posts around the country.

In the station square outside Coventry station there were a number of office blocks along with a Chinese take away, which I used to frequent, especially when I was working a twelve-hour night shift. The staff got to know me. I would telephone my order and then go and collect it. One evening I was called to two Chinese men who had travelled from London on a train and failed to produce a ticket. I took them to the office where they refused to speak in English.

I rang the Chinese take away and when I introduced myself, the voice on the other end said, "Ah, Mr. Bill, the usual?" I explained about the two people in the office. The owner came across and started talking to them in Mandarin and began banging his fists on my desk. Shortly afterwards they spoke with near perfect Cockney accents. Needless to say, they were reported for prosecution.

One evening in July 1975 I was called to a gunpowder van that had been detached from a freight train, which had a hot axle. The train went forward with the van still in the platform. None of the rail staff appeared to do anything. I could feel the heat coming from the smouldering axle. So, myself and the duty station supervisor pushed it out of the platform to a more accessible place for the Fire Brigade to deal with. Fortunately, they were very quickly on the scene; otherwise Coventry station might have been the scene of a nasty explosion.

One wet Sunday afternoon in the winter of 1975 as PC Frank James, based at Northampton, was on annual leave, I went on a train patrol to Northampton. The office at Northampton consisted of two offices and did not have a cleaner, therefore it was up to the duty officer to make sure the offices were kept clean and tidy. On this occasion, I duly mopped the two rooms and generally cleaned them. I then made myself a cup of coffee prior to returning to Coventry. The door opened and in walked a very wet London based dog handler and an equally wet dog, who lived in Northampton, on their way to work by train. The dog suddenly gave an almighty shake and all the rain which had soaked into his fur was unleashed all over one of the offices, covering the papers, furniture, and the floor. A few choice words were spoken before I cleaned the mess up from the canine culprit.

November 1975 saw me attending Force Headquarters at Park Royal, North London, for an interview for a Detective Constable's vacancy at Leicester. I was told to enter FHQ by the rear door, which I did. It was not very impressive as there was a milk bottle crate full of bottles containing sour milk. I went to the foyer and introduced myself to the receptionist. I was told to wait until I was called in to see Mr. Basil Nicholls, the Detective Chief Superintendent. I sat down and put my overcoat on the coffee table in the waiting area and a big cloud of dust flew off the table. Perhaps it was the force's way of getting its own back from when I nearly showered DS Hart with dust on the bus going to school.

The parcels and mail traffic on the railway was, on the approach to Christmas, particularly the focus of attention from thieves. On the days leading up to Christmas 1975 I was on duty at Northampton railway station one evening on late turn standing in the shadows of the approach road, when I saw a Railman riding a bike along the road away from the station, nothing unusual about that, except for the fact that the bike was a brand new one and still had its cardboard wrapping and name and address of the consignee. He stated that he was taking the bicycle home for safe keeping. He was arrested and charged. He cleared up a couple of other offences.

Around about the same time I and another officer arrested a Railman from Coventry for stealing parcels. We performed a strip search on him. Not a pleasant sight as he was not wearing any underpants and the back of his uniform trousers were heavily stained with deposits from a certain rear orifice.

They were like a relief map of the Alps and the Himalayas rolled into one. We did not have plastic gloves in those days, only our black leather gloves. So, it was a case of using the office cleaner's bright yellow marigolds. He was suitably dealt with at Coventry Magistrates' Court.

Towards the end of December, I received notification that my application for the Detective Constable post at Leicester had been successful and that I would be appointed as from 1 February 1976. The year was fast drawing to an end, and I began preparing for my move to Leicester. I used some of my outstanding annual leave and lieu days to take an extended Christmas holiday.

CHAPTER 9

THE LEICESTER YEARS. FEBRUARY 1976 – JULY 1977

In the shit again. Saving the Government

Monday 2 February 1976 saw me reporting to the Inspector at Leicester, Victor Charles Colbourne. I was amused by the nameplate on his door, '*Inspector Colbourne. V.C.*' A lot of people were also amused, thinking he had a Victoria Cross.

At Leicester, there was an establishment of one Inspector, one Detective Sergeant, four uniform Sergeants, three Detective Constables and I believe eight Uniform Constables. We had two vehicles there, one uniform car, a Ford Cortina, which was 'grass green' in colour, with a force crest on the front doors. Apparently, a couple of years previously there was a shipment of these Cortina's bound for Hong Kong, but the buyer backed out and the British Transport Police bought them rather cheaply. The only snag was, that they were different colours, ranging from, light blue, dark blue, grass green, dark green, purple, orange, bright yellow and pink, all marked up with the force crest. The 'mickey' was taken out of the force at the locations they were based at including Leicester. The CID had a little Ford Escort, grey in colour registration number JJU 202N.

The police accommodation was in old railway offices and appeared to have never been renovated since the day they were built, except for the odd lick of paint. One of the entrances to the police office was from the main London Road. Outside the door was a BTP sign. It was not unusual for members of the public to come in mistaking our office for the Leicestershire Police station, which was across the road in Charles Street. Our Detective Inspector, Mr. Brown was based in Nottingham and he covered the police office at Derby as well. I had to lodge in Leicester, as I was told it was too far to commute about an hour each way in those days. I was found some accommodation with Mrs Cath Woods, the widow of Dougie Woods, who had been a PC at Leicester. The area we covered was from Stanford on Soar on the Nottinghamshire/Leicestershire border to Sharnbrook on the Northamptonshire /Bedfordshire border, with railway stations at Loughborough, Leicester, Market Harborough, Kettering, and Wellingborough. Corby freight sidings came under our district. On the Birmingham to Peterborough line we covered, Hinckley, Narborough, Melton Mowbray and Oakham stations. We also covered the freight line from Leicester to Burton on Trent as far as Coalville.

Shortly after arriving I met up with Detective Sergeant John Wright, a local man, who had recently been promoted from Oxford. My other two colleagues were DC Don McKim and DC Frank Melling, a fellow Lancastrian from Wigan. John Wright was just going out on a routine investigation into a theft, so he took me along, nothing like hitting the ground running.

Being the junior detective, I got all the 'non-detected' and 'hard to detect crimes' such as parcels going missing in transit. The rail staff at the receiving station would issue a form called a 'Flash Report' detailing the loss of the parcel, and these would be sent to the nearest British Rail Claims Investigator. If he suspected a crime, he would then send them onto the Divisional Police Headquarters. The Investigator based at Leicester, was Ron Crooks, yes really. He would pass them direct to us. I would then have the task of working with Ron to try and establish where the theft took place, a nigh on impossible task especially if the parcel had been sent from Inverness to Leicester or Penzance to Leicester. However, we did have a little success, passing the details back to the station where the suspected theft had taken place. Sometimes the theft was right on our own doorstep.

At Leicester I transferred my membership of the International Police Association to the Leicestershire Branch and joined the committee.

One of the ongoing investigations at Leicester when I arrived, involved a signage firm from the West Country. They were tasked with replacing old station signs with new ones and taking the old ones to Collectors Corner at London Euston. However, some of the signs never reached Collectors Corner, the workmen sold them to the enthusiasts direct and pocketed the money. What they had not realised was that the staff at Collectors Corner had made a full inventory of the signs and when a full audit was made against the returned signs, the alarm bells started ringing. They were arrested and charged and dealt with at court.

Another investigation involved a parcels delivery driver from Kettering railway station who lived in Corby. He had furnished his house with stolen household items from mail order parcels in railway transit. He had also sold some of the stolen property onto people in pubs. It was easy for him to discover what was in the parcel. As well as the senders name and address along with the consignee, the catalogue number of the items would be on the label. All he needed to do was to obtain a mail order catalogue and look for a corresponding parcel in transit. In the pub, he would take a catalogue and pass it round and then take orders, charging a much lower price. For the property going to his house, he would relabel the parcel with his address. One of his neighbours became suspicious of his actions and reported him. His house was visited, and property recovered. About the only thing left was a pair of curtains which he had bought legitimately from Woolworths. He was suitably dealt with at Court.

Friday 4 June 1976 saw John Wright and myself going to the Enderby area of Leicester to arrest a male person who was suspected of theft. It turned out this man had stolen some fishplates and baseplates and other bits of metal from the railway line at Enderby. His Land Rover vehicle had been seen in the vicinity. We went to his house and nothing was found. However, we checked the back of his Land Rover and found traces of moss in the back. Controlled samples were taken for forensic analysis. We then went to the scene of the actual crime and took controlled samples of the moss from the scene.

After enquires we found the baseplates in a local scrapyard and they had traces of moss on them, again controlled samples were taken. The base plates were seized as evidence. All the samples were then sent off to the British Railways Forensic Science Laboratory at Derby for analysis. We would have to wait around a month for the result. The results came back positive, great, they all matched up. On 5 July 1976, myself and John Wright attended Wigston Police Station where we formally charged the defendant. He appeared before the court and was fined.

On the 28 July 1976, following the losses of money, namely 'straight one pounds' from the till and excess fares when a certain booking clerk was on duty, at the booking office at Hinckley railway station, Frank Melling and myself interviewed the booking clerk concerned. He was questioned about the theft of excess fare monies and the money from the till. He claimed that he had issued the wrong tickets and denied stealing the money and pocketing the excess fares. After being questioned about the thefts further he admitted several offences, stating that he had been short of money, He made a voluntary statement, He was then charged with several offences. He was suitably dealt with at court.

On Saturday 21 August 1976 at 17.20 hours, I was on Platform Two of Leicester railway station awaiting the arrival of football supporters, with Frank Melling when we saw a local youth sat on a bench. In his possession he had a hook shaped metal rod about 15 inches in length. He stood up and began to walk along the platform still carrying the rod close to his right hip. He was arrested for possession of an offensive weapon. He was later fined at court.

After securing his detention we returned to the platform. At 17.30 hours, the 15.30 hours London St Pancras to Nottingham passenger train arrived at Platform Two. The train contained a large number of Leicester City fans. At this time, there were a large number of Manchester City fans on Platform Two. A group of approximately 130 Leicester City fans began chanting obscenities and making obscene gestures towards the Manchester City fans who surged forward towards the train.

Because of this Frank Melling and myself boarded the train and went towards two youths who were particularly vocal and who appeared to be the ring leaders of the group. Both came out with a string of very foul expletives and doubted our parentage. We identified ourselves as police officers, this made them even worse with their obscenities and expletives. We got separated. We were heavily outnumbered. I did not have my handcuffs; they were being used on a previous prisoner and it was virtually impossible to draw our truncheons.

One of the youths lashed out at Frank with his right arm, which was in a plaster cast, hitting Frank in the chest. He continued with his expletives and grabbed Frank around the waist. Both Frank and I shouted that we were police officers. The youth again struck Frank with his arm, in the chest and face. I went to Frank's assistance and was grabbed around the waist by the other youth. He started to incite the others in the carriage to attack me. He then struck me several times in the middle of my back with his fist, which left me with very bad bruising. I managed to free myself.

The youth leaned against a seat and started lashing out at me with both his feet, shouting yet more obscenities. We were then joined by Sergeant John Evans who helped me restrain the youth who had attacked me. The youth then kicked John on the left shin. He was removed from the train and continued to struggle violently and managed to wrench his right arm free of John's grip and lashed back with it, hitting John in the stomach, still shouting expletives. We managed to restrain him. We took him up a flight of stairs and as he was being taken across the concourse, again he began to struggle violently. He got free from my grip and made a grab at John's throat. Pulling his tie from his shirt. I regained my grip and managed to restrain him. In the police office, he calmed down and stated that he thought Frank and I were Manchester City fans (No doubt because of our Lancashire accents) and wanted to 'get the boot in'. He apologised for his actions. He was seen in the presence of his parents and reported for numerous offences, including Assault on Police and Public Order. The youth who had attacked Frank was also arrested and dealt with.

In 1976 whilst I was serving at Leicester, I had an Old English Sheepdog as a pet and on occasions I would take him on the train when visiting the family in Lancashire. One day, I had to laugh at one of the railway staff, who shall I say was a little gullible. He saw me on the train with my dog. He said to me that it was unusual to see me on the train with a dog. I told him that as I was a C.I.D officer and this was a German Shepherd in disguise, and we were on a case. He seemed to believe me and often asked if I still used the dog for duty.

One Saturday in August 1976 I was rostered late turn 16.00 hours to 24.00 hours. I came into the office at around 15.30 hours only find my other three colleagues there with a young lady who alleged that she had been raped on a train between London St Pancras and Leicester. She was taken to the Leicestershire Police station at Charles Street where she made an identikit of her attacker. I took one look at it and said, "That is not her attacker". She had in fact given a perfect description of one of my colleagues who had been talking to her about her ordeal. Suspicion for the attack fell on her boyfriend. I don't think we ever caught her attacker.

At Coalville, there was a freight depot, which employed a number of staff including drivers and guards for the coal trains. British Rail took on some trainee guards and after a few weeks of training they would be appointed full time. Two of the trainee guards went to a flat in Melton Mowbray and committed an aggravated burglary, by putting on face masks and using a knife to threaten the elderly occupant and steal several hundred pounds from him. It transpired that the occupant was the grandfather of one of the assailants, but he did not recognise them. He called the local police who were very quickly on the scene. At the scene, they found a railway free pass in the name of the grandson's accomplice. A phone call to our office at Leicester, resulted, within five minutes, me obtaining the details they required i.e. the full personal details of the pass holder. Armed with the information, two arrests were quickly made. Both the assailants were charged with the offence. They were then dismissed from the service of the railway.

However, for a number of weeks the wages office in Derby kept paying wages for both of them and they were sent to the office at Coalville and placed in the safe. Following an internal audit at Derby a few weeks later, it was realised that wages were still being paid for the two men. A clerk was despatched to collect the wage packets. On arrival, he found that they were missing from the safe. We were called in and enquiries were commenced. Suspicion fell on a clerk in the office at Coalville. He was arrested and admitted the thefts stating that he was heavily in debt. He was charged and bailed to appear at court. The railway authorities suspended him from duty. During his suspension, his job was regraded to a higher grade. At court, he pleaded guilty and was suitably punished and ordered to pay back the wages along with his fine. He was subsequently dismissed from the railway. However, his union successfully appealed against his dismissal and he was re-instated. He could not go back to his original position due to his dishonesty, so he was found another job in the yard at a higher grade. Who says that crime does not pay?

A senior employee of the Jaeger knitwear factory in Leicester had a nice little scam going. He would send knitwear to a couple of fictitious firms in London via the railway Red Star parcels service to London St Pancras station. He would go to London, usually on a Friday, collect the parcels and sell the contents on, making a few pounds for himself. In fact, it was around one hundred thousand pounds by the time we arrested him. When Jaeger's accountant realised that the 'firms' were not paying their invoices, the alarm bells started to ring. A joint operation was set up between the British Transport Police at Leicester and London St Pancras along with the Leicestershire Police. He was eventually arrested and convicted at court.

A Member of Parliament had the misfortune to have his wallet and contents stolen from his unattended jacket pocket whilst he was on a northbound train from London St Pancras. The wallet minus his cash was recovered from the lineside near to Wellingborough. This was the usual Modus Operandi of thieves, steal the wallet, take what they wanted and throw it from the train window. The task of returning the wallet to the gentleman concerned fell to me as I was going to the area where he lived on some other enquiries. On arrival at his home, I handed over the wallet and contents against a signature on a Property Recovered and Disposal Form. His wife went to the kitchen to make us a cup of coffee. It was at this juncture that I gave him another piece of property from the wallet, a packet of condoms. He was clearly very embarrassed as I handed them over and stated that he admired my discretion very much and further stated that I would go far. Perhaps I saved the Government some potential embarrassment and the early retirement of the MP concerned.

I was tasked to make some enquiries into the theft of metal from the railway line at Glenfield, on the Leicester to Burton on Trent freight line. My enquiries took me to a Romany caravan in a layby nearby. It was immaculate inside; you could have eaten your dinner from the floor. The solid gold rings on the gentleman's fingers and thumbs were worth several thousands of pounds each. He informed me that it was not him or his wife that were responsible for the theft but advised me to look a mile or two down the road at the itinerant travellers who were in another layby. I had a cup of freshly ground coffee from him. His information proved correct it was indeed the travellers. They were subsequently dealt with.

The Highfields area of Leicester, just around the corner from the railway station was the location of the red-light district and the residence a large student population. A request for a couple of witness statements from the London Underground Division of the force in respect of a riot on a tube train, landed on my desk. As it was a nice evening, I decided to walk down to the address, going past a number of houses each with a red light in the window, along with the young and not so young ladies of horizontal virtue sat in the window, openly soliciting for business. The Leicestershire Police had tried to prosecute them for soliciting, but on appeal the cases were dismissed. The appeal court stated that it could not be proved they were soliciting and that they were entitled to have a red lamp in their windows.

I arrived at the address of the witnesses, who were a couple of students. It was a large terraced house, divided up into several flats and bedsits. In the entrance hall, there was a professionally printed poster, entitled 'What to do when arrested by the pigs' with pictures of pigs, with police helmets on their heads and captions giving advice under each picture.

Another witness statement request, this time from the 'Knife and Fork brigade', as they were affectionally known, from Force Headquarters. They were a squad of detectives that investigated frauds in restaurant cars, railway hotels and buffets. A railway enthusiasts train had run from London up north and conveyed a restaurant car. The Chief Steward had been for some time, suspected of fiddling the receipts and undercover officers travelled on the train. Two men from the Leicester area were on the train and ate in the restaurant car. It was my job to obtain witness statements from them. I rang one of them up to make an appointment. The time and date was duly arranged. The gentleman asked if I would be taking a statement from his travelling companion to which I told him I would be. He very kindly arranged for him to come to his house so that I could take both the statements on the same night.

I arrived at the property, a three-storey Edwardian detached house on the outskirts of Leicester, a few minutes early. The gentleman of the house invited me in and took me to the front room and stated that he had to run the '7.30' before I could record the statements. In the front room, he had an 'O' gauge clockwork railway system which went around the room and into another where his friend was waiting to accept the train.

One afternoon in the Autumn of 1976, Frank Melling and myself found ourselves at the northern extremity of our patch near to Stanford on Soar as we had received reports of a person discharging a gun at trains. A search of the area proved negative. As we were leaving, the car got stuck in the mud and I got out to give it a push. Yes, you have guessed it, the wheels of the car spun furiously in the mud covering me from head to toe in mud, I slipped and fell in the mud. I had to have a shower and had to take my suit to the cleaners.

I was on duty from 16.00 hours to 24.00 hours at Leicester on Saturday 18 December 1976. At 19.20 hours, I was on duty keeping observations on the concourse at Leicester station when I saw two boys, one aged 14 years and one aged 9 years walking along the concourse, each carrying a London North Eastern Railway *'Omitting to shut and fasten the gate'* metal sign, which were about four-foot in length.

After identifying myself, I asked where they had obtained the signs from. They told me that a man at March locomotive depot had given them the signs. They then admitted stealing the signs from a scrap heap at the depot. They were interviewed in the presence of their respective parents and reported for the offences disclosed.

Some personal items belonging to a member of the permanent way staff based at Nottingham were damaged on Friday 21 January 1977, in a trackside cabin at Croft, adjacent to the Birmingham to Peterborough line. The offender had slashed his wellington boots, coated grease on the inside of his donkey jacket sleeves, coated grease inside his gloves, cut the fingers off the gloves and drilled several holes in his drinking mug. Enquiries were made, and it transpired that an ex colleague of his who he did not get on with committed the damage just before he left the employment of the railway, as a parting shot. The offender, an Italian who spoke very little English, was interviewed at Nottingham police office on Tuesday 1 February 1977 by myself and Don McKim, and he admitted the offence. To assist with the interview, we had the services of a Nottingham based PC who spoke fluent Italian.

Valentine's Day, Monday 14 February 1977 at 20.45 hours, following the report of theft of foodstuffs from the Buffet on platform one at Leicester, Don McKim and myself stopped a female employee whilst she was walking across the concourse on her way home. A search of her bags revealed three large bags of tea concealed in her shopping bag. She claimed to have purchased them earlier in the day. However, we were to quickly disprove that explanation, as they were a brand only issued to British Rail refreshment rooms. She was taken to the police office where she was interviewed and admitted that theft and other thefts on previous occasions. She appeared before the local Magistrates and was suitably dealt with.

A railway employee was seen in a depot at Wigston on Saturday 19 February 1977 loading coke into a railway lorry. At 10.40 hours on Tuesday 22 February 1977 Frank Melling and myself went to the Knighton area of Leicester where we interviewed the employee and recovered a quantity of coke from his coal bunker. We had to shovel it into several sacks and retain it as evidence. He claimed to have bought it from a local coal merchant. He was unable to produce receipts and later admitted the theft.

Frank Melling and I went to the permanent way office at Leicester, on 2 March 1977 where we arrested a railway employee suspected of a Burglary, whereby he entered a building and stole a coat belonging to another employee. During the subsequent interview, he admitted entering the office and stealing the coat and selling it to a man in a pub as he was short of money. He was charged with the offence.

Ten days later on Saturday 12 March 1977 at 18.10 hours Frank Melling and myself went to an address in Leicester where we arrested a man on suspicion of entering a cabin at Beal Street locomotive depot, unlawfully between 14 and 15 February and stealing a coat. He was taken to Wigston police station where he was interviewed during which he admitted the offence stating that he stole the coat to keep warm. He was formally charged with the offence of Burglary.

In late March 1977, we received a complaint that monies had been stolen from the booking office at Narborough railway station. Suspicion fell on one of the railway employees. Enquiries were commenced, and evidence was gathered. At 18.05 hours on Monday 4 April 1977 Frank Melling and myself went to the home of the suspect. His reply to my caution was an absolute classic. He said, 'I've been expecting you gentlemen". He readily admitted his guilt to us, stating that he was short of money and was due to get married and that his overtime had been stopped. He was arrested and taken to Wigston police station where he elected to make a voluntary statement admitting his guilt. He was then formally charged with theft and deception. He cleared up some more offences for us.

One evening, one of the uniformed officers was checking the waiting rooms on Leicester station and he came across a woman who was breast feeding her baby. The baby was reluctant to take mother's milk. She said to the baby, "If you don't want it this nice policeman will have it". The look on the officer's face was an absolute picture. I wish I had my camera with me.

The new town of Corby with a population of around 48.000 grew from a small village which dates back to the Roman times. Locally mined iron-ore gave the town its importance, the ore was used in Roman times and the Middle ages. In modern times, the ore was mined by the British Steel Corporation. A majority of the townsfolk are Scots and are employed by British Steel. The local police had a regular liaison with the Strathclyde Police and received their daily crime bulletins. There were two trains a day that ran between London St Pancras and Glasgow Central, via, Kettering, Sheffield, Leeds, the Settle to Carlisle railway line and Dumfries. It was a long journey, but a lot of people used to travel between Kettering and Glasgow on it. The uniform lads used to pick up a few ticket frauds from it.

The steel works had its own railway network which connected to the British Rail freight sidings. The brass wagon bearings were regular targets of local thieves. They would jack up the empty wagons and steal the brass bearings. On a couple of occasions, they even jacked up a wooden cabin where the bearings were stored and stole them. On Easter Monday 11 April 1977 Frank Melling and I kept observations on the sidings from an exceptionally large oak tree. Now I know what Robin Hood felt like. We did not catch anyone on this occasion, but we had some later success.

1977 was Her Majesty the Queen's Silver Jubilee year and she travelled extensively around the country in the Royal Train. One such visit was to the Nottingham area. Sergeant Dick Powell from British Transport Police based at Nottingham and I, were rostered duty in a siding at Holme Pierrepont, on the outskirts of Nottingham to guard the Royal Train when it arrived, whilst Her Majesty had tea. However, at the appointed time there was no sign of the train and we had no radios. After about an hour or so we were advised by a railway official that Her Majesty was running late with her engagements in the city, so it was decided to keep the train at Nottingham Midland station.

In the early afternoon of Saturday 14 May 1977, a group of boys were seen on the disused Great Central railway line, where it crossed over the Birmingham to Peterborough line at Whetstone.

As a Birmingham to Norwich train was passing under the bridge a large stone was thrown onto the top of the train causing a large dent in the cab roof and causing the driver to make an emergency brake application. PC Keith Berry a motorcyclist with the Leicestershire Police was quickly on the scene and enquiries were commenced. At 16.20 hours that afternoon I went with Keith to an address where we saw a boy in the presence of his father. He admitted being at the scene but denied all knowledge of throwing the stone. He went onto implicate two others. The other two boys were seen in the presence of their parents and because of what they said we returned to the home of the first boy and, he, after a time admitted throwing the stone onto the top of the train. He stated that he only did it for a lark. He elected to make a voluntary statement. He was later reported for Endangering the Safety of Persons upon the Railway. Keith later resigned from the Leicestershire Police and joined the British Transport Police at Leicester.

Commencing in May 1977, British Rail were recovering copper wire from the telegraph poles along the Midland Main line between Kettering and Sharnbrook. They used a third-party company to recover the wire. Most of the employees of this company had dubious backgrounds and a lot of cable was being stolen by them. So, most of May and June, we were on regular nights keeping observations, in the Kettering and Wellingborough areas. We had the use of a lime green coloured Thames van which was nicknamed the 'Parks and Gardens van' because of its colour. We dressed in appropriate clothing for the observations. In fact, we looked like thieves ourselves. On a couple of occasions after returning from the observations at around 03.30 hours in the morning we were stopped by the Leicestershire Police, thinking we were up to no good.

To relieve the boredom of being in one place all of the time our locations were changed at different intervals. The Railway Technical Department at Derby set up a device called a 'Pulsator', in the Signal and Telegraph office at Kettering station, which was connected at intervals to the copper wire. Whenever the wire was cut, the location would show on the screen of the 'Pulsator'. Whoever was monitoring the 'Pulsator' would give the location to the teams that were out near to the lineside. We used officers from Birmingham, Nottingham, and Derby to assist us along with officers from the Northamptonshire Police.

One night, I was in a vehicle in a field between Kettering and Wellingborough when my colleague who was out in a field, radioed in and stated that there was a suspect at the top of a telegraph pole. Another officer and I joined him and observed the telegraph pole. There was no one there. It transpired that he had been staring at the pole too long and had convinced himself that an arm of the pole was in fact a thief.

A few nights later, as we were keeping observations, I teamed up with a dog handler from the Northamptonshire Police, in his van. It was not a very pleasant experience as the dog kept emitting foul odours from its rear orifice. However, as we were about to call it a night, we had a call from a colleague to the effect that the suspects had been seen on the railway line. We made our way across a potato field, this was one of the roughest rides I have ever experienced, I was bounced from side to side, going over rows of potatoes and this did not help the dog's flatulence one little bit.

By the time we got to the scene the suspects had made good their escape. we caught them a couple of nights later. The unofficial ploughing of the farmer's field invited a public complaint from him about his ruined crops. No doubt the force had to pay some compensation to him.

Early one morning after we had returned to Leicester, we received a telephone call from the police at Kettering to say that they had arrested a man in a van with a load of copper cable in the back. The man's explanation was he'd heard that there had been a lot of thefts of cable from the area and that he was taking it home for safe keeping and would be bringing it back the next morning – pull the other one my friend!, he was charged with the theft.

17 June 1977 was a momentous day for me. I arrived home at about 04.30 hours absolutely knackered having done a month of continuous 10 or 12-hour night shifts and was just dozing off and Shirley, who was pregnant with Alison our daughter, woke me to inform me that her waters had just broken. I remember saying "Okay I'll crime them in the morning" (In my daze thinking she was reporting a crime!), and started to go back to sleep. I was awoken, and she was taken to hospital where she gave birth to our daughter, Alison.

On Thursday 30 June 1977 at 11.10 hours, I went to the railway line at Desborough, Northamptonshire where I met up with PC Percival of the local police. He pointed out to me some grease on the line and he took possession of broken glass aspects from two coloured light signals. It transpired that at around 20.30 hours on Wednesday 29 June, grease had been spread on the railway lines, wooden sleepers had been placed across the London bound line, pieces of wood, stones, some small concrete blocks and an oil drum had been placed on the same line. These had been knocked clear by a London bound train. He said that he would make enquiries in the village for me. Thank goodness for the local village bobby, they are worth their weight in gold.

It was off to Wellingborough Police Station on Thursday 7 July 1977 at 20.30 hours with John Wright where we spoke to a man who had been arrested by the local police for stealing some copper cable from the railway at Wellingborough. He readily admitted his guilt and implicated an accomplice as well. He was charged with receiving stolen property and his accomplice was later charged with theft of cable.

The following day, Friday 8 July 1977 at 18.25 hours, following information received from PC Percival at Desborough in respect of the incident on the 29 June, I attended a house where I saw a juvenile in the presence of his parents. He was informed as to the reason for our visit and he immediately denied all knowledge of the incident, He was questioned at length stating that he was at the local leisure centre. He was informed that he would be seen again. We then went to another house where we saw another juvenile in the presence of his parents. Again, he denied all knowledge of being at the scene but had read about it in the local newspaper. He stated that he had been out on his bike.

So, it was back to the drawing board, I was convinced that the two lads we had seen were the culprits, but proving it was another matter. Armed with further evidence, on Thursday 21 July 1977 at 14.35 we, by arrangement saw the two boys and a third suspect in the presence of their parents at Kettering Police Station.

I was dreading the interview, as one of the mother's had the most loud, penetrating, and unmelodious voice known to mankind. After initial denials, they all admitted their part in the incident. They were reported for summons for Endangering the Safety of Persons on the Railway, Obstruction of the Railway, and Trespass. Due to the seriousness of the incident the case ended up at Northampton Crown Court. Initially they pleaded 'Not Guilty' but changed their pleas at the last minute. The Judge stated that he was going to be lenient with them, by sentencing them to six months youth detention. The mother of one of the defendant's, the one with the unmelodious voice, doubted the judge's parentage and was told by him in no uncertain terms to leave the court or she would be joining her son.

Due to domestic circumstances within the family I transferred to Heysham Harbour on the 31 July 1977.

CHAPTER 10

THE HEYSHAM YEARS JULY 1977 – SPRING 1978

Meeting the Russians again and working in Scotland

The last day of July 1977, saw my transfer, at long last, to Heysham Harbour, I was back home. I had a great patch to cover. Bay Horse, south of Lancaster to Tebay on the West Coast Main Line, including the Morecambe and Windermere branches, the Lake Windermere Steamers, the Carnforth to Skipton line inclusive and the line from Settle Junction to Kirkby Stephen and the Furness Main line from Carnforth to Millom.

There were actually two police posts, one at Heysham and one at Lancaster. There was one Sergeant, Walt Girdley, and eight constables. Four based at Heysham and four based at Lancaster. The Inspector and CID officers had been withdrawn a few years earlier. We now came under the Inspector at Preston, and CID assistance was afforded from Preston as well.

However, one constable, Jim Morris, covered Barrow in Furness and the Furness area. The police establishment at Barrow had been withdrawn some years earlier although we still retained an office there. It was the old ladies' public toilet. The bench where the ladies used to sit to apply their makeup, was used as our desk. One toilet cubicle was used as an actual toilet and the other was used as a property store / general storeroom.

We would work a seven - week roster, four weeks at Heysham and three weeks at Lancaster. We worked a night shift one, in every seven weeks, the other shifts being made up of lates, earlies and days.

The office at Lancaster had recently been reopened. I believe it closed in 1965. It was just one room with a desk and a sink. We had no toilet. We had to use the public toilet on Platform Three. It was a typical railway toilet. I went to a cubicle one day. The rear of the door and the walls had the usual graffiti associated with railway toilets etched on them. The brush had, what I shall best describe as, historical deposits from a previous encounter with the pan, from someone who had had a curry from the Indian the night before!! The Heysham accommodation was much better. A mess room, toilet, Sergeant's office, and two general offices.

We had one vehicle to be shared between the two stations, it was a Ford Cortina, part of the Hong Kong batch. It was much more in keeping with the force it was light blue and had a crest on each of the front doors. I think the registration number was HBT 921N, it was formally the Area Commander's car at York.

One feature of the Heysham office was that there were no signs indicating to the public where it was. Due to the Irish troubles of the 1970's the BTP signs were removed, and a spy hole was inserted into the front door, but we were never allowed to use this door. The only door we could use was the rear door which had two large windows in it.

Prior to transferring to Heysham my colleagues regularly escorted the ships to and from Belfast and the trains to and from Manchester Victoria, this was because George Best, who played for Manchester United, was from Belfast and had a large following from the City and Northern Ireland in general.

We were repeatedly called upon to assist our colleagues at Preston to cover for sickness and annual leave there. Other duties included covering football traffic around the North West. All these additional duties entailed overtime or rest day workings. The shifts at Heysham where officers had been used for mutual aid duties would be covered by overtime as well. Other mutual aid duties would see us working at Blackpool North railway station in connection with the football and illuminations traffic. We had two officers stationed at Blackpool North. A Sergeant and I believe six constables were based at Fleetwood Docks. We used to return to Preston on the last service to Manchester Victoria which was affectionally known as the '*Blackpool Belle',* full of courting couples and the like. Howard Broadbent and Jimmy Smith wrote a song about this train and its antics and it is regularly sung by the northern folk group from Westhoughton, '*The Houghton Weavers'.* We rarely experienced any trouble on this train as the passengers wanted to round off a perfect day by the seaside, by doing what comes naturally.

One evening as I read the parade book I looked at some back entries. One memorandum stuck out in my mind. It was from the days when there was an Inspector based at Heysham. '*Due to the high number of rear collisions with other vehicles on the promenade at Morecambe; it advised officers not to drive along the promenade during the summer when going to Hest Bank, Bolton Le Sands or Carnforth'.* It appeared that officers were distracted by the young ladies who were scantily dressed, on the promenade.

When I arrived at Heysham the passenger ferry service to Belfast had been withdrawn a few years earlier. There was only a British Rail Freight Roll-on-Roll-off service to Belfast, operated by the vessel 'Penda'. We used to suffer a few thefts from the freight vehicles on the vessel, and we would end up liaising with our two colleagues in the British Transport Police at Belfast, Detective Inspector Alec Manning, and PC Brian Palmer.

Other vessels that used Heysham, came into the James Fisher of Barrow, quay, they brought oranges, grapefruit, bananas, potatoes, and other general cargo. The James Fisher's compound was surrounded by palisade fencing and there was a 24-hour security presence at the main gate. We had a good liaison with the security officers and used to get called to some of the seafarers who had been stealing goods from the vessels and the quayside.

Since the withdrawal of the passenger ferry service to Belfast and the associated trains we only saw one train a week at Heysham and that was a freight train on a Monday morning.

Just after I arrived at Heysham I had not been issued with a uniform, so I was patrolling in plain clothes which was useful, as I apprehended a local lad for being in possession of cannabis. He was jointly dealt with between the British Transport Police and Her Majesty's Customs and Excise Officers, with whom we had a particularly good liaison.

One Sunday afternoon I went to the main West Coast Railway Line between Hest Bank and Bolton le Sands where I caught two boys playing on the tracks near to a caravan park. I took them to the caravan where their grandfather was. It turned out that he was a very senior officer in the West Yorkshire Police. They received a caution.

I believe it was in October 1977 that I was part of a serial at Liverpool Moorfields underground station when Her Majesty the Queen came to officially open the station and the Merseyrail system. I was on duty on the deep level platform, where Her Majesty was due to leave a train, unveil a plaque and then re-join the train. The red-carpet was in place. Ordinary passenger trains were running through the station at five miles per hour and not stopping. The train in front of Her Majesty's came through at about twenty-five miles per hour, blowing the red-carpet across the platform. Panic set in from the railway officials as Her Majesty's train was right behind the offending train and was entering the platform. I have never seen a red-carpet replaced so quickly. The rest of the ceremony passed off without incident.

The prostitutes from Liverpool used to come and visit the ships at Heysham. I remember being on an extended late turn in November 1977. I was on a rostered eight hours late turn but volunteered to cover four extra hours for the night turn officer who had attended the retirement function of Detective Sergeant Hart, late of Carnforth and Heysham, but had been transferred to Preston some years earlier.

At around about 18.00 hours there was a foreign registered ship berthed alongside the James Fisher's quay and the gangway was level with the quay. I was informed that a prostitute went on board looking for business. During the next few hours, a ferocious storm blew up. I have never seen anything like it, oil drums, pallets, in fact anything that was not fully bolted down was being blown through the air by the severe gale force wind. Even the pier in nearby Morecambe was destroyed. Just before I went off duty at 02.30 hours, it was a high tide and I have never seen a tide so high in Heysham. The gangway was now vertical, and I could see the prostitute trying to leave the ship, she was as white as a sheet, being sick all over the place. I thought that will teach her. We would only prosecute if we had a complaint from the Master of the vessel, no such complaint was forthcoming on this evening.

One of our most common offences was that of Oil in Navigable Waters, contrary to *The Oil in Navigable Waters Act 1955*. This law was introduced so that the United Kingdom Government could honour the agreed provisions laid down by the international convention for '*The prevention of pollution of the sea by oil 1954*' *and the sea includes all navigable waters.*

Vessels from abroad would on occasions, leak oil into the harbour waters and on receiving a complaint from the Harbourmaster, we would have to collect sets of oil samples, two sets from the actual water, for this purpose we would use a rowing boat, collect the samples in glass jars, then board the vessel, collect two samples from the bilges in glass jars and finally collect another two samples in glass jars from the fuel tank. We were completely at the mercy of the Master of the vessel. You had to be on your guard as the Master or one of his officers would try and frequently mislead you into taking a different sample. It was always advisable to try and take one of the marine engineers from the harbour with you. The Master of the vessel would then be given a set of samples and the other set of samples would then be taken by hand to the British Railways Forensic Science Laboratory at Derby for analysis. This would take a couple of weeks. It was a pointless exercise really, by the time the results came back, usually positive, the vessel had set sail and next time it came into port the Master had been replaced. We had quite a few of re-issued summonses on file and 'Sine Die' (adjourned indefinitely) cases.

One of the unusual features of Heysham was that we charged and bailed our own prisoners from our office. The Sergeant would be called out from home to accept the charge. If they had to be kept in custody, they would be taken direct to Morecambe police station.

One morning I arrived for early turn duty at 05.30 hours. My tour of duty was not due to commence until 06.30 hours, but the officer on nights, Terry Booth used to relieve me early on some occasions so I obviously reciprocated and this particular morning was one of those occasions.

On arrival, I saw the Sergeant's car outside the office. I went into the office to find that Terry had arrested a Russian Chef from a Russian ship, for stealing a one-hundredweight bag of potatoes from the quay-side and was in the process of taking it back to his ship, which funnily enough had brought a cargo of potatoes in. It transpired that the chef had Egyptian potatoes in his galley but he did not like these so he took a bag of Cyprus potatoes from the quay which were better quality.

He could not speak much English, except for 'Liverpool Football Club', apparently, he followed the club. The Political Commissar came off the ship and was told that his chef was going to be charged with the offence of theft. The Commissar asked if he could take the chef back on board the ship and put some decent clothing on him for his court appearance. Nice try Ivan! He must have thought we came off a banana boat.

We needed an interpreter, so I was asked to ring the Lancashire Constabulary at Lancaster to obtain one. I spoke to the duty PC who duly supplied me with the name of a gentleman that lived in the Lancaster area. I rang the number and spoke to a male person and explained that we needed an interpreter. The person on the other end of the telephone was the son of the man I was after, but he advised me that his father who had been an interpreter, had been dead for five years. Profuse apologies proffered. A call back to Lancashire Constabulary to ensure that they checked their records to make sure that they were kept up to date.

I eventually found an interpreter from Lancaster University. He came down and the interview went ahead. The man was charged and taken to Morecambe Magistrates' Court. Permission had to be obtained from the Russian Embassy in London before he pleaded 'Guilty'. I believe he was fined £25 and this was paid for by the James Fisher Group, who were the agents for the ship. The case attracted a lot of attention locally in the press.

Back at the harbour we handed the man over to the Captain who stated that he would be put in irons until the ship arrived back in Russia. The Captain informed us that he too would lose his job, even though he was asleep at the time of the offence.

Talking of the Russians, the local Ribble bus company used to run an hourly service from the harbour gates to Lancaster University and they used a double - decker bus for this service. It was not unusual for the Russian seafarers who were regular visitors to the port to leave their ship and go for a bus ride to, either Morecambe or Lancaster. A double-decker bus was quite novel to them. They would be followed by an officer from the ship, no doubt making sure that they did not defect. Also, when they left the quayside via the James Fisher compound, they would have to pass the security office and show their pass to the Security man on duty. If we were on patrol at the location, they would automatically open their bags for us to search. There was very little conversation between us. I often wondered if they had any political motives for going to Morecambe or Lancaster!

There was rather an eccentric gentleman known locally as 'The Professor', he lived in Lancaster and travelled to Preston by train. He would usually dress in a mortarboard and gown. Sometimes, he would buy a ticket, but more often than not he would try and avoid his fare by hiding in the toilet for the eighteen-minute journey. One day returning from Preston he locked himself in the toilet of a two-car Diesel Multiple Unit and would not come out. On arrival at Lancaster he came out and produced a valid ticket. However, somebody came forward and stated that they could not use the toilet because of his actions. Bingo! we obtained a statement and successfully prosecuted him under the Byelaws for 'Interfering with the comfort and convenience of persons upon the railway'.

I was outside the police office at Lancaster one afternoon and a gentleman came up to me and asked if I had seen the back of my tunic. I took it off only to find that a seagull had left its calling card. Worse than that the acid in the poo had started to eat into my tunic.

Unfortunately for some reason, I let my membership of the International Police Association lapse.

Saturday 20 May 1978 Scotland were playing England in an international match at Hampden Park, Glasgow. I and a contingent of officers from, Heysham, Lancaster, Preston Liverpool and Manchester went on secondment to Glasgow to assist our Scottish based colleagues in dealing with the crowds using Glasgow Central station. We all travelled up on an early morning train to Glasgow for the afternoon kick-off. 'Ginge' Ablard and his dog 'Ben' based at Preston, travelled on the train with us.

On arrival at Glasgow, we were given a briefing and assigned to a Scottish officer. All went well dealing with the supporters on the outward leg of their journeys to Hampden Park station. On the return I, along with some other English based officers was assigned to the main concourse with some of our Scottish based officers.

The returning supporters were quite high after indulging rather heavily in whisky, beer and lager. Thankfully due to our tact and tolerance with them they gave us no trouble. However, unknown to us on the concourse, a disturbance was taking place between the Scottish and English supporters in Union Street near to a side entrance to the station.

I then saw some officers coming from the direction of the disturbance, laughing their heads off. It transpired that 'Ginge' Ablard and 'Ben' had been assisting in dispersing a crowd, when a senior officer from our force, who was also assisting in the dispersal of the crowd, but due to his position 'Ben' bit him on his arm as he was in 'Ben's' 'line of sight'. The crowd dispersed and the senior officer had to receive treatment for his wounds, which included having a tetanus injection, the only snag was that he had a phobia about needles.

Shortly afterwards it was time to catch our train home south of the border. Whilst we were on the train dealing with some English supporters, two Scottish officers came running along the platform looking for 'Ginge' who by now thought he was on a discipline charge. The officers shook him warmly by the hand and asked if his dog was alright. 'Ginge' breathed a huge sigh of relief.

In the summer of 1978, the late motorcycle ace Geoff Duke from the Isle of Man started up a shipping line called Manx Line. He bought a vessel called '*Monte Castillo*' from Spain and renamed it '*Manx Viking*', for the service to Douglas. This service was in competition with the Isle of Man Steam Packet services from Liverpool. However, the vessel was very unreliable and kept breaking down, leaving passengers stranded at Heysham and they had to be taken by bus to Liverpool. During the busy holiday season on the island, we certainly had our work cut out maintaining law and order with the disgruntled passengers.

One afternoon we were informed that the vessel had broken down and that the passengers were to be taken by coach to Liverpool. One of the harbour officials came to the office to inform us of this and stated that there might be trouble from a gentleman, who was none other than the late Wrestler, Giant Haystacks. I drew the short straw and went to inform him of the problem. He could not have been more understanding of the situation. Phew!

During a late turn at Heysham I received a telephone call from the signalman at Hest Bank to the effect that he had seen on the Close Circuit Television Cameras, monitoring the level crossing at Bolton Le Sands, a young boy who kept putting his bicycle in the metal skirt of the barrier every time it was raised. I went to the crossing and the boy was still there. He was ashen faced and pleaded with me not to take him home, but as he had been committing a couple of offences, I felt it was my duty to act. I put his bicycle in the back of the police vehicle and he sat in the front. I asked where he lived, and he told me Slyne Road. Now, Slyne Road, on the main A6 road into Lancaster is quite a long one.

As I was driving along, he became more and more agitated and withdrawn. I was fast running out of houses on Slyne Road. Then he pointed at one and informed me that he lived there. My heart went into my mouth, it was only the local police station and he was the local Policeman's son. As I drew up his dad came out. I explained what had taken place. It was decided to deal with him as a verbal warning and leave his dad to deal with him further.

Another telephone call took me to the quaintly named station of Giggleswick on the Carnforth to Skipton line. The lady residing in the station house had reported people living in the old goods shed in the station yard. So, I drove over. It was a really hot evening, so I had all the windows in the car open. On arrival, I went into the house where I spoke to the occupant. When I came out to go to the goods shed, I found six hens in the back of the car, and some of them had left their calling card on the back seat. I made my enquiries in the shed and established that there was no one there. I then had to clean the back of the car, before going back to Heysham.

The docks at Barrow in Furness were still owned by the British Transport Docks Board so we had jurisdiction there especially at Buccleuch Dock. In the glory days of the British Transport Police, we used to have officers stationed at Barrow Docks and Barrow railway station. It was an Inspector's post a few years ago.

During my time at Heysham, Vickers Armstrong were building submarines including nuclear ones, not only for the British Navy, but for foreign Navy's as well. They built one submarine for the Israeli Navy. I was on duty on launch day. There was a large ceremony, with dignitaries invited from all quarters. The Israelis had an armed guard, the local police were there, armed, the Royal Navy Police were there armed, and the good old British Transport Police there also armed – with our truncheons!

On Bank Holiday weekends, duty was often performed at Cark and Cartmel station on the Barrow line in connection with the horse racing at Cartmel. People would travel by train from all over Britain to attend the races. We never experienced any real problems; everyone was good humoured.

I was called to a foreign lorry with a forty-foot refrigerated trailer, one evening, which was blocking the entrance to the loading ramp of the 'Penda'. On arrival I saw the driver slumped over the wheel, it was obvious that he was drunk. I arrested him for being in charge of the vehicle and removed him from the cab. An officer from the Lancashire Constabulary at Heysham police station came to my assistance, whilst I tried to move the lorry. It had an extraordinarily complex gear system and no matter how I tried I could not move it. A couple of the Lancashire Constabulary traffic officers came to try and move it, it even perplexed them. In the end I found another lorry driver and he moved it for me. The drunk driver was taken to Morecambe police station. After discussions with the duty sergeant, it was decided, as the driver was from a foreign country, to charge him with being found drunk. He was suitably dealt with at Morecambe Magistrates' Court the next morning.

There was an open prison at Haverigg near Millom. Whenever there was an escape, we used to get notification from the Cumbria Police to be on the lookout for the escapee as many a time they would catch a train taking them to Lancaster. On the other hand, whenever an inmate was released legitimately, they would go to the nearest pub, down a few pints, then travel by train to Lancaster. More often than not, we would be called to the train to sort out their drunken behaviour.

Talking of prisons, Lancaster Castle, which overlooked the railway station was still an operational prison and some of the inmates on release would travel home by train. One or two tried to escape and we were informed to be on the lookout for them. Incidentally, this station was called Lancaster Castle to distinguish it from Lancaster Green Ayre station which was on the old electrified line from Lancaster Castle to Morecambe Promenade and Heysham.

The Spring of 1978 was drawing to a close. Preparations were being made to cover the Lake Windermere Steamers on Sundays and during the August Bank Holiday weekend.

CHAPTER 11

THE HEYSHAM YEARS - SUMMER 1978 – SUMMER 1979

The police car with the rude registration number and trying to tame the Scots

The Lake Windermere pleasure steamers, Swan, Teal, Swift and Tern were owned by British Railways and plied the lake every day in the main tourist season. The Swan and Teal were the biggest and did a full trip of the lake from Lakeside to Ambleside via Bowness, while the Swift and Tern would usually sail between Bowness and Ambleside. The former two vessels had full bar facilities on board and due to the licencing laws they were open all day whilst sailing on the lake. The local pubs in Bowness used to close at 14.00 hours on a Sunday and Bank Holiday Mondays. At closing time, the landlords would have no trouble in getting rid of their customers as they were told to go to the lake, purchase a cruise ticket and then they could drink to their hearts content. This is where the British Transport Police came in. We used to cover the boats as some of the clientele were worse for wear coming from the pubs and we would prevent them from travelling, others would board the vessels and start drinking and get inebriated on board, so we would travel on the vessels to maintain law and order.

It was a glorious day one Summer Sunday in 1978. I was on duty at Bowness Pier, when a prim and proper lady, approached me and requested that I go to the lake at the side of the pier as there was a most disgusting site. She would not elaborate on what this sight was. On arrival, I found a youth having a clothes-free dip in the lake. He had been drinking and had stripped off for a bet. I removed my helmet to cover a strategic part of his anatomy, but having nothing else, his rear was on show, so I had to walk behind him. There was much cheering from the assembled crowds on the promenade and I received a round of applause when I reached the promenade. I quickly found a towel and reunited him with his clothes. He was later cautioned for a Breach of the Peace.

Again, I was at the entrance to Bowness Pier in full uniform, watching the activities on the lake prior to the arrival of one of the vessels, when I heard the Japanese language being spoken by several people behind me. As I turned around about forty cameras clicked in unison. No doubt I was on a couple of dart boards back home.

The things that people said to me whilst I was on duty at the piers:-

I was stood on Lakeside Pier one day and a lady came up to me and said, *"Excuse me officer, what time does the two 'o clock boat to Ambleside depart?"*

I was at Ambleside pier, one afternoon, stood by a large sign which stated that 'Boat trips go from here'. A member of the public asked me where the boat trips went from.

Again, at Ambleside Pier a male person came up to me and said, *"How long does the two-hour cruise last for?"*

At Heysham in the summer of 1978 we took delivery of a brand-new police car, a dark blue Hillman Avenger. The registration plate left a lot to be desired *'ARR 511T'* which was written in italics. It turned a few heads as we were out and about. We were well a truly ribbed over this by all and sundry. We tried to have the registration number changed but to no avail.

Being based at Heysham, we used to go on mutual aid to Preston, Blackburn, Burnley, Bolton, Blackpool, and the Manchester stations to cover the home and away football supporters using these stations. At Manchester on some occasions, we were lucky enough to get into the ground of Manchester United and watch part of the games. Privately I supported the team they were playing.

I remember the first Saturday of the 1978 season a group of us arrived back at Lancaster after an uneventful day (which was unusual) on football duty at Manchester Oxford Road and Victoria Stations.

The Sergeant, Walt Girdley and I were just about ready to go home when the Guard of the 19.30 hours train to Barrow in Furness came to our office and asked for a police escort as he had got a number of Barrow in Furness and Furness based Manchester United supporters on board.

Walt decided that we would travel to Barrow. It was extra overtime for me. Walt was not too keen about going and he made this clear. He did not want to spend his other Saturday evenings during the football season travelling to and from Barrow as he was due to retire shortly.

As the train left Carnforth, I struck gold, there was a young man who was a supporter persistently annoying the ordinary passengers. I saw my chance. The train stopped at Silverdale station, which was in the middle of nowhere. In accordance with the Byelaws I ejected him. Despite his pleadings and those of his companions I would not let him back on the train. The train set off, leaving him on the platform. There was not another train from Silverdale until the following Monday morning and there were no buses until Sunday afternoon. My plan had paid off, we did not have any more trouble from the Barrow based supporters for the rest of the season and Walt was happy.

Whilst performing duty at Manchester Oxford Road one Saturday afternoon, there was a ticket barrier check. One supporter came to the barrier and offered to pay from Deansgate, the previous station, which was 'closed' for the purpose of the ticket check. Ticket Inspectors would be on duty there to ensure that everyone joining the train at that station had a ticket. This supporter gave false details to my colleague. It transpired that he had travelled from Altrincham and was a serving constable with the Greater Manchester Police.

Covering the Bolton Wanderers home matches had its perks. After dealing with the incoming fans, we used to go to the Catholic Club across the road from the station for pie and chips and a mug of tea. Then we would go to watch the game, as the ground, in those days, Burnden Park was situated next to the main line to Manchester and the west goal mouth was situated at the rear of the old Bolton to Bury railway line. (This can be seen in the film 'The Love Match' staring Arthur Askey).

The permanent way staff had built a stand on the railway embankment out of old railway sleepers and we, along with the staff used to stand on these watching the games. I remember one Saturday afternoon watching a game and the BBC were covering the match for Grandstand, from in front of where we were standing. Our Inspector was 'effing and blinding' at the referee and we had to point this out to him as was being picked up by the microphones and the cameras.

Another Scotland v England match saw me policing the concourse at Glasgow Central Station, making sure that the fans queued in an orderly manner to buy their tickets. Again, relatively trouble free, but I have never seen as many large whisky bottles in my life, some were two and three litre sizes. The fans were consuming the contents as if it was water.

Another visit to Glasgow, the week before Christmas 1978, saw me patrolling the trains to Hampden Park, for a Rangers v Celtic match. One train, with three carriages was absolutely crammed packed of both sets of supporters, that were a little noisy to say the least. I boarded the train and shouted in my best Lancashire accent, "Can you keep it down lads please?" All went quiet and I gave myself a mental pat on the back for taming some of Glasgow's finest. Suddenly, they all started hand clapping and chanting in unison "Sassenach, Sassenach" and the train began to rock from side to side. The next thing I knew I was pulled off the train by one of my colleagues from Glasgow who said "If ye dinna want your heid kicking in get off the train" – lesson learnt.

On the return, I was at Hampden Park waiting to escort one of the last trains back to Glasgow. As I looked down to the track, I could not see the ballast or the sleepers for whisky bottles and Tennent's lager tins.

One morning in early 1979, I was called to the road over rail bridge at Helmside, Oxenholme. A local, young man had been on the bridge and had fallen through the 25.000-volt overhead wires and landed on the track. He was still alive when I arrived. He had broken both arms and both legs along with a few other bones. He was lucky to be alive, miraculously he did not receive any burns from the wires. He was incredibly lucky. He was taken to Lancaster Royal Infirmary, where I interviewed him a few days later. He could not remember anything of the incident. No further action was taken against him.

On the 16 March 1979 I received a telephone call to inform me that I had been successful in passing my Sergeant's exam. I was speechless and ecstatic at the news.

I received a memorandum on 27 March 1979 from the Divisional Commander in Manchester congratulating me on passing my promotion exam to Sergeant. Almost immediately I was asked to go to Manchester as an Acting Sergeant. I stuck my career on the line and turned the offer down. I'm, glad that I did. During the year Sergeant Walt Girdley had spells of sickness followed by annual leave and I was assigned Acting Sergeant's duties whenever the occasion arose. I was now officially sat at the very desk where I had my initial interview to join the force by Inspector George Smith-Leach

In April 1979, a man was employed in the District Civil Engineers Office at Lancaster as a bridge examiner. He had a particularly good job, which was to visit bridges and other structures in the area, using a British Rail van. If he found a suspected fault, he would take a photograph and take it back to a more qualified person. One evening he was seen on the roof of Morecambe Promenade railway station removing lead. When challenged by the Station Supervisor, he produced a memorandum purporting to be from and signed by the Divisional Civil Engineer at Preston, giving him permission to remove the lead. The Supervisor allowed him to continue with his actions. However, he was suspicious of him and reported his suspicions to his superiors who made further enquiries into the matter. No such authority had been given. The matter was reported to us. Initially the CID at Preston were informed but they did not take any interest in the matter and stated that the uniformed officers at Heysham could investigate it.

A couple of days later I was on early turn at Heysham and Walt Girdley instructed me to come out the next day in plain clothes, pick him up at 08.00 hours at his home and take him to Lancaster. On arrival, I was told by Walt to go to the suspect's office and arrest him on suspicion of theft and take him back to the police office for an interview. Back at the office we interviewed him, and he maintained his innocence. So, we took him to Lancaster police station and booked him into the cells and left him there for a couple of hours, whilst we continued with our enquiries. On returning he was a changed man; he admitted the offence and others. I went back to Heysham and Lancaster to collect the crime registers. He was further interviewed, and, in the end, he admitted to around thirty crimes, some of which had not even been reported to us. One crime that he admitted to, was a burglary of his own office, whereby a camera and other equipment was stolen. He had reported this crime to us some weeks earlier. We bailed him for further enquiries to be made.

Our enquiries took us to Dent and Blea Moor Signalboxes on the Settle to Carlisle railway line, where some clocks and other equipment had been stolen. We arranged to meet up with Norman Greenhough the local British Rail traffic manager. Dent Signalbox was situated around four miles from the actual village of Dent. He stated that he could not offer us a brew as the locomotive with the fresh water had not arrived but was on its way. Sure, enough about five minutes later a class 40 diesel locomotive running as a light engine pulled up at the Signalbox and the driver unloaded two containers of fresh water and took the empty ones for refilling. So, we had our brew and Norman gave us some valuable information to assist us with our enquiries.

A couple of days later we returned to the area in plain clothes, to go to Kirkby Stephen police station to meet up with officers of the Cumbria Police who were going to take us to the home of a local antiques dealer, who we believed had some stolen railway property. Before we went, Walt and I called in at the local pub for a bar snack. We went to the main bar and I saw a chap in plain clothes stood at the side of the bar consuming a pint. We ordered our meal of steak pie and chips and an orange juice. I asked the barman where the police station was. He gave me directions. I noticed that the man stood at the side of the bar disappeared rather quickly.

After lunch, we went to the Police Station and the duty sergeant was none other than the man at the bar. We introduced ourselves and he breathed a sigh of relief he thought we were Complaints and Discipline Department from Headquarters at Penrith. The officers whom we had arranged to take us across the moors to the antiques dealer's house made themselves known to us. We set off in convoy, the Cumbria Police panda car, the BTP car, the local dog handler, and a village bobby in his mini car. As one officer commented it made a change from sheep rustling.

We recovered several items from the antiques dealer's house. Feeling really chuffed with a job well done we returned to Heysham and prepared to interview our suspect further. The CID got wind of our successes and tried to muscle in on the job, but they were told in no uncertain terms that they were not welcome as they did not take any interest at the start of the case. One of them did come sniffing round, desperate not to be embarrassed when the file eventually went in. Again, he was told to go away or words to that effect. Walt and I stood our ground against the CID hierarchy and we eventually won. Our name was mud.

Our suspect came to Lancaster police station to answer his bail. He was charged with one count of forgery, four counts of Burglary and four counts of theft. He was then bailed to appear at court. At his court appearance, he pleaded guilty and he asked for sixty-nine other crimes to be taken into consideration. The proceedings were adjourned for sentence. On the next court appearance, he was sentenced to six months imprisonment, suspended for two years, and ordered to pay compensation and costs amounting to £356.93p. Walt and I received a commendation from the Area Commander for our work in the case.

It was the late spring bank holiday Monday in May 1979, when I was on late turn at Heysham in shirt sleeve order. I remember it was a very warm evening, a cloudless sky and the sun was shining. At about 19.30 hours I had just finished my meal break when I received a telephone call from the Signalman at Carnforth East Junction Signalbox, to say that he believed there were intruders in the Signalbox at Wennington on the borders of Lancashire and North Yorkshire, on the Carnforth to Skipton line. His suspicion was aroused, due to the fact that this box was only staffed between 08.00 hours and 16.00 hours and that he had an indication through the instruments in his box, that the signal equipment was being operated at Wennington. The scene is about eighteen miles from Heysham. I went up in the Preston dog van which was on loan to us. On arrival, I saw the most spectacular sight. There was a covering of snow in the station yard and on the tracks. There had been a freak snowstorm. The sudden change in the air pressure had caused the signalling equipment to operate and this was confirmed by the Signal and Telegraph staff who also attended.

Back at Heysham I wrote the message up in the telephone book and one of the phrases I used in the action taken column, was '....and no footprints were found in the snow'.

The next day, Walt had me in and asked if I had been drinking, making mention of snow, as he and his wife had been enjoying a family barbeque in the sunshine at their house.

One evening I was on patrol of the harbour when my attention was drawn to a forty-foot wagon trailer which was on some waste land near to the Marine Yard. There was movement coming from underneath the tarpaulin. I pulled it back only to find a local courting couple going 'hell for leather'. Well, for all I knew It could have been a burglar sorting out their ill-gotten gains!

Arnside viaduct over the Kent estuary, on the Carnforth to Barrow line always attracted a lot of fishermen, who used to walk along the viaduct and go fishing from the track side. We had several successes with reporting them for trespass.

The town of Kendal and the village of Burneside on the Oxenholme to Windermere branch line are only 2 ¼ miles from each other and the train took around three minutes. That journey was an exceptionally long three minutes when the school children travelled on the train to from the high school at Kendal. Some of their antics would put the girls of 'St Trinian's' to shame. We regularly had to travel on the afternoon train from Kendal to Burneside to maintain law and order. We had a few successes in prosecuting offenders for Disorderly Conduct and Ticket Fraud.

One Tuesday in June 1979 I was asked if I would like to work my rest day, the following day to assist in the removal of travellers from the old railway yard at Haslingden on the long-closed Accrington to Ramsbottom railway line.

Early the next day I went with a colleague Gerry Bains, an ex-dog handler himself, to Preston, where we met up with Sergeant Madge Dowling and 'Ginge' Ablard and his dog 'Ben'. We went off in 'Ginge's' Police vehicle, which was a Ford Escort estate car, painted bright yellow! On arrival at Haslingden we found that the travellers had left. Whilst discussing our next course of action, we were approached by officers of the Lancashire Constabulary who were looking for jewel thieves who had robbed a nearby jewellers. 'Ginge' offered assistance with his dog and started tracking through the disused railway tunnel. The robbers were apprehended in a nearby field. A job well done.

By this time, it was time for lunch, and we went to the town of Padiham near Burnley and the four of us purchased a meat and potato pie from a local pie shop. We sat in the car to eat our pies. Madge and 'Ginge' were in the front whilst Gerry and I were in the rear seats, with 'Ben' in the rear portion of the vehicle. Gerry took a bite out of his pie and was chewing it slowly, obviously enjoying this Lancashire delicacy, when all of a sudden 'Ben' lurched forward, licking his lips and snatched the rest of the pie from the hand of a mesmerised Gerry. The three of us could not eat our pies for laughing. Gerry's face was an absolute picture.

British Rail ran several excursion trains hauled by steam locomotive along the Cumbrian Coast Line from Carnforth to Ravenglass and to Skipton in North Yorkshire. One such train was the 'Cumbrian Mountain Express'. It ran from Blackpool North to Skipton then to Grange over Sands and sometimes up to Ravenglass. A variety of steam locomotives were used on the train and were attached at Carnforth.

We had the task of riding with the train to Skipton and Grange over Sands and performing duty whenever it stopped to prevent trespass incidents. Despite our presence one or two people were daft enough to go onto the tracks to take photographs, they ended up autographing my pocketbook, after being interviewed.

A heart-warming story comes to mind. At Barrow in Furness, there was a small local team called Greengate United. In 1979 there was a young boy, from the Barrow area, who was sadly suffering from a life-threatening illness (not sure what it was), but treatment was only available in America. So Greengate United organised a charity evening whereby they invited Manchester United to send an autographed ball for the raffle. Manchester United went one better and sent a team up to play them. Admittedly, none of the first team players played, but two or three of them came up and walked onto the pitch to a rapturous applause.

I was Acting Sergeant at the time and covered Barrow railway station for the game with one Constable. There was no trouble whatsoever, in fact it was a carnival atmosphere.

I recall one occasion during the summer of 1979 I was acting Sergeant but not wearing any insignia and was on the vessel 'Swan' on Lake Windermere, for public order duties, with Jim Morris, who is a few years older than myself, in the crowded smoke-filled bar. Jim informed me that he was going upstairs on deck to get some fresh air but would stand at the entrance keeping me in view if I needed assistance. I was standing at the side of the actual bar when I felt a tap on my shoulder. I turned around it was the barman, who handed me a pint of best bitter and said, "Get this down you, now that your sergeant has gone". Cheers.

During my time at Heysham the Royal Train arrived at Lancaster. I cannot for the life of me remember the date or which member of the Royal family was on board. After completing protection duty on Platform Three at Lancaster station I was given the task of travelling with the Royal Train to the sidings at Carnforth, remain with it and patrol the area until it returned to Preston. I did manage to dine on the train, not in the main dining room, but in the guard's van eating my locally purchased steak and kidney pie.

In the summer of 1979, a General Order arrived, inviting suitably qualified officers to apply for the Promotion Board and to choose a vacancy from the list should they be successful. I applied and chose Crewe from the several stations that were listed. I attended the Promotion Board at Force Headquarters and on 9 July was advised by the Chief Constable Eric Haslam that I was successful in passing the board. On 21 August 1979 I was advised that I was to be promoted to Uniform Sergeant at Crewe with effect from Monday 3 September 1979.

CHAPTER 12

THE CREWE YEARS SEPTEMBER 1979 – 1981

A baptism of fire and enquiring into the CIA

My first day as a Sergeant, Monday 3 September 1979, I was supposed to report to Chief Superintendent George Smith-Leach at Divisional Headquarters, Birmingham at 12.00 hours. However, the train was late, and I was late arriving, which did not bode well. However, after being welcomed back to the Division I made my way to Crewe where I met Inspector Ted Locke. The establishment at Crewe consisted of One Inspector, One Detective Sergeant, four Uniform Sergeants, four Detective Constables, eight Uniform Constables and two dog handlers. There was also a civilian clerk. The Crewe District was also responsible for the police posts at Stoke on Trent, where there was a Sergeant and four constables, and Shrewsbury where there was a newly introduced Sergeant's post and four constables. I had put in for the Shrewsbury post when it was advertised after my Promotion Board but was unsuccessful.

I already knew one of the Sergeants, John Simpson, who originates from Lancaster. Ken Paxton had been promoted the same day as me, and 'Mac' McMullen had been in post for about twelve months, the same as John Simpson.

I was allocated to a shift. My Constables were the late Alan Perkins (shortly to go into CID at Crewe) and Albert Ryan. Albert was currently on a course at Tadworth, so I did not meet him for a couple of weeks. My Detective Constable was Eric Kendrick and my dog handler was Eddie Howell and Police Dog 'Rick'. The Constable who usually worked round with me at Stoke on Trent was Charlie Emery and the Constable who usually worked round with me at Shrewsbury was Gordon Beharrell.

I quickly got to know my fellow officers, their strengths, and weaknesses. Each and every one was unique in his or her own way. You could always tell when the CID had been drinking at night, they came in eating a bag of chips from the chippy on Nantwich Road. I also got to know the station staff quickly as well.

The retired officers and probably a few serving officers will remember the CRO (Criminal Records Office) 74 form (Modus Operandi and Descriptive Form) which was to be filled in when a person had been arrested. One of the sections to be completed was '*How criminal left the premises*'. This could be answered simply such as '*egress as ingress*' '*via an open door*' '*by forcing the back door open*' etc. However, we had one CID officer, who fancied himself as a comedian. On one occasion, when he made an arrest in conjunction with one of the Crewe dog handlers he wrote in the CRO 74, in respect of his prisoner, 'In handcuffs, in a compartment in the rear cage of the dog van with the dog in the other'. It was never queried. Someone at New Scotland Yard, no doubt had a good laugh.

We had three vehicles at Crewe, a dark blue Hillman Hunter saloon car, which was used by the uniformed officers, a dark blue Ford Escort estate car which was used by the CID and a dark blue Vauxhall van which was used by the dog handlers.

Most of my work was to supervise the Constables and to assist the Inspector with prosecuting cases at the courts in the area.

I also established that we had an exceptionally good working liaison with the Cheshire Constabulary and officers from both forces used to help each other out on Mutual Aid. It was common for them to come up to our office for a chat and a cuppa.

On our patch, we had the following football league teams; Crewe Alexandra, Port Vale, Stoke City and Shrewsbury Town. The supporters of these clubs gave us plenty of work, as well as the passing football traffic.

Crewe as we all know was and still is a remarkably busy railway junction, ordinary passenger and football special trains from all the four corners of Britain used to converge there conveying football supporters to and from their matches. It was almost a seven day a week operation dealing with football traffic. We had to carefully plan with the railway authorities the position of trains at Crewe station, whilst the locomotives and train crew were changed, so that opposing fans did not clash. Sometimes it was necessary to have a uniformed police presence and if possible, dogs and their handlers on the platforms to quell any potential disorder. On the odd occasion they did clash we had fun trying to sort them out and round them up. Some occasions it was like a scene from a wild west movie. The only thing missing was John Wayne.

Some of the travelling supporters would leave the trains at Crewe and whilst waiting for connecting services would go onto Nantwich Road, outside the station, and fight between themselves or the local youths. This caused no end of problems for the Cheshire Constabulary.

I had no trouble in finding lodgings in the Crewe area, my late mate, Graeme Brocken, let me have the use of a room at his house about a mile away from the station. Graeme at this time worked in the train planning office at Rail House, Crewe, which was especially useful for when we were arranging football specials. Graeme would find us the appropriate stock for the journey and the best possible route.

The week following my appointment I was supposed to go on annual leave for two weeks but postponed it towards the end of the month, as Ken Paxton was moving to a new house from the Potteries to Crewe, so I covered for him as well as my shift.

Just before my long weekend, I was approached by Terry Belcher one of the Station Supervisors at Crewe, he was also the Scout Master of the local scout troop, who requested a presentation at his next meeting, Thursday 20 September 1979, on railway safety. I said that I would arrange one. There was nobody at Crewe who could do this, so I made up a presentation from material that I had at home and went to the meeting and made my first railway safety presentation.

Before going on annual leave, I went onto a run of seven night shifts. My first night, a Tuesday night was reasonably quiet. But Wednesday 19 September 1979 was a real baptism of fire. There was only Alan Perkins and myself on duty. The shift started off quietly at 22.30 hours. Then at around 22.40 hours we were called to 'The Mail Bach' ('The Small Mail'), the nickname for a passenger/mail train from Holyhead, this train consisted usually of about three TPO vehicles and two passenger coaches, hence its nickname.

Up to three or four years previously, Holyhead based officers used to travel on this train as far as Crewe, in the main mail coach. This was a requirement following the Great Train Robbery. There was an off-duty Soldier on the train from Chester who had started to smash up a compartment. Alan Perkins and I arrested him and took him to the police office, where we had a semi-secure room. As we were documenting him, we received a telephone call at around 23.30 hours to go to a local train from Liverpool which had just arrived on Platform Five and had about fourteen Feyenoord football supporters from the Netherlands on board, who were returning from a 1 - 0 victory against Everton in a UEFA Cup match and were travelling to London on a later service. It was alleged that they had been causing some disorder. We began to deal with them the best we could, as my Dutch is non-existent, we managed to calm them down using sign language. The train departed empty stock to the sidings.

Then at 23.52 hours the overnight sleeping car train from Barrow in Furness to London Euston arrived at the same platform and the guard called us to a drunk male. Fortunately, he was too drunk to cause any problems. Due to his drunken condition, I thought the best course of action was to get him to hospital for a check-up. An Ambulance was called. We went back to dealing with our football supporters, when at around midnight, we received a call to go to the 'The Irish Mail', London Euston to Holyhead passenger train on Platform One as there was an elderly woman, travelling with her daughter, en-route to Ireland, in a collapsed state and un-responsive. By this time, the football fans had quietened down somewhat after their victory, they were, very tired. I think they had been without sleep for a couple of days and went forward to London on the Barrow in Furness to London train without further incident.

We went over to the Holyhead train to find that the lady had sadly died. Another ambulance was called for and she was taken to the Mortuary at Leighton Hospital, Crewe, we then arranged for her daughter to stay in the area, whilst some of her family came to collect her.

We then went back to the soldier who fortunately at this time was fast asleep. He was taken to Crewe police station, where he was formally charged with Criminal Damage. He was denied bail and appeared the next morning at Crewe and Nantwich Magistrates' Court. I cannot remember how the case was disposed of, but the Military Police came to collect him after the court hearing.

It was then up to Leighton Hospital to arrest our drunk who by now was in a conscious state and take him to Crewe police station where he was charged with being Found Drunk. He was then detained in custody and appeared at the court the following morning and was fined five pounds.

Back to the office and we attacked the mountain of paperwork that lay before us. It was certainly a busy night for the two of us. The rest of the week passed off quietly.

One Saturday, evening shortly after being promoted, I was travelling back off duty, after performing football duties at Stoke on Trent, on a late-night train from Crewe to Preston, with 'Ginge' Ablard a colleague of mine, who also had been recently promoted from dog handler at Preston to Sergeant at Stoke on Trent, after the retirement of Norman Steele. We were travelling in 'half blues', in an open plan coach, which was not too busy. Sat opposite us was a Clergyman. The train came to a sudden stop somewhere around the Hartford area, north of Crewe. We seemed to stay there for ages. There was no information forthcoming from the train crew as to what the delay was. The Clergyman leaned over to us and asked if we knew what the problem was. I said to him "I was rather hoping you might know something with your connections". He smiled, put his hands together in a prayerful position, looked heavenwards and said, "Even the good Lord has given up on British Railways". We all had a good laugh and shortly afterwards the train departed - divine intervention?

Shrewsbury football club had recently been promoted to the old English First Division, playing, such teams as Chelsea, Manchester United, Liverpool and Leeds. Apart from bringing big money in, this was a novelty for them, but a big headache for the West Mercia Police finding extra officers.

It was either in September or October of 1979 I attended a Shrewsbury home game against Chelsea, which was a big match for Shrewsbury. West Mercia Police had drafted officers from every corner of the three counties they covered (Worcestershire, Shropshire and Herefordshire) some of these officers had never had experience of football traffic in their careers; it was a wake-up call for them, seeing the fans from the big city whose behaviour they had only seen on the news bulletins.

Leeds supporters were the most troublesome and they usually travelled on the overnight Friday, York to Aberystwyth TPO train, which came via Leeds and Crewe arriving in Shrewsbury around 03.50 hours on a Saturday morning. On their first encounter, the supporters wreaked absolute havoc in the town centre of Shrewsbury, as the local police were totally unprepared for them. On subsequent meetings the local police had the ground opened for their arrival. I remember one Saturday evening I was on duty at Shrewsbury for the return of the supporters to Leeds and the Military Police from Catterick, Yorkshire were on the station to assist us. I still do not know to this day why they were there. Probably looking for some squaddies amongst the supporters.

During November 1979 whilst on patrol of Crewe railway station and in particular the station forecourt, I became aware of a lot of plain clothes police activity. Some looked suspiciously like the American FBI and CIA agents, dressed exactly as you would see them in the films. They stuck out a mile. So, I wanted to know what was taking place on my patch and I started to make some enquiries.

It transpired that they were in fact CIA agents working with detectives from New Scotland Yard into a case of gun dealing. The Scotland Yard detectives had raided four premises in the immediate vicinity of Crewe town centre, and another being the Hunters Lodge Hotel, a couple of miles away from the station. The Hunters Lodge Hotel was owned by an American gentleman who was an ex-CIA Agent but had been dismissed from his job in 1971. They also believed that the hotel had actually been operated by a clandestine CIA network in Britain, but this was not proved. The hotel's owner was, a week before Christmas in 1979, put before a Federal Grand Jury in Washington accused with others after being arrested in New York city for attempting to sell ten-thousand machine guns to city detectives posing as Latin American Revolutionaries. It transpired that the CIA men and Scotland Yard officers were using Crewe station as a rendezvous point.

As there were only four Sergeants at Crewe, we usually worked 09.00 hours to 17.00 hours and 22.30 hours to 06.30 hours on a Sunday. I went on long weekend after seven days of early turn and was looking forward to four days off before going onto nights for seven nights. However just before I went off, on the Thursday afternoon, I was asked by the Inspector if I would work my rest day on the Sunday as the day turn Sergeant was taking a lieu day. I agreed, but it meant that I had to drive back from my home in Morecambe as there were no suitable trains.

I arrived at Crewe at about 08.30 hours on the Sunday morning, only to find that the Inspector was on duty and that the night Sergeant was still on duty along with the night turn Constables and the early Constables. It transpired that during the night the Sergeant and a PC had come across two male persons from the Liverpool area on the station and their story about being on the station did not ring true. They were taken to the police office, where they were placed in the interview room. When left unattended they saw their chance and escaped from the office via the fire escape and not realising there were overhead 25.000-volt wires nearby, one of the suspects touched the wire and was killed outright. His friend was so traumatised that he returned to the office on his own accord. It transpired that both were wanted by the Merseyside Police for armed robbery. The survivor was later picked up by officers from the Merseyside Police.

On Friday 14 March 1980, Her Majesty the Queen and His Royal Highness Prince Philip The Duke of Edinburgh travelled to Leicester by Royal Train to perform five official duties in the city and surrounding areas. I and three other officers from Crewe went to Leicester station to perform protection duties in connection with the visit. I was able to renew some old acquaintances on this day.

One of my hobbies, was Crown Green bowling and we had a team in the railway league. Alan Perkins and myself regularly partnered one another in the league and won a couple of trophies.

British Rail ran a network of Motorail services throughout the country. They were a good way of transporting your car without the long drives on the motorways. You could travel from Inverness to St Austell all the way by train, with your car on an open-air low loader attached to the rear and then relax in the passenger coaches. One such service ran overnight from Stirling to Crewe.

As usual, one morning the train arrived at Crewe at around 06.00 hours. An elderly gentleman who owned a Bentley car, drove his vehicle off the low loader and reversed it into a crash barrier, which was made from a length of old railway line, on the loading bay. There was considerable damage to the rear of the car. Rolls Royce were contacted, and they attended the scene, covered the vehicle with a sheet, and left it on the loading bay until the hours of darkness. Apparently, they did not like their damaged vehicles being seen in public during daylight hours.

We had a PC at Crewe who had transferred from the Cheshire Constabulary. He was mad keen on firearms and his hobby was shooting game in the fields near to where he lived. He submitted a memorandum to the Divisional Commander, requesting to be considered as a firearms officer should our officers in the provinces be trained in the use of firearms. (We did have trained officers in London at the time). The Divisional Commander sent a memorandum back thanking him for his interest but stated there were no immediate plans to have trained firearms officers in the provinces, but should the need arise he would be considered.

A few months later, myself and another PC saw our chance to play a practical joke on the PC. We typed up a memorandum purporting to be from the Divisional Commander, stating that the force was now considering the possibility of training officers in the use of firearms. We placed it in an envelope addressed to him. When he came on duty, he opened it and read it. His face was a picture, full of anticipation then he noticed the date, 1 April. I will not tell you what he said. but you can imagine.

The Liverpool to Manchester Railway was officially opened on Monday 13 September 1830. Throughout 1980 British Rail staged several commemorative events. One of the highlights was the Rainhill Trials re-enactment and a Grand Cavalcade between the 24 May and 26 May 1980, which was a bank holiday weekend. This event consisted of several replica locomotives, some retired steam locomotives, active diesel locomotives and active electric locomotives (hauled by a diesel). I and some officers from Crewe went on Mutual Aid as a serial for this event. We along with other officers were accommodated at Bruche, Warrington, the Number One Police District Training School, which was closed to students for the weekend. This is where I did my initial training in 1971. The British Railway Board did us proud for our evening meals, three course meals, with waitress service and wine. We had full use of the bar facilities. On the three days, we were working at Rainhill we were taken by bus from Bruche after breakfast, to Bold Colliery, where we had temporary accommodation. Lunch was provided in the canteen. Pie, chips, peas, and coal dust! This was some four years before the miner's dispute, so we had no problems from the miners.

My serial was to cover a stretch of the line just outside of Rainhill station. Once in position I was approached by a member of the railway staff who stated that the control room at Liverpool wanted to speak with a BTP Officer and as I was the nearest, I went to the booking office to contact them. The radio system was abysmal in those days. The office was full of railway staff and I said to one gentleman, "May I use the phone to ring our office in Liverpool, please my friend?" He scowled at me and said, "I'm Detective Inspector Stephenson". Oops, well, I had never met him before.

I never worked with DC Tony Robinson, on a regular basis as he was on an opposite shift to me. One thing that I learned about him was that he was a great practical joker and one evening I found myself covering a night turn for a colleague of mine who was on annual leave. At around 01.00 hours we received a call from the Cheshire Constabulary to the effect that the burglar alarm at the Permanent Way Sports and Social Club in Gresty Road, Crewe had been activated. As this was on our patch we were obliged to attend. Tony made a head start in the CID car whilst myself and two Constables went in the uniform car. On arrival, I put one Constable at the rear of the premises and one at the front whilst I walked around the building. I did not see Tony, but I knew he was more than capable of looking after himself, as he had served in the Palestine Police in World War Two.

We put our force radios on to channel two which meant that we could talk to each other (normally they were on channel one so that we could be contacted by the control room at Birmingham). I walked round the building and found that it was secure and joined the Constable at the front of the premises. We remained in situ to await the keyholder of the premises. The Constable at the rear of the building radioed me and stated that there was an intruder on the roof who was throwing empty beer bottles in his direction. (The bottles did not smash as they were landing in a rubbish pile). I went around to the rear to weigh up the situation and to plan my next course of action. I caught a glimpse of 'the suspect' in the moonlight, it was none other than Tony. Apparently on arrival he collected some empty beer bottles and put them in his coat pocket, shinned up a drainpipe and when the opportunity arose, he started throwing them at this particular Constable. The incident turned out to be a false alarm, due to the burglar alarm being faulty.

In November 1980, Detective Constable Tony Robinson retired from the force. During the evening of Thursday 6 November 1980, he held his retirement party at a local hostelry. I attended along with several other officers, after which we went to a night club in Nantwich, arriving back home in the early hours of the morning. The following day Friday 7 November 1980 I was on 09.00 hours to 17.00 hours as the duty Sergeant, for obvious reasons, I was looking for a quiet day. At around 10.50 hours one of the Constables came into my office and informed that there had been a train crash on the lines known as the 'Salop avoiding lines' which run behind Crewe station and in front of Rail House. We went to the scene and found that a light engine had run into the back of a stationary oil train which was at a set of red signals. Three members of the crew of the light engine were killed. The local police Chief Superintendent and Superintendent, with whom we had an excellent liaison attended. They asked if my senior officers would be attending. I told them that they would be in due course as they were coming from Birmingham. They laughed and stated that they would leave it in my capable hands and left. My superiors eventually attended but left very soon afterwards. After the scene was cleared, I submitted a report to the local Coroner and one to the BTP Area Commander in Bristol, as we were under the Western Area at that time. A short time afterwards, I received a memorandum from him, congratulating me on my well-presented report, which was also endorsed by the Divisional Commander in Birmingham.

On the 17 February 1981, I re-joined the International Police Association and became a member of the Cheshire Branch. I became the Social Secretary of the branch for a short while. Shortly after re-joining I answered an advert in the Association's magazine from Karl Frimberger a police officer with Deutsche Bundersbahn Polizei (German Railway Police) Criminal Investigation Department, in Regensburg, who was looking for a pen friend. Karl and I had a couple of things in common We both joined the Police and the IPA in 1971 and we were of a similar age. I began corresponding with Karl, a friendship which still lasts. I have been out to his home in Bavaria on a couple of occasions to meet him and his wife Margit.

Ted Locke our Inspector had retired, and his place had been taken by Inspector Andy Bicknell who had transferred from Southampton Docks.

In June 1981, I attended a newly promoted Sergeants Course at Tadworth. This was a contradiction in terms as I had been promoted in September 1979.

Following their return from honeymoon after their marriage on the 29 July 1981, His Royal Highness the Prince of Wales and Diana the Princess of Wales toured Wales in the Royal Train. A couple of their destinations were Machynlleth and Aberdovey in Mid-Wales, which were covered by the Shrewsbury office. I was instructed by Inspector Andy Bicknell to go to Shrewsbury, one Tuesday, team up with Steve Wilson, the Sergeant there, and go off to Machynlleth and Aberdovey and draw up plans of the station and sidings in readiness for an operational order in connection with the royal visit. I went on the train and teamed up with Steve. We went over to Machynlleth, drew up our plans. We then went to Aberdovey, this is a one platformed halt on a single-track railway line with a path leading to it from the main road. The plans took us less than five minutes to draw up.

As we were both in plain clothes we then adjourned to the local pub for a pie and a pint. I sat facing the entrance door and Steve had his back to it. We were waiting for our food to arrive and generally chatting about different things, when the door opened, and a very tall man walked in. I said to Steve, who at this time was taking a sip of his drink, "He's a big bloke, I wouldn't like to meet him on a dark night". Steve turned around and spat his drink back into the glass and said, "It's the Superintendent from Birmingham". It was Jim Hoath, who I had never met. My pension flashed before my eyes. Following Mr. Hoath was Detective Chief Inspector Hulin, sadly both men are no longer with us. There was a pregnant pause and Mr. Hoath turned to Mr. Hulin and said, "Don't just stand there get the lads a drink" Phew! That broke the ice.

In the early 1980s, I forget the exact year the British Transport Police from Crewe entered a team in an 'It's a Knockout' style competition in the grounds of Leighton Hospital, Crewe, against the local police, local fire service, the local ambulance service and the staff at Leighton Hospital, to raise funds for the kidney unit there. We had a fantastic day getting soaked from the fire brigade during some of the games. More importantly we raised several hundred pounds for the unit.

Sometime later on, a cabaret night for the kidney unit was held at the Rolls Royce social club in Crewe. I went with Shirley and en route picked up a colleague of mine and his wife.

On arrival at the club, unknown to me, I should have gone to the public car park across the road from the factory. Instead, I went to the main gates and told the security man that I was for the cabaret, he let me in and pointed to where I could park my car, which was a metallic grey, 1725 cc, Hillman Hunter, registration number BMS 521R, and the paint was peeling off. I had recently purchased the car from a colleague. I parked it next to a line of twelve brand new Rolls Royce's and went to the cabaret. When we came out the car was still there, but the Rolls Royce's had been moved. The company were particular what was parked next to their vehicles. The Security man thought that I was part of the actual cabaret and that is why he let me park where I did.

Graeme, my mate, still had connections at 'STEAMTOWN', Carnforth, and he arranged for my vehicle to be resprayed in the paint shops there, at the same time that the London North Eastern Railway A4 class Pacific, 'Sir Nigel Gresley' was being repainted. I had a lovely gleaming blue coloured car.

One evening on a Saturday in November 1981 I was on duty on the station platforms when I was called to a small disturbance between two sets of football supporters who were in the process of changing trains. That evening, I had a dog handler on duty with me. Both the handler and dog accompanied me to the disturbance, and we began to split them up. The dog suddenly flew at a man who was particularly vocal and waving his arms around in the air like a windmill in a gale force wind. The dog took hold of his arm and the handler brought the situation under control as he was trained to do. The man then complained that the dog had torn the sleeve of his brand-new leather jacket. The dog handler very unsympathetically said to him "Your fault, go to the hardware shop and buy some vinyl weld" The man was arrested for disorderly conduct and subsequently dealt with at court.

Crewe Magistrates' Court had four courtrooms one of which was designed to be used as a Crown Court, however a Judge, in civil and family cases only used it. All the furniture in court four was removable, including the witness box, which was on castors.

One of our officers entered the witness box and the thing started to move towards the Magistrates' bench, but it was stopped in time. On another occasion, a colleague of mine from the Cheshire Constabulary who was about 6'6" entered the box to give his evidence. The Clerk of the court asked him to take the oath in the usual way. However, the Bible and the card for reading the Oath from were on the Clerk's desk. The Sergeant leaned over to obtain the items, only for the box to fall forward and for the sergeant to fall out. Fortunately, he was not injured and on discovering this, their Worships had a good laugh to themselves, as did the rest of the court. The court was adjourned for coffee.

Each year, during an evening on the week before Christmas all the furniture in court number four would be removed and there would be a party in there. Representatives from the police and the legal profession and others would attend, the invite being via an official summons. It always seemed strange prosecuting drunks in that court!

Just before the Christmas party the Magistrates' Clerk ran a caption competition and the cartoon for the caption to be appended to, would be circulated a couple of weeks beforehand. It had to be submitted a couple of days before the party for judging. One year, the cartoon had a Clerk addressing the Magistrates.

My caption was on the lines of. *'This is typical of the British Transport Police cases, dirty, smelly, downright drunk, offensive, uncooperative and totally impolite, and that's only the prosecuting Sergeant'.* To my surprise I won it. My prizes were, a book entitled *'Cucumbers are better than men because...'* and a small square game in a plastic case, where I had to put two small metal balls in two holes on a shelf across the middle. (I still have both).

The female clerk announced to a packed courtroom that I had won and when she presented me with the game she said, "Sergeant Rogerson can play with his balls at the back of the court whilst waiting to present his briefs to their worships". Well, the whole court was in uproar. I always had a job to keep a straight face when I went to her court in the future. I was often asked if I still played with my balls.

Here are a few of the cases I dealt with at the local courts.

I remember going over to Stoke on Trent court at Fenton one day to prosecute, as the Sergeant at Stoke was on holiday. I was in full uniform in the upstairs courtroom waiting for my cases to be heard. The Magistrates adjourned for coffee, so, I went downstairs to the police room to obtain a coffee for myself.

As I was descending the stairs a youth ran out of one of the downstairs courtrooms hotly pursued by a constable from the Staffordshire Police, shouting "Stop that man". I was a little fitter in those days and joined in the chase outrunning the Staffordshire PC. I saw the youth cross the main A50 road, but a double decker bus blocked my view. When the bus had gone the youth was nowhere to be seen and I presumed that he had gone into the first building in the side street across the road. I ran in, not taking any notice of what the building was. As I entered, I heard this girl shout, "It's a raid" and she pressed a bell. The next thing there were all these men with towels around them being followed by scantily dressed women, of horizontal virtue running for the exits. Yes, unknown to me, I had gone into a massage parlour in pursuit of this lad and the receptionist thought I was part of a raiding party. It was like a scene from the Keystone Cops. All that was missing was the Benny Hill theme tune. The offender was caught a couple of weeks later.

I went to Crewe court one day to prosecute a simple case of ticket fraud. The defendant had failed to turn up at a previous hearing and it was my job to prove the case in his absence. So, I put my chief witness, a constable from Liverpool, in the witness box. As usual, I asked the Chairman if the officer could refer to his notebook. The Chairman of the bench agreed and asked the officer when did he make up his notes. To which the officer replied, "I didn't make them up they are true". If only the floor could have opened up and swallowed me up. Fortunately, the Chairman and the other two Magistrates saw the funny side of it.

A forestry worker from Sandbach threw a punch at a British Rail guard and knocked his glasses off when challenged about his fare. He then ran off but was traced by British Transport Police officers and appeared before Sandbach Magistrates' Court where he pleaded guilty to behaving in a disorderly manner at Sandbach station.

I prosecuted the case and the facts were, that he had alighted off the Altrincham to Crewe train at Sandbach. He went to the guard, gave him 34 pence, and said he had got on at Holmes Chapel. When the guard challenged the amount of the fare the defendant threw the correct amount of 40 pence at him and then threw a punch at the guard and ran off. He was fined £30 and bound over to keep the peace for 12 months in the sum of £50.

One of the cases I prosecuted at Crewe Magistrates' Court was that of a 46 year-old man of no fixed abode. He was a schizophrenic. The day in question he was sat alone in the crowded buffet on Platform Four of Crewe station. Also, in the buffet were women and children. He then got up and started to mess around with his trousers, he undid them, and they fell to the floor. He was not wearing any underpants and he exposed himself for about a minute. A man and woman nearby thought it was disgraceful and disgusting and contacted the BTP. He admitted exposing himself in Wolverhampton and on the train to Crewe. His defence solicitor said that his client had received treatment for schizophrenia as a voluntary patient in Wolverhampton. He was sent to prison for forty-two days.

I prosecuted a case involving a ticket fraud at Crewe and Nantwich Magistrates' Court, involving two local men. A ticket collector at Crewe station told police officers that two men had offered to pay the fare from Alsager to Crewe. When he challenged them, they left without paying the fare. Enquiries revealed that only one person boarded the train at Alsager, and one ticket had been issued. Both men who had been previously dealt with by the court, initially denied doing anything. It transpired that they had actually travelled from Stoke on Trent. A platform ticket from Birmingham was found on one of the men. Both had not offered any payment from Stoke on Trent. For making off without paying a £1.80 train fare they were fined £50, ordered to pay the £1.80p fare and £10 costs.

Another case I had concerned three juveniles aged 13, 14 and 16 who had absconded from the Redlands Assessment Centre at Willaston near Nantwich. On the day in question the three had been on a railway bridge on the Crewe to Shrewsbury line near to Willaston level crossing, when they threw stones at a train which was travelling at fifteen mph under the bridge. The stones smashed the cab window of the locomotive. The driver was unhurt and reported the incident to the British Transport Police at Crewe. Officers attended and within ten minutes the juveniles had been arrested. The Chairman of the bench described the incident as 'stupid and dangerous'. The two youngest were each fined £16 for damaging the window, valued at £232; throwing stones at the train; Endangering the Safety of anyone on board a train and trespassing on railway land. The Chairman of the bench warned them that if they had been older, they would have faced a prison sentence. The older youth was given a supervision order for two years.

At the Cheshire Constabulary police station in Crewe, there was a particularly good canteen. I went down there one day after being at court for a spot of lunch. I joined a colleague of mine from the local force. He began to eat his sweet which was rhubarb crumble, liberally covered with what appeared to be custard and which had just been brought over for him.

He said it tasted rather strange but not uneatable; in fact, he had almost finished when one of the canteen assistants came over with an apology. The covering on the rhubarb crumble was not custard, it was in fact salad cream, and she had taken it from the wrong container.

I am not sure of the year, but during the 1980s a majority of the buildings of the famous railway works at Crewe were being demolished. A large chimney in the works compound, near to the town centre, was to be demolished one Sunday morning. The Cheshire Constabulary evacuated some vulnerable residents. I was on duty down at the works. When it was time for the chimney to come down, I made sure that the staff on duty went to the designated place of safety. I spoke to the gentleman who was carrying out the demolition, I cannot remember who it was, but it certainly was not Fred Dibnah or Derek 'Blaster' Bates. He showed me exactly the line that the chimney would fall along and where it would land. I went to the place of safety to witness this spectacular site. The next thing it was 'boom', 'boom', a cloud of dust and the chimney fell towards where I and others were. It was breath-taking to see it fall, and it landed just a few feet from the building we were in, at the exact spot the demolisher had said.

CHAPTER 13

THE CREWE YEARS 1982 – 1985

Joining the Army - well not quite

It was a very foggy morning in February 1982 at around 08.50 hours when I was on early turn at Crewe. I took a telephone call from the railway control at Stoke on Trent to the effect that a Manchester Piccadilly to London Euston express had hit someone at Coppenhall on the outskirts of Crewe. I went to the scene with a PC. On arrival, sadly we found the lifeless body of a young male person, who appeared to be a schoolboy. He had no identification on him whatsoever. We removed him to the mortuary at Leighton Hospital. We then set about making enquiries into his identity. We went to the local schools and checked the registers to see who had not registered for the morning lessons, then after lunch we checked them again to see who had not registered for the afternoon lessons. One name from the local high school came up and we went to his house. We discovered that our deceased person was the fourteen-year-old son who resided at the house. A check of his bedroom discovered that he had left a suicide note. An incredibly sad case indeed.

Shortly after this incident I contracted chicken pox and was off work for ten consecutive days. This was the only period of sickness I have experienced in my working life.

Most of 1982 was taken up with routine police work dealing with football supporters, ticket frauds, people behaving disorderly and prosecuting at court etc.

In August 1982, I went to Southampton Docks with some other Midlands Division officers on Mutual Aid assistance in connection with 'The Cutty Sark Tall Ships Races', which was being held at the docks. We were accommodated at Marchwood Army Barracks. On arrival at the barracks, we had to queue up at the stores and we were given; a foam mattress, a couple of sheets, a hairy blanket, a foam pillow and a pillowcase, along with a tin mug, a plastic knife, fork, and spoon, which we had to sign for. There was a probationer from the London Underground Division in the queue in front of us. I asked him if he had signed for his equipment to which he replied that he had. I asked him if he had checked the small print. He stated that he hadn't, I told him, that was it, he was now in the Army for three years. He went white as a sheet. I reassured him later on that there was no small print. Then it was across to the hut we were staying in. All the Sergeants were in one hut and the PCs were in another. There were no separate rooms or en-suite facilities. It was quite novel for us. Breakfast each morning was taken at the barracks. We had to fry our own eggs as the chef said that there were too many fussy people or words to that effect, in the Army nowadays. The bacon was awfully hard, and I broke my plastic knife on the first morning, very reluctantly I was given another one.

We were then taken by road transport to Southampton Docks each day, where we were given a briefing at the Divisional Police Headquarters prior to performing our duties.

On the first morning, I looked out of the window and saw Ian Bixter a Sergeant from the Cheshire Constabulary walking down the main dock road. Ian was my counterpart back at Crewe. He was surprised to see me. The serial I oversaw was a relief serial, so it meant that we went around the docks relieving the other serials for their meal breaks. This gave us a good overview of the docks.

One day we were on duty at number one gate which was at the far end of the docks. This was one of the most isolated places on the docks. The local officers dreaded performing duty there. Another day I was on duty on the roadway directing traffic when a passenger ferry from France arrived and discharged the motor vehicles. I was stood in the middle of the road and I had to dive out of the way as a little Citroen CV 1 motor car was heading straight for me. The driver had forgotten to drive on the left, I think he must have thought he was still in France. Our evening meals were taken in a large catering marquee on the docks. After dinner each evening, we were taken back to Marchwood Barracks. We were then invited to have a drink in the Sergeants Mess. A couple of us ended up arresting a soldier for breaking a chair, whilst being drunk. The Military Police were soon on the scene and took him away. We saw him in the cells the next morning at the Guardroom as we were waiting for our transport, he was a sorry sight.

Whilst stationed at Crewe, which was in the Midlands Division, it was normal practice for us on a Saturday to go on Mutual Aid football duty to places such as Wolverhampton, Birmingham New Street, and Smethwick Rolfe Street (for West Bromwich Albion's ground). These duties were usually covered by overtime. We usually returned on the 18.05 hours Birmingham New Street to Glasgow Central, Inter–City train, which conveyed a buffet car. It usually arrived in Crewe at 19.05 hours.

More often than not, football supporters from the Northwest of England who had been watching their team playing in the midlands would usually return on this train escorted by the returning officers to Crewe. However, there were occasions when there were no police officers on the train and the supporters took advantage of this fact and would steal whatever they could from the buffet, when the Steward's attention was distracted. We would usually end up recording the crime at Crewe - not too good for our figures.

One Saturday evening in the winter months of 1982 after performing duty in the Midlands I returned on this train with a couple of officers and a dog handler along with his trusty companion. There were some Northwest based supporters who were travelling on the train and changing at Crewe. I, sticking my neck out, as the dog was supposed to travel in the brake van, put the dog and handler to work in the buffet. The dog just sat on the floor opposite the counter, no doubt thinking about the meat pies on display. The supporters got a shock when they saw the dog sat there. It was a case of form an orderly queue lads. A few days later I received a telephone call from the British Rail Catering Manager responsible for the buffet car, thanking me for the initiative and stating that for the first time in ages the buffet made a profit that evening.

When fans from the Manchester area were travelling on this train, they had a connection almost immediately to Manchester. However, for fans from the Merseyside area it was a different story as they had to wait well over an hour for their connection, which gave them time for potential mischief, especially if there were fans coming in from the north and going south. Fortunately, we had a good working relationship with the railway staff at Crewe. On being advised of the departure from Birmingham and the number of fans on board, contact was made with the duty Station Manager, who quickly arranged a train and crew for Liverpool, and we provided an escort. Everyone was happy. I do not think it can be done today in the era of privatisation.

At about 23.15 hours on Monday 6 December 1982 a terrorist bomb estimated to be between five to ten pounds exploded in the *'Droppin Well'* pub in Ballykelly, Northern Ireland. The blast brought down the roof, killing seventeen people and injuring about thirty persons some of whom were seriously injured. Of the persons that died there were eleven soldiers and six civilians. Of the soldiers that were killed, eight were from the 1 Battalion Cheshire Regiment, two from the Army Catering Corps and one from the Light Infantry. One of those on the scene was Company Commander Stewart from the Cheshire Regiment. That night he lost six soldiers from his company and was deeply affected as he tended to the dead and injured. It went without saying that the incident sent shock waves around the world, especially in the County of Cheshire. Everyone in the force especially at Crewe were deeply shocked at the bombing and wanted to do something constructive to help the injured and bereaved families.

On Sunday 2 January 1983 at 08.45 hours, myself and thirteen of my colleagues mounted a 20-mile sponsored walk from Blue Stone crossroads Nantwich, and arrived six hours later at the Cheshire Regiment's Headquarters at Chester Castle. The object of the walk was for us to carry our Crewe district plaque to the regimental headquarters as a token of respect for those soldiers killed and injured at Ballykelly, and to raise funds for the families of the victims of the blast. There were no incidents on the walk. On arrival at the Headquarters, Inspector Andy Bicknell presented our plaque to Lt. Col. Bob Peel, the regiment's secretary who in turn presented the regimental plaque to Andy as a gesture of thanks to the police officers. The plaque was hung proudly in the police office at Crewe.

We expected to raise around £200 but, in the finish, we raised £873.60. On Tuesday 01 March 1983, a cheque for the amount raised was presented by Chief Superintendent Douglas Harrow, Divisional Commander at Birmingham, to Lt Colonel Bob Peel, of the Cheshire Regiment at their Headquarters at Chester Castle. I attended the ceremony along with two other officers. Our cheque was the second largest sum received by the soldiers and all the money raised was used to help the families of the victims and the seriously injured.

Figure 5 Bill and colleagues setting out on the Sponsored Walk from Nantwich to Chester Castle to raise money for the victims of the Ballykelly bombings. Bill is on the back row 2nd from the right.

One Saturday morning during the football season, I was on duty by myself at Crewe, I am not sure why. I arrested a Portsmouth football supporter travelling to Liverpool to watch his team play. He had kicked the door of a gent's toilet cubicle off its hinges, on Platform Two. I conveyed him to Crewe police station where he was charged with Criminal Damage. He was bailed to appear at court in a few weeks' time.

I was over at Stoke on Trent in connection with a Stoke v Brentford football match one Saturday evening. The sixty or so fans from Brentford travelled up unescorted. On the return, the Guard of the Inter-City train to London Euston refused to take the train without a police escort and I was the only officer left, so I travelled on the train to London Euston, without incident. On arrival at London Euston, I have never seen as many Metropolitan Police or BTP officers in my life. It transpired that the Station Supervisor at Stoke had told our control that the fans were rioting. I spoke to the senior officer, who I believe was an Inspector and he asked where the rest of my men and women were. To which I informed him that I was by myself. His face was a complete picture of bewilderment. I was the talk of Euston concourse for the evening. 'The Skip's by himself'!!!

Crewe station during the night dealt with more trains, both passenger and parcels than most stations deal with during the day. A lot of northbound parcels traffic was handled at Crewe on Platforms One and Two during the night. The trains would usually be in the station for anything up to forty-minutes.

One night, during the height of the activities of the IRA, I was on duty when I was called to a parcels train by the duty Station Manager, the late Bob Brien. His staff had come across a mail bag that was emitting a ticking noise from the interior. There were two courses of action open to me. One was to close everything down and call the bomb squad thus causing massive disruption to the operations of the railway network or think logically and have a look at it myself. I took the latter course of action. I have never seen as many rail staff disappear so quickly.

I obtained a pair of scissors and carefully cut open the mailbag. Inside there were three parcels. I found the one that was ticking. Examination of the label showed that it was being returned from a lady in the Midlands to a mail order company in Manchester. I asked Bob to obtain for me a mail order catalogue from the company the parcel was going back to, these were readily available in staff room on the platform. I looked at the catalogue number from the label and it corresponded with the number in the catalogue. My suspicions were ninety-nine per cent confirmed. I opened the parcel, very gingerly and yes it was a clock which had still got the battery in it. It was a clock being returned as not required. Everything was resealed and back to normal within fifteen minutes and the train still had twenty minutes to departure time. Time for a cup of tea.

Another night turn myself and a constable were called to one of the overnight trains from Glasgow to London Euston, as there was a drunk person on board. He was arrested for being Drunk and Disorderly. He was placed in the back of the car with the Constable and taken directly to Crewe police station. As I was driving along the main road the drunk passed rather a large amount of wind from his rear orifice followed by an almighty stench, made up no doubt of bitter, whisky, chips, deep fried Mars bars and curry. He had 'followed through'. Some of his 'evacuation' had seeped on to the car seat. The Constable was not impressed when he had to clean it up.

Just before midnight, on one night turn, I was called to the buffet on Platform Four of Crewe railway station; a black man, from London, had stolen a watch from a passenger who was asleep. I obtained the details of witness who saw the incident. I then arrested the man concerned. The watch was not on him. Armed with the information received I took the man to Crewe police station where he was charged and bailed. The watch was later recovered in the buffet. When he appeared at court the defendant pleaded 'Not Guilty' but was found guilty. He later appealed against his conviction and sentence. A few months later I received a witness summons to appear at Chester Crown Court for the appeal. I arrived at the court and was told to wait in the witness room until the case was called. Time went on. I spoke to the Usher who informed me that as the defendant had not turned up the Judge had dismissed the appeal.

A call to an altercation in the buffet on Platform Four at around midnight, myself and a PC on entering saw the alleged offender, a railway guard, and the victim. It transpired that they were both in the queue at the counter. The allegation was that the guard who was only around 5' 5" had hit the passenger who was about 6'0" on the head with his handlamp. The guard was arrested and charged with Assault Occasioning Actual Bodily harm. He was later acquitted of the charge.

On one of my night shifts, I was called over to Sideway occupational crossing on the main line south of Stoke on Trent railway station. A male person had been hit by a train and was killed outright. On arrival, the local police were on the scene and the Inspector was an absolute nervous wreck. He was chain smoking and kept offering me cigarettes, which I politely refused. We got the body onto a stretcher and arranged for the deceased to go to the local mortuary, where I commenced the necessary documentation and enquiries.

Every so often, the British Rail Engineering Company would hold an Open Day at the world-famous Crewe works. We were rostered duty there. Usually everything was peaceful, but we still had to keep an eye out for the light-fingered enthusiasts who thought they could take an unofficial souvenir or two.

One mid-morning, I was called to a train due to a suspected ticket fraud. I went with a PC and saw a youth from Liverpool, who had travelled all the way from Holland, via the Hook of Holland ferry to Harwich Parkestone Quay, then to London Liverpool Street, and via the Underground to London Euston. At Euston he boarded a Liverpool bound train. He was in possession of an official looking Dutch document. When he was approached by a Travelling Ticket Inspector during the journey, he purported that it was a travel ticket which had been issued to him by the Dutch Railways as he had lost his original one. The Inspector became suspicious of his story. He was invited to the police office where I looked at it and not knowing any Dutch, I called Graeme my mate, in Rail House as he knew of a colleague who was fluent in the Dutch language. It transpired that it was a charge sheet from the Dutch Police, and he had conned his way back home. He was reported for Ticket Fraud.

I was working a 16.00 hours to 04.00 hours shift at Norton Bridge, Staffordshire guarding the Royal Train, which was conveying HRH the Duke of Edinburgh, to some engagements in the Stoke on Trent area. For the first part of my duty I was stood in an adjacent field. To pass the time of day, I started pulling the husks off the top of the grass, which was knee high. The door window of a carriage opened, and the Duke put his head out of the window and said, "Are you enjoying yourself Sergeant?" He had obviously been watching me from behind the net curtains of his carriage. I just said, "Hello Sir", rather sheepishly. He then said. "I know that you would be rather be down the pub than stood there". I smiled but did not reply. He said, "I know where I would rather be, I'll have one for you", waving his hand and shut the window. Also on duty was a PC who feared the dark and the supernatural, and we would wind him up whenever we could. After midnight I was on duty at another static location, near to the Royal Train with PC Gordon Beharrell, who sadly is no longer with us. One of Gordon's hobbies was ghost hunting. He would spend hours whilst off duty in old houses etc., looking and waiting for ghosts. We were due to be relieved by the PC who feared the dark and I saw my chance as he approached. I said to Gordon, when the PC was in earshot, "So this is roughly the location of the crossroads, where they hung people, on the old coaching road that ran from Birmingham to Stoke and where the ghost of the headless robber from Stoke roams?" On hearing, this he ran back to the van which was being used as the control point. The next thing was I was summonsed to see the Inspector who gave me a tongue in cheek rollicking for upsetting the PC.

I remember working a mid-week football special to Wembley Central from Crewe, I am not sure what the occasion was. The force had laid on an open plan coach in the bay platform for us to relax, but for food we had to find our own. Three or four of us found ourselves in a kebab house a couple of streets away from the station. The following day we were all struck down with mild food poisoning.

A Sunday evening in 1983 found me on a twelve-hour night shift, probably covering for a PC who was off sick. The only other person on duty with me was DC Alan Perkins. At about 19.15 hours we were called to a seven-year old child on Platform Four. Apparently, he was travelling with his mother and two siblings to London. His mother had put the siblings, her luggage, and a pram, on the train, leaving the boy on the platform. The train set off. We arranged for his mother to be taken off the train at Stafford and we took the boy to our mess room, where we had a small shop of confectionary. I bought him a Mars Bar and gave him a glass of milk, whilst we waited for a train to Stafford to reunite him with his family. For amusement Alan showed him his truncheon and handcuffs. The lad asked if we hit people on the head. We told him most definitely not as it was too dangerous. Alan pointed out the places on the arms and legs where we could restrain people with it if the need arose. The lad picked up Alan's truncheon and hit him, on his left arm, saying, "Like this mister?" Alan went a whiter shade of pale and gritted his teeth. Fortunately, he only had minor bruising. The lad was soon reunited with Mother.

Just north of Crewe station adjacent to the West Coast Main line is Crewe cemetery. One evening I was called to some youths who were throwing stones at trains from within the cemetery grounds. I went in the car and walked into the cemetery and made a search with a negative result. I must point out that I was in full uniform complete with helmet. As I returned to the car an old lady came up to me and asked what time I was closing the cemetery. She must have thought I was the cemetery keeper. During my career, I have been mistaken for many things, but a cemetery keeper!

After all the overnight northbound passenger trains had left Crewe, we had a little breathing space until the southbound passenger trains arrived, we usually managed to grab something to eat. One night I had two PCs on duty with me. We were enjoying our refreshments when a sleeping car attendant came to the office to report that a naked woman was running up and down his train, which had just arrived from Glasgow. Well, I have never seen police officers so keen to get to a job, they were like dogs out of the trap in the '2.30' at a dog racetrack. By the time the bobbies had got to the train the woman was nowhere to be found. The railway authorities thought that it wasn't serious enough to hold the train any longer than necessary.

In my time at Crewe, amongst the many passenger trains that used the station was a train with the headcode '1M10', an overnight sleeping car service from Glasgow Central to London Euston via Kilmarnock and Dumfries. It would arrive in Crewe at around 02.00 hours and would have to be met by police nearly every night due to problems of one sort or another.

I received a telephone call from BTP in Glasgow, one evening, to say that it was full of Glasgow Celtic supporters on their way to the continent. Subsequent messages were received stating that the police had to be called to the train at Kilmarnock, Dumfries, Carlisle, and Preston due to disorderly behaviour. By the time it arrived in Crewe it was well over two hours late. I boarded the train with a couple of Constables, to find that it was all incredibly quiet and that the fans were fast asleep. The whole train stunk like a brewery and a distillery. To top it all there was vomit all over the floors throughout the train. I did not envy the carriage cleaners in London.

We were called to this train on another occasion which was full of Glasgow Celtic supporters when it arrived at Crewe, in the early hours of a Saturday morning. An elderly couple and their friend, en route to a holiday in Jersey had suffered verbal and physical abuse from three of the supporters in particular. Fortunately, I had two Constables on duty that night. The assailants were quickly identified and arrested. They were taken to our office in Crewe, along with the witnesses. We had them in separate rooms and we then started documenting the assailants prior to taking them to the local police station. Whilst I was documenting my prisoner, one of the Constables came in, white as a sheet and asked if he could have a word with me. It transpired that his prisoner was a serving Strathclyde police officer. The three prisoners were bailed pending further enquiries. On the following Tuesday afternoon after doubling back off nights, I received a telephone call from one of the Strathclyde Police Assistant Chief Constables, in respect of the officer who had been arrested. I assured him that all the 'i's' had been dotted and all the 't's' had been crossed. He was happy. It turned out that the prisoner was on bail from the Lothian and Borders Police for theft and had been suspended from his force. I then had to prepare a file for the Director of Public Prosecutions, which I was complimented on.

One duty as Sergeant at Crewe, was to escort a train of Crewe Alexandra fans to London Euston with a female police officer, for a Millwall v Crewe Alexandra mid-week evening kick-off. On arrival at Euston we walked down to Soho in half blues and bought a bag of fish and chips and stood in a doorway eating them. Whilst we were there, several men approached the door and on seeing us quickly turned away. It transpired that we were stood in the doorway of a massage parlour.

During the early part of 1984 I was on night duty as the Duty Sergeant at Crewe, when I received information from the British Transport Police at London Euston that there were a number of unescorted Glasgow Rangers fans on a service train from London Euston to Glasgow Central headcode '1S18', via Dumfries and Kilmarnock, returning from the continent. The group of about forty supporters were described as, 'high in spirits'. During the journey to Crewe the police had to be called to the train at Rugby due to their behaviour. On arrival at Crewe at around 01.20 hours there was a train crew change. The Guard taking the train forward to Carlisle had got wind of the trouble and refused to take the train forward without a police escort. The fans were still very noisy.

A Constable and I travelled with the train to Carlisle. Before the train set off I located a fan who appeared to be the ringleader and told him in no uncertain terms that I was no 'Sergeant Wilson' and the Constable was no 'Private Godfrey' from Dad's Army and that we would stand no messing and they would be dealt with accordingly. I also informed him that I had, had previous experience of dealing with Rangers and Celtic supporters when I worked in Glasgow on secondment from Heysham. The ringleader knowing that I meant business went back to his fellow supporters said a few words to them and they all quietened down. The journey to Carlisle was one of the best football escorts I had undertaken. We returned from Carlisle in the rear cab of an electric locomotive hauling a freightliner train.

In 1984, I was looking for a change from Crewe and kept applying for district posts as a sergeant at places such as Westbury, Lincoln, and King's Lynn, but was unsuccessful.

On a sad note, one Sunday in early 1984 I was duty Sergeant at Crewe from 09.00 hours to 17.00 hours. On reporting for duty, I was informed that there had been a very serious assault on a local person at Shrewsbury railway station, just before midnight, following a Shrewsbury v Leeds football match. I was instructed to go to Shrewsbury with DC Alan Perkins to start the investigation off. On arrival at Shrewsbury, I reported to the local police Superintendent and visited the hospital to see the victim. Enquiries were commenced and I finished duty at midnight. The following day I handed the enquiry over to our Detective Sergeant. Sadly, the victim died exactly one year and one day later following the assault.

The Ford cars that were built at Halewood near Liverpool would be transported on open air low loader wagons and taken to another plant in the south of England for completion. You can imagine that around one hundred and fifty cars on a train in the open air were a tempting target for the vandals. At one stage, in the late spring of 1984 the cars were being hit by people throwing stones at the train whilst it was in the Nuneaton area. Windows were smashed and the bodywork dented. An operation was set up to catch the culprits. On one occasion, I rode in the back cab of the locomotive of the train from Crewe to Nuneaton to keep a look out for the culprits in the area and if I saw anything would radio a mobile squad who were waiting in a nearby lane. On this occasion, nothing was seen. I believe that they were seen on another evening and were caught. Soon afterwards Ford used covered wagons.

During the month of June 1984 copper telephone wire was being stolen from the telegraph poles situated alongside the Chester to Shrewsbury railway line, in the Gobowen area of Shropshire. The CID from Crewe naturally took charge of the investigation and arranged observations during the forthcoming nights. One night I was part of the observations team, which also consisted of a dog handler from Birmingham. One of the team spotted two thieves on the embankment. The order was given to release the dog to chase them. The dog ran for a few yards and decided to cock its leg up against a telegraph pole and relieve itself for what seemed an eternity, much to the annoyance of the dog handler and the CID officer. By the time the dog had finished the thieves made their getaway in a Ford Transit Van. They were caught a few days later.

One morning I was on early turn at Crewe during the height of the miners' strike in 1984. I was informed via Divisional Headquarters in Birmingham that intelligence had been received to the effect that large numbers of pickets would be attending Ironbridge Colliery in Shropshire to try and blockade a coal train that was leaving later in the day. A Mobile Support Unit (MSU) in full riot gear was being sent to the scene.

Due to the fact that a majority of our officers were engaged in picket duty in Yorkshire, I was to form a hastily arranged back up serial to the MSU, with two PCs from Crewe and Eddie Howell and his dog 'Rick', along with a couple of officers from Shrewsbury. All we had was our wooden truncheons as protection. The senior officer, who briefed me, as the serial commander, informed me that our location was to be the car park of a disused public house some two miles away from the colliery railhead. Fortunately, the pickets never materialised, and our services were not required.

Whilst I was on a twelve hours night duty one Saturday night at Crewe, in November 1984, after all the football traffic had died down, I received a request from the duty Inspector at Crewe police station for assistance to search for armed robbers who had attacked the Landlord of a Public House in Nantwich, whilst he was cashing up at about 02.00 hours. It was believed that the suspects had made their way onto the Crewe to Chester main railway line. After a briefing by the Inspector the dog handlers from both forces made their way onto the railway line. I and one of my constables followed on foot a few yards behind. Upon reaching a village with the grand name of Aston-Juxta-Mondrum, near Nantwich, the search was called off and we went onto a dark unlit country lane. As I was walking along the lane, I lost my footing and fell into a ditch. Yes, you've guessed it I was covered in slime.

Another night I was on a twelve-hour night shift when myself and a PC who, shall we say, was really too nice to be a police officer, as he had the qualities of being an Ordained Minister, a bit like 'Sergeant Wilson' from the Television programme, 'Dad's Army', were called to one of the platforms at around 21.30 hours, due to a drunk making a complete nuisance of himself. It turned out that he was a Scotsman from Glasgow, who was well and truly inebriated on the Scottish amber neck oil. He wanted to fight the world. He was arrested for being drunk and disorderly. On the way to the police office, he started struggling violently with the two of us. We managed to get him into the office and began to search him before putting him in the interview room (no luxury of cells in those days). However, as we were beginning to search the prisoner, the duty dog handler, Eddie Howell, and his dog 'Rick' walked in for their meal break. The prisoner became more and more violent and Eddie put his dog in the 'down' position to come to assist us. As we were restraining the prisoner, he lashed out with his feet kicking 'Rick' in the side. The PC who had assisted me initially went red in the face with rage and it seemed to swell up to twice its size and he screamed at the prisoner "You've hit a police dog, you've hit a police dog" and I could see that he was about to hit the prisoner, so I pushed him aside to prevent him assaulting the prisoner, thus saving a lot more paper work. Fortunately, 'Rick' was none the worse from his unpleasant episode.

Periodically we used to provide officers to escort high value bullion which had been sent by rail from the Royal Mint at Llantrisant, to the Ministry of Defence base at Radway Green, Alsager, in freightliner containers. The containers were then sent by road to the Trafford freightliner depot, Manchester. One officer used to ride in the cab of the road lorry whilst the other one followed in the police car. Both Officers would then return in the police car to Crewe. The only equipment we had in case of attack, was our radios and truncheon. One day in December 1984 there was only one PC available for the escort, so I was designated as the second officer and I chose to ride in the cab of the freightliner lorry. As we were going along the main road towards Manchester, we were informed that the Ministry of Transport in conjunction with the Cheshire Constabulary were carrying out spot checks on road lorries in a lay-by ahead of us. I radioed the PC in the car and told him to go and check to see if the checks were genuine and not a set up to attack us and secondly to let us pass unheeded with our cargo. Yes, they were genuine, and they let us carry on without being checked.

In January 1985, it was officially announced that a major track, re-signalling and station facility scheme for Crewe costing £14.m that would ensure the famous station continued to play a major role in the railway network. Part of the work called for a virtual shutdown of Crewe station in the weeks between 2 June and 21 July 1985 in order to remove the existing track work, signalling and overhead electric wiring and new equipment put in place. By concentrating the work in this short period, disruption to passengers would be kept to a minimum and nearly £1m would be saved. A majority of trains would therefore call at Stafford to connect with a shuttle service from Crewe. The force decided to establish a temporary 24 hours police post at Stafford, and it was agreed that I would be the Sergeant in Charge for the weeks during the work at Crewe. Officers from all over the Midlands area would be rostered to perform duty at the police post. Andy Bicknell and I attended all the planning meetings. The police post at Stoke on Trent would still have overall responsibility for the rest of the area. All our crimes and summary offences would be recorded under Stoke's references. A suitable office at Stafford was found. In fact, it was two rooms of the old refreshment room staff accommodation, on the first-floor offices, of the station. Rosters started to be prepared. Towards the end of May, I began to furnish the office at Stafford.

Just prior to the partial closure of the station, British Rail and their contractors began preparatory works on and around the platforms. One such work was to erect hoardings around the buildings of the platforms. One of the contractors, 'Pochin's' put up hoardings around the buildings on Platform Five. Their name was prominently displayed at eye level in block capital letters on the hoardings at intervals, of around ten-foot. One night I was patrolling Platform Five when the 'Irish Mail' from Holyhead to London Euston passenger train arrived. This train remained at the station for around ten minutes whilst the diesel locomotive was replaced with an electric locomotive for the onward journey to London.

As I was walking along the platform an Irish gentleman came up to me and asked if I knew when the train arrived at Crewe. I told him that he was at Crewe, but he insisted that he was not and pointed to the 'Pochin' sign. I then pointed to the Crewe sign which was above the hoardings. He still seemed unsure as to where he was.

Another incident which came to my attention involving the 'Irish-Mail' was one night, I was patrolling Platform Five when the train arrived. Whilst the locomotives were being changed, I saw some Irish children climbing on the outside of a coach towards the roof. I immediately told them to get down and gave them a very stern lecture on the dangers of the railways especially the overhead live 25,000-volt wires. I often wonder what the outcome would have been if I had not been there at the time.

Peter Bowman, one of the Cheshire Constabulary's Inspectors at Crewe was also the Chairman of the Crewe branch of the Royal National Lifeboat Institution (RNLI). He recruited me to assist with the house to house collections in the Crewe area. In the spring of 1985, he invited me to go with members of the Crewe branch and the Burton on Trent branch of the RNLI to Hartlepool, Lifeboat Station for an organised visit. The Burton on Trent branch were in the process of raising funds for a new lifeboat which would be called 'The Burton Brewer' I took my son, Stephen, with me. We had a fantastic day. I think that the trip ignited the enthusiasm for Stephen to join the crew at Trearddur Bay when we eventually moved to North Wales later that year.

On 2 June, I began duties at Stafford working the same shift pattern I had worked at Crewe, nights, lates, earlies and days. The first couple of days were incredibly quiet. I then I realised why it was so quiet, the station staff were calling the Staffordshire Police to incidents, as they had been used to, since the police establishment at Stafford was withdrawn in the early 1970s. We soon remedied that.

Whilst on duty one night the late PC Geoff Turner from Stoke on Trent and myself came across a youth who had come to our notice as having an out of date ticket. He was searched and numerous other tickets were found on him. Our enquiries led us to his home in Preston, which we searched, and we found several more tickets and date stamps, which he was using to travel around the country. The youth admitted several ticket frauds. Fortunately for us, he had kept a diary of all his journeys which made the interviewing of him easier. He was reported for summons and was dealt with at court for Ticket Fraud and Forgery, asking for quite a number offences to be 'Taken into Consideration'.

One afternoon, whilst at Stafford, a male person came to our notice, when he offered to pay for his train from the north of England by using a forged cheque. He was charged with Forgery and Obtaining a Pecuniary Advantage and the case was disposed of at Stafford Magistrates' Court.

One evening I received a telephone call from the railway control to say that some wooden sleepers had been placed on the London bound track at the entrance to Shugborough tunnel on the main West Coast Railway Line. As there were no officers on duty at Stoke, I went to the scene to commence initial enquiries. The follow up enquiries were made by the Stoke officers, which led them to meeting Lord Lichfield whose land was above the tunnel.

One of the features of the closure of Crewe, was that the York to Aberystwyth Travelling Post Office train was diverted via Stafford. Consequently, a special mail franking stamp was issued to endorse mail carried by the train for the weeks during the work at Crewe.

After I had closed down the office at Stafford, I returned to Crewe to continue with my normal duties.

Just after I returned from Stafford it was announced that the Police and Criminal Evidence Act of 1984 (PACE) would become law as from the 1 January 1986. All the police officers in England and Wales needed to receive five days intensive training in respect of the act. It was one of the biggest changes to hit the police in decades.

I went over to the railway offices at Derby in September of 1985 to undergo my training from Inspector Brian Hiley, who was an excellent trainer. He had a manner which made it easier to absorb all the information. He injected a bit of humour into the lessons which helped. One day the fire alarm went off and we thought that it was one of Brian's little jokes. One of the officers looked out of the window to see the rest of the occupants of the building leaving. It was a real alarm. There was a malfunction on the alarm system.

At the beginning of October 1985, the force underwent yet another re-organisation. This time the Crewe District was to come out of the Midlands Division and go to the North-West Division and become part of the Liverpool Sub-Division, which also took in Chester and Holyhead.

Shortly after this re-organisation, I was on early turn and was out on patrol on the station at Crewe, when I received a radio message from one of the PCs who stated that the Inspector wanted to see me as a matter of urgency. Well, all sorts of things ran through my mind. I went to see Andy Bicknell and he asked me if I would like to go to Holyhead for a week, in a couple of weeks' time as the Inspector there, Ian Griffiths, was on leave, one Sergeant had retired and the other was on long term sick, thus leaving the station without supervision. I was an ideal candidate as I had experience of maritime law from my days at Heysham. I jumped at the chance.

I think it was the 15 October 1985 when I went to Chester to meet Inspector Ian Griffiths, the Officer in Charge of the BTP at Holyhead, who briefed me on the workings of the Holyhead District.

CHAPTER 14

THE HOLYHEAD YEARS OCTOBER 1985 – FEBRUARY 1986

Eating 'Dog shit'

Monday 21 October 1985 saw me travelling to the Port Holyhead to take charge of the BTP at the port for five days. On arrival, I met a couple of the officers. I stayed in a local guest house for the week. The Sergeant's office was in a corridor opposite the main police accommodation. I worked from the Inspector's office. On Wednesday 23 October Bangor City FC took on the Spanish giants Athetico Madrid in a European Cup winners cup, second round game at Farrar Road, Bangor, which Athetico Madrid went onto win 2 - 0. This was a big day for the residents of North Wales and crowds were expected. British Rail even laid on a special train from Abergele and Pensarn station. To be fair, Ian Griffiths, the Inspector came off his annual leave to assist with the policing of the fans. All passed off very peacefully.

I returned to Crewe on Friday 25 October 1985 to commence my own annual leave for a week. On returning to work, Ian Griffiths contacted me and asked if I would like to go back to Holyhead for another week during the second week of November, as the officers there were going to receive their week's training on PACE. Instead of sending the officers individually to Liverpool or Manchester for training it was decided to send a trainer to Holyhead. I agreed to this request which had the blessings of the senior officers at Divisional Headquarters in Manchester.

It was back up to Holyhead again and I took up residence once again in a guest house in Newry Fawr, Holyhead, about one mile away from the port, The landlady, sadly now deceased, and her husband had other rooms and would take in mainly workmen and British Transport Police officers who were assisting us in the area.

I worked twelve hours per day with DC Mike Rhodes to assist me, and PC Geoff Davies worked twelve-hour nights, with me on call should the need arise. These two officers would receive their PACE training at Liverpool later in the month. It was a fairly quiet week, with no arrests, just a couple of people reported for byelaw offences.

During this time, the position of the Sergeant who had retired was advertised in General Orders. Out of the blue, I received a call from Chief Superintendent, Peter Featherby the Divisional Commander, who asked me to stay at Holyhead until the sergeant's vacancy had been filled. I agreed to this request. After some deliberation I applied for the position. I had to tell the family about my decision, and they backed me wholeheartedly. I was appointed to Holyhead from the 31 December 1985. My colleagues at Crewe and Holyhead thought I was absolutely mad to do this as the writing was on the wall for the police establishments at the Sealink ports. The Government of the day had recently privatised the British Transport Docks and all the officers had been made redundant and transferred to other stations.

The government had their sights set on the Sealink ports as the next asset of the British Railways Board to be privatised. I was ready for a change of scenery and at least I had escaped from Crewe. I began house hunting.

I began to familiarise myself with the stations and locations on the patch. I went to Ty Croes railway station, which serves a small hamlet and surrounding villages, and introduced myself to one of the Signalmen there. He made me welcome with a cup of tea. I then requested to use the toilet, which was a small cabin made out of galvanised corrugated metal sheets, situated on the track side. He asked if I could wait until the express from Holyhead to London went past. The express duly went through at 60 mph and I could see the toilet cabin shaking violently from side to side. Close shave!

The police establishment at Holyhead consisted of One Inspector, two Sergeants, a Detective Constable, six Constables and one Clerical Officer. A few years ago, the establishment was much greater. The Inspector then used to cover Holyhead, Dun-Laoghaire, Dublin North Wall, Chester, and Shrewsbury.

An office with an enquiry counter, two detention rooms, facilities for photographing and fingerprinting prisoners and an interview room was situated in the main embarkation hall. This office was very modern, built in the early 1970s and fit for purpose compared to some accommodation around the force. The administrative offices were situated on the first floor of the embarkation hall. A small office was located at Salt Island in the centre of the harbour, which was named after an unsuccessful 18th century experiment to produce salt from the sea. At Salt Island, which was connected to the rest of the harbour, there were holding facilities for the road wagons and large vehicles going to Ireland.

The 'Z' shaped breakwater, nearly two miles long, had its own standard gauge railway system, which was built to transport building materials for the breakwater whilst it was being built. The railway line remained in situ until the early 1980's for maintenance purposes. This railway line was not physically connected to the main line. Any movement of locomotives and rolling stock had to be carried out by road transport.

The breakwater had its own engineering workshops which stored heavy duty plant and road cranes; every so often the cranes would have to be taken along the main Newry Road, which was owned by Sealink. The job of escorting them would fall to us, using the van, which did not have any warning lights on.

Two vehicles were based at Holyhead, a dark blue 1800cc Vauxhall Cavalier and a dark blue Leyland Sherpa van which was used for transporting prisoners, mainly drunks, to the North Wales police station at Holyhead. This vehicle was marked up with the force crest. The North Wales Police would repeatedly call on us to borrow the van for transporting some of their prisoners. They only had Morris Mini cars. Not very practicable when dealing with drunks as I was to experience. During my second week back at Holyhead, after completing duty I was walking home to my guest house and went to assist the local police who were in the process of arresting a drunk. They were trying to get him in the back of a Mini. At first, they thought I was a friend of the drunk who was trying to snatch him away from them. I quickly identified myself. They were incredibly grateful for the assistance rendered.

The passenger traffic from Holyhead to Dun Laoghaire (Fort of Leary) in Ireland was provided by a 9,000-ton multi-purpose ship M.V. 'St Columba', built in Denmark. The vessel at full capacity could take 2400 passengers and 335 cars in the peak season. Services (except on Christmas Day) operated twice in each direction, every day at 03.15 hours and 15.00 hours from Holyhead to Dun Laoghaire and 08.45 hours and 20.45 hours from Dun Laoghaire to Holyhead arriving at 11.55 hours and 23.55 hours, respectively.

British and Irish Line, known as B+I line, operated a multi-purpose ship called the 'Leinster'. This would sail to and from Dublin leaving Holyhead at 03.30 hours and 15.45 hours. This vessel would have a Master at Arms on board and a brig for detained persons. We very rarely went on this ship as the Master at Arms tended to deal with incidents on board. It was only the drunken or unruly passengers after embarkation that we had to deal with.

Passenger trains from London Euston, Birmingham, and Manchester as well as local services would connect with the sailings.

A five days a week container service operated to Belfast and Dublin using two purpose-built vessels M.V. Brian Boroime and M.V. Rhodri Mawr. These vessels were built specially to carry 184 20-foot, or equivalent number of larger, containers. Freightliner services to and from London (Willesden and Stratford), Birmingham, Manchester, Seaforth, and Southampton and by connecting services to other terminals, operated in connection with the sailings.

There were other facilities at Holyhead, such as dry dock and marine workshop facilities. There was also a 2,800 feet long jetty for the Anglesey Aluminium company. There was a fish dock for the local trawlers.

We had an excellent relationship with the North Wales Police and their Special Branch officers along with HM Customs and Excise. The Divisional Commander for Anglesey was Superintendent Trefor Edwards, who became a very good friend of mine and later on introduced me to the Rotary Club of Llangefni.

From Holyhead we were responsible for covering: the North Wales Coast Line from Holyhead to just east of Rhyl (55 miles); The Conwy Valley Line from Llandudno to Blaenau Ffestiniog (31 miles); the freight line from Blaenau Ffestiniog to Trawsfynydd (5 miles) and the Cambrian Coast Railway Line from Pwllheli to Barmouth (32 miles).

Over the 1985 Christmas period, whilst I was back at Crewe on leave, some of the North Wales Police Special Branch officers visited our office for a Christmas drink. One of the female officers had a puppy and she placed it in the Inspector's office, where it did its business. The Inspector was not too impressed when he came to his office the next day.

On returning to work after the Christmas holiday, I was informed of this incident by some of the PCs. Being somewhat of a joker, I brought in some chocolate Angel Delight, and placed it on the Inspectors carpet and retreated to the Mess Room. A short time later in a rather loud and fearsome voice I was summoned to the Inspector's office and pointing to the Angel Delight desert on the floor, He said "What's this"? I bent down, put some on my finger and licked it. I said, with a straight face "It appears to be dog shit sir". I will not tell you what he said, but you can imagine.

The Police and Criminal Evidence Act of 1984 came into existence on the 1 January 1986. This was a very steep learning curve for all of us.

I remember interviewing an Irishman suspected of theft in early January 1986. I told him that I was going to interview him contemporaneously under the new law and he replied, "Will it hurt, sir, I'm not a violent man?" Once I explained what it meant he was alright.

Part of my duties at Holyhead consisted of prosecuting at the Magistrates' Courts in the area; Holyhead, Amlwch, Llangefni, Menai Bridge, Beaumaris, Bangor, Llandudno, Abergele, Colwyn Bay, Prestatyn, Caernarfon, Pwllheli, and Barmouth. Menai Bridge court was on the quay side and this posed a problem when navigating the small streets with the van, this could be particularly challenging at times. Barmouth court was a single courtroom on the main road. I learned a very valuable lesson there. On the Clerk's desk, there were always a selection of boiled sweets and the prosecutors and defence were always invited to take one. I took up the invite and selected a barley sugar. No sooner had I put it in my mouth, my cases were called. Moral of the story never eat a sweet in Barmouth court until the conclusion of your cases. Beaumaris court was the oldest court that sat in the British Isles. We occasionally had our cases held there.

One useful lesson I learned was that all the railway staff and some of the North Wales Police officers had nicknames due to the majority of them having the surname of Jones, Hughes, Rowlands, and Roberts. All the four train drivers at Pwllheli were called Jones. Some of the staff even had the same first names. I wanted a statement from a guard and asked for him by his full name and I received a puzzled look from the Station Supervisor. I mentioned that he was known by a nickname. I was soon put in touch with him. The North Wales Police officers were always known by their collar number.

It is said that the Cambrian Coast Line from Pwllheli to Machynlleth is one of the most scenic on offer in Britain. For most of the route it offers scenery which is breathtakingly out of this world, as it hugs the seashore passing golden beaches and windswept dunes. At one point it passes the magnificent Harlech Castle. People come from all Britain and the world to travel on this line. However, like most railways it has its problems; if we include the Aberystwyth to Dovey Junction and the continuation of the line to Shrewsbury it is said that there are over four hundred and twenty level crossings of varying kinds. Needless to say, on our patch we were kept busy with motorists failing to comply with the warning lights and signs.

One of the main schools on our patch was Ysgol Ardudwy (Harlech High School). Due to the geography of the area, it was always quicker to travel by train than road to the school. The local school children, who could number up to around three hundred, by arrangement with the local county council would travel by train. It went without saying that this was an open invitation for them to cause disorder. When I first arrived at Holyhead, the Cambrian Coast Line was still operated by the old type Diesel Multiple Units with 'slam-doors', which could be operated by the passengers. The rear red warning light was a removable paraffin one and the passengers had access to the guard's brake van.

There had been cases of children setting fire to the seat cushions, removing the rear warning lamp, opening the doors in-between stations, general disorder and pressing the warning buzzer in the guard's compartment; sometimes the guard would be on the platform and the driver sat in his cab. On occasions it was not unknown for the driver to set off when he received the 'right of way' from the buzzer. And the doors would still be open.

In conjunction with the school, a bi-lingual, one page 'Code of Conduct' was devised. The local Council employed a warden on the train and the Deputy Head, Doctor Peter Williams, was appointed discipline officer for the train. He appointed six boys from the sixth form to act as prefects on the train and at Harlech station to assist the British Rail staff. We had regular meetings with all concerned at the school. This went a long way to reducing the problems. Punishments for the offenders ranged from a verbal warning, detention after school, being banned from the train (this had a financial impact on the families as they would have to pay for the bus fare or take the offending pupil themselves depending where they lived), writing out the 'Code of Conduct', a written caution or even prosecution. Once the new Sprinters were introduced on the line the problems eased a little.

One Saturday at around 23.45 hours PC Doug Worster and myself were on a patrol of the Cambrian Coast Line stations when we visited Barmouth. We saw a youth on the station and asked what he was doing, he stated that he was doing nothing and would leave immediately. It transpired that he had been in trouble on the school train one day and he was made to write out the railway byelaws. We thought he meant the 'Code of Conduct' but it turned out that he had been made to write out all the thirty-two British Railways Board byelaws including the sub-sections.

One morning, myself, Inspector Ian Griffiths, and PC Frank Seery went to Barmouth and reported twenty-four school children for trespass, as they walked from their homes to the station to catch the train to Harlech. They all received official cautions at Barmouth station, some weeks later.

After a few days on duty, on Thursday 6 February 1986 I returned home to Crewe on the 16.15 hours London Euston train. At around 18.00 hours I was approached by the guard who stated that the buffet car attendant had been assaulted by a youth with a scouse accent. On arrival at the buffet car, I noticed that the attendant had a small cut across the bridge of his nose. When the train arrived at Chester, I made arrangements for other BTP officers to attend and to continue with the enquiries as the assailant could not be found. Whilst on the platform near to the train's buffet, the assailant, who was unsteady on his feet and smelt strongly of alcohol, came up to me and admitted hitting the buffet car attendant. As I was in 'half-blues', he must have thought I was a member of the railway staff. I identified myself as a police officer and arrested him for Assault Occasioning Actual Bodily Harm. I was then joined by two BTP Officers from Chester. The two officers then took the assailant away but as they were about to ascend the footbridge, the assailant started to struggle violently with the officers and shout obscenities. I went to their assistance. He was eventually restrained. As we were walking towards the police office, the assailant continued shouting obscenities.

I travelled back on the train to Crewe, where I made further enquiries with the buffet car attendant, who advised me that some wine and champagne had been stolen by the assailant. I made further enquiries into the case at Crewe. The assailant was later charged with Assault Occasioning Actual Bodily Harm, being Drunk and Disorderly and Theft. He appeared at Chester Magistrates' Court on Thursday 8 May 1986 and formally pleaded 'Not Guilty'. I was required to give evidence. He was found guilty and handed a substantial fine and ordered to pay compensation to the buffet car attendant.

Back on duty at Holyhead, on Tuesday 11 February 1986, I worked a 16.00 hours to Midnight shift. During a routine patrol of the diesel depot at 22.25 hours I reported a local youth for trespass. This location was the subject of local residents stealing the diesel from the tanks for their vehicles.

Whenever the Wales Rugby Union team played at home in Cardiff, playing the home nations and teams like the famous All-Blacks and the Springboks, British Rail would run a special train from Holyhead to Cardiff at a cost of £10 per person. This was an absolute bargain compared to the normal passenger train fare. We used to escort these trains, with a Sergeant and two or three Constables, which could have around six hundred supporters on board, It was a long day as we had to book on duty at 05.00 hours and we would not return into Holyhead until around 23.30 hours. The majority of the journeys went without incident. Rugby supporters overall, even in drink are far better behaved than football supporters. Those days there was no restriction on the amount of alcohol that could be taken on the trains. The one or two incidents were quickly dealt with, using a good dose of robust policing, good humour, and common sense. We could have held a court on the train, as some of the passengers consisted of the local Magistrates, The Magistrates' Clerk and Solicitors! On the return journey if Wales had lost the fans were subdued. However, if they won, they were jubilant and we would have a good old sing song, singing great Welsh classics such as 'Calon Lan', 'Guide me O thou great Redeemer', 'We'll keep a welcome' and 'Men of Harlech'. You cannot beat the Welsh for singing. I had a group of them in stitches on one trip, I told them that the previous week, I had actually sung with the great Sir Harry Secombe, yes me and Harry Secombe sang together... I was in the bath and he was on the radio.

Thursday 13 February 1986 saw me booking on duty at 23.59 hours and I performed duties in the terminal in respect of rugby supporters travelling to Ireland on the 03.15 hours sailing to Dun Laoghaire. This vessel was escorted by myself, PC Doug Worster and PC Pete Morris. I estimated that we had around 1500 rugby supporters on board. On arrival in Ireland, we supervised the disembarkation and liaised with the Garda Siochana (The Irish National Police). We took our well-earned meal break, then at 08.45 hours returned to Holyhead maintaining a plain clothes surveillance on the vessel, in particular the duty-free shop.

We arrived back in Holyhead at 12.25 hours the following afternoon and booked off at 12.30 hours. This was my first taste of escorting rugby supporters on the high seas.

The following day, Valentine's Day, Friday 14 February 1986, I booked on duty at 23.59 hours and again performed duty in the terminal in respect of rugby supporters travelling to Ireland.

Myself, PC Doug Worster and PC Beattie from Liverpool escorted around 1700 rugby fans to Dun Laoghaire on the 03.15 hours sailing from Holyhead. Again, the fans were very well behaved. On arrival in Ireland, we supervised the disembarkation of the supporters and again liaised with the Garda. We returned to Holyhead at 08.45 hours maintaining plain clothes surveillance on the ship.

Saturday 15 February 1986 saw me booking on duty once again at 23.59 hours and monitoring rugby supporters returning from Ireland. With PC Worster and PC Beattie, we travelled over to Dun Laoghaire maintaining plain clothes surveillance on the ship. On arrival in Dun Laoghaire we took our meal break after which we supervised the embarkation of around 1700 rugby supporters returning to Holyhead. The passage was without incident. We booked off duty at 13.00 hours. The supporters travelling forward by train, were escorted by other officers from the force.

The following day, Sunday 16 February 1986, I reported for duty at 21.00 hours to monitor rugby supporters returning from Ireland. Although they were in high spirits the evening was relatively peaceful. I booked off at 05.00 hours.

I was back on duty at 13.00 hours on Monday 17 February 1986 for a late turn until 21.30 hours. We just had a few stragglers returning from the rugby match in Ireland. Like me they were all tired and looking forward to a good night's sleep.

On Tuesday 18 February 1986, I worked 07.45 hours to 16.00 hours prior to taking two well-earned rest days off after the busy weekend.

Friday 21 February 1986, I visited the Magistrates' Clerks Office at Holyhead to sort out some summonses and to get to know the staff there a little better. Then off to Valley station yard to make enquiries into a Burglary of the offices used by the local Coal Merchant.

One of our duties was the cash escort from the ship to the booking office. An officer would escort the cashier from the ship who took a trolley full of money through the ship, and through the embarkation hall to the booking office. Usually, this duty was performed by a Constable, but on some occasions, it fell to yours truly.

On Friday 28 February 1986, I booked on duty at 14.00 hours and at 15.00 hours went with PC Keith Roberts to Dun Laoghaire on the St Columba to escort back Irish rugby supporters. At around 19.30 hours Keith and I supervised the loading of around 1750 Irish rugby supporters and then escorted them back to Holyhead. Fortunately, there was no trouble on board. If my memory serves me correctly it was a force ten gale out there and most of the fans just wanted to have a lie down. Several of them could be found on the big white telephone calling for 'Huey' or 'Ruth'. (I always advised my officers not to have a curry before they sailed). Personally, I am a particularly good sailor, the rougher the better for me. Keith and I then supervised the loading of the train to London which was escorted by our colleagues. Due to the bad weather the fans were incredibly quiet going down to London.

Another problem we encountered was on a Saturday evening. British Rail had a fifty pence evening rover ticket for travel on the Cambrian Line, which were operated by the Diesel Multiple Units with 'slam doors', which the conductor had no control over.

The local youths, sometimes up to forty in number, would travel from Porthmadog to Criccieth, a journey of around eight minutes. They would offer the conductor a £20 note for the fare. On arrival at Criccieth they would leave the train by opening the doors and leaving the train without paying. They then made their way to the nearby pub and catch the train on the return, again offering a £20 note for the fare. The conductor did not stand a chance collecting all the fares. On arrival at Porthmadog they would again leave the train without paying.

Following complaints from the railway management about the youths evading their fares on the Cambrian Line between Porthmadog and Criccieth, we mounted an operation to deal with them. Fortunately, as from the 17 March 1986, two months ahead of schedule, British Rail introduced new class 150 Sprinter trains on the line, which could accelerate faster than the old Diesel Multiple Units. They ran under the old Diesel Multiple Unit times until the new timetable came into existence in May. This was ideal for us as it gave us around an extra five minutes at Criccieth. Armed with a couple of police officers and around six revenue protection officers along with a lot of loose change we managed to collect all the revenue from the youths. As the doors on these new trains could only be operated by the conductor. The youths were kept on the train until their fares were paid. On the return journey all their tickets were checked. We carried out this operation on and off for a few weeks and this cured the youths.

CHAPTER 15

THE HOLYHEAD YEARS MARCH 1986 – DECEMBER 1986

Cutting off the IRA's income

During my time at Holyhead from October 1985 to February 1989, the ship escorts mentioned in the previous chapter, were typical of what I was involved in. We could be escorting the ship to and from Ireland around four to five times a year especially when the home Rugby Union teams were in action and when there were large football fixtures involving Ireland. The English domestic football league had supporters from Ireland but on the whole these supporters were well behaved and did not need an escort. It was not unusual for the fans, sometimes in excess of eighteen hundred, to be escorted by a Sergeant or the Inspector and one Constable or at the most a Sergeant and two Constables. The only exception was when England football fans travelled, we had to bring in extra officers to assist us. Once on the high seas there was no back up. I suppose we could have called on the North Wales Police who would have been flown to the ship by helicopter from RAF 22 Squadron at RAF Valley. In fact, looking back there was no such plan in being.

There was no doubt about it, we had to have a touch of the blarney when dealing with the supporters, have our wits about us, a thick skin and above all else a large dose of common sense. Also, a good old force ten gale would assist as well. The jurisdiction was doubtful as well, but we worked under the command of the Master of the vessel. On the whole there were no real problems. What helped a lot was that the 'St Columba' had a capacity of two thousand four hundred passengers. There was less trouble and less drunkenness when she was running to full capacity as the passengers were unable to drink as much due to the queues at the bar. On a Sunday morning in the winter months, I have seen as few as seventy five foot passengers, on the ship.

I remember working a night shift early in 1986 in connection with rugby fans travelling to Ireland, on returning to Holyhead on the ship, I had occasion to deal with a youth for a minor offence. I went back to my lodgings for a well-earned sleep and used the same bedroom and same bed linen as the sergeant who was on day shift! That is how it was in those days. Things have altered drastically now.

Other sporting traffic using the Port of Holyhead were people coming from Ireland and going to the races at Chester, Cheltenham, Aintree for the Grand National, Ascot and Epsom. All were very well behaved and just wanted to shake your hand or hug you.

We had a very good liaison with the Royal Air Force Police at the RAF Valley base. We regularly assisted them with RAF personnel from the base returning from Ireland, who had travelled over to the Emerald Isle without authority. On arrival back at Holyhead they would be arrested by the RAF Police and Court - Marshalled by the Commanding Officer.

The National Express coach company operated coaches to London via Birmingham and Leeds via Manchester to coincide with arrival of the ships.

For some reason the drunks always made their way to the back of the coach. We would get called to them. Taking them off the coach down the narrow aisle was always difficult. So, we used to park the van at the rear of the coach and take them off through the emergency exit at the rear.

One night I was in pursuit of a man wanted in connection with a theft. He was outrunning me. So, I commandeered the National Express coach and instructed the driver to 'follow that man'. The passengers thought it was great being involved in a police pursuit. As we drew alongside him, he was very surprised to see me jump off the coach and arrest him.

We were regularly called to the overnight train to London Euston due to the fact that people who had second class tickets, used to make their way to the first class and started to settle down, once in drink they became more difficult to move. With some gentle persuasion they would move. It got to the stage where I requested that the first class be locked out of use, as not many people actually used it, and only let genuine first-class passengers in.

Sometimes the trains, both the overnight and daytime ones to London Euston would be awash with vomit especially after a rough crossing. I will not go into the gory details, but you can imagine.

Bomb scares relating to the 'St Columba' were a regular feature. We used to receive telephone calls via the North Wales Police or the Sealink telephone exchange stating that there was a bomb on board. They turned out to be hoax calls, from disgruntled passengers who had been refused boarding to the ship, disgruntled members of crew for one reason or another, usually crew who had been dismissed, a drunk passenger, local youths etc. All had to be taken seriously and we had a well-rehearsed procedure for searching the vessel with the crew and the officers. One particular occasion I received a call to say that a person with an English accent had stated that there was a bomb on board the 'St Columba'. Only one snag, the 'St Columba' was half-an-hour into her journey across the Irish Sea. The Master was advised, and the vessel was searched by the crew and officers. Fortunately, nothing was found. Every so often a training exercise would be held involving all the relevant agencies.

Around March 1986 my colleague who had been on the sick since early 1985 decided to retire. His place was taken by Sergeant Phil White who transferred from Liverpool. Phil stayed in the same guest house as myself. There was not much time for socialising as we were on opposite shifts.

St David's Day Saturday 1 March 1986, I booked on duty at Holyhead at 23.59 hours, to deal with the returning Irish rugby supporters from a match in Cardiff. Myself, PC Pete Morris, and PC Frank Seery escorted the 03.15 hours sailing to Dun Laoghaire with around eighteen hundred Irish rugby supporters on board. They were all in high spirits but manageable and a bit of banter and a touch of the old blarney from the three of us, especially from Frank who was Irish himself, kept them in order. On arrival in Ireland, we supervised the disembarkation of the supporters and partook of a well-earned breakfast on the ship. The return journey saw us carrying out plain clothes observations on the ship. We booked off at 12.30 hours.

Sunday 2 March 1986, it was back on duty at 23.59 hours to escort the 03.15 hours sailing to Dun Laoghaire with PC Morris and PC Seery. The fans were arriving back in Holyhead between 22.00 hours and 02.10 hours and required supervision on the station. Again, the passage was quiet, most of the fans were exhausted after their weekend away and just wanted to sleep. On arrival in Dun Laoghaire we supervised the disembarkation of the fans, after which we enjoyed breakfast with DS Tom Doyle from the Garda Special Branch and the Irish Customs officers on board the ship. We then returned to Holyhead, maintaining plain clothes surveillance in the retail areas.

Monday 3 March 1986 was just a short routine night turn from 22.30 hours to 01.00 hours as I had to be back on duty at 08.45 hours the following day.

I booked on duty at 08.45 hours on Tuesday 4 March 1986 and travelled to Crewe on the 12.45 hours train in plain clothes keeping observations on the ship's crew in respect of thefts from the duty-free shop. Most of the crew for the 'St Columba' were drawn from a pool of staff at Liverpool and they regularly travelled by train to and from Holyhead. It was not unknown for them to liberate items of spirits and cigarettes by unlawful means from the ship. My findings were reported back to the CID. I then booked off at Crewe and spent a night at home.

Friday 14 March 1986 I was on duty from 17.45 hours until 04.30 hours. The shift was fairly quiet dealing with the normal type of shipping traffic. At 03.45 hours I was called to Salt Island re travellers being abusive to staff. They were given suitable advice and allowed to board the B+I vessel. There were large numbers of travellers who used both ferry lines to travel across the Irish Sea. We used to get called to them on a regular basis. On the 'St Columba', there was an up-market lounge called the 'Pullman lounge' where on payment of a supplement of £5 you could go in there and drink unlimited tea and coffee along with biscuits. The travellers used to push their way into the lounge and 'go to the toilet' on the seat where they were sitting. Many a time we have been called to them where they have soiled the seats and the walls with excrement and urine. Depending on the mood of the Master they would be warned, made to clean up the mess or reported to us for process.

I worked from 17.30 hours to 02.00 hours on Saturday 15 March 1986 covering the railway stations along the North Wales Coast for revellers returning to Bangor and Holyhead from the night club at Colwyn Bay. They would usually travel on the last train into Holyhead arriving at around 02.10 hours, which was also a boat train. Fights would be picked with the other passengers and there was a need for a police presence on the train.

It was back to Crewe on Tuesday 18 March 1986. I travelled on the 12.45 hours train to London as far as Crewe, keeping observations on the ship's crew returning to Liverpool, following reports of disorderly behaviour on previous occasions.

A certain terrorist organisation in Ireland was forging rail and sea tickets and selling them at knock down prices in bars in Dublin and other towns in the Republic of Ireland, to fund their terrorist activities. Liaison was undertaken with the Garda CID in Dublin.

On Friday 21 March 1986 I booked on duty at 12.00 noon and travelled with DC Mike Rhodes and a couple of Ticket Inspectors to Chester, on the 12.45 hours train checking all the tickets of the passengers. All had valid tickets. At 15.05 hours, we then, in company with the late DS Pete Hempton travelled from Chester on a relief train which had originated at Holyhead, to Crewe. A check of the tickets proved negative.

We returned to Holyhead on the 16.20 hours train from Crewe and we arrested around six of the passengers who were in possession of forged tickets from London or Birmingham to various locations in Ireland. They were all taken to Holyhead police station where they were interviewed and charged with various offences. They were detained in custody to appear at Holyhead Magistrates' Court the following day. I finished duty at 01.00 hours

The following day Saturday 22 March 1986 proved a busy day for me. I booked on duty at 09.00 hours and at 11.30 hours I attended a special sitting of Holyhead Magistrates' Court where I prosecuted the arrested persons who were suitably dealt with. Sentences ranging from Conditional Discharges to fines and costs were handed out.

After drawing breath and a general patrol of the port, I along with a couple of officers met a train from London Euston and arrested seven people for being in possession of forged tickets from London or Birmingham to Ireland. After being documented they were taken to Holyhead Magistrates' Court, where another special court was convened at 19.20 hours. At the court I prosecuted the seven. Again, the punishments ranged from Conditional Discharges to fines and costs. I booked off duty at 21.45 hours.

The cases which were only the tip of the iceberg, as many more slipped the net, attracted media attention from both sides of the Irish Sea. The local press in Holyhead had the good sense not to mention my name in the press reports. However, the Irish Press splashed my name all over the front page of the Dublin Irish Press newspaper. The local Special Branch, 'tongue in cheek', told me not to expect from the terrorists, an invite for their Christmas dinner. The Garda, I believe traced the forgers to a house in Dublin. After that we did not see any more forged tickets.

Monday 24 March 1986 saw me at Llandudno Magistrates' Court with some prosecutions for people failing to comply with the level crossing warning lights at Deganwy level crossing.

Most of our cases on a Monday and a Thursday were those of motorists who drove across the level crossing at Deganwy in contravention of the red flashing lights, under the Road Traffic Act 1972. We would send them a summons along with a Statement of Facts and a Mitigating Circumstances form. If they accepted the facts, they could send in a plea of guilty along with the completed Mitigating Circumstances form and the case would be heard in their absence.

Some of the excuses on the Mitigating Circumstances form were amusing. *'I wanted to get to the promenade before my fish and chips got cold'. 'I wanted to meet my wife who had just bought the ice creams and I wanted to get to her before they melted'. 'I thought the train would stop for me', I had just driven two hundred miles and needed to use the toilet'. 'The dog was barking in the back of the car'*

The most commonly used excuse was '*I didn't see the lights or the barriers*'. I questioned the fact, if their eyesight was that bad, they should not be driving at all.

One man pleaded 'not guilty' and contested the evidence of the Signalman. He was found guilty, fined and his licence endorsed. After the hearing he went to the beach at Deganwy, completing ignoring the red flashing warning lights. He was again reported and pleaded guilty.

The Easter weekend of 1986 Friday 28 March 1986 to Monday 31 March 1986 was fairly busy at the Port of Holyhead with passenger traffic travelling to and from Ireland. Several visits were made to the sidings at Valley, due to reports of children playing there. Also, we had several containers in the Freightliner Terminal containing coins and spirits and these needed checking periodically with Customs Officers to make sure that the seals had not been tampered with.

I headed out to Amlwch with DC Mike Rhodes on Thursday 10 April 1986 to investigate the theft of wooden sleepers from the trackside. The passenger service on the Amlwch to Gaerwen line was withdrawn in 1964. However, it was still open for the Associated Octel Works freight traffic. Whilst there, we caught a local man trespassing on the tracks. He was questioned about the theft of the sleepers but denied all knowledge. He later appeared at Amlwch Magistrates' Court for trespassing on the railway.

Since transferring to Holyhead, I made frequent visits to the Ethylene Dibromide processing plant at the Associated Octel premises in Amlwch for liaison meetings. On arrival at the plant, you had to surrender any matches or lighters to the security man at the entrance. The train conveying the substance ran once a day in the early mornings between Monday and Friday. On approach to the plant the train had to travel over two level crossings at a speed of no more than twenty miles an hour. Situated by the one of the level crossings was a motor vehicle repair garage and the owner used to complain that the train travelled over the crossing too fast and the vibration caused tins of paint to fall from the shelves onto the floor. This was not really a police matter but an internal railway one. The railway management investigated it. They sent a traction inspector to the scene on a regular basis armed with a speed gun, similar to the ones used by the North Wales Police to detect speeding motorists. The Inspector would hide in some bushes and as the train approached, he would point the speed gun at the locomotive. On each occasion it was proved that the train was only travelling at around fifteen miles per hour. Like the roads, the railway system had speed restrictions. These speed guns were used throughout the railway network to detect speeding train drivers. The operator would hide in bushes, stand on bridges, behind signals and on station platforms. To ignore a speed restriction could have disastrous consequences, such as a derailment involving loss of life. Nowadays the locomotives, diesel and electric units are fitted with sophisticated computer equipment which can tell if a driver has been disobeying the speed restrictions. The offending drivers are given endorsements on their train driver's licence.

PC Frank Seery and myself were in the Maesgeirchen area of Bangor at 15.35 hours on Friday 11 April 1986 due to reports of trespass on the main line.

We found a well-worn unofficial path leading from the river bank up the railway embankment to the side of the track.

The next thing I knew, Frank had gone up another path nearby and had slipped in some human excrement, covering his uniform and hands. Needless to say, he was not best pleased, coming out with a string of expletives. He had to be cleaned up before he was allowed back in the car.

Following information received, on Monday 14 April 1986, PC Bob Bastable and myself went to Amlwch police station where we interviewed a local man for the theft of wooden railway sleepers from the area. He was reported by process.

PC Doug Worster and I on Saturday 19 April 1986 carried out a late-night station patrol of the stations on the Cambrian Coast Line between Pwllheli and Harlech, these stations tended to get neglected over the years by the force. All was quiet.

On Monday 21 April 1986 I commenced 15 days leave in readiness to move into my new house in Valley, near Holyhead, the following day, 22 April 1986.

When it came to shopping, this came as quite a shock, the nearest large major supermarket was in Llandudno, some forty miles away. There were only about six miles of dual carriageway, so it was a full day to go shopping once a month. We had smaller shops in Holyhead but no major supermarkets. A few years later we had a large supermarket chain move into Bangor.

However, on Tuesday 29 April 1986 I returned to work to attend a meeting at the North Wales Fire and Rescue Headquarters, Colwyn Bay in connection with the planning of a simulated table-top train accident training event. On our patch we had two Nuclear Power stations, one at Wylfa, Isle of Anglesey and Trawsfynydd, near Blaenau Ffestiniog and the aforementioned Ethelyne Dibromide (EDB) works at Amlwch. Ethelyne Dibromide, a highly toxic compound, is a naturally occurring (small quantities can be found in oceans) colourless liquid used in pesticides and leaded petrol, (now banned). Both the nuclear fuel and EDB are lethal in their own right. The scenario involved both trains colliding head-on, on the North Wales Coast main line.

Around May of 1986, I had occasion to visit Llangefni on the Amlwch branch line to investigate the explosion of six detonators which had been clipped onto the line and which had been detonated by a freight train travelling from Amlwch. People arriving in Llangefni town centre for the popular Thursday market clearly heard a rapid series of explosions as the 09.20 hours freight train from Amlwch passed over the detonators. It was believed that the detonators came from a haul of sixty that were stolen from Bangor railway station in March, which the CID were actively investigating.

In June of 1986 I had to attend a three-day Custody Officers' course at Chester. This stood me in good stead with the North Wales Police as I was able to book our own prisoners in at Holyhead police station when they were short officers in their custody suite.

We have all heard about people impersonating police officers, but a Labrador impersonating a police dog! During the summer of 1986 whilst stationed at Holyhead I was on duty on late turn on the station, when I was approached by officers from HM Customs and Revenue, from Liverpool, who, out of courtesy, informed me that they were carrying out a drug related operation with their passive drugs dog, a black Labrador called 'Max'.

The boat train from London Euston arrived on Platform One and a number of passengers alighted and made their way to the embarkation hall, where myself and the customs team were on duty. However, there was a large group of particularly noisy Irish youths, who no doubt had been sampling a certain black stout, from their home country, during their train journey from London. The Customs Officer with the dog looked at me and said, "These may be a problem Sarge, but 'Max' can impersonate a BTP dog and sort them out". Sure, enough the handler commanded 'Max' to let out a couple of barks, which was enough to sober the youths up pretty quickly.

Usually on Friday and Saturday nights, the local youths from Holyhead would come down to the Port looking to pick fights with the Irish youths arriving off the ferry. We were usually waiting for them and they took the hint and left.

Committing offences whilst driving on Dock Road at Holyhead Port was always a contentious issue with the local Magistrates. They believed that it was not a road within the meaning of the Road Traffic Act 1972, but it clearly was. On Thursday 31 July 1986, a lorry driver from the Gwynedd area appeared at Holyhead Magistrates' Court after being summoned by us for Driving whilst being Disqualified and Driving without Insurance. He readily admitted the offences. The Magistrates fined him a total of 20 pence, 10 pence on each offence. In his defence, he stated that he thought that the dock road on which he was caught, was a private road, as he had only driven the lorry from the compound to the ferry. Our prosecuting Solicitor stated that the defendant had been previously disqualified for six months by the same bench, under the totting up procedure, after being found guilty of speeding. On the day in question, he was checked by one of our officers and produced a duplicate driving licence and was allowed to proceed to the ship. Lady Cledwyn chair of the bench said that the situation had occurred many times before and felt that the road is not adequately signposted to show that it is a public highway. She went onto say that in the past, repeated requests for notices to be displayed had been ignored. She further commented that the case was a waste of the bench's time.

There were twenty two sections within the Road Traffic Act of 1972 which applied within the port, but it would have been a sheer impossibility to list them all and a danger to anyone reading a list of that length whilst driving. Sealink officials stated that they were not prepared to put up signs stating that it was a public road. There was no legal requirement for such a sign to be displayed in any case.

On 14 August 1986, Manchester United supporters travelled from Manchester and Liverpool via Holyhead to go to Dublin to watch their team play a local team in Dublin. Sealink did not relish the fact that fans would be travelling on the ferry and we had made no provision for a police escort as we believed that there would only be a small number travelling.

Just in case there was any disorder on the trains along the North Wales Coast, the force laid on extra officers to travel from Crewe and Chester up to Holyhead. The fans were well behaved, in fact we did not even know they were on the train. At Holyhead Sealink made a half-hearted attempt to stop them by putting out a chalk written notice *'SPL NOTICE 14-8-86 FOOTBALL SUPPORTERS WILL NOT BE ALLOWED ON BOARD SEA LINK SHIPS'.* Around fifty fans not wearing any identifiable clothing, slipped through the net and boarded the ship. We believe that they were genuine football supporters and not the usual hooligan element. There was no trouble at all. Even the North Wales Police had laid on extra officers in the town.

In late 1986 a local man from Maesgeirchen, Bangor, placed a sleeper on the main line between Llandegai and Bangor Tunnel. A local train spotter removed the sleeper just as a train was about to leave Bangor station. I was tasked with bringing the sleeper back in the van. I lifted it into the back of the van and on arrival at Holyhead, as I was pulling it out of the van, I noticed something moving on the floor of the van. I discovered that it was a lizard that had made its home in the sleeper. The offender was fined a total of £100 for Obstructing the Railway and Trespass at Bangor Magistrates' Court.

On Monday 1 December 1986 DC Mike Rhodes and myself took part in a Police Schools open day at the Plas Arthur Sports Centre, Llangefni, Isle of Anglesey, where we saw a number of children from around the island and educated them in the dangers of the railway. We received a letter of appreciation from the local police and were congratulated by our Area Commander.

The rest of the year was taken up by dealing with drunks and persons behaving in a disorderly manner travelling home for Christmas and the New Year.

CHAPTER 16

THE HOLYHEAD YEARS 1987 – 1989

Meeting Cilla Black

The New Year of 1987 started off fairly quietly for us with just routine matters to deal with.

Just after midnight, one night in February 1987, I caught a 28-year-old man from Holyhead urinating against a train on Platform Two of Holyhead station in full view of passengers using the buffet bar, when the gent's toilet was only twenty yards away. He stated that he went to the station to get some cigarettes and that he could not wait. He was arrested and appeared at the Holyhead Magistrates' Court the following week where he was fined £10.

On Friday 6 March 1987, the day of the Zeebrugge Disaster, involving the 'Herald of Free Enterprise' I was on night turn at Holyhead. On arrival of the vessel 'St Columba' myself and a Constable were called to the vessel, as a citizen of the Irish Republic from Dublin had been attacked very severely, for no apparent reason by two youths from Holyhead who had been on a day trip to Ireland. Both youths were arrested and charged with Grevious Bodily Harm. I believe they received suspended jail sentences.

Another case I was involved in, was that of an Australian lady who had her suitcase stolen from the embarkation hall by a local youth, who was arrested shortly afterwards. A statement was obtained from her and I included the fact that she would be willing to return to the United Kingdom to give evidence. At court, the defendant pleaded 'Not Guilty'. The defence were playing on the fact that we, the prosecution, would not bring back the witness all the way from Australia. I contacted her by telephone to see if was still willing to attend and she stated that she was and I received written confirmation from Divisional Headquarters in Manchester that the force would be willing to pay her air fare and accommodation and that we would seek costs should the defendant be found 'Guilty'. This information was presented to the defence and at the next hearing the defendant entered a plea of 'Guilty'.

The North Wales Coast Line was not exempt from unruly behaviour from schoolchildren. The 08.10 hours Holyhead to Scarborough passenger train, which consisted of a locomotive and six passenger coaches, would stop at all stations across the Isle of Anglesey, picking up schoolchildren for Friars High School, Bangor and the two independent schools in Bangor. Sometimes we could have as many as two hundred travelling on the train. Around thirty would board the train from the eastbound platform at Valley station. This platform was exceptionally low down and passengers had to use the portable wooden steps to board trains. The children were generally well-behaved travelling to school. On the return journey they would travel back on the 16.05 hours from Bangor to Holyhead, this was when their behaviour was at its worse.

Having been cooped up in school all day they would run riot on the train, putting the girls of 'St Trinians' to shame. We regularly had to travel on the two aforementioned trains.

PC Pete Morris and myself in early 1987 had to interview a railway guard who had worked the Scarborough train. Owing to the fact of the low platform at Valley, he assisted a young schoolgirl who was wearing a short skirt, up the wooden steps. And shall I say that the guard became a little too familiar with her. He was reported for the offences disclosed.

In May 1987 British Rail ran a series of steam-hauled passenger trains on the Cambrian Coast Line between Machynlleth, Aberystwyth and Pwllheli. This necessitated extra police resources to the area, which was covered by overtime and rest day working, On the whole the enthusiasts were very well behaved.

On Thursday 21 May 1987 at 00.15 hours a lady from London and her six children, whose ages ranged from 11 months to 13 years, arrived at Holyhead from Ireland. It was the intention of the lady to travel to London on the National Express coach departing Holyhead at 01.00 hours. Upon boarding the coach, she informed the driver that she had purchased a single ticket from Cavan to London but had lost it. The coach driver did not believe her story and refused her entry onto the coach. She was allowed to spend the night in the ladies waiting room on Platform Two of Holyhead railway station until she could contact her friend.

At 10.10 hours that morning I was informed by Mr. William Beckett the Railway Traffic Manager, that the lady was at the ticket barrier in a distressed state. I ascertained from her that she had been unable to contact her friend in London. She stated that the baby and the five other children had not been fed since 20.00 hours on Wednesday 20 May, when they joined the ship and that she only had 75 pence in her possession.

I then made immediate arrangements for warm milk to be supplied to the baby and food for the rest of the children. I contacted the Gwynedd Social Services, Isle of Anglesey Area Office, in Llangefni and related the circumstances to them. They stated that they would contact their counterparts in London to see if the family were known before deciding on further action.

Contact was made with the ticket office at Cavan bus station and the duty clerk verified the fact that the lady had in fact purchased a ticket. I managed to contact a friend of the lady and he planned to come to Holyhead to collect her but would not be there until around 18.00 hours.

Social Services were informed of this fact, they stated that they would not be able to send a Social Worker until 15.30 hours and asked if I could use money from the office petty cash, to be re-imbursed later, to buy food for them. I told them that this was not possible. I informed Social Services that the family were desperate for food and drink. I was assured that a Social Worker could not attend until 15.30 hours at the earliest. Having regard for the welfare of the children and in particular the baby, I agreed to buy food for the family out of my own pocket. The Social Services agreed to this offer. I purchased fish and chips, sandwiches, mineral water, crisps, chocolate, milk and fruit to a total value of £18.94.

At 12.50 hours, I received a telephone call from the lady's friend stating that his car had broken down and was not able to travel to Holyhead. Arrangements were then made for the lady and her family to travel to London on the National Express coach departing Holyhead at 16.00 hours. At 16.20 hours, a Social Worker attended the Police Office and re-imbursed my money.

Shortly afterwards I received the following letter from Social Services: -

Dear Sgt Rogerson,

'I am writing to you regarding the lady and her six children who arrived in Holyhead in the early hours of Thursday morning.

I would like to express our sincere thanks for all the time you spent organising their return to London and also for the practical help and care you showed the family. As a Department, we are very grateful for your assistance in this matter and I am sure the family involved will not forget your kindness'.

I believe it was in June 1987 that I was sent on a two-week Sergeant's refresher course at Tadworth. I think the reason for this was that the intake was short of candidates and the Superintendent just decided to send me to have a break. It was just like having an extra two weeks holiday as the course was very informal.

Between 20.00 hours and 21.00 hours on 12 July 1987 a group of youths managed to gain access to the Port and got hold of a forklift truck and drove it for around twenty yards finally colliding with a fence and lamp post causing damage to the value of £250. I took the lead in the enquiry. The youths who were local, were eventually traced and dealt with through the court system.

On our patch, we have what is reputed to be the village with the longest name in Britain and the railway station in the world reputed to have the longest railway station sign.

'Llanfairpwllgwyngyllgogerychwyrndrobwllllantysiliogogogoch.'

(It means 'St Mary's church in a hollow by the white hazel close to the rapid whirlpool by the red cave of St Tysilio'). Its proper name is Llanfairpwllgwyngyll. The other letters were added by a local man in the 19 century as a tourist attraction. The name has stuck and has become the longest name in Britain. The station is more commonly referred to as Llanfair P.G. or Llanfairpwll.

The village and the railway station are visited by people from all over the world. The coach tours used to pull up in the old station yard, which was still railway owned, adjacent to a famous woollen mill retailer. The local school children had permission, when not at school, to meet and board the coaches and pronounce the name of the village to the tourists and hold out their hands for a tip. However, things got out of hand when some of the older children from another village started to abuse the system by going onto the coaches and would not let the younger children onto the coaches and also would not let the passengers off until they had given them a tip. Talk about a junior mafia. After consultation with the management of the woollen mill, they were all banned from the premises and a full-time welcome host was employed.

On the 29 September 1987 I received a letter from the British Rail Area Manager at Shrewsbury, who in turn had received an anonymous letter from a rail enthusiast, stating that on Saturday 3 October 1987 there was going to be serious disorder on the 10.55 hours Shrewsbury to Pwllheli locomotive hauled passenger train service, by so-called railway enthusiasts. The author of the letter alleged that the offenders were going to turn up in Nazi uniforms and to have a heavy drinking session along the coast and turn a coach into a disco on the return journey. It was also alleged that an attempt was being planned to steal a 'single line token'. (These tokens are issued by a Signalman and handed to a driver giving authority to travel along a portion of single track). A couple of offenders were named by their first name only. I made enquiries and ascertained the identity of the two persons named. Due to previous disorder on this train and our success in apprehending the culprits, the contents of the letter were taken seriously and an operation jointly with British Transport Police Officers from Shrewsbury was undertaken. If my memory serves me correctly only a handful of enthusiasts turned up and the journey was without incident.

One afternoon in September 1987 whilst on passenger control duties at Holyhead myself and a PC were called to an Irishman, who had disembarked from the B+I vessel 'Leinster', who was drunk, but on the border line of being arrested. I had a word with the Master at Arms on the 'Leinster' and he agreed to take him back on board. I have a great sense of humour and as we were taking him to the ship through the embarkation hall, where there was quite a crowd waiting to go on the ship I said to him "Come on captain, I'll get you sobered up before the ship sails". A lot of passengers started making a sign of the cross, across their upper bodies. On the ship, he asked if he was going to get a nice cabin. The Master at Arms assured him that he was. We took him to the top deck, and he was placed in the brig, which was about the size of a telephone kiosk, with a small ventilation plate at the top and bottom of the door.

Just after the 'St Columba' arrived at lunch time on another day I was on duty in the embarkation hall. After all the passengers had disembarked, PC Bob Bastable and I were making our way to the platforms for a general patrol, when the Sealink supervisor came to us and stated that our presence was required in the Pullman Lounge of the ship. I enquired as to what the problem was, and he stated that he did not know. All sorts of things go through your mind. We boarded the ship and went to the Pullman Lounge where we saw the Bosun, who pointed out a Nun, in full habit, who was inebriated and couldn't stand without assistance. Apparently, she had consumed a full litre bottle of duty free gin. I thought 'the North Wales Police are going to really thank us for this one'. So, my next course of action was to ring the local Catholic Priest from St Mary's Church in Holyhead to see if he would accept her and to be looked after by his housekeeper. Being a good Christian gentleman, he agreed. Bob and I placed her in a wheelchair and put a blanket around her and wheeled her from the ship to the station entrance. As we were passing through the embarkation hall there were several passengers waiting to embark. I told them that the sister was ill and many of them started to sign themselves with the cross. She was handed over to the Priest, who on seeing her shook his head from side to side and 'tut-tutted' in disgust.

I had a report of an alleged rape, involving a female from the beautiful south-west area of Ireland, on the 'St Columba' whilst it was on the high seas en-route to Dublin. From initial enquiries, it appeared that the incident took place whilst the ship was in Irish territorial waters. It was decided that the Garda would take primacy with our assistance. Initially I was to go to Ireland for a couple of days to assist the Garda. I rang the Garda station in the small village where the victim lived. There was no direct line to the Garda station, so I had to go through the telephone operator in the village. I asked the operator to put me through to the Garda station and she told me that there was no one in, as she had just seen him cycling by the telephone exchange. She got him to ring me back. The powers that be from our force decided against sending me or anybody else to Ireland. I am not sure how the case was finalised.

Between Llanfairfechan and Abergwyngregyn on the North Wales Coast Railway Line there are a couple or so occupational farm level crossings. The users of the crossing have to ring the signalman at Bangor to obtain permission to cross the line. One particular day the signalman granted permission for a farmer to use one of the crossings. As the farmer began to cross with his tractor and trailer, an express train bound for Holyhead, was approaching. Both the farmer and the train driver had a shock. Fortunately, the farmer managed to clear the crossing. I had to interview the signalman under caution and report him for Endangering the Safety of Persons on the Railway. He claimed that he had forgotten that he had a 'train in section' when he gave permission to the farmer to cross. He was dealt with at the local Magistrates' Court.

When a report published by Loughborough University named Holyhead as 'The most depressed town in Britain' in 1988. A lot of people in the town were shocked and upset at the news. The report claimed that Holyhead came bottom of the list in all aspects, and that North Wales especially was in a very poor state compared with the rest of Britain. A champion of the town decided he would lift the town's spirits with a 'lorra, lorra' help from a TV favourite.

Determined to prove that, while Holyhead 'may well be depressed' economically, it certainly was not a depressing place to live and neither were the townsfolk depressing, the directors of the popular ITV show 'Surprise Surprise' came to the town.

Having been shown the local attractions, the programme returned to the area with host Cilla Black in February 1988. Cilla 'arrived' by train. She boarded a specially laid on train at Valley and travelled to Holyhead with her husband Bobby on board. I was rostered to travel on the train with them. I can recall that the train did at least three journeys from Valley to Holyhead to get the shots of her arriving in Holyhead exactly right. It was a great success, which saw hundreds of people take to the streets despite bad weather. I had quite a long chat to Cilla and Bobby.

One case that came to our notice, in which we assisted Her Majesty's Customs and Excise, was that of a worker from Crewe railway works. He would regularly travel to Ireland with his wife and teenage son, purchasing duty free spirits and cigarettes for his work colleagues. They used to get their son to carry them off the ship in a suitcase.

The Customs Officers became increasingly suspicious of them as they were all too frequent travellers across the water. On one occasion, the son could hardly carry the suitcase, as it was packed to the gunwales with spirits and cigarettes. The father was getting a little too greedy. The family were arrested, and the case was disposed of at Caernarfon Crown Court.

Mike Rhodes and I had a nice enquiry to conduct. Duty free cigarettes and tobacco worth £2,600 were stolen from a container whilst in an isolated part of the container terminal. The containers' custom seals were found to be broken. We were tasked to visit all the pubs in Holyhead, around twenty-seven in all, and tobacconists, to warn them about the stolen cigarettes. Enquiries failed to trace the culprits.

We received a report that about ten-thousand pounds was missing from the Sealink booking office at Holyhead. Enquiries were commenced and with the help of PC Geoff Davies we had two suspects, but not enough evidence to arrest them straightway. We bided our time and lo and behold we had a breakthrough some weeks later. One of the suspects was seen, in Holyhead driving a large American car, not the sort of thing you see every day in Holyhead. It transpired that he could not wait until things had quietened down for his share of the money. His accomplice gave him some of his share. Both suspects were arrested and charged with the offence. The case was disposed of at Caernarfon Crown Court with them receiving jail sentences.

It transpired that the suspects, one employed by Sealink and the other by British Rail had stolen the money one Saturday evening whilst they were on duty and had wrapped it up well in plastic bags and had hidden it in a lobster pot in the Irish Sea. A few weeks later the money was then brought back to the railway station and placed in the clothing locker of the suspect employed by Sealink. During the interview, they admitted the offence and I was immediately dispatched to the clothing locker to recover the ill-gotten gains which was wrapped up in plastic bags. My colleagues and I along with an independent person had the task of counting around nine thousand pounds. The suspect with the car had also bought some other expensive items including a Russian Leica camera.

Another noteworthy case I was involved in, was the million-pound fraud on the 'St Columba' involving the duty-free shop staff altering the credit card details on the till and pocketing cash. Twelve crew members, only one of whom came from Holyhead the rest coming from Liverpool were arrested and charged with Theft, Forgery and False Accounting.

Superintendent Tom Baker from Manchester oversaw the operation. We brought in our own arrest team and custody team who worked at Holyhead police station. The North Wales Police were extremely impressed with the whole operation. It did have a knock-on effect because during some house searches, we recovered goods stolen from well-known clothing chain stores in Bangor and Llandudno, also drugs and drugs paraphernalia were recovered from houses. They all appeared at Mold Crown Court, all but one was convicted.

The outer harbour at Holyhead came under our jurisdiction as did the boats that were berthed there. The pleasure craft were subject to numerous break-ins. One incident which was the latest in a string of thefts from the boats was discovered at 09.25 hours on a Sunday morning. Items stolen included a navigator worth £900, a ship's radio worth £400 and a bearing compass worth £100 from a yacht. The culprits had forced open a padlock on the cabin door to gain access. As the yacht was moored out in the outer harbour the culprits must have had some form of craft to get out to it. Around the same time another yacht was broken into, but nothing stolen. I commenced the initial enquires. The CID then took over the enquiry.

In March 1988, the news that we were expecting came, the new owners of Sealink had given the force notice that they were terminating their contract with the force at all their ports with effect from the 1 February 1989. Although it was expected it came as a shock, nevertheless. Protest about the termination of our contract came from the local Member of Parliament, Gwynedd County Council, The Holyhead Town Council and the rail unions.

We were all called to a meeting at Holyhead with Assistant Chief Constable Tom Buckle from Force Headquarters. At the meeting, the Redundancy and Resettlement agreements were discussed. The Force was obliged to offer us three alternative postings. The first post offered to us was London Waterloo, which we refused, the second post was Baker Street on the London Underground, which we refused, and Liverpool Lime Street (Merseyrail) which we refused. After a tense few minutes, Mr. Buckle stated that the force were prepared to retain a post on the North Wales Coast, but not all officers could be accommodated.

The question was where to locate the post. Force Headquarters favoured us remaining at Holyhead in Portacabins on Platform One. But this did not go down too well with the Midlands Division senior officers and the officers at Holyhead. We could see that Sealink would try and get policing on the cheap, as professional police officers we could not really refuse a request for assistance. Llandudno Junction was looked at as a possible location as well. However, it was agreed that a police post at Bangor would be established, thanks to Sergeant Phil White, who was one of the executive members of the British Transport Police Federation and who had fought our corner for us. I, PC's Doug Worster, Keith Roberts and our clerical officer, Alison Jones were advised that we would be retained for North Wales with effect from the 1 February 1989. The other officers took postings elsewhere in the country.

The 21 April 1988 proved a busy day. It began at around 12.45 hours when the 11.20 Holyhead to Hull train which was formed of a Sprinter unit was pelted with stones as it was travelling between Abergele and Rhyl, causing a forty-minute delay because of the brakes on one of the carriages being damaged. At 16.53 hours that day. I had a case where four youths laid down on the main railway line on the approach to Rhyl railway station as another Holyhead to Hull train was approaching. The driver applied the emergency brakes. The youths got up at the very last moment and ran off.

I was on early turn at Holyhead on Monday 14 June 1988 when I received a telephone call from the North Wales Police control room at Colwyn Bay informing me that an explosion had occurred in one of two nitroglycerine mixing houses at the Cookes explosives factory at Penrhyndeudraeth, which is situated adjacent to the Cambrian Coast Railway Line. The blast which was heard twenty miles away sadly killed two employees and injured eight others. The North Wales Police declared a major incident and were looking for our assistance should the need arise later in the day. As it happened our assistance was not required. Cookes used to dispatch Gunpowder in specially designed vans on freight trains along the Cambrian Coast Line and we were always advised of their movements.

In July 1988 we had a spate of children playing on the railway lines between Bangor and Llanfairpwll and I visited several primary schools in the area warning the children about the dangers of the railway.

During the summer of 1988 two youths aged thirteen and fifteen took a rowing boat from the harbour at Holyhead and rowed it in the path of the Irish Ferries vessel 'Leinster' as she was waiting to leave the port. The Captain refused to leave until the youths had been apprehended. I went out in another rowing boat with a member of the harbour staff to them. I took them home and reported them. The youths later received formal cautions.

Having two Nuclear power stations on our patch at Trawsfynydd on the Blaenau Ffestiniog branch line with its own rail head and Wylfa on the beautiful Isle of Anglesey with a railhead at Valley, near Holyhead, we exercised regularly with the other emergency services, just in case there was an incident involving the nuclear fuel that was transported by rail. Reproduced below is an article that I wrote for the Spring 1989 edition of the British Transport Police Journal, following one such exercise.

'Wednesday 19 October 1988 was a typical autumn day in North Wales. The weather was heavy drizzle and there was a slight breeze. During the morning trains were running normally along the Conwy Valley Line. The line, which covers 28 miles from Llandudno Junction to Blaenau Ffestiniog runs alongside the Conwy estuary through the lowlands of the Conwy Valley and up through Llanrwst and Betws y Coed to the slate town of Blaenau Ffestiniog. Trains conveying nuclear flasks carry on past Blaenau Ffestiniog to the Central Electricity Generating Board, Nuclear Power station at Trawsfynydd.

The British Rail staff employed on the line were working normally and were looking forward to a normal day of operations. A British Transport Police Mobile Support Unit from Liverpool was on routine patrol in the area, as was an officer from the Holyhead District Police Post.

Then at a quiet level crossing somewhere on the Conwy Valley Line, a road lorry packed with drums of explosive kerosene hit a nuclear waste train travelling from the Power Station at Trawsfynydd to Sellafield in Cumbria, head on. The ashen-faced lorry driver, who was badly shocked, crawled out of his cab. The drums of kerosene began to smoulder, only yards from a flask of deadly uranium rods. The lorry driver's heart went into his mouth when he thought of the possible consequences. He then lapsed into a state of unconsciousness.

The guard of the train, not seriously injured, but suffering from shock, manages to ring the duty Area Operations Controller, British Rail, Chester, who alerts the emergency services.

A radio message is picked up by the Liverpool Mobile Support Unit and the Holyhead Officer. They race to the scene, reaching there at the same time as their colleagues from the North Wales Police. Immediately a police cordon is put around the area. Ambulance and Fire crews arrive. Two firemen from the Gwynedd Fire Brigade in breathing apparatus run towards the lorry driver with a stretcher and strap him to it.

As the driver is being taken away, the kerosene drums explode in a ball of fire and fierce flames envelop the nuclear flask. The Fire Brigade are now under intense pressure to bring the blaze under control as quickly as possible. The intense heat causes the pressure to build up inside the flask until it cracks and a jet of contaminated steam spurts out from the steel cube of the flask.

There is no time to waste, a race against time is now on. More fire appliances arrive at the disaster scene. The 'ice-cool' Gwynedd fire fighters in protective suits move in with a high-pressure hose and tackle the blaze. The fire on the lorry is quickly brought under control, the hose is then trained on the nuclear flask. Foam is sprayed over it to cool it and to prevent the contaminated steam from escaping.

Meanwhile fifty metres away the British Transport Police Officers hold back the spectators, members of the press and television, whilst their colleagues from the North Wales Police start to set up roadblocks and diversions to keep the roads in the area clear for emergency back-up ambulances and fire appliances from other parts of Gwynedd and the neighbouring County of Clwyd.

Officers from both forces keep a watchful eye on the situation, coordinating the emergency operation. As the Firemen are cooling the flask a Central Electricity Generating Board action team of experts in nuclear accidents races to the scene. On arrival, they check the level of radiation around the accident scene and make sure that the flask is safe.

After a couple of hours everything is brought under control and the emergency services breathe a sigh of relief. A welcome cup of tea and sandwich is provided by the Women's Royal Voluntary Service.

Fortunately, on this occasion the 'Accident' was in fact a 'mock-up' of a crash to test the reflexes of the emergency services and to drill their response in case of a genuine incident.

The exercise which was codenamed 'FLASK EXERCISE 88' was staged in a siding at the British Rail Freight depot at Llandudno Junction and was organised in conjunction with British Rail, by the Central Electricity Generating Board at Trawsfynydd.

The Police Officers from both forces found the exercise very beneficial and learnt many valuable lessons. During the last 26 years approximately ten thousand tons of radioactive waste has been carried by British Rail. To date there has not been one case of radioactivity being released.

On Monday 18 July 1988 at Old Dalby, near Melton Mowbray, Leicestershire, British Rail, and the Central Electricity Generating Board, crashed a class 46 diesel locomotive and a carriage into a nuclear flask at over 100 mph. the locomotive was crushed but the flask remained intact.

In 1987 over 200 loaded flasks carrying 200 tonnes of spent nuclear fuel passed through Llandudno junction from Wylfa power station on the Isle of Anglesey and Trawsfynydd heading for re-processing at Sellafield. There is nothing like a 'good exercise to keep everyone on their toes'.

One late Friday evening in November of 1988 one of our officers had an incredibly lucky escape. He was on patrol by himself on the unlit quay of the fish dock, when he slipped on some discarded fish and ended up in the water. Fortunately, there were two anglers nearby who went to his rescue.

I think it was November 1988, an Irishman joined the 00.50 hours train to London Euston which was formed of slam door stock with door windows that opened from the inside. As the train was leaving Holyhead, he stuck his head out and it came into contact with the overbridge abutment. He fell unconscious into the vestibule and was discovered by another passenger who alerted the guard. The train was stopped at Rhosneigr station. PC Frank Seery and I attended. An ambulance attended and conveyed him to Ysbyty Gwynedd (Gwynedd Hospital) Bangor. He remained in a coma for a few weeks and was eventually taken back by ambulance on the ferry to his home in Ireland, still in a coma. I never knew what happened to him.

It was off to Liverpool on 9 December 1988 where I successfully completed a day's training course there on the force's new computerised Police Information System (PINS).

In December 1988 just before Christmas, I was on duty in the embarkation hall when a member of the railway staff came to me and handed me a lady's handbag. A search of the bag revealed the details of the owner, who lived on the east coast of the Isle of Anglesey and a quantity of cannabis resin. It was then booked into our property system. PC Pete Morris and I went to her address and she completely denied all knowledge of owning the bag. On returning to Holyhead, we booked it back into the property store and as we were doing so the owner turned up and admitted that the bag was hers and that the cannabis inside was also hers. It transpired that she was the daughter of a very high-ranking police officer from the home counties and did not want to cause embarrassment to her family. She received a caution for possession of the cannabis.

During my time at Holyhead, I visited many schools and attended many exhibitions promoting rail safety. One occasion stands out very vividly in my mind, but I cannot recall the exact date. I was on the stage at a primary school in Rhyl giving my presentation from the stage to the assembled children who numbered about one hundred and twenty in total. The scenario was, I was supposed to be playing football in a park adjacent to the railway line which was separated by a fence. The ball after I kicked it, went onto the railway line instead of going to another player. My question to the children was "Should I climb the fence and go and get the ball back or leave it there". Simple!

In reality, I kicked the ball and lost my balance and fell off the stage onto the floor, sliding a few feet, narrowly missing some seated children on the floor. The teachers, all took a sharp intake of breath and the children thought it was hilarious. All I needed to complete my actions was to get up and shout "Mr. Grimsdale". (Recollections of Norman Wisdom). I was lucky that I did not break any bones, but my pride was dented and my uniformed covered in dust. The children wanted an encore, they were in absolute hysterics, but I told them that I only do it once per visit. For some reason, I was invited back a few weeks later! I went back a couple of years later, but by this time I had changed my script.

An incident, the date I cannot recall, was one of the most despicable acts of football violence I have ever come across, was from a group of supporters who had travelled from Ireland overnight and boarded the early morning train to Cardiff. During the journey across the Isle of Anglesey to Bangor they went to the brake van and badly assaulted a defenceless man in a wheelchair. The supporters were detained at Bangor by the North Wales Police, I was called out from home. They were all dealt with at Bangor Magistrates' Court.

I spent most of Christmas 1988 drawing up plans for the three rooms we were to occupy in the new police accommodation at Bangor. The accommodation was not ideal, but it was better than nothing at all. Brian Ashton, the British Rail Area Works Supervisor at Bangor and his team did a fantastic job in fitting the rooms out for us in the short time they had available.

Most of January 1989 was taken up removing items from Holyhead for disposal and ordering new equipment and preparing for the move to Bangor.

On the 31 January 1989 I completed my tour of duty at 16.00 hours, when Sergeant Phil White booked on. At midnight, he put the lights out at Holyhead police office for the last time thus bringing the curtain down on the end of an era at Holyhead which had begun some one hundred and fifty years ago.

CHAPTER 17

THE BANGOR YEARS FEBRUARY 1989 - MARCH 1991

Arriving at Bangor and preparing for the Cold War

I opened the police office of Bangor station on Platform One without ceremony at 08.00 hours on 1 February 1989. There had been a police establishment at Bangor up until 1965 and the office was located on Platform Two. I believe that the officers were transferred to Holyhead.

I moved there with two Constables, Doug Worster and Keith Roberts and a clerical officer, Alison Jones. They joined me a little later in the morning, and we had a cup of coffee and a chocolate biscuit to celebrate the official opening! The rest of the staff from Holyhead went to other stations around the force area and one took his redundancy and left the force. I was now under Inspector Andy Bicknell at Crewe, which was part of Midlands Division.

Whilst we were at Holyhead, the rail policing side of things was largely neglected as the contract with Sealink stated that there must be a police officer in the port every time there was a passenger vessel in the port. This did not give us much scope for visiting the rail stations on a regular basis. It went without saying that the rail crime and summary offence figures were abysmal. Had, we had been able to devote more time to the rail side of policing our figures would have been much higher and I am convinced that we would have had more officers at Bangor.

It was decided by the powers that be, that I would supervise the three uniformed officers at the Chester police post, as they had lost their supervision some two years previously with the retirement of the Detective Sergeant. The Detective Constable at Chester was supervised by the Detective Sergeant at Crewe. So, I had one of the biggest patches of any Sergeant in the force to cover.

My area stretched from Holyhead along the North Wales Coast to Chester, through to Beeston Castle on the main Chester to Crewe railway line; Chester through to Wrexham and Chirk on the Shrewsbury line; out to Lostock Gralam on the line from Chester to Altrincham; Winsford, Hartford and Acton Bridge on the main West Coast Railway Line; Runcorn East on the line to Warrington Bank Quay; Bache and Capenhurst on the third electrified rail line to Liverpool Central; Llandudno to Blaenau Ffestiniog and finally the Cambrian Coast Line from Pwllheli to Barmouth. It was an exceptionally large area to cover.

Shortly after moving to Bangor, I remember the Divisional Commander, Chief Superintendent Jim Hoath, coming from Birmingham, and taking me for a coffee and bacon sandwich in the refreshment room at Bangor, stating that I must make the Bangor patch work or otherwise it would be closed. A nice simple task and no pressure then! I had broad shoulders. Shortly after Mr. Hoath's visit, following a reorganisation of the force we went back under the command of the North West Division at Manchester.

With having such a large area and two police posts to cover most of my duties between 1989 and 1992 were administrative ones.

Bangor is situated on the Chester to Holyhead railway line and was incorporated by an Act of Parliament in 1844. Work commenced building the railway on appropriately St David's Day 1 March 1845. There were no railway police on the line at the time. On the 22 March 1846, the navvies were fighting between themselves at Bangor and the Military had to be called from Chester to restore order. Two sets of contractors were ordered to employ policemen during the period of construction. In total ten regular Constables and over one hundred special constables were employed from the work force to maintain law and order. They were later absorbed into the London and North Western Railway Police when that company took over the Chester and Holyhead Railway in 1859.

17 September 1856 saw a train accident at Bangor railway station. As today, there are four lines going through Bangor station, the two centre lines are used for through running and two are used for the platforms. The centre lines were used for the storage of wagons. In those days, a Policeman was used for regulating trains. On the day in question, Policeman Myddleton who was on duty at the mouth of the south tunnel lowered the signal for the night mail train to enter the platform but forgot to change the points which were set for the through line. The train ploughed into the wagons causing injury to a Post Office Inspector a Mail Guard and four passengers. Having watched the crash, Myddleton absconded from the scene and has not been seen since. I told my officers should he come to the office to see if the coast is clear, at least give him a cup of tea.

There was much to sort out, we needed our own toilet facilities. We had to share with the railway permanent way Inspector and his staff or use the public toilet situated along the platform. I made arrangements to take delivery of a toilet Portakabin, which had separate facilities for both male and female and had a shower facility as well. This was placed on the platform near to our office. On rainy days, we had to brave the rain. It was only when the office at Bangor was refurbished and extended in 2005 that I found out that the toilets were illegal, as Bangor station is a listed building and special permission should have been sought beforehand.

I did hear that a few days after we had left the Port of Holyhead there was a sudden death on the 'St Columba'. The North Wales Police were called, but due to other duties they did not attend immediately. As the ship was being delayed from departing Sealink staff kept ringing them and stated that if the British Transport Police had been called, they would have been on the scene straight away. Sealink were in no uncertain terms, reminded that our services had been dispensed with.

During the early years of the charitable Victim Support Scheme, the British Transport Police had a nationwide policy of referring all victims of crime to the local Victim Support Scheme. The North Wales Police only made selective referrals. At a meeting of the Môn Gwynedd (Isle of Anglesey and Gwynedd) Scheme, the Chairman, the late Eldred Boothby, a retired Chief Constable, asked the North Wales Police representative as to why the BTP were referring more victims to the scheme than the North Wales Police and why was there no representative from them.

The next thing I knew, was that Superintendent Trefor Edwards was on the telephone to me inviting me to join the committee of the scheme.

There was a lot of fundraising to be carried out to assist in the running of the scheme. Over the years I rose to become Vice-chair of the scheme until it underwent a reorganisation and became an all Wales Scheme.

Whilst I was based at Holyhead, the Inspector was responsible for attending meetings at the RAF base at Valley, which is in fact in Llanfair yn Neubwll, near to Valley. Valley is much easier to pronounce. One of the meetings he attended was 'MOLEPLAN' the defence of the Anchorage of Moelfre, Anglesey. This was a joint plan between the Royal Navy, the Army, and the Royal Air Force, along with the local police, BTP, Sealink, and the local council. It was a plan to be initiated should the Cold War break out and the Isle of Anglesey was invaded by the enemy. The plan, which was supposedly top secret, had to be kept under lock and key so it was kept in the office safe. After we moved to Bangor, I became the British Transport Police representative. Although we had moved away from the Port of Holyhead, we still had jurisdiction within the port under the British Transport Commission Act of 1949 and obviously we had jurisdiction at the adjoining railway station at which we still provided a police service. The offices of Sealink would be taken over by the military and the emergency services. I thought to myself, that would be nice walking into the Sealink offices and evicting them – payback time.

The meetings were held twice a year in the Officers Mess at the base and usually commenced at 11.00 hours with coffee and cake followed by a hot buffet lunch. The meetings were coordinated by the Officer Commanding, HMS Devonport, Plymouth. The notice of the meetings would arrive by first class post. For my first meeting I attended in uniform, but felt out of place, when I met the representatives of the other services who were laden with medals and 'scrambled egg' on their tunics. The North Wales Police representative was the local Superintendent. For my subsequent meetings I attended wearing my three-piece suit with a rose in the lapel. Although I was immensely proud of my uniform, I felt much more at ease with the top brass.

After coffee, the Chair opened the meeting with the usual words of welcome and we went around the table introducing ourselves. He then told us that there was nothing to report about the Cold War, as all that we needed to know, could be found in the *'Daily Telegraph'*. I made a mental note, go to the newsagent a few minutes earlier each morning and scan the *'Daily Telegraph'* before picking up my copy of the *'Daily Mirror'*. He then informed us for the next few minutes we would all update our contact details on a form which he passed around. After this we adjourned for lunch.

A few weeks later, minutes of the meeting, along with our contact details would arrive on my desk. What amused me was the envelope was clearly a standard Ministry of Defence, A4 issue one and was stamped *'Confidential' 'Top Secret'* and *'For the eyes of the addressee only'* and it arrived by first class post!! In the years I was involved, never once did it fail to arrive. Was it a coincidence that our postman for the Bangor station area was called Ivan? After the thaw of the Cold War, we were informed by a letter sent by first class post that 'MOLEPLAN' had been disbanded and we had to shred our copy and advise the Ministry of Defence that we had done so.

I could now sleep a little easier at night knowing that I would not be worrying about Ivan and his comrades invading Anglesey. Funnily enough we did get a new postman on the round.

In 1989, I was selected to become a PINS (Police Information System) Trainer for the force's computer system. I had to spend one week at Tadworth on a training course. On arrival, back at Bangor I had to train officers, particularly probationary Constables from the North West Division for one day on the system at Bangor.

During the summer of 1989 British Rail introduced regular steam-hauled passenger trains along the North Wales Coast. This in turn attracted several lineside enthusiasts, who caused no end of trespass problems. Some of them were very cooperative whilst others were downright awkward with us. There was no reasoning with them, once that far away glazed look came into their eyes on seeing a steam locomotive. The actions of these idiots not only put their lives at risk but delayed the steam trains and the ordinary passenger trains as well. This had a knock-on effect for the travelling public wishing to make connections.

Figure 6 Bill at Valley sidings with 'Merchant Navy' locomotive 35028 Clan Line

With my limited resources at Bangor, I was able to secure the use of a 'Q train'. These trains were named after the disguised armed merchant ships that wreaked havoc in World War Two. They looked like any other passenger train or diesel locomotive that ran on the North Wales Coast to blend in. They did not run to a timetable and the only passengers on board were a squad of British Transport Police Officers. Mostly, I used a twin carriage diesel multiple unit. (DMU). I or another officer rode in the cab as a spotter and radio contact was made with two police cars following on the adjacent roads, on sighting the offenders. Whenever possible the 'Q train' would stop and the officers on board would deal with them. The trains were highly effective.

Figure 7 Bill at Valley Sidings with 'Merchant Navy' locomotive 35005 'Canadian Pacific'

On one 'Q train' trip, on a Sunday morning, which ran in front of the 'Flying Scotsman' steam train, we caught around thirty offenders at Mold Junction. One of which, was a man seen lying on his stomach inches from the track in readiness to take a photograph of the steam excursion. A couple of officers went to speak to him, and he refused to get up. He was forcibly lifted and arrested, where upon he assaulted one of the officers. He was taken to Mold Police Station and pleaded with the officers not to tell his wife as he was not supposed to be out photographing trains.

He later appeared at Mold Magistrates' Court where he was fined. This incident took around three-quarters of an hour to deal with at the lineside, thus delaying the trains behind us. We were put in the first available loop and had to follow the steam excursion. Shortly afterwards the 'Q trains' were disbanded.

Figure 8 Bill by 'Black Five' locomotive 5407 at Holyhead station. Fireman Tom Slavin can be seen on the footplate

It was around 15 July 1989 when I received a call that someone had cut the track circuit cable near to the Maesgeirchen housing estate on the outskirts of Bangor, an area notorious for trespass and vandalism. This act of mindless vandalism certainly caused several hours of delay and inconvenience to the travelling public. The local press assisted in an appeal for us to trace the offenders. It took me some persuasion with the railway authorities to erect palisade fencing in the area. This certainly reduced the incidents at the location.

Duty at the opening of the new station at Llanrwst was the order of the day on Thursday 29 July 1989. Llanrwst, on the face of it, is a pleasant market town in the Conwy Valley, but has been the scene of serious disorder on weekend nights. The town is served by trains on the Llandudno to Blaenau Ffestiniog branch line. The original Llanrwst station is situated on the outskirts of the town. It was decided to build a new station, more convenient for the town. It opened just in time for the National Eisteddfod which was being held in the town in August. The original station was kept open and renamed Llanrwst North / Gogledd Llanrwst, as it has the line's only passing loop. The locals quickly nicknamed the new station Llanrwst International because of the Eisteddfod. Overseas visitors on arrival were surprised to find a single platform halt and were looking for a metro station and airport!

Early in the afternoon of Friday 4 August 1989 I was in the office at Bangor mulling over some paperwork when I received a call to the effect that two Campaign for Nuclear Disarmament (CND) activists went into the sidings adjacent to Llandudno Junction station and daubed anti-nuclear protest slogans in both English and Welsh and chained themselves to a nuclear flask which had just arrived from Valley on its way to Sellafield. The two protesters had walked unnoticed across the tracks to the sidings.

The local Police attended, as did the local Fire and Rescue service. I attended a short time later. The members of the fire service refused to use bolt croppers to release the protesters as they were sympathetic to their cause. After speaking to them and with a member of the rail staff, the bolt croppers were handed over to a member of the rail staff and the protesters chains were cut. They were arrested and taken to Conwy police station where they were interviewed in Welsh and both made a no comment interview. They were later convicted at court, which they refused to recognise.

The protestors and local councillors made a big play that the flask had been unattended, and the local press obviously made a big fuss about it as well. I told them that it was impossible to guard the flask with a presidential forcefield all the time and that it was perfectly safe, citing the test at Old Dalby a few years earlier.

Like a lot of seaside resorts, the popular resort of Rhyl would attract several thousand visitors especially on a Bank Holiday Monday. The normal passenger trains would arrive at intervals disgorging their passengers from the North West and the Midlands. On the return they would all turn up at the station at around the same time trying to board the already overcrowded trains from Llandudno and Colwyn Bay and we had to queue them to prevent disorder. Some were drunk others were disorderly, so we had our work cut out preventing them from travelling and arresting the worst of the offenders. I used the MSU from Liverpool on several occasions to assist myself and my officers. Before the days of privatisation British Rail used to lay on a special three coach DMU based at Rhyl to be used as a special to go to Crewe or beyond to ease the overcrowding and disorder on the normal passenger trains.

The problems with the behaviour of the school children travelling on the Cambrian Coast Railway Line began again. On the 28 September 1989, a complaint about the behaviour of the children was received by the Transport Users Consultative Committee (TUCC) for Wales, Cardiff, who in turn sent it to the British Rail Provincial manager at Cardiff, from a member of the public who was on holiday. The complaint was forwarded onto me.

I was a little perturbed about the letter, because whilst stationed at Holyhead I and my colleagues worked extensively to curtail the unruly behaviour of the pupils travelling on the trains. For around eighteen months or so prior to the complaint we did not receive one single complaint from anyone regarding the behaviour of the pupils. In fact, several letters praising the pupils had been received by the Headteacher.

On Wednesday 11 October 1989, I visited the Ysgol Ardudwy, Harlech and in conjunction with the school management I investigated the matter and found that the culprits had only been at the school for three weeks, they were a brand new intake.

Thursday 16 November 1989, Thursday 23 November 1989, and Thursday 7 December 1989 saw me visiting Ysgol Ardudwy and present rail safety talks backed up by a video to over six hundred pupils at the school.

Following these visits, I received a genuinely nice letter of appreciation from Mr. J.B. Davies, the British Rail Provincial Manager for Wales, thanking me for my efforts. The incidents were virtually eradicated.

The innocence of children. A couple of amusing incidents spring to mind. I went to a Roman Catholic primary school in North Wales, which was run by Nuns, to deliver a rail safety talk. I told the children that it would not be very nice if I had to go to their homes and tell their mummy and daddy that they had been killed or hurt whilst playing on the railway. One little lad put his hand up and told me that he did not have a daddy. I told him that I was deeply sorry. He then went onto tell me that mummy slept with Uncle Jim (name change). The nuns did not know where to put their faces.

When I visit schools, I like to take a few minutes to introduce myself to the children and tell them a little about my job and the equipment that I carry. One day in a primary school, I showed the children my accoutrements as usual, including my handcuffs. One little girl told me that her mummy had a pair of handcuffs in her bedside table. I thought at this stage it would be unwise to show her my truncheon.

During my time in North Wales, we didn't really have the need for a regular dog handler, anyway the nearest ones were at Crewe (86 miles away), Liverpool (72 miles away) and Manchester (98 miles away), so we used the North Wales Police dog handlers with whom I had a very good liaison.

However, whenever there was a Royal Visit on our patch in North Wales, our own dog handlers would attend.

In late 1989 a 'triangle' was added to the railway sidings at Valley, the village where I live, near Holyhead, mainly for the purposes of turning the steam locomotives working the excursion trains along the North Wales Coast.

This extension to the sidings was an ideal opportunity to stable the Royal Train when any members of the Royal Family visited the Isle of Anglesey. On the first opportunity of such a visit I, as the local Officer in Charge at Bangor, was invited to a planning meeting, as naturally I had local knowledge of the area, which later proved to be invaluable.

During the meeting, the question of searching the railway lines by an explosive's detector dog was discussed. For security reasons, I will not elaborate on the procedure, but suffice to say the dog would be set to work to do its 'sniffing out' duty. The Officer in Charge of the meeting asked the dog handler if there were any questions. He stated that he was happy as it seemed to be a routine matter. I chirped up and informed the meeting about the adders that reside in the adjacent fields and on the railway embankment. There was a stunned silence and the search scenario was quickly re-written.

1990 started off with a spate of vandalism on the North Wales Coast. Trains were hit by stone throwing; objects were placed on the lines. Myself and my two officers' PCs Doug Worster and Keith Roberts had our work cut out. School visits to deliver safety messages were arranged.

It was around Wednesday 14 February 1990 at Penmaenmawr when a driver narrowly escaped serious injury, when a stone was hurled through the window of his locomotive which was in the freight sidings. Sadly, enquiries proved negative.

A week later, on Wednesday 21 February 1990, during half-term week in North Wales, I remember it was a very warm and sunny day. I was on duty with PC Doug Worster in the office at Bangor. At around 12.30 hours I received a telephone call stating that conductor David North of Llandudno Junction had been severely injured at Colwyn Bay. It transpired that he was working a two-coach train from Bangor to Stalybridge and was stood in his cab near to the open window at the rear. As the train was passing Penrhos College, on the approach to Colwyn Bay station, he was hit in the face by a stone. On arrival at Colwyn Bay he collapsed on the platform. Doug and I went immediately to the scene. David had been taken to the Glan Clwyd hospital at Bodelwyddan where it was found that he had a serious injury to his eye. We went to the hospital to interview David. As the incident happened so fast, he could only recall seeing two young persons on the roadway. David was then taken to HM Stanley eye hospital in St Asaph, where it was discovered, after a while that his sight had been saved by his plastic spectacles. He was completely blind for the first few hours and then had to lie completely still in a hospital bed for six days while the internal bleeding stopped. It was a worrying time for David.

Doug and I commenced enquiries in the area, and we were joined by the CID officer from Chester. He stated that due to the poor description given by David there was no point in continuing with the enquiries. The culprit could have been one of around two hundred youths in the area plus any youths on holiday from outside the area. Having an attitude like that I sent him back to Chester. I told Doug Worster to come out in plain clothes the next day.

The following day, Thursday 22 February 1990 at around 10.00 hours, Doug and I went to a local café in Colwyn Bay where we planned our strategy in peace and quiet, away from the office. As people are creatures of habit, we went to the scene of the crime just before the same train involved in the incident was due. Sure enough 'Mrs. Jones' was walking her dog, the Postman was delivering his letters, 'Mrs. Hughes' was on her way to the shops and the breadman was delivering his bread. They all had been in the area at the same time the previous day. They gave us some valuable information. Armed with our further information we made further inroads into the identity of the culprit. We knocked on a few doors and narrowed the suspects down to around half a dozen or so. We finished late that evening.

Friday 23 February 1990 saw Doug and I returning to Colwyn Bay knocking on few more doors. Finally, our breakthrough came we had the name of two fourteen-year-old boys. It was just the matter of apprehending the right one, otherwise the case could be in jeopardy. This is where our sixth sense came into play.

We had a feeling who the culprit was, and we went to his friend first, who for a time denied being in the area, but after being questioned, further admitted being there and that his friend had actually thrown the stone. Lady Luck was certainly on our side.

We went to see the main suspect and arrested him on suspicion of Endangering the Safety of Persons on the railway and took him to Colwyn Bay police station where he was interviewed in the presence of his father, who it turned out was a railway worker in the locality. After initial denials, he fully admitted the offence. He was reported to the Crown Prosecution Service (CPS), who decided that an official caution be administered.

The CID officer got wind of our success and tried to 'muscle' in on the case so that he could have his name and number on the paperwork. I told him in no uncertain terms to 'get lost', or words to that effect.

Following the case David was 'over the moon' that we had managed to apprehend the culprit and asked how we did it. I told him that it was just old fashioned, standard basic police work, painstakingly knocking on doors and wearing out the shoe leather, which we had been trained to do.

Doug and I received letters of appreciation from David, the railway management and Superintendent Tom Baker, Divisional Headquarters, Manchester, for a job well done.

There was a serious assault in Colwyn Bay late one Saturday night in early April 1990. An argument ensued between one youth and five others outside a public house in Station Road, Colwyn Bay. The five youths chased the victim onto Platform One of Colwyn Bay Station, then pursued him across the tracks to Platform Two and to the bottom of the steps leading to the Signalbox. There, they severely assaulted him by kicking and punching him all over his body from head to toe. The assailants then ran off. The North Wales Police were quickly on the scene and obtained some valuable information as to the identity of some of the assailants.

Following receipt of the information, I called in the services of the MSU from Liverpool to assist me with the enquiry. After making further enquiries, we identified all the assailants and ascertained where they lived. We went around Colwyn Bay early one morning arresting them and taking them to the custody suite at the town's police station. One of them resided in a three-storey guest house on the promenade. Sergeant Tony Barratt and myself went to the house to arrest him. We were informed by his parents that he was still in bed. Just in case he tried to escape from his bedroom we put three officers on the rear lawn and two officers on the front lawn, whilst Tony and I made the arrest. We arrested him and as we were making our way to the van we saw the officers on the front lawn, sat down enjoying a pot of tea and cake, whilst the officers on the rear lawn were doing the same. It transpired that the mother of the accused took the refreshments out to the officers. One of the officers remarked, "If this had been in Liverpool, they would have been throwing stones and bricks at us". All five were charged and subsequently appeared at the Magistrates' Court in the town.

One afternoon in May 1990 I had to go to a very remote part of Snowdonia to interview a female who had driven her motor car across an unmanned level crossing in front of an oncoming train on the Cambrian Coast Line.

I had to park the police car in a lay by on the main road and walk quarter of a mile through the woods to her cottage. On arrival she offered to make me a cup of tea, which I accepted. She left the cottage and went to the nearby stream to collect water directly into the kettle. I interviewed her contemporaneously after which I handed her the notes to read to make sure that they were an accurate record. She handed them back pointing out that I had missed out some full stops, commas, and had not inserted colons etc. (When you are writing fast, you tend to miss these out). She then said, "It's okay I used to be an English teacher and old habits die hard". I thought 'Rogerson take five hundred lines'. Incidentally the tea was one of the best I've ever tasted.

During the second week of July 1990, I was called to a fatality at Ty Newydd Road, overbridge at Rhyl. Apparently, a male person had stepped out from behind the road bridge that goes over the railway line into the path of an express train. On arrival I spoke to the train driver from Manchester, He said to me "It's my sixth one this year". At the subsequent inquest, a verdict of suicide was returned.

On Wednesday 18 July 1990 I booked on duty at 06.00 hours looking to complete my tour of duty at around 18.00 hours. I was the only officer on duty that day at Bangor and had the world famous 'Flying Scotsman' locomotive hauling an enthusiasts special along the North Wales Coast to and from Holyhead. I dealt with all the routine paperwork and performed train patrols along the North Wales Coast until I met up with the 'Flying Scotsman' special. I travelled with the train from Llandudno Junction to Holyhead performing duties at Bangor and Holyhead station in connection with the enthusiasts. I then travelled back with the train from Holyhead to Llandudno Junction, intending to finish there and return to Bangor in time to book off at 18.00 hours, after the train had departed.

However, as the train was about a mile or so from Llandudno Junction station a passenger came to me and stated that a man in the rear vestibule of the first coach required first aid. I immediately went to the coach and found the man lying on the floor. I thought to myself this man does not require first aid, he requires an undertaker, as three-quarters of his head had been ripped away from his shoulders and there was a large pool of blood on the floor around his head.

When the train arrived at Llandudno Junction, I arranged with the North Wales Police to call out the duty undertaker to convey him to the mortuary at Ysbyty Gwynedd, Bangor. As I was obtaining the details of witnesses and arranging for the carriage to be detached from the train and secured for examination, the usual circus of press and television reporters arrived. The phones from Force Headquarters, the British Railways Board and the Rail Accident Investigation Department were red hot. I could have done with an extra three or four pairs of hands.

It transpired that the man, from London, who was about 6'2" was leaning out of the carriage window, with his back to the direction of travel, taking a photograph of the carriages, when his head came into contact with the rocks on the side of Penmaenbach tunnel, between Penmaenmawr and Conwy. When I carried out a profile of the scene for the Coroner's report, I found that there were only nine inches between the rocks and the side of the carriage. The poor man did not stand a chance.

The body of the man was removed from the train into a hearse. As I did not have the police car with me, I asked the undertaker if I could obtain a lift in the hearse to the mortuary at Bangor. Alan Lambert, the undertaker agreed but stated that he would have to go via his office, which was next to the station, to change his clothing. No problem at all. On arrival at his garage/funeral parlour, he invited me in for a drink. I politely refused, seizing the opportunity to get my pocket book up to date. A short time later he arrived with his assistant. Now most people only travel in the back of a hearse once in their lifetime. I had my first trip when I was very much alive. I sat in the back of the hearse with my helmet resting on top of the coffin. I received some startled looks from the motorists who overtook us on the dual carriageway, as I waved to them.

During the journey Alan Lambert asked me if I was okay sat in the back, to which I stated that I was. His assistant, who was driving, turned around with a startled look and said, "Bloody Hell, I don't usually get any replies from the rear of a hearse!". Just keep your eyes on the road!

On arrival at the mortuary the deceased was booked in. Alan very kindly dropped me back at the office. As soon as I walked through the door the telephones were red hot, with Area Headquarters, Force Headquarters and the press and television. After dealing with them, I booked the deceased's property into the property room and began to compile the report for the Coroner, ready to open the inquest the following day. Whilst I was in the process of doing this at around 21.30 hours, I answered the telephone, this time it was the Duty Inspector from Colwyn Bay Police Station. "Hello Sarge, I've got a sudden death to report to you" I replied, "Thanks sir, I know all about it, I just returned from Llandudno Junction". He said, "This is another one". I will not repeat what words went through my mind, but I am sure you can guess. It transpired that a dumper truck driver who was working on the sea wall at Towyn between Abergele and Rhyl had suffered a fatal heart attack. The sea wall, which was owned by the British Railways Board, was breached by sea water and heavy floods the previous winter and was in the process of being repaired. The Inspector agreed for his officer who attended the scene initially, would continue with the investigation and hand the paperwork over to me in due course. Such was the excellent cooperation I had with the North Wales Police.

I eventually finished duty at 23.30 hours that day and I certainly earned my commuted allowance. This was a regular allowance paid for unforeseen overtime to certain officers of the force.

The following day, Thursday 19 July 1990, which was red hot weather-wise, was taken up with speaking to the local Coroner, dealing with the press enquiries and preparing further reports in connection with the incident. The Post-mortem was arranged for 14.30 hours. I went to the Mortuary for about 13.30 hours and received a cup of tea. The staff, who I had met on previous occasions regaled me with tales of the vicissitudes of their profession. During our tea break, a couple of helicopters from 22 Rescue Squadron at RAF Valley landed with dead bodies of elderly people who had collapsed and sadly died on Mount Snowdon. One of the morticians with a dead-pan expression (excuse the pun) said, "It's like F*****g M.A.S.H. here today." (There was a fictional American television programme about a Mobile Army Surgical Hospital in the Korean War).

As they were short of staff, I was then called into the Pathologist's examination area to assist him with recording the organ details of another body. I then dealt with my client.

In October of 1991, the local coroner held the inquest into the death and after hearing all the evidence in front of a jury, he returned a verdict of Misadventure. In open court the Coroner congratulated me on an excellent file, stating that his understanding of the complex case had been made all the easier.

I received letters of congratulations from the local railway Area Manager and The BTP Area Commander.

Between Tuesday 13 November 1990 and Thursday 15 November 1990, several England football fans travelled from all over England to go to Ireland to watch their national team play Ireland on Wednesday 14 November 1990 at Landsdowne Road, Dublin in a Euro 92 qualifying match. The game ended in a 1-1 draw. Many of the fans travelled by train, and the force policed the fans to and from Holyhead. During this time Doug Worster, Keith Roberts and myself found ourselves back at Holyhead Station and port monitoring the fans along with the North Wales Police who mounted an operation called 'Operation Cybi'. At the conclusion of the operation, we received a nice letter of appreciation from Chief Superintendent Larry Davies, Divisional Commander, North Wales Police, Caernarfon, for our involvement and professionalism in the operation.

Early 1991 saw me preparing for my forthcoming Rail Dash around the country to raise funds for the RNLI Police Lifeboat Appeal.

CHAPTER 18

THE BANGOR YEARS - THE RAIL DASH 1991

Raising funds for the Police Lifeboat Appeal

What made me want to spend just over two days continually travelling around Great Britain by train in 1991?

In the mid 1980s, I just happened to find myself reading a copy of 'The Railway Magazine', and in the magazine, there was an article by a railway enthusiast, who had travelled by train and visited for pleasure the most Northerly, Westerly, Easterly and Southerly terminal stations on the British Rail network, these being Thurso, Mallaig, Lowestoft and Penzance. (Morar, the neighbouring station to Mallaig is in fact the most westerly station on British Rail. It is a through station and not a terminal).

As I enjoy travelling by train and never having ventured north of Dundee or east of Norwich, I thought that this would be a good idea to do a sponsored event to raise money for a worthy charity, such as the Royal National Lifeboat Institution (RNLI), which is a charity close to my heart. My family have been associated with the Lifeboats since its inception in 1824. I have the sea in my blood, being born and bred in Morecambe, and at the time working in Bangor and living in Valley, the RNLI was a natural choice. Also, I am a Governor of the Institution and my wife Shirley, is the Secretary of the Holyhead and District Ladies Lifeboat Guild. Both my son and daughter served on the crew at Trearddur Bay. I am on the management and operational committees at Trearddur Bay lifeboat station and still undertake several voluntary roles there.

I obtained a copy of the British Rail timetable and began making a few notes. It was my intention to visit lifeboat stations nearest to the aforementioned railway terminals, a journey of over 1600 miles.

However, before I got my idea off the ground, Neil Harvey, who was a Police Constable with the force at Nottingham, had been severely attacked by some vicious and cowardly thugs and left for dead. To show his appreciation to the dedicated doctors and nurses who saved his life at the Nottingham University Hospital, Neil had planned and was in the process of executing a similar venture to raise funds for the Hospital. So, I put my idea on hold for a few years, so as not to steal any of Neil's thunder.

In August 1990, whilst selling raffle tickets for the RNLI at the Isle of Anglesey agricultural show, I mentioned the venture to Richard Polden, who at the time was the Deputy Regional Organiser for RNLI Wales. It was at that point that Richard informed me about a National Police Appeal, which was in the process of being set up by Doctor Ian Oliver, Chief Constable of the Grampian Police, to raise money to fund a Mersey Class Off-shore Lifeboat at a cost of £450.000. I told Richard that I would use the venture to raise funds for the police lifeboat.

Richard was very enthusiastic about the idea and I asked him to accompany me on the trip, which without any hesitation he agreed to do. Prior to joining the RNLI Richard served as a British Railways Booking Clerk in the south of England and had been a Special Constable.

When I arrived home, I mentioned the venture to Shirley, who at the time thought I was quite insane and thought I must have been struck on the head by a hay bale at the show. As she was about to ring the local psychiatrist to have me certified, I mentioned the magic words to her, "It's all in aid of the lifeboat". Well, those few words threw a different light on the matter entirely. I received her full support.

I decided to hold my 'dash' in April 1991. This was usually a quiet time of year as far as rail travel was concerned. After consultation with Richard, the 'dash' was arranged to take place between Tuesday 16 April 1991 and Thursday 18 April 1991.

As the railway timetable had altered quite drastically since my initial planning stage, I had to revamp my original programme. Originally, I was going to begin my journey in Thurso, then on to Mallaig, then on to Lowestoft and finally to Penzance. There followed a couple of evenings where an intensive study of the British Rail timetable was undertaken to work out suitable routes and times. I wanted to complete the journey in the least possible time. Nowadays, I would just feed the information into a computer for the best route for my needs, it would be back in a few moments time all worked out for me.

Finally, I decided on the route Richard and I were to embark upon. We were to commence the 'dash' from Lowestoft lifeboat station at 08.45 hours on Tuesday 16 April 1991, walk to Lowestoft railway station to arrive in time to catch the 09.00 hours train to Ipswich, where we would change for the 10.49 hours train to London Liverpool Street, which was scheduled to arrive at 11.50 hours. A journey on the Circle Line of the London Underground would take us to London Paddington in time to catch the 12.35 hours service to Penzance. On arrival at Penzance at 18.04 hours, a car would take us to Penlee lifeboat station, where after formalities we would return to Penzance station in time to catch the 19.05 hours train to Plymouth, where we would catch the overnight sleeper train departing at 21.00 hours to Glasgow Central, due to arrive at 06.25 hours. A Leisurely walk to Glasgow Queen Street in time to catch the 08.10 hours service to Mallaig, arriving at 13.20 hours. A walk across to the lifeboat station, where after formalities we would return to Glasgow Queen Street, arriving at 19.39 hours, time for a wash and brush up followed by a meal. The final leg of the journey would see us catching the 23.50 hours service to Inverness, thence forward on the 07.02 hours to Thurso, where on arrival at 10.45 hours we would be met and transported by car to Scrabster lifeboat station, arriving at about 10.55 hours.

Did it seem possible? Well on paper it looked as if it would work out. The only tight connections was the journey between London Liverpool Street and London Paddington on the tube. In practice, it could be completely different, only executing the plan would tell.

My next task was to promulgate the details of the 'dash' to the late, Archie McKenzie, our Assistant Chief Constable in Scotland, who was secretary of the appeal and who was a member of the Scottish Lifeboat Management Committee. Mr. McKenzie gave me a lot of valuable help, assistance, and encouragement with the planning of the venture, for which I was very grateful.

I received approval from the Chief Constable to perform the 'dash'. So, it was all systems go. I used the long winter months that lay ahead to write begging letters for sponsorship. The RNLI were kind enough to provide me with the necessary stationery. Annual leave for week ending 20 April 1991 was booked. A bank account in the name of the 'RNLI Rail Dash' was opened with Barclays Bank in Holyhead to deposit sponsorship money. Richard very kindly arranged accommodation in Lowestoft for the night before the 'dash' commenced, and in Thurso for the night after the 'dash' was completed, he also arranged for the cars to transport us between Penzance station and Penlee lifeboat station and return: also, between Thurso railway station and Scrabster lifeboat station.

Inter-City and Regional Railways very kindly donated free tickets for Richard so that he could accompany me.

I sent out the begging letters in January and almost immediately the sponsorship money started rolling in. I was very encouraged by the amount that I had received in the first month.

During February of 1991 I travelled to Glasgow to finalise the loose ends with Mr. McKenzie. The big day was fast approaching. On 3 April 1991, I visited the British Rail Anglia Region, Headquarters, London Liverpool Street to finalise my plans as far as the journey between Lowestoft and London Liverpool Street was concerned. Whilst I was at Liverpool Street Station, I noticed that the 10.49 hours train from Ipswich, the one we were due to travel on during the 'dash', was fifteen minutes late. Also, there were delays on the Circle and District Lines. If we had carried out the venture on that day, we would certainly not have made it to Paddington in time to catch the 12.35 hours to Penzance. 'Plan B' would have had to have been put into operation, the only snag being, there was no 'Plan B' at the time.

A drastic re-think of my plan was called for. After taking advice from British Rail, Anglia Region and London Transport, I decided that Richard and I would depart Lowestoft at 08.00 hours and travel via Norwich to London Liverpool Street and thence via the Circle line to Paddington to catch the 11.35 hours train to Penzance. If the train from Norwich was late and there were delays on the Underground, we would have the 12.35 hours to Penzance to fall back on. I informed our colleagues at Norwich of my new plans, as they were arranging to meet us and give us a send-off at Lowestoft.

Well, Monday 15 April finally arrived. My neighbour, Jim Thomas, very kindly took Shirley and myself to Holyhead railway station in time to catch the 09.02 hours train to London Euston. Waiting to send me off on the platform at Holyhead was Lord Cledwyn of Penrhos, Goronwy Parry, Deputy Mayor of Anglesey, British Rail Line Manager, Steve Delves and members of the Holyhead and District Ladies Lifeboat Guild.

I felt like royalty. The train left on time. The train was nearly late into Fflint, where Richard was joining me, due to a suspect suitcase on the train. I dealt with it, it turned out to be some dirty washing belonging to someone who had travelled from Ireland.

Figure 9 Holyhead Station Manager Steve Delves wishing Bill 'Bon Voyage' on his 'Rail Dash'

We arrived in Lowestoft at 18.49 hours, where we were welcomed to the pleasant seaside town by Inspector Derek Hackett, British Transport Police, Peterborough and Sergeant Trevor Reid, British Transport Police, Norwich.

A visit was made to the lifeboat station where final arrangements were made for our departure. Lowestoft lifeboat station was founded in 1801, 23 years before the establishment of the RNLI. I worked it out that we could walk from the lifeboat station to the railway station in two minutes.

After spending a very pleasant evening in Lowestoft we arrived at the lifeboat station at 07.30 hours, on Tuesday 16 April 1991, ready to commence the dash at 07.55 hours. We were welcomed to the Lifeboat Station by the Station's Honorary Secretary, Michael Chapman, and by Inspector Derek Hackett.

At 07.45 hours, horror struck, the lifting road bridge between the inner and outer harbours was raised to let a ship through. Was the 'dash' to be aborted before we had even set off? Silly me, no contingency plan. No, we were saved, the bridge went down, and the road opened to road traffic. Phew! first panic over. With our certificate duly signed by Mike Chapman, the Honorary Secretary of the lifeboat station, we left the station with Inspector Hackett at 07.55 hours, arriving at the railway station some two minutes later, where we were met by Sergeant Trevor Reid and Constable Pat Lumsden of Norwich.

Sergeant Reid on behalf of the Norwich officers, presented me with a beautiful book entitled 'Lowestoft Scrapbook'. Well done lads. The book was very much appreciated during the long hours ahead.

We left Lowestoft right-time at 08.00 hours. The 'dash' had begun well and truly. The thirty-five-year-old diesel multiple unit we travelled on did not appear to 'dash' very much. We arrived in Norwich on time at 08.39 hours. A visit was made to the police office, where we were introduced to Police Constable Mel Dobbs.

After a quick chat with Mel in the office, it was time to board the 09.05 hours Inter-City service to London Liverpool Street. We were safely seen on our way by Inspector Derek Hackett and Constable Dobbs. The train made good time until Chelmsford, where it stopped at signals for about five minutes, which seemed like an eternity. Then we ran on yellow signals to Stratford. Then it was all clear to Liverpool Street arriving at 11.58 hours, some eight minutes late. The conductor apologised for the delay which was due to a defective train in front of us. A quick dash to the London Transport booking office, where tickets to Paddington were purchased from an empty window. What no queue, was this a record?

Having purchased our tickets, we made our way to the Circle Line platform. Great! a Circle Line train had just arrived. The train certainly dashed along the Underground for the first part of the journey. Every time the train accelerated it sounded worse than the dentist's drill. On arrival at Baker Street, the train stopped for over two minutes. Great doors closed, away we went. At Edgeware Road, the doors opened, passengers disembarked and embarked, doors closed, oh no, doors re-opened, trains either side of us departed. A quick look at the watch, we still had fifteen minutes to get to Paddington, no real panic at this stage as we had the 12.35 hours train to Penzance to fall back on. Doors closed and away we went. Oh, that dentist's drill! We arrived in Paddington at 11.25 hours. As lady luck appeared to be on our side, we decided to travel to the West Country on the 11.35 hours 125-Inter-City service to Plymouth. We settled back to enjoy the magnificent scenery of the West Country.

The county of Devon certainly lived up to its title of 'Glorious Devon'. The sun was shining brightly. Plenty of menfolk stripped to the waist working in their gardens. We arrived in Plymouth at 14.58 hours. The Sprinter to Penzance was waiting in the adjacent platform, so we boarded it just in case the 12.35 hours ex Paddington was late. At the stroke of 15.08 hours, we were off on our way to Penzance. Arrival at Penzance was on time at 17.14 hours. As we arrived in Penzance earlier than expected, we decided to partake of a local delicacy, Cornish pasty and chips.

At 18.00 hours, we went to the car park at Penzance Railway Station, where we met Peter Garnier, Chairman of the Penlee lifeboat station, who welcomed us to Penzance and took us to Penlee lifeboat station in his 1970 Rover, which was in excellent condition. On arrival at the lifeboat station, Peter signed our certificate and gave us a brief history of the lifeboat service in the area. It was incredibly sad to learn that 1991 was the tenth anniversary of the Penlee lifeboat disaster. In December 1981, the lifeboat 'Solomon Browne' set sail from Penlee Point lifeboat house, during a ferocious storm, with her eight-man crew to go to the aid of the coaster 'Union Star'. Sadly, the eight-man crew were lost during the rescue.

The lifeboat's Coxswain, Trevelyan Richards was awarded a posthumous gold medal, the RNLI's equivalent of the Victoria Cross. Our thoughts at that moment were with the members of the crew and their families.

Peter took us to his house, where we met his wife and partook of some liquid refreshments. Peter then took us back to Penzance station in time to catch the 19.05 hours 125-Inter-City service to Plymouth. We were now back on the original schedule. Arrival in Plymouth was on time at 20.50 hours. We made our way to the 21.00 hours overnight sleeper service to Glasgow Central. We were welcomed aboard the train by a Stewardess who showed us to our previously booked berths. After making ourselves at home, we were invited to make use of the lounge car. As we made our way to the lounge car via two other sleeping cars, the Stewardess informed us that she could do with a lifeboat at that moment in time as the water tank had burst and had flooded the galley and the corridor. The car was removed from the train and we eventually departed Plymouth for Bonnie Scotland at 21.34 hours, some thirty four minutes late. After patronising the buffet facilities, we returned to our berths to get a good night's sleep, as this would be the last night until late Thursday that we would see a bed. It was not too bad sleeping on a train, this was the first time in my life I had travelled in a sleeping car.

At 05.45 hours on Wednesday 17 April 1991, the Stewardess awoke us with a refreshing cup of tea and biscuits. We were informed by her that the train was now virtually on time. Great, this would give us time to have a leisurely breakfast in Glasgow. However, we stopped outside Motherwell for about fifteen minutes, then ran under yellow signals all the way to Glasgow Central. We eventually arrived at 06.55 hours, some thirty minutes late. No panic though as our train to Mallaig was not due to depart from Glasgow Queen Street until 08.10 hours.

We were welcomed to Glasgow by Sergeant Alistair Buckle, who took us to the police office for a welcome cup of tea. We then made our way to Glasgow Queen Street station where we had breakfast. We were now ready to face the journey to Mallaig. A check of the departure board revealed that our train was to depart from Platform Two, on time at 08.10 hours and was called 'The Lord of the Isles'. This conjured up in my mind a luxury Pullman train of bygone days with all the trimmings. My dream was soon shattered when the train arrived from Edinburgh, it was a two coach 156 Sprinter unit. The dream was nice while it lasted.

Once on the train we settled down to enjoy the magnificent scenery of the West Highland Line. The sky was blue, and the sun was shining. The conductor of the train informed us that the weather was perfect for seeing the breath-taking scenery at its best. Arrival in Mallaig was three minutes early.

A hearty Highland welcome was extended to us at Mallaig railway station by Archie McLellan, the Honorary Secretary of Mallaig lifeboat station, and Coxswain Tom Ralston, who took us to the lifeboat station, which was situated in the fish market just across the road. Our certificate duly signed, we joined Archie and Tom for lunch at a local hostelry. The whisky tastes better north of the border!

Figure 10 Bill and Richard Polden during a break in the 'Rail Dash' at Mallaig

Archie made sure that we were back at the station in time to catch the 14.30 hours train to Glasgow. On arrival, back at Glasgow Queen Street at 19.39 hours exactly on time, we were welcomed to Glasgow by Archie McKenzie. Mr. McKenzie ensured that we received a square meal in a nearby bar. As our next train was not until 23.50 hours, we waited in the mess room in the Scottish Divisional Police Headquarters where we watched the television news to catch up on the world events during the last couple of days.

At around 23.30 hours we made our way back to Glasgow Queen Street station where we boarded the 23.50 hours service to Inverness. This service used to be a sleeping car service but was now relegated to, two, two-car 158 Sprinter express units, which had not been in service all that long. Sergeant Alistair Buckle turned out to see us safely on our way from Glasgow.

Upon departure from Glasgow we made ourselves comfortable the best we could, as we had four hours on this service. We hid our bags out of sight of any would be thieves. (it would have been embarrassing to say the least to have had our bags stolen, especially as it was national crime prevention week). I dozed off only to be awoken at Stirling, by fitters who were attending to the train. After about twenty minutes, the train headed north once more, and I went back to the land of nod. The next thing I knew it was Perth, when two men in orange overalls and each carrying a handlamp in one hand and a spanner in the other, awoke us. As I was not fully awake, my first thought was that they were psychiatrists who had finally tracked us down and were going to certify us. However, this was not the case. They were genuine British Rail fitters who informed us that the unit we were on had failed. (It had only been in service for a matter of months).

We were directed to the front unit. Would we arrive in Inverness in time to catch the 07.02 hours to Thurso? Yes, the fitters assured us. Automatic pilot was switched on and we made our way to the front unit. Shortly afterwards we were on our way northwards. By this time, the train was about forty-five minutes late. I dozed off again and the next thing I knew, we had arrived in the highland capital of Inverness, only about ten minutes late, in the early hours of Thursday 18 April 1991.

Upon leaving the train we made our weary way to the police office mess room on the station for breakfast, which had been previously prepared for us by PC Richard Mansfield. His homemade marmalade and bread was delicious. After breakfast, a visit was made to the bookstall where we purchased papers. We returned to the police office to read the papers which helped pass the time until 06.45 hours, when Richard Mansfield arrived. He directed us to the 07.02 hours train to Thurso. This train carried the grand name of 'The Ocardian'. Another vision of a splendid train of by-gone days. On arrival at the platform the vision again was shattered. Yes, it was another 156 Sprinter unit.

Richard saw us off on the last leg of our journey to Thurso, in the far north. The train left on time at 07.02 hours. We were well and truly on the last leg of our journey. 'Would Lady Luck stay with us?' I asked myself. As the train departed from Dingwall station, the main road was alongside us and, looking bleary-eyed out of the window, I saw a yellow pick-up van heading north with the words 'Holyhead Boatyard' painted on the side. Small world.

The train arrived in Thurso at 10.40 hours, a full five minutes ahead of schedule. At Thurso station, we were met and received a very warm welcome from George Gibson, Honorary Secretary of Scrabster lifeboat station. George very kindly conveyed us to Scrabster lifeboat station, which is about four miles from Thurso. We arrived there at 10.55 hours, exactly 50 hours and 55 minutes after leaving Lowestoft. George signed our certificate. Our marathon journey was well and truly over. We could now relax.

George took us to a local hostelry, where we tucked into a delicious lunch of homemade steak and kidney pie. After lunch, we returned to the lifeboat station where we met the Coxswain William Farquhar. We were given a conducted tour of the station and a very informative history of the lifeboat service in the area.

George very kindly took us on a conducted tour of the area. One of the places we visited was Dunnet Head, the most northerly point on mainland Britain. I, like most people, believed that John O'Groats was the most northerly point. Dunnet Head extends nearly two miles nearer the Arctic Circle. John O'Groats can only claim to be the most northerly mainland village. After a most enjoyable afternoon in the company of George, we went to our digs at a Bed and Breakfast establishment by the station, where we freshened up. The local Police Chief Inspector had offered us a cell for the night in the police station, but we declined his kind offer.

A visit to a local hotel was made where we treated ourselves to a slap-up meal and sampled some of the local whisky.

After a good night's sleep, we were up at 05.00hours on Friday 19 April as we had to return to North Wales. The journey back home was a marathon.

We left Thurso at 05.59 hours, arrived in Inverness at 09.48 hours, departed at 10.10 hours, arrived in Crewe at 18.31 hours, departed Crewe at 19.26 hours and arrived in Holyhead at 21.43 hours, five minutes early. Richard had left the train at Chester. By the time I had arrived back in Holyhead I had clocked up well over 2,800 miles.

The late Ted Rowe, a retired Customs and Excise Officer from Holyhead, met me and took me home. On arrival, back home I celebrated my trip by opening a bottle of malt whisky which I had been saving for a special occasion.

Back at the office in Bangor, whilst dealing with the mail which I had received in connection with the 'Dash', Alison, the clerical officer handed me a letter from the safe. It contained two-hundred pounds in ten-pound notes, which had been sent in by a lady pensioner from Wrexham. This marvellous donation certainly put the 'icing on the cake' for me. I arranged to send her a nice bunch of flowers.

Several people asked me if I would do it again. The answer was 'yes'. Richard and I thoroughly enjoyed ourselves and the receptions we received from the British Rail Staff, fellow colleagues in the British Transport Police, the lifeboat service, and the public, was tremendous.

I raised £3500, which included a donation from the British Transport Police Federation. Later that year I went to the BTP Scottish Area Headquarters in Glasgow to present my cheque to Doctor Ian Oliver, Chief Constable of the Grampian Police.

Shortly afterwards, the RNLI arranged for me to perform a local presentation at Holyhead. A presentation cheque was arranged for a ceremony at Holyhead lifeboat station followed by a buffet at the Holyhead Sailing Club, which the force very kindly sponsored. An invitation was extended to the Chief Constable, but he was unable to attend. He was represented by Mr. Coles the Deputy Chief Constable.

Figure 11 Bill handing over the sponsorship money raised from the 'Rail Dash' to BTP Deputy Chief Constable Ted Coles

Superintendent Tom Baker, from Manchester, Chief Inspector Mick Griffin from Liverpool, Acting Inspector 'Mac' McMullen from Crewe, PCs Doug Worster and Keith Roberts from Bangor along with Chief Superintendent Larry Davies from the North Wales Police came to the ceremony, which was hosted by the Holyhead lifeboat crew and the ladies of the Holyhead and District Ladies Lifeboat Guild. The late John Parry the Honorary Secretary of Holyhead lifeboat station then arranged for the invited guests to have a trip in the lifeboat.

Figure 12 Bill and PC Doug Worster on the Holyhead Lifeboat following the presentation of Bill's sponsorship money

CHAPTER 19

THE BANGOR YEARS APRIL 1991 – JUNE 1993

Suspected of being a terrorist. Being certified at long last!

Recovering from the Rail Dash, it was back to work dealing with the paperwork that had accumulated in my absence. The usual train patrols and meetings occupied me for the next couple of months. Throughout the force I became known as 'Bangor Bill'.

Figure 13 Bill on duty at Llandudno Junction in connection with a steam special

As you will read in the chapters of this book, regular training was undertaken to prepare for a train crash. Some of these exercises were held in sidings or a tabletop version. However, the management of the North Wales Fire and Rescue Service approached British Rail requesting to do an exercise with their staff. British Rail found a suitable day and location, which was one Sunday morning at Llysfaen, near to Old Colwyn, on the main line, when it was closed for maintenance. It was also agreed that they could use a passenger carriage that was due to be scrapped soon. On the day of the exercise, I and a couple of officers were on duty at the scene to stop any onlookers coming too close.

The exercise commenced with the Fire and Rescue service arriving at the scene on the 'blues and twos'. To make it look realistic they broke down the post and wire boundary fencing at the lineside, which had only been erected about two weeks previously.

Once inside the coach, to continue with their realism they 'went to town' with their equipment smashing side panels, doors, and windows. They were only supposed to carry out the minimum amount of damage. At the end of the exercise the carriage was unable to be moved due to the extensive damage caused. It was sometime later in the day that it was moved and taken to Holyhead where it was scrapped on site. I believe that the North Wales Fire and Rescue Service ended up with a large bill for the repair of the fence and other associated costs.

I had reports on Monday 8 July 1991 of children walking along the Britannia Bridge, which connects the mainland to the Isle of Anglesey. A visit to the area proved negative.

More reports of trespass came in on Wednesday 10 July 1991 of children walking across the main North Wales Coast Line at Maesgeirchen on the outskirts of Bangor. Area visited two local children reported for trespass. They were later cautioned for the offence.

It was back to school on Thursday 11 July 1991, the Anglesey Sub-Division of the North Wales Police had organised an 'inter-schools', 'It's a Knockout' competition at Ysgol David Hughes, Menai Bridge (David Hughes High School). This competition was organised to promote a better understanding between the police and pupils by giving them the opportunity to mix freely with police officers and hopefully learn a little about the work of a police officer. Approximately four hundred pupils between the ages of 11 and 16 from five high schools on the Isle of Anglesey attended.

The British Transport Police had a major involvement in the day. I exhibited a bi-lingual rail safety display. Our divisional incident vehicle attended and was staffed by two officers from Liverpool. A dog handler from Manchester provided a dog display. Also, myself and a female police officer acted as judges for the actual competitions. Despite the appalling weather, the day proved a success in its intentions, with all our displays proving extremely popular.

Following the competition, I received a nice letter of appreciation from Chief Superintendent Larry Davies, the Divisional Commander, for the North Wales Police, Caernarfon, thanking us for our involvement in the day. This was followed by a letter from Chief Superintendent Geoff Griffiths, Divisional Commander, BTP Manchester, thanking the officers involved for ensuring that the safety message was sold to our communities in person.

The lives of a train driver and his passengers were put in danger on Sunday 14 July 1991, by stone-throwing teenagers. The driver of a Holyhead to London Inter-City train spotted the youths between Llanddulas and Gwrych Castle throwing stones at his train, although little damage was done, he halted the train at Abergele to report the incident. By the time we arrived at the scene the offenders had decamped. Enquiries in the area proved negative as the holidaymakers were beginning to arrive at the holiday parks in the area. With an increase in the population at this time of year it was always difficult to trace offenders.

One afternoon towards the end of July 1991, PC Doug Worster and myself were called to the derelict crossing keeper's house at Penrhyndeudraeth, on the Cambrian Coast Railway Line, as a resident nearby had reason to believe that there were squatters on the premises.

On arrival we found no such evidence except for a few broken wooden boards across the windows, which we arranged to have boarded up.

We went to see the complainants, whose house overlooked the estuary of the Afon Glaslyn (River Glaslyn) and over to Portmeirion, the ornate Italian village, where the original series of *'The Prisoner'* was filmed. I recall it being a very warm day and we were invited to take tea and cake with the residents of the house, in the garden. I said to Doug "Do you feel guilty about taking tea and cake whilst our colleagues on the London Underground are chasing after robbers?" He said "No sarge, more tea?"

Construction of the two Conwy A55 Expressway tunnels costing £190 million to build, commenced in 1986 and were to be opened by Her Majesty the Queen on 25 October 1991. Her Majesty was due to arrive at Llandudno Junction station by Royal Train. Prior to the opening an Operational Order for the day had to be prepared and work on this began in September 1991. Myself and Acting Inspector 'Mac' Mullen from Crewe visited the area, in plain clothes, in early September to begin the preliminary work. 'Mac' thought it would be a good idea if we went onto the ramparts of Conwy Castle to get a 'birds eye' view of the railway line, which passes by the castle and surrounding area. We went to the entrance gate and 'Mac' told them in his Northern Ireland accent, who we were, warrant cards were produced and the reason we wanted to visit the castle without payment. The cashier on the desk at the gate let us in. We both climbed up to the ramparts. As we were drawing up our plans for the order we were approached by two North Wales Police officers who asked who we were and what we were doing at the castle. We quickly told them who we were and what our business was. It transpired that the cashier had become suspicious of us, and thought we were terrorists especially with 'Mac's' accent. On the way out the cashier did apologise to us, I told her that it was better to be safe than sorry.

When I first arrived in Holyhead in 1985, the nearest decent supermarket was in Llandudno over forty miles away. A few years later a national chain opened a branch in Bangor, near to the railway station, on the site of the old Caernarfon and Anglesey Hospital. Shirley and I used this one. On Thursday 7 November 1991 at 17.40 hours after completing my tour of duty, I met Shirley from the Holyhead train and we went to do our monthly shopping. Whilst I was in the Supermarket my pager went off requesting me to contact Area Headquarters urgently. I made contact and I was informed that a lorry driver had been killed on a level crossing on the Cambrian Coast Railway Line. I took Shirley to the station with some of the shopping for her to catch a train back home, whilst I carried onto to Minffordd between Porthmadog and Penrhyndeudraeth.

At around 17.50 hours that evening, a two car Sprinter 150 unit was travelling at about 40 mph from Machynlleth to Pwllheli with ten passengers on board, when it struck a thirty-tonne lorry laden with granite waste from the Wimpey Asphalt's Minffordd granite quarry, near to Penrhyndeudraeth, which was being driven by an employee from Caernarfon over the private crossing.

The crossing was normally controlled by barriers operated by the quarry staff. The cab of the lorry was sliced in two and dragged along the railway track for twenty yards ending on top of a concrete wall.

The lorry's engine dropped off on the side of the track and metal parts from the mangled cab were still lying on the track for around two hours. The train driver escaped injury, despite being only inches from the impact, which caused damage to the front of the train, with one piece of metal ripped away. The lorry driver's body was recovered from the cab and he was certified dead by a local doctor. A young boy on board the train suffered a slight bump on his head in the impact.

Following the incident, DC Tom Brookshaw from BTP Crewe was assigned to the case and we commenced further enquiries. Following the completion of our enquiries, a week later a quarry worker was charged with manslaughter and he subsequently appeared at Caernarfon Crown Court, where he was suitably dealt with.

In 1991 the force underwent a major reorganisation. Divisions were being replaced by Areas and police offices would be designated as police stations and the person in charge at the police station would be known as an 'Officer in Charge'. All those in charge of a police station had to apply for our jobs. On the 6 December 1991 I was informed that I was successful in retaining Bangor and that I would become the 'Officer in Charge' with effect from the 5 April 1992.

Originally Colwyn Bay railway station had four platforms. Due to the remodelling of the station in the 1980s two of the platforms were closed, one being swept away completely. The old Platform Four was renamed Platform Three and turned into a shopping complex, which included a model shop and other shops and a café bar and restaurant in an old railway carriage. At the head of the carriage was an old industrial steam locomotive. I was not too happy about the café bar and restaurant arrangement as this woud be open late at night, well into the early hours at the weekends. I could foresee trouble from the local youths, with trespass and disorder. I made this known to my superiors and others concerned. My protestations were ignored. But I was later proved right when it was open late on Friday and Saturday nights, we had reports of people running across the main line, which is on a sharp curve. Also, there were drink related offences in the premises. Having to provide officers here was a drain on my resources. Security officers were employed. The complex did not last too long and was boarded up.

On 2 January 1992 British Rail announced a major campaign to stop North West and North Wales schoolchildren and others from vandalising the railway and putting lives at risk. At that time trespass and vandalism was costing British Rail nationally in the region of £40m. A special committee on Trespass and Vandalism was set up by the British Railways Board. New child safety and anti-vandal educational packs were produced to be used as part of the national curriculum. I was to be involved fully in this campaign in North Wales.

Trespass and vandalism were no exception in North Wales. Being a popular tourist destination, it attracts people from all over England, Wales, Scotland and indeed the world. It is said that the largest concentration of caravans and chalets in Europe, are located between Colwyn Bay and Prestatyn. The good people of the Lincolnshire coast may contest this. It is reputed that there are over thirteen-thousand of them and with the population changing weekly/fortnightly we could have an extra fifty-two-thousand visitors in the area. Catching miscreants was difficult, as a lot of them were on holiday from out of the area.

Shortly after the campaign was launched, I walked along about four miles of railway line between Rhyl and Colwyn Bay with Alan Bullimore the local Traffic Manager, identifying locations as to where palisade fencing should be erected. It was great spending other people's money! I am pleased to say that my suggestions were taken up by the powers that be.

I remember in early 1992 escorting the overnight 'Irish Mail' train from Holyhead to London Euston, which was full of Irish based football supporters for a match in Wembley. On arrival in London, we were taken to the Bonnington Hotel in Holborn where we stayed the rest of the day until the evening when we had dinner and then returned with the supporters on the 'Irish Mail' train back to Holyhead. The accommodation was far superior to what I had experienced previously with the force.

Another problem that I faced, was that of luggage thefts from trains and station platforms. With the aid of CID officers assisting myself and my officers working in plain clothes, and high-profile uniformed patrols, we mounted an operation and were successful in reducing the thefts and arresting the culprits.

In 1992 my establishment was increased by fifty per cent. I received the good news that I was to have two more constables on my establishment. One was a probationer and the other was a transferee from another area.

One morning, in the early spring of 1992, I was preparing to go out on train patrols when there was a knock at the door, it was a member of the railway permanent way staff who handed me a large green leaf. I immediately recognised it as a cannabis leaf. I asked him where he had got it from, and he informed me that he found it with some others on the embankment of the mainland side near to the Britannia Bridge.

I took him to the scene, and I discovered that there were six growbags each containing three cannabis plants in a polytunnel, well hidden in the bushes. I contacted our CID in Chester and the late DC Gordon Roberts came up and kept observations. The culprits believed to be from the university were never caught despite enquiries in the area and with the local drug squad.

A few weeks later the local Permanent Way Supervisor drew my attention to six large packages each containing a brown substance, on the steps leading to the booking office boiler room at Bangor railway station. I went over, and my initial thoughts were that the contents were cannabis or some other similar drug. After enquiries it turned out that the contents were crushed dates from Africa.

The 5 April 1992 arrived, and I officially became the 'Officer in Charge' (OIC) at Bangor. The area I had to cover was reduced somewhat in size. On the North Wales Coast Line, I only covered to Rhyl, still retaining the Llandudno to Blaenau Ffestiniog line. On the Cambrian Coast Line, I only covered the portion between Pwllheli and Porthmadog. I also became a member of the North West Area Management Team, which meant I had to attend monthly meetings in Manchester with all of the other OICs and BTP senior management of the area.

Between May and September in 1992 when the main summer timetable was in operation, several additional trains ran along the North Wales Coast Line and the Cambrian Coast Line. One such train on the Cambrian Coast Line was 'The Snowdonian', which ran from London Euston to Pwllheli via Shrewsbury.

It was locomotive hauled, usually by a pair of class 37 diesel locomotives. This train attracted several so-called railway enthusiasts who travelled all the way to Pwllheli and back. Sometimes their members were in excess of twenty and their behaviour left a lot to be desired. Over the weeks the train ran, it required police officers to travel on it. The duties were shared between BTP officers from Shrewsbury, Bangor, Crewe, and Liverpool.

I was fortunate enough to have the officers from the Mobile Support Unit (MSU) at Liverpool to assist me on the train on Saturday 6 June 1992. We reported eight youths for various offences. One youth from Oxfordshire was reported for using offensive language in front of women and children. Another youth from Stockport admitted waving a condom in front of a young girl, stating that it was for a bit of fun. A youth from Cumbria was reported for running up and down the train waving a condom embarrassing the other passengers. One 18-year-old youth from Buckinghamshire ran up and down the train and on the platform at Criccieth with a water filled condom. A youth from Derbyshire who dropped a water filled bottle onto the tracks, with the words '*Cambrian Bomb*' written on the side, whilst the train was moving, using offensive language, and behaving in an offensive manner was reported. Others were reported for disorderly conduct.

A prosecution file was submitted to the Chief Inspector at Liverpool and proceedings were authorised under the Byelaws. I laid the Informations and Summonses before the Magistrates' Clerk at Caernarfon, for the offenders to appear at Porthmadog Magistrates' Court. By the time I arrived back at the office in Bangor there was a message requesting me to ring the Magistrates' Clerk at Caernarfon. He asked me all sorts of questions about the punishments under the Byelaws. I explained to him what they were. He was so incensed with their behaviour, that he wanted to ask the Magistrates to send them to jail. At a subsequent court appearance, the youths were all fined.

A few weeks later, a different set of so-called enthusiasts left the train at Pwllheli and went to the local Co-op supermarket and purchased cartons of double cream. On the return journey they ran up and down the train smearing the cream on the windows of the carriages and cushions of the seats. I could not comprehend their mentality for doing this–what a waste of cream. They were reported and subsequently appeared before the Magistrates where they were fined.

The penultimate train of the day along the North Wales Coast Line to Holyhead was the Scarborough to Holyhead train and was usually hauled by a class 45 diesel locomotive, which attracted several so-called enthusiasts. This train also conveyed local youths who had been to the night club in Bangor. Sometimes disorder would break out between the two groups. Again, a police presence was required on the train. One occasion we caught a so-called train spotter ripping out a toilet pan from a carriage toilet and throwing it out of the window onto the Britannia Bridge. He was arrested. At Holyhead police station where he was interviewed it transpired that he was a locomotive driver from the south of England. When asked what he thought, if it had gone through a window of a train that he was driving. He just shrugged his shoulders and said, "So what". What an attitude to have. He was subsequently dealt with at Court. I believe he received the sack from his job.

My two new officers did not last too long at Bangor. The probationer who was from South Wales requested a transfer to Cardiff, as he had baby back home with a heart problem. The request was refused, so he resigned. The transferee from another area went on long term sick. So, I was back to two operational officers. Not much had changed.

One Saturday afternoon PC Doug Worster and myself were on duty in the downstairs office at Bangor, which overlooked the car park. We had the rear door open and a car drew up and the driver alighted and asked us where the racecourse was. He was actually looking for Bangor on Dee racecourse. I told him that he was miles out and gave him suitable directions. He gave us a tip, which was a horse called 'Space Kate'. We passed this onto a member of the rail staff who was an avid racehorse fan. He went to the bookmakers to put a bet on. The horse was a non-runner. But a few weeks later it won at another racecourse at some decent odds.

A train driver escaped serious injuries when a rock about the size of a house brick shattered the outer windscreen of a 70 mph 125 Inter-City Express train, as it emerged from the tunnel entrance at Penmaenrhos near Colwyn Bay and was slowing down for the station stop at Colwyn Bay on Sunday 26 July 1992 at 20.05 hours. Hundreds of passengers had to leave the train at Llandudno Junction and had to wait for a replacement. I and my officers began an investigation into the incident. I remember describing the offenders to the local press as 'Mindless Morons'.

Talking of morons, shortly after this incident at around 23.20 hours on a date I cannot remember, a 125 Inter-City train from London Euston to Holyhead travelling at 40 mph struck a builder's wheelbarrow and a forty pound bag of sand which had been left on the tracks on the Britannia Bridge, causing the brake pipe of the leading power car to fracture. The barrow was carried one hundred yards along the line and crushed to around eighteen inches square. Subsequent trains were delayed until 04.00 hours. Again, I described the offenders as 'Mindless Morons', to the press.

With the school holidays beginning and being conscious of the above incidents I put out a general warning about the dangers of the railways in the local papers.

In late August 1992 at about 20.30 hours, a group of five or six children narrowly missed being hit by a train as they crossed a railway track at the Foryd Bridge, Rhyl. The train driver applied the emergency brakes and the train stopped. The driver of the train thought he had hit one of them, as they were only a matter of inches away from the train. An immediate search of the area proved negative. Subsequent enquiries also proved negative.

During the month of September 1992, I was approached by the Principal of Hillgrove, Independent School, Ffriddoedd Road, Bangor, to see if I could attend a railway themed evening that the school were holding during the evening of 15 October 1992. Prior to the evening, I arranged, for the pupils to design a Rail Safety Poster for a competition and arranged with Ben Davies the station manager at Bangor to provide some prizes, such as book tokens and free rail tickets for the winners, in the various age groups. I also arranged for rail safety goody bags from the force to be given to all the pupils.

The week before the evening I took pupils from the junior forms to Llandudno Junction by train for an educational visit. My efforts were rewarded with a nice letter of appreciation from Mr. Jim Porter, Principal of the School.

Being the Sergeant in Charge at Bangor, apart from my normal duties I was on call as well. In early September 1992 I was due to take a well-earned Saturday off as a rest day, but a few days before, I was contacted by Lew Baxter, a freelance Journalist who had been commissioned by Regional Railways to write an article on the British Transport Police for their in-house newspaper 'FOCUS North West'. Lew had chosen my rare Saturday off to come to Bangor to write his article.

Figure 14 Bill briefing PC Doug Worster at Bangor Station

The finished article appeared in the October 1992 edition of 'FOCUS North West'.

He entitled it – **'Incident at Bangor! With the Thin Blue Line'**

'Minutes after settling down to talk about the problems of covering an area about 2000, square miles, winding mostly along the remote North Wales coast, flanked by the mountains of Snowdonia and across Anglesey, with a tiny squad of five officers, Sergeant Bill Rogerson was grabbing for his hat after a trilling telephone call alerted him to trouble on a train arriving from Holyhead.

Several drunken youths were upsetting passengers, flouting the rules on smoking, generally making a nuisance of themselves and needed ejecting. Further down the line an unidentified Land Rover was reported to have made a death-defying dash across a level crossing, missing an oncoming 158 express by inches.

And this was a supposedly quiet Saturday afternoon at his base in Bangor Station, indeed Bill Rogerson had only popped into the office on his day off, to chat to 'FOCUS' about running one of BT Police's rural outposts.

Bill's team really do fit the description of the Thin Blue Line rather well, with the resources stretched to the limit. In fact, at present he's down to a compliment of three, including himself, due to sickness and a vacancy.

"People assume because we are mostly rural that we don't have any problems. But that is far from the truth", he explained. "Of course, we're not like Manchester or Liverpool or the large conurbations but we certainly have our share of incidents".

In fact, he reveals, the total number of reported incidents last year on his patch was close to sixty and that, he stresses is only scratching the surface. "Apart from the early morning boat train, Rhyl has a big population and between the town and Abergele there is the largest assembly of holiday caravans in Europe, something like 13,000. During the season we do have to be on our toes. Trespass is a big problem, for wherever you go along the North Wales coast to get to the sea people have to cross the railway line".

His main problem areas include Abergele and Rhyl but there's also a sharp watch kept at Holyhead, Colwyn Bay, Bangor and, surprisingly the genteel sea-side town of Llandudno. Offences range from trespass, stone throwing – youngsters pitching rocks at high speed trains is one of his particular nightmares – vandalism and luggage theft.

Bill's been in charge at Bangor for six years and admits he relies heavily on support from railway employees tipping him off about incidents and back up from the local community and police forces.

He's now helped set up a community based public forum which will examine the dangers and problems of running a railway in the area and suggest ways to make it safer.

It's all part of increasing the profile of the Force in the public imagination. "There are still many who don't know who we are and when they see a uniformed officer on board a train or at a station think the worst is happening", he remarked.

"The Forum programme is to publicise what we do and seek assistance from the community in setting objectives which will benefit everyone".

Bill explains that apart from himself as chairman, members will include representatives of the TUCC, the local press, the Station Manager and trade union representatives from the TSSA and ASLEF.

The last attack on a member of the public was several months ago and the culprits were quickly apprehended and charged. But only weeks later constable Keith Roberts, one of Bill's team at Bangor was assaulted within the station confines after arresting a drunk one evening for disturbing the peace.

Keith takes up the tale "I'd brought in the man when he suddenly went berserk and began kicking, me wildly. I was on my own and taken completely off guard. Fortunately I managed to get a call out to the North Wales Police, and they came to my aid to suppress this violent character".

This isn't a common occurrence, admitted a relieved Bill Rogerson, but highlights the dangers of such limited resources. "That's why we need the backing of the local community", he added.

One of Bill's main targets has been to reduce luggage thefts, a frequent problem on the 158's speeding along the route. "We carried out a programme of high-profile policing on trains earlier this year and the number of incidents has fallen enormously".

But he also has the logistical problem of controlling a short twelve miles stretch of line from Pwllheli to Barmouth which serves the huge Butlins Holiday Camp.

On the map it's a short 35 miles hop from Bangor by car, but the route crosses narrow twisting mountain roads that hinder the speed. "It's another example of how our resources are stretched", he went on. "Really all we can do is maintain 'fire-brigade' policing in a way, which is far from satisfactory".

Meanwhile on the platform at Bangor, Bill, the two on duty constables Keith Roberts and Doug Worster had sorted out the problem of the drunks – not without a little difficulty, it must be said.

There was, though, a brighter note to the end of the day. A distraught passenger had reported losing his wallet, crammed with credit cards and cash, on a train heading to Anglesey. Keith Roberts came striding down the platform wielding it triumphantly above his head after finding it down the side of a seat.

"It's not all rough and tumble", he declared with a huge grin.'

Figure 15 Bill with PC Doug Worster and PC Keith Roberts in the police station at Bangor

Figure 16 Bill takes a moment from his paperwork to look at the camera

Following the launch of the safety campaign earlier in the year, the force established School Liaison Officers, (SLO) throughout the force area to assist in promoting the dangers of the railway. These officers would be working full time in their duties and would be only used for other operational duties in an emergency. The force drew up a policy in respect of the officers. One of the policies was that they had to undergo a weekend's assessment at Tadworth. If they were successful, then they had to undergo a week's intensive training at Tadworth to be suitably qualified.

I successfully applied for a Child Liaison Officer's post to be based at Bangor, which would take the pressure off me as I had been visiting schools and other establishments for the last thirteen years on a part time basis.

One of my officers at Bangor applied for the post and failed his weekend's assessment at Tadworth. The post was advertised in General Orders, but no one applied for the post, so I carried on visiting schools. Over the years I was very well received and was being booked by headteachers twelve months ahead to address new intakes of pupils.

The powers that be in the force realised from my annual appraisals and letters of appreciation that I was visiting the schools but was not qualified under the force's rigid policy. I was told to stop my visits.

A difficult dilemma arose, there was no one available to visit the schools which was having an adverse effect on our credibility which I had built up over the years.

Superintendent Mick Griffin, Support Services, Area Headquarters, Manchester, successfully applied to the Assistant Chief Constable (Support Services) at Force Headquarters for a relaxation in the rules and for me to carry on visiting schools until such time a suitably qualified officer was in place. However, there were still no takers for the post.

I received a memorandum on 7 December 1992, from Superintendent Colin Thomas Force Training Officer at Tadworth, that he was running a school's assessment centre at Tadworth between Friday 8 January 1993 and Sunday 10 January 1993 primarily for London Underground officers but could find spaces for myself and an officer from the Midlands Area.

Between Friday 8 January 1993 and Sunday 10 January 1993, I duly attended the assessment for a Schools Liaison Officer. There was a trainer from the British Transport Police, a retired headteacher and a psychologist. It was a very, very demanding three days. I passed with flying colours. I passed the subsequent Child Liaison Officer's, weeklong course. I received my certificate. One senior officer commented that after several years, 'I had been certified at long last'!

Figure 17 Bill and colleagues performing a man management task on the School liaison course at Tadworth

In January 1993, to assist with combating trespass and vandalism on the railway in the North Wales area, the late Peter Hicks, the owner of a model shop on the refurbished Platform Three complex at Colwyn Bay railway station built a portable '00'-gauge model railway, fraught with miniature safety hazards, to be used by the force as a teaching aid during school visits and exhibitions. The local area works department at Bangor made a carrying case for the model.

I believe it was at the beginning of 1993, that Alison Jones, the clerical officer approached me and stated she and would like to take six months leave of absence whilst she and her boyfriend travelled around India and the Himalayas. This was granted by the force, who sent me a temporary replacement. Whilst she was in India a couple of coincidences occurred. Sadly, their passports were stolen, and they went to the British Embassy in Delhi to obtain new ones. The clerk who dealt with them was from Four Mile Bridge, near Holyhead. The second coincidence was whilst they were in the Himalayas. They were sat down having something to eat at the side of a path and were joined by another couple. It transpired that the couple were from Bangor and had heard about yours truly through a cousin of theirs who worked for the railway in Bangor.

During the months between January and March 1993 there was an upsurge of crime on Rhyl railway station, particularly in the late evenings. I was not aware of this until I was contacted by a local town councillor. The railway staff were reluctant to report these crimes. Following her complaint, I stepped up patrols at the station and arranged for a full crime prevention survey to be carried out. I also held an exhibition to advise people how to travel safely. Later in the year the whole station was redeveloped with a lot of improvements made.

St David's Day, Monday 1 March 1993 at 08.10 hours, a security officer from 'Arm-a-Guard' was walking across the footbridge from the car park to the booking office at Llandudno Junction railway station, with a quantity of money in a secure box, when he was rugby-tackled from behind. He was then slammed against the bridge's steel girders before being pushed to the ground. The attacker tried ripping the cash box from the guard's hands, and when he refused to let go of the box, he was kicked in the chest and showered with abuse. The guard then fought with the assailant, swinging the heavy cash box at the attacker. At this point two youths ran onto the bridge from the station platforms, and the startled raider fled empty handed. The attacker is reported to have run from the station to the pub car park opposite. The guard received bruising to his ribs. Enquiries were commenced in conjunction with the local police CID.

The following week, I arranged with Crimestoppers Wales to make a reconstruction of the incident. I played the part of the Security Guard; a member of the railway staff played the part of the assailant and my son along with another member of the railway staff played the part of the two youths. The reconstruction was shown on Welsh television for a week. Despite this and extensive local media coverage the assailant was never caught.

In the summer of 1993 Regional Railways erected a new phonetic sign at Llanfair. P.G., railway station, Anglesey, to assist visitors in pronouncing the station name which in its entirety consists of fifty seven letters. I was present at the launch of the sign along with Ben Davies the local Station Manager and the local Girl Guides.

Due to the large volume of holidaymakers travelling by train into North Wales and going onto Ireland we suffered spates of luggage thefts from the trains to and from Holyhead. In 1993 we relaunched a *'Travelsafe'* campaign and issued leaflets to passengers incorporating the safest way to travel by train particularly in the dark winter months and to be extra vigilant over their luggage.

During the period between January and June 1993, two Probationary constables, albeit at separate times, PC Sean Morgan and PC Sean Braithwaite were allocated to Bangor. PC Doug Worster became their tutor Constable and he made a fantastic job of training them.

One morning in the early summer of 1993, I attended a meeting at Tygwyn level crossing on the Cambrian Coast Railway Line. British Rail, were going to upgrade the crossing and there were representatives from British Rail, the local council, the Welsh Office and the local North Wales Police officer. As we were in discussions, the level crossing began to close for an oncoming train, with the activation of the red alternating flashing lights and the descent of the barriers. At this juncture a local farmer on his tractor came along the road, waved at us, and shouted some words of greetings in Welsh, completely ignoring the closure procedure of the crossing. We all looked at each other in total amazement. After the train had cleared the crossing myself and the North Wales police officer went on the 'blues and twos' after the farmer. We caught up with him further along the road. I interviewed him and it was the first time in my career that I had given a verbal 'Notice of Intended Prosecution' (NIP) under the Road Traffic Act 1972, but I remembered the wording from my training days. Normally an 'NIP' would be issued in writing. He was later convicted at court and fined with his licence endorsed.

CHAPTER 20

THE BANGOR YEARS - A MEMORABLE JULY 1993

Going Dutch and visiting the Palace

For a variety of reasons, July 1993 was one of the most memorable months of my life. Tuesday 6 July 1993 at 13.55 hours saw me flying from Manchester Airport for a six-day visit to a friend of mine, who was the equivalent of a British police constable in the Nederlanse Spoorweg Polite (Dutch Transport Police).

I first met Paul De-Vette and his then wife Sonya (who originated from Manchester), one evening in August 1992 whilst I was on patrol of an early evening train between Bangor and Holyhead. Paul and Sonya joined the train at Llanfairpwll (The station with the longest name) He made himself known to me. An immediate friendship was struck up. We began exchanging letters.

In October 1992 Paul's then Chief Superintendent, Hans Hattink who was a friend of Geoff Griffiths, Area Commander, British Transport Police, North Western Area, came to Manchester and addressed the British Transport Police, Area Management Team, of which I was a member, on the work of the Nederlanse Spoorweg Polite. I was extremely impressed by what Hans had to say. (Shortly after this meeting Hans retired and came back as a civilian employee).

Early in 1993, Paul, after speaking to his superior officers, invited me to Amsterdam to study the working of his force. Arrangements were put in motion for the trip.

On arrival at Schiphol Airport, Amsterdam, I was met by a colleague of Paul's, who informed me that Paul had been unable to meet me personally as he had been injured (not seriously, thankfully) whilst arresting a German citizen for evading his train fare - a common occurrence in both in the Netherlands and Britain.

As Paul's colleague whisked me through the heavy commuter traffic of Amsterdam, he informed me that he had a Bordeaux Dog as a pet, which was the nephew of 'Hooch', from the film 'Turner and Hooch'.

On arrival at Amsterdam Centraal railway station, I was taken to the police bureau, which was in temporary accommodation, whilst their permanent accommodation was being refurbished. I was made welcome by the duty Sergeant, who gave me a welcome cup of coffee. A short while later I met Paul who was busy preparing a file in respect of his arrest. I then met more of Paul's colleagues.

Once Paul had completed his prosecution file, he signed off duty and we went to his house in Almere, on a Sneltrain, which was a fast commuter train. Holland's railway system is one of the world's most efficient and most extensive in the world.

Approximately fourteen million people were living in this very densely populated country at the time of my visit.

The train we were on was about twelve months old, a four-coach double-decker and was hauled by a class 1700 locomotive. Almere station was around six years old. The city itself is a new one, situated on reclaimed land from the sea, north of Amsterdam.

Paul lived approximately two miles from Almere Centraal Station. The quickest way to the station from his house was by bicycle. Paul then presented me with a mountain bike for the duration of my stay. A mountain bike in Holland, that is a novel idea! Our force plaques were also exchanged.

The next day, Wednesday 7 July 1993, we set off from Paul's house by bike at 08.00 hours to catch the 08.22 hours train to Amsterdam. I stopped at a couple of junctions to let the cars go by. Paul informed me that the cyclists have preference on the road over the car driver.

We left our bicycles in the unmanned police bureau (The bureau at Almere was currently used by Amsterdam officers when they are on patrol or there is a special event on). The train to Amsterdam was right on time and soon whisked us into the Netherlands most exciting and lively city.

On arrival at Amsterdam, we changed trains for a semi-fast service to Utrecht. On arrival at Utrecht, we went to the Information Room of the Spoorweg Polite, which was situated in the headquarters building of the Dutch Railways. The Information Room covered the whole of the country.

The duty Inspector gave me a very thorough insight into the force computer and communications systems. Hardly any paper to be seen at all. After spending an interesting ninety-minutes in the Information Room I was given a guided tour of the Dutch Railways Control Room. They were gradually changing over to computers. Even so, their operations were still extremely efficient.

We then had time for lunch and time for a little sightseeing in Utrecht before making our way back to Amsterdam. We alighted at Amsterdam Amstel railway station and visited the shooting range of the Spoorweg Polite. All their officers are armed. I was lucky enough to be shown around the range and to witness some officers who were undergoing their regular six-weekly training.

The Sergeant in Charge asked if I had ever shot a gun before. I told him only a couple of air rifles at the fairgrounds in Blackpool and Ffestiniog when I was still at school.

He handed me a standard police issue pistol, loaded with six rounds, and gave me a set of ear defenders. I took aim at the target. After discharging the rounds, we walked over to the target only to find that it was untouched by the bullets.

I followed his eyes down to the floor and lo and behold I had splintered the skirting board. He laughed and said, "When the people of Amsterdam see you, they will climb up the lamp posts where they will be safe!"

Figure 18 Bill with the Firearms instructor examining the skirting board on the shooting range at Amsterdam Amstel Station

After leaving the shooting range we then went to the police bureau on Amsterdam Centraal Station, where I was given a full guided tour of the bureau. After the tour, I was to join the late-turn shift (15.00 hours to 23.00 hours) in full British police uniform. I was introduced to the shift, of one Sergeant and five patrol officers. The Sergeant commenced his briefing, during which coffee and gateaux was served. The Chief Superintendent joined us for part of the briefing. I was then allowed to accompany Paul on his patrol of the station. At 15.20 hours, I set foot on to Platform One and almost immediately heads started turning in my direction and I soon became the centre of attraction. All was quiet until 15.30 hours when an American couple approached us and complained that their camera had been stolen. A search of the station and likely hiding places proved negative.

Whilst I was in the main subway an English lady came up to me and asked for directions to a platform. Looking at the signs, I was able to direct her to where she wanted to go. She thanked me and walked away, stopping suddenly, looking round in my direction, with a very puzzled look on her face, shaking her head from side to side and carried on walking. I knew what she was thinking "I've just spoken to an English police officer in Amsterdam!"

We patrolled the station subways and platforms for a short while. Later we patrolled an international express whilst it was in the station. Paul was then called back to the bureau to complete more reports in respect of his arrest the previous day. I spoke to some of his other colleagues regarding the work of the British Transport Police, all spoke perfect English.

At 17.00 hours after the day shift had completed their tour of duty, Paul and I went on a mobile patrol around the suburban stations of Amsterdam. Observations were kept for a short while on the level crossing at Diemen.

This crossing is notorious for motorists ignoring the red flashing warning lights and barriers. No offenders were detected. A patrol was carried out of the nearby carriage sidings. Upon returning to Centraal station, a radio message was received to the effect that two youths had stolen a bag from a tourist. A search of the surrounding streets proved negative. However, two officers later arrested the suspects on the station.

Figure 19 Bill with Officer Paul De-Vette of the Nederlanse Spoorweg Polite at Amsterdam Centraal Station on the occasion of Bill's visit

After a short meal break, another foot patrol of the station was carried out. Again, heads were turned. We then patrolled a local train to an ultra-modern station called Duivendrecht. This station was only opened in May of 1993 and was the show case of the Dutch Railways. A visit to the unstaffed police bureau there was made. We then patrolled a local train to Schiphol Airport. A patrol of the airport station and the concourse of the airport was made before we returned to Amsterdam Centraal on an Inter-City train.

On arrival back at Amsterdam Centraal another short patrol was undertaken before partaking of a cup of coffee in the bureau. We finally completed our tour of duty and headed out to Almere for a well-earned beer or two at Paul's house.

Early on Thursday morning, saw me on the mountain bike once again. From Almere station, we travelled out to a village called Maarn, via Amsterdam and Utrecht. The dog training school of the Spoorweg Polite is situated at the old railway station approximately fifteen minutes' walk from the new station. The school is also surrounded by beautiful woodlands and makes an ideal location for training dogs. On arrival, we were given a full conducted tour of the school.

Two dog handlers and the Chief Instructor gave Paul and I a very entertaining two-hour demonstration, with their German Shepherd dogs. No other breed of dog was used at that time and they are only trained for criminal and search work. The training appeared to be the same as for the British Transport Police dogs, with one very noticeable exception, their dogs are also trained to catch criminals who make their getaways on bikes – most of the Dutch population own bicycles.

After lunch with the dog handlers, we returned to Amsterdam for an afternoon's sightseeing on the canals. After leaving the canal cruise I fancied a cup of coffee and a piece of cake. I saw a bar which looked friendly. Paul stated categorically that we were not going in. Yes, we could have a coffee and cake – cannabis cake. We would have walked in and floated out. We found somewhere else.

On Friday 9 July, we spent the day sightseeing in The Hauge, (De Haag) a city where the Dutch Parliament and Royal family are based. After the sightseeing, I was given a conducted tour of the police bureau of De Haag Centraal Station. This bureau had only been open for about three years.

Saturday 10 July 1993 was taken up with sightseeing in Amsterdam with Paul and Sonya visiting such sights as the Van Gough Museum, Anne Frank House, and other places of interest.

Sadly, on Sunday 11 July 1993 I had to leave the Netherlands. Little did I know that I would be returning in a few years' time. I was extremely impressed with the hospitality and friendliness of the Dutch, they are a very warm race, the work of the Nederlanse Spoorweg Polite and the British Transport Police is very similar in many respects. Such as, trespass, stone throwing, fare evasion, graffiti, luggage thefts. public order, burglaries, train obstructions, failing to comply with traffic signals at a level crossing, etc.

At the beginning of June 1993 whilst I was on annual leave at home, slaving away decorating the hallway of my house, the Postman delivered a large bundle of letters, a majority of which were the usual unsolicited 'Junk Mail'. However, one letter stood out, it was a large cream coloured envelope, bearing the crest of the Lord Chamberlain, Buckingham Palace and addressed to Shirley. Inside was an invitation card which bore the Royal Crest and Cypher in gold and proclaimed, 'The Lord Chamberlain is commanded by Her Majesty to invite Mr. & Mrs. William Rogerson, to a Garden Party at Buckingham Palace on Thursday 15 July 1993 from 4 pm to 6 pm.' A little bit of detective work revealed that the invitation was in recognition of our voluntary work for the Royal National Lifeboat Institution.

Shirley and I travelled down to London on Wednesday 14 July and stayed overnight. Prior to going to the Palace, we left our suitcase at the police station at Victoria station. We then had a walk through St James' Park. There were many Royal look-a-likes walking through the park. As we were walking along a pathway a person called out to me, "Bill!" I looked round and said "Walter". It was Walter Girdley and his wife Beat, who were on holiday in London. Walter was the Sergeant at Heysham during my time at Heysham.

At 15.00 hours on Thursday 15 July 1993 Shirley and I found ourselves outside the grand entrance to Buckingham Palace, where a photographer, arranged by Simon Lubin, the then Press and Public Relations Manager for the British Transport Police, took our photographs.

After the photographic session, we walked through the grand entrance into an inner courtyard where our personal tickets were surrendered, we then walked up a red carpeted staircase into a hallway. After a brief look at the fine paintings in the hallway we made our way via a large pair of open French windows on to a magnificent expanse of lawn. Two military bands were sited at different ends of the lawn, they took it in turn to play a continuous selection of music.

On the lawn, we joined thousands of other guests in a line to await the arrival of Her Majesty the Queen and other members of the Royal family. Promptly at 16.00 hours Her Majesty the Queen appeared on the terrace accompanied by His Royal Highness the Duke of Edinburgh and the late Diana, Princess of Wales. After the National Anthem had been played, Her Majesty the Queen stepped on to the lawn and walked along a line of guests.

Diana, The Princess of Wales, walked along the line that Shirley and I were in. She spoke to guests at random. We were not selected, but just content to be there and share in the atmosphere of the afternoon.

After the Royal party had made their way to their tea tent, Shirley and I went to a refreshment tent, which seemed to stretch for miles. At the tent, we sampled a selection of mouth-watering dainty sandwiches, strawberry tarts, other cakes and ice-cream. Tea and coffee along with iced drinks were available. All food and drink was served on bone china crockery.

After tea, we had a stroll around the magnificent gardens. People were there from all walks of life and from all over the world – office cleaners to senior police officers, tea ladies to lords.

Time was passing so quickly, so we made our way onto the terrace for one final look at the lawns and gardens. We were lucky enough to see Her Majesty the Queen and her party leave their tea tent and walk into the Palace.

At 18.00 hours, we left the Palace via the grand entrance, just in time to witness the changing of the guard. After the guard had changed, we left the Palace, taking with us memories of a most memorable and spectacular experience for us both. Little was I to know that I would be making two further trips to Buckingham Palace.

Upon departing Buckingham Palace, we made our way to Victoria station, collected our suitcase and then travelled to Ramsgate, for an overnight stay before attending the naming ceremony and dedication of the Mersey Class Lifeboat 'Her Majesty the Queen', on Friday 16 July 1993. Money for the Lifeboat was raised from the National Police Lifeboat Appeal. I had raised some funds via my 'Rail Dash' in 1991. In March of 1993 the Chief Constable of the British Transport Police, Desmond O'Brien, OBE, QPM had nominated me to represent the British Transport Police at the naming ceremony.

Her Majesty the Queen had graciously consented to the Lifeboat being named after her as a fortieth anniversary gift in connection with her accession, from the appeal steering committee on behalf of the police service. This honour had been received with pride and satisfaction by everyone associated with the police service, as it joined with the RNLI in the provision of a caring and compassionate service dedicated to the wellbeing of everybody both on land and at sea.

At 10.50 hours on Friday 16 July 1993 on what could only be described as a perfect summer's day, Shirley and I arrived at the ceremony site at Ramsgate Harbour. We took our seats to await the commencement of the actual ceremony at 11.30 hours. During the half-hour or so, we were entertained to a selection of music from the Kent Police Band.

At 11.30 hours prompt Her Majesty the Queen accompanied by His Royal Highness the Prince Philip, Duke of Edinburgh, arrived at the harbour and the National Anthem was played. Her Majesty and the Duke of Edinburgh were presented to selected guests. Lieutenant Commander Brian Miles, the then Director of the Royal National Lifeboat Institution, opened the proceedings. Doctor Ian Oliver QPM, Chief Constable of the Grampian Police and Chairman of the Police Lifeboat Appeal committee, presented a commemorative parchment to Her Majesty.

The parchment was inscribed as follows:

'To Her Majesty Queen Elizabeth 11 as a token of their continuing loyalty and to mark the fortieth anniversary of Her Majesty's Accession, the officers and staff of the United Kingdom constabularies are honoured by Her gracious permission to give the name for the RNLI Lifeboat 'Her Majesty the Queen' provided from funds raised by the National Police Lifeboat Appeal 1990-1992'.

Dr Ian Oliver then handed over the Lifeboat to the RNLI. Mr. Michael Vernon, the then Chairman of the RNLI accepted the Lifeboat on behalf of the Institution for use in the relief fleet.

This meant that the Lifeboat would visit many Lifeboat stations around the coast on active duty covering for those which had gone for overhaul. This would give police officers a chance to see the vessel when it was at a station near to them.

There followed a service of dedication which was conducted by the Venerable Michael Till, the then Archdeacon of Canterbury, after which Her Majesty named the Lifeboat. Mr. Michael Vernon then invited Her Majesty the Queen, accompanied by His Royal Highness, the Prince Philip, Duke of Edinburgh, to inspect the Lifeboat. After the inspection, Her Majesty attended the local yacht club for lunch.

Shirley and I, along with other fund raisers who came from the other police forces in Great Britain, attended a special buffet lunch, kindly provided by the Chairman of the Thanet District Council and the Ramsgate Royal Harbour Board, which was hosted by Mr. Ted Crew, Deputy Chief Constable of the Kent Police. The lunch gave Shirley and I the chance to have a talk with the other fund raisers.

Sadly, at 13.28 hours it was time for us to leave Ramsgate for the long journey back home to Holyhead. Again, the day was full of fond memories that will live with us forever. Little was I to know that I would be attending another ceremony involving the Lifeboat in a few years' time.

Upon my return to the office at Bangor on Monday 19 July 1993 I opened a letter which stated that I had qualified for the Police Long Service and Good Conduct Medal, for twenty-two years' service with the British Transport Police.

Indeed, a memorable July.

CHAPTER 21

THE BANGOR YEARS SEPTEMBER 1993 – DECEMBER 1994

A surprise letter from the office of the Prime Minister

Shirley and I attended the Euston Plaza Hotel, Upper Woburn Place, London WC1 on Monday 13 September 1993 for the presentation of my Police Long Service and Good Conduct Medal, by Mr. Trefor Morris CBE, QPM, CBIM, Her Majesty's Chief Inspector of Constabulary. The medal is presented to officers of the British Police Service who have rendered long and meritorious service as members of the police forces of the United Kingdom for at least twenty-two years.

The award is in enpro-nickel, in the form of a circular medal, bearing on the obverse the Crowned Effigy of the Sovereign and on the reverse the inscription, 'For exemplary Police Service' with the design showing the figure of Justice holding, with outstretched hand, an emblem of laurel, thus honouring the forces of law and order.

The medal is to be worn on the left side suspended from a ribbon one and a quarter inches in width, which shall be in colour dark blue with, on either side, a white stripe on which is superimposed a narrow stripe of dark blue.

In 1986, the then Chairman of the British Transport Police Committee, Derek Fowler, CBE, consulted with the force regarding a form of recognition which could be presented to the family members of officers who qualified for their Police Long Service and Good Conduct Medals.

It was decided to recognise the services of the family and support they gave the individual officer by way of a Family Accolade Medallion. This is presented to the officer at the same time as the Police Long Service and Good Conduct medal.

Figure 20 Bill being presented with the family accolade medal on the occasion of his Long Service and Good Conduct medal presentation by Trevor Morris CBE, QPM, CBIM

There were twenty-three officers on the medal parade that memorable day.

My presentation was featured in the local newspapers as per a press release supplied by Force Headquarters.

Following the presentation and newspaper articles, local North Wales author and newspaper correspondent Joan Stockdale wrote the following article about me and the family in her 'Reflections' column in the Holyhead Chronicle.

'Next Sunday is the official launch of the International Year of the Family. Continuing a little on last week's theme, I wonder, do families as a whole receive accolades from one another, for their support to each other? Too easily and too often family "back-up teams" are forgotten in the face of glory and success. One should more often hear the winner's words: "Without family help this wouldn't have been possible". It is wonderful when exceptions do occur as shown in the piece covering the presentation of Sgt Bill Rogerson's Long Service and Good Conduct Medal.

This was awarded in recognition of his 22 years' service with the British Transport Police. Bill is the boss of the Bangor Transport Police Station. He lives in Valley where he works tirelessly for the community and many charities. He's closely involved in activities at St Michael's Church.

But the sergeant's medal wasn't the only Rogerson medals presented by Her Majesty's Chief Inspector of Constabulary at the special London ceremony a few weeks ago. He also received one which will have made the transport policeman deservedly happy.

The Family Accolade Medallion. A unique British Transport Police Force award was given to the Officer's family in recognition of their support throughout his service. To those knowing the Rogerson's, the most dominant factor in their hectic hardworking lives is the support given to each other, and, the obvious friendship which exists between Bill, his wife Shirley and their grownup son and daughter, Stephen, and Alison. Theirs's is a close, fun-type example of family pride and respect.

One can see why the Police Force recognised the Rogerson "Unit" to be special because it certainty is. But I abhor the fact that there has to be a year of national family awareness. We shouldn't need a nudge. In all walks of life in whatever we do, we should stop and think if we could have achieved what we have without the encouragement of the family.

When in the affirmative, then we should say so loudly and triumphantly and then maybe, more families might stick together, more marriages survive, and inter-family competition to be first and best in everything, would not exist'.

To end the year there was a sad incident involving the theft of luggage that occurred on Wednesday 29 December 1993, A seven-year-old girl was travelling with her mother on a train from Cleethorpes to Colwyn Bay for the New Year. The little girl had a rucksack, containing five hundred pounds-worth of presents stolen from near the doorway of a stationary train at Rhyl. The family looked on helplessly through the window of the crowded two-coach train, as a woman in her 20s walked away with the teddy bear shaped rucksack, which the girl had called 'Henry', whom she had since she was two. Sadly, there was no CCTV at Rhyl or on the train. Unfortunately, the culprit was not located despite local enquiries.

I booked on duty at Holyhead at 05.00 hours on Saturday 15 January 1994 due to the fact that Wales played Scotland in the rugby five nations at Cardiff Arms Park. I and one officer escorted the local North Wales fans travelling to Cardiff on this day as far as Shrewsbury, where we were relieved. There were no problems with the fans.

Wednesday 19 January 1994 saw me attending Holyhead High School to talk to half the pupils regarding railway safety, due to trespass and other related issues at the town's railway station.

I was on duty in the sidings at Llandudno Junction on Tuesday 25 January 1994 which saw me involved in a regular multi-agency simulated train crash between a Nuclear Flask train from Valley and the Ethelene Dibromide train from Amlwch.

A return visit to Holyhead High School was made on Wednesday 26 January 1994 to address the rest of the pupils on railway safety and other issues.

Between Friday 4 February 1994 and Sunday 6 February 1994, I was on duty along the North Wales Coast in connection with Welsh rugby fans traveling to Dublin for the Wales v Ireland five nations rugby match. All the fans were in good spirits.

An early start was called for on Saturday 19 February 1994 which saw myself and a couple of officers escorting Welsh rugby fans to Cardiff for the Wales v France five nations rugby game. The train consisted of ten coaches. The front of the train was used for the supporters joining at stations between Holyhead and Chester. The middle of the train was reserved for supporters joining at stations between Wrexham and Hereford and the rear portion was reserved for supporters joining from the Welsh Valleys at Abergavenny. No arrests, just a few friendly warnings dished out to the more vocal ones.

A nice lunch was provided on Thursday 24 February 1994, as I was invited to address the Holyhead Probus Club at the Trearddur Bay Hotel, after their lunch, on the work of the British Transport Police.

On Monday 7 March 1994 I held a public forum in the Ffordd Las Community Centre, Rhyl. The meeting was well attended from a cross selection of the local community who used the railway system in the area. The usual problems of trespass and vandalism along with late night disorder were raised.

During the evening of Thursday 24 March 1994, I attended the Rhyl supper club to address them on the work of the force. After the talk I enjoyed a nice dish of piping hot lob scouse on that cold dark night.

Saturday 26 March 1994 saw me attending a workshop for cub/scout leaders at Ysgol David Hughes, Menai Bridge. I gave the participants an input into railway safety.

Good Friday 1 April 1994 and Easter Sunday 3 April 1994, events were held by the Steam Locomotive Operators Association at Llandudno Junction using five locomotives to mark the passing into history of the Inter-City business and indeed of British Railways as a publicly owned National Rail Network. On each day, over three thousand persons attended the events, which were successfully policed by myself and six officers from Bangor and the area.

A genuinely nice letter of appreciation was received from the Chairman of the Steam Locomotives Operators Association. A real change from the letters of complaint.

One Sunday morning I was off duty at home enjoying my morning cup of coffee when I received a telephone call from the BTP Control Room at Manchester advising me that the body of a fourteen-year-old girl had been found in Belmont Tunnel at the west side of Bangor railway station. I immediately went to the scene. On arrival in the freight yard, which was the nearest access, I saw Emrys, a local North Wales Police officer from Bangor and a young female officer from the same force. Emrys and I exchanged greetings in Welsh and the female officer smiled at me. I was advised that the 'girl' was in fact a thirty-two-year-old, petite woman who was missing from the psychiatric ward of the local hospital. I went into the tunnel to view the body and to make my own notes. On returning to the freight yard, Emrys advised me that the undertaker was on his way. The female officer again smiled at me and said, "I'm scared of railways". I said, "Why's that?" She replied, "I remember you coming to my school and showing us a gory film about the dangers of the railway". To add insult to injury it was her primary school that I had visited in Rhyl a few years ago. I thought to myself 'you old so and so you should be retired'. But the main thing was that the message had sunk into her.

Thursday 12 May 1994, I attended a safety-first day at Ysgol Gogarth, a special needs school in Llandudno, which was attended from pupils from primary schools in the area. The local Crosville bus company provided transport free of charge for the pupils. This was a real opportunity to spread the rail safety message to at least five hundred children.

Between Monday 23 May 1994 and Tuesday 5 July 1994, a lot of my time was spent visiting schools and cub packs in North Wales, giving rail safety talks to the members.

I found that during my police career people would make complaints against the police for the least little things. Some of them made a hobby of it. So, it was always really pleasing to receive letters of appreciation from members of the public. One such letter arrived in connection with a theft. On Wednesday 18 June 1994 an Irish lady with homes in both Istanbul, Turkey, and Ireland, was travelling on a Holyhead bound train from Chester to catch the ferry to Ireland when her suitcase was stolen. The matter was reported to the force. Enquiries were commenced by myself and PC Morgan, and whilst doing so the lady in question had caught the ferry to Ireland, not expecting to see her luggage again. During our enquiries we recovered all her luggage, intact on the lineside, in the Conwy area. The problem was now getting this large suitcase and contents back to her and to obtain a statement. Permission was granted for me to travel to Ireland from Holyhead one Sunday morning and meet up with the lady and obtain a statement from her. On arrival in Dun Laoghaire, I met the lady and obtained a statement from her using the office of the Dun Laoghaire Harbour Police.

Shortly afterwards she wrote a lovely letter to the force.

Dear Detective Chief Inspector,

'Last June 18 while travelling home to Ireland, my suitcase was stolen from the Holyhead bound train.

Thanks to the action of the railway staff and the police everything was recovered.

This is just a note to thank everyone involved for the courtesy with which I was treated. A policeman went to the trouble to get my suitcase released to me and to bring it to me in Dun Laoghaire. The theft was one of those events which was horrible in itself, but which was almost completely ameliorated by the kindness and help I received afterwards.

Thank you and your staff very much'.

The slate town of Blaenau Ffestiniog suffered from disorder on the streets and on the railway station. I had the use of the MSU from Liverpool on a couple of occasions to deal with the problem at the railway station and to assist the North Wales Police in the town.

Their reputation preceded them, as soon as their van rolled into town word got round that *'The English police are in town'* and the potential troublemakers would be nowhere to be seen.

I was on duty during the evening of Sunday 3 July 1994 at Llandudno Station for the Royal Train. His Royal Highness the Prince of Wales was in the resort opening the new theatre at Llandudno, now called Venue Cymru. Whilst at the station I met a gentleman, the late Alf Burgus, and his wife Jean, who were on holiday in the resort. He informed me that he used to drive the Royal Train when he was based at Carnforth. After speaking to him further, it transpired that he was my Grandfather's fireman. I spent some time reminiscing about the 'old days' at Carnforth.

The following day, Monday 4 July 1994 I was in attendance at one of the caravan parks in Pensarn, Abergele, adjacent to the North Wales Coast Line for the launch of a safety leaflet aimed at holidaymakers, informing them how to use the level crossings safely. This was covered extensively in the local press.

Figure 21 Bill at Abergele with members of the public on the launch of 'Operation Railcross' a campaign to educate people use level crossings safely

For two weeks during the 1994 school summer holidays myself and my officers along with our counterparts from Chester had an operation between Prestatyn and Colwyn Bay to catch trespassers, mainly holidaymakers. We caught twenty-eight people in all.

Being a member of the Môn Arfon Victim Support Scheme, which is a registered Charity, I successfully applied to the Police Property Act for a donation, during the month of July 1994. The Chief Constable Desmond O'Brien authorised £2000 for the scheme.

The money was made available through the fund, where unreturnable belongings are auctioned. The force works closely with the Victim Support Schemes on a national level to help the victims of crime. A national referral scheme was set up at the beginning of 1993 with money from the Home Office and the British Railways Board to deal exclusively with crime on the railways.

Tuesday 6 September 1994 saw me in Manchester on a driving course led by ex-Chief Inspector Peter Lyons of the Cheshire Constabulary, learning how to drive the Area's safety transit van and trailer. I had to drive to Stockport and Macclesfield and around some of the narrow streets in the localities. Reversing techniques were carried out in the Trafford freightliner terminal, where I had to reverse in between stationary containers. I passed the course.

Between Thursday 22 September 1994 and Friday 23 September 1994 an Area Team building exercise was held at the Deganwy Castle Hotel. Deganwy. This was attended by the senior officers from Area Headquarters and all the OICs from the area. Thursday 22 September was my birthday and it was my turn to buy a round of drinks after dinner, Ouch!

Friday 23 September 1994 was a different matter. The RMT Union had decided to call a national rail strike of signalling staff. The rail management were unable to staff the Signalboxes on the main North Wales Coast Line. However, to make a point to the union, they staffed the Signalboxes at Llandudno Junction and Llanrwst along with the level crossing at Tal y Cafn on the Blaenau Ffestiniog line with management staff. The RMT put pickets out at the entrance to Llandudno Junction Signalbox and Tal y Cafn level crossing. The latter had a police presence from my officers at Bangor.

However, I had to perform picket duty at Llandudno Junction near to the entrance to the Signalbox. I was not too pleased, as I had consumed a quantity of ale the night before and I had to be on the picket line at 06.00 hours, which meant getting up at 05.00 hours and walking from the hotel to the Signalbox a distance of approximately two miles. My colleagues from the Area Management Team were still fast asleep. I went across to the newsagent in Deganwy to purchase a paper and the newsagent was incredibly surprised to see a police officer on foot duty at that time of the morning.

On arrival at Llandudno Junction, I met up with the union convenor and about six or seven pickets, who I knew very well. I told them that I was there under sufferance due to having a heavy night before and that I had another day of team building ahead of me. A short while later the convenor brought me a nice bacon and egg roll and a large mug of coffee from the local Crosville bus garage canteen.

At about 08.00 hours the pickets withdrew and went home. I returned to the hotel and had breakfast with my colleagues. The following week I received a nice letter of appreciation from Geoff Griffiths the Area Commander.

At a small ceremony in the Bangor police station, on Thursday 30 September 1994 Area Commander Geoff Griffiths presented a cheque for £2000 from the Police Property Act Fund to Betty Williams, Chairperson of the Môn Arfon Victim Support Scheme. Shirley came along and prepared the buffet for the assembled guests.

Like most car parks on the railway system, the car parks in North Wales suffered theft of vehicles and from the interior of them. A National Operation called 'Operation Hyena' was set up at the beginning of October 1994 to stem vehicle crime and was to last for two months. I selected the car parks at Bangor, Colwyn Bay and Rhyl railway stations to be the North Wales focus of the operation. At that time vehicle crime accounted for twenty per cent of all recorded crime to the force, in England, Scotland and Wales. Extra resources and publicity were afforded to the operation. We made a few arrests in North Wales and nationally.

Between September and November 1994 apart from my normal supervisory duties and patrol duties I was kept busy with school visits and various liaison meetings.

During the evening of Monday 7 November 1994, I attended the offices of the Aberconwy Borough Council, Conwy, where I made an illustrated presentation on the work of the force to the Council's Public Protection Committee. Following this meeting I received a complimentary letter from the Borough Secretary thanking me for an interesting and informative talk.

I was in for an unexpected surprise on Tuesday 15 November 1994. I arrived home at around 16.30 hours after a relatively quiet day at work. As I walked through the front door, Shirley said to me "There's a letter from the Prime Minister along with the other mail". I ignored it, changed from my 'half blues' and went to the kitchen to polish my boots ready for the next day. After doing this, I went to read my mail. The letter from the Prime Minister was in an envelope entitled 'On Her Majesty's Service,' with 'Urgent, Personal and Prime Minister' typed on it. I noted that it had been franked London S.W.1, on the 14 November 1994.

My first thought was that John Major, the then Conservative Prime Minister was writing to me regarding the various liaison forums I held, which included the local North Wales Members of Parliament.

On reading the enclosed letter, it stated that the Prime Minister had it in mind, in the strictest confidence on the occasion of the forthcoming list of New Year Honours, to submit my name to The Queen with a recommendation that her Majesty may be graciously pleased to approve that I am appointed a Member of the Order of the British Empire. If I agreed I had to return a form to the Honours Committee. If the recommendation is accepted, I would not hear anything else until the New Year Honours List is published.

My first thought was that one or more of my colleagues were having a joke with me. But the more I read it the more convinced I became that it was genuine. I was numb with shock; I was truly taken aback. I was speechless. I did not expect such an honour. I returned the form of acceptance.

During the middle of December 1994, the results of 'Operation Hyena' were published and it was pleasing to note that a near fifty per cent reduction in car crime was reported at Bangor Railway Station car park alone. Throughout the force it was a great success with the Force's North Western Area (including Bangor and North Wales) witnessing the best results with a drop of thirty seven per cent in recorded incidents. I was incredibly pleased with the results for North Wales as we had involved a range of initiatives, including crime prevention improvements, high profile patrols, public awareness campaigns and the latest forensic techniques.

Following on from the success of 'Operation Hyena', 'Operation Tindale' was launched to target the theft of luggage on trains throughout the rail network. This involved high profile patrols of stations and trains along the North Wales Coast as well as a public awareness campaign with the handing out of specially produced warning leaflets, which paid particular attention to the dangers facing lone women travellers late at night. The local press gave me some good publicity.

I took part in a severe weather exercise on Wednesday 7 December 1994 organised by the Clwyd County Council, in the Nuclear Bunker, which formed part of the Council offices in Mold. This exercise was to test the emergency services response if towns and villages were cut off due to flooding.

I had a report of youths discharging a firearm at a London to Holyhead passenger train whilst it was leaving Rhyl railway station, between Marsh Road and Westbourne Avenue, on Thursday 29 December 1994 at 21.10 hours. This is an area where objects have been thrown at trains in the past. A window in one of the rear carriages was cracked. A passenger was badly shaken but not injured. Investigations were commenced, and the local press informed.

Whilst in the downstairs office at Bangor on Friday 30 December 1994 with my PCs, one of them answered the telephone. He said, "It's for you Sarge". I said to him "It will be the Daily Post (The daily newspaper for North Wales) or Rhyl Chronicle ringing up about yesterday's incident". I asked him to put it through to my office upstairs, where I had the papers relating to the incident. I went to my office and answered the phone and the voice on the other end said, "Its Tom Bodden here from the Daily Post, congratulations on your award of the MBE, I am very pleased for you". I went into a state of shock, it was true, I had actually been awarded the MBE. He went onto ask for a quote from me and asked for some personal details, but for a few seconds I was absolutely stunned and speechless. He arranged for a photographer to attend later that afternoon. The MBE stands for Member of the Order of the British Empire: a British honour given to a person by the Queen for a special achievement.

My appointment was published in a supplement of The London Gazette of Friday 30 December 1994, Number 53893.

The following day, Saturday 31 December 1994, I was front page news of the Daily Post and took the centre spread of one of the inside pages, complete with photograph, putting the then Chief Constable of the North Wales Police, Michael Argent, who had been awarded the Queen's Police Medal in the same honours, in the shadows with a one-line entry. The telephone at home was nonstop with people ringing me up to congratulate me. One of the first callers was Desmond O'Brien the then Chief Constable of the British Transport Police.

CHAPTER 22

THE BANGOR YEARS 1995 – 1996

Off to the Palace again

The New Year of 1995 started off on a high for me after the Christmas and New Year holiday. I returned to work on Monday 2 January 1995, still on a high after the news that I had been appointed an MBE. I read the telephone messages from the last couple of days. One was headed 'VIP VISIT TO BANGOR'. I quickly glanced at it I said to PC Sean Morgan, "Why wasn't I told of this before, there are certain people to inform and protocols to adhere to". He said, "Read it again Sarge". I did, and I realised that it was a spoof message and related to me on my return to work. We had a good laugh about it.

The letters and telephone calls of congratulations followed for months afterwards. In fact, people are still congratulating me today.

Early January 1995 saw me booking in several schools and other youth groups for rail safety talks through to April.

The evening of Tuesday 24 January 1995 saw Bangor City playing Wrexham in the Welsh Football Cup quarter final. I was heavily involved in supervising the supporters from both clubs who had arrived at Bangor by train. There were no serious incidents. Words of guidance were given to a few supporters.

The results of 'Operation Tindale' were published and they showed that we had had some success in reducing luggage thefts along the North Wales Coast, which was reassuring for the general public.

Each year, officers had an annual appraisal with a senior officer. The officers under my command were seen by myself and if there was anything adverse in my comments they would be seen by a higher-ranking officer. For two consecutive years all the 'Officers in Charge' of police stations had to go to Force Headquarters for an interview with one of the Assistant Chief Constables. The intention was also, that 'Officers in Charge' of police stations should gain a wider appreciation and knowledge of the departments at Force Headquarters, during the day of their appraisal. Monday 30 January 1995 saw me travelling to Force Headquarters, staying overnight in the Force Headquarters accommodation, a single room, with not enough space to swing the proverbial cat. The following day Tuesday 31 January 1995 at 10.00 hours I had my appraisal with an Assistant Chief Constable which lasted around an hour. Then I was to visit the various departments at Force Headquarters with an included lunch in between. I returned to Bangor at around 15.00 hours.

Between Friday 3 February 1995 and Sunday 5 February 1995, I was on duty at Holyhead and the North Wales Coast Line monitoring Irish rugby fans travelling from Ireland to Scotland for the Scotland v Ireland five nations rugby union match. The Irish fans were their usual friendly self and caused no problems.

On Wednesday 15 February 1995 there was a so called 'friendly' international football match between Ireland and England at Lansdowne Road, Dublin. At least eight hundred fans supporting England travelled by ferry from Holyhead to Dublin. A majority of whom travelled by train. They were escorted along the North Wales Coast by myself and other officers from the British Transport Police. North Wales Police had a heavy presence at Holyhead Port.

One group of English fans did not even get across the Irish Sea, after rival supporters clashed at Holyhead station. Fighting broke out between Huddersfield Town and Stoke City fans on the station concourse on the afternoon of the match. Stena Sealink refused to let the Huddersfield group on to the ferry, and they were escorted back to the train while the Stoke supporters were allowed to continue.

After the game there were riots in and outside the ground. The first set of fans came back on the night of the match, but the rest came back in dribs and drabs during the next twenty four hours – looking very much like the morning after the night before. It was obvious that many of them had been fighting. Black eyes, blood on clothing, bumps, swellings, and abrasions were obvious. Surgical dressings obviously covering stitches were seen on others. Some of the fans seemed to be thoroughly ashamed of themselves and tried to cover their faces from the cameras of both television and press photographers. But others flaunted the Union Jacks they had taken with them to Dublin and expressed no shame for what happened. The only time any of them reacted was when someone from the large crowd on the station concourse shouted, "I thought Sealink had banned the transport of animals on their ships".

One photographer was hit by a fan he had photographed, but otherwise there was no trouble. Officers from the British Transport Police were on hand to escort them back on the trains. A rough crossing might have had something to do with the hangdog expression on some faces. In fact, it had been so rough that the 'Stena Hibernia' was nearly two hours late arriving in Holyhead.

Wales played England in a five nations rugby union match at Cardiff Arms Park on Saturday 18 February 1995. The North Wales based Welsh fans were monitored on the early morning trains by myself and my officers. There was no trouble from the fans.

I received a letter on 22 February 1995 from the Central Chancery of the Orders of Knighthood, St James's Palace, SW1A 1BH informing me that my Investiture would be held at Buckingham Palace on Tuesday 2 May 1995 at which my presence was requested. I was advised to arrive at the Palace between the hours of 10.00 hours and 10.30 hours and that I was permitted to bring three guests with me. I sent a copy of the letter to Force Headquarters.

Towards the end of February 1995, the driver and passengers on a late afternoon train travelling from Holyhead to Crewe had a lucky escape as it was travelling between Rhosneigr and Ty Croes, when a young male who was stood on a road bridge threw stones at the train shattering the cab window of the diesel locomotive. Fortunately, the driver was unhurt, but he was badly shaken and shocked. Enquiries in this isolated location failed to trace the youth responsible.

At the end of February 1995 'Operation Rhino' was announced. This operation was a nationwide initiative by the force aimed at stamping out trespass and vandalism. It was to run from March, through the Easter Holidays until the end of April. In North Wales we concentrated on the railway line between Colwyn Bay and Rhyl, paying particular attention to the Rhyl area. Trespass was rife near to Rhyl railway station. Shortly before the initiative was launched a pram was dumped on the railway line at Sandy Lane Prestatyn and caused damage to a train. The area around Penmaenmawr station was also targeted, as several offences had been reported there.

On one Saturday evening during the month of February 1995, Sean Morgan and myself were on patrol of Rhyl Station, as part of 'Operation Rhino'. At this time Rhyl was undergoing extensive refurbishment and wooden safety hoardings had been erected all around the station. Some of the hoardings had been damaged by the local youths. I went behind one of them on Platform One to see if any equipment had been tampered with. As I entered, I stepped in a large pile of human excrement. I liberally peppered the air with a string of four-lettered profanities. Standing nearby was an elderly gentleman from the locality called Geoff (not his real name) who was well known to us. He used to travel frequently by train to Chester in the first class with a valid ticket. Sadly, Geoff was severely autistic, had a club foot, a glass eye, and spoke very slowly with a high pitched voice. He said to me, "I've just done that". That could be taken two ways, one, he could have deposited the offending material there or he could have stepped in it like myself. I didn't want to ask. Sean Morgan was doubled up with uncontrollable laughter.

During the evening of Monday 13 March 1995, I held a public forum at the Ffordd Las Community Centre, Rhyl, where the public and rail staff were briefed on 'Operation Rhino'. I informed them that one of the major problems was, that people obstructed the railway tracks with all kind of objects such as mattresses, push chairs, bicycles, wheelbarrows, traffic cones, metal objects, etc. They were totally aghast at the scale of the problem and promised to be vigilant.

The two-month clamp down was a great success, as we used a combination of high-profile police tactics, school visits and undercover officers to reduce the crimes. Yes, it did mean extra work for us, but it had been worthwhile. Several offenders were caught and reported for various offences from Trespass to Obstructing the Railway. Over the Easter Holidays several youths were caught trespassing at Llandegai, near Bangor and on the Britannia Bridge.

St Patrick's Day Friday 17 March 1995, a number of Irish supporters travelled over from Ireland to go to Cardiff for the Wales v Ireland five nations rugby union match at Cardiff Arms Park, on Saturday 18 March. High profile policing from myself and my officers on the trains along the North Wales Coast ensured that they caused no problems. No doubt they boosted the profits of a certain brewer of stout from Ireland, sold in Cardiff.

The following day, Saturday 18 March 1995, I was on duty early morning, with my officers to escort the North Wales based rugby fans to Cardiff for the Wales v Ireland rugby match. We had a few Irish fans on the train as well. Both sets of fans got on well with each other, unlike football fans. As usual the Welsh were in fine voice singing their hearts out.

In March 1995, the then Welsh Under Secretary, Gwilym Jones launched the 'National Springclean 95', backed by the Tidy Britain Group and the Keep Wales Tidy campaign. More than forty thousand volunteers were to take part in the most extensive footpath litter-pick ever undertaken in Wales. As part of the clean-up, which began on Saturday 1 April 1995, Gwynedd County Council began an investigation into the problem of litter along the footpaths in the county. The force was involved in this campaign and I chose the Cae Mawr sidings and embankment adjacent to the running line at Llandudno on the Llandudno Junction to Llandudno railway line. This was an ideal location as there was a lot of rubbish and potential ammunition for vandals. I approached the local railway managers and at first, they were very reluctant to become involved, even though the line was closed to rail traffic on the day I had in mind, Sunday 2 April 1995. However, with persistence I finally managed to persuade them to cooperate. I contacted the local council and they provided me with two skips in a nearby car park, the local high school, Ysgol John Bright provided me with a dozen pupils. Railtrack provided a couple of staff and a four-wheeled trolley. I, along with PCs Sean Morgan, Bangor and Bill Reed from Crewe, assisted by the pupils, began collecting rubbish from the location. It was amazing what we found, old prams, supermarket trollies, chain link fencing, a moped, bed frames, mattresses, paint cans, lengths of wood. You name it we found it. During the clean-up which lasted until around 16.00 hours we managed to fill the two skips with the rubbish we collected.

Figure 22 Rubbish picked up from the lineside at Llandudno during 'National Springclean 95'

In late April, I received a letter from Force Headquarters advising me that I would be looked after by the force for my Investiture at Buckingham Palace.

All the arrangements were kindly made by Fred Keeler who was the Chief Administration Officer for the force.

Shirley, Stephen, Alison, and myself travelled by train to London on Monday 1 May 1995 where we were met by PC Colin De'ath and conveyed to the Bonnington Hotel in Holborn, where rooms and a booking for dinner were awaiting us.

Tuesday 2 May 1995 on the day of the Investiture, after breakfast at 09.15 hours PC Colin De'ath picked us up and conveyed us to Buckingham Palace. I sat in the front, in shirt sleeve order next to Colin, who was also in shirt sleeve order, whilst Shirley, Stephen and Alison sat in the back. The force even provided corsages for Shirley and Alison. On arrival at the Palace gates, Colin had to stop for security checks. Outside the Palace there were large crowds of onlookers, complete with cameras. Upon seeing Colin and myself in police uniform the focus of attention was on the family in the back of the car. They must have thought that they were very important persons from Royalty, the world of television or the film industry. Little did they know. On arrival in the Palace grounds, I put on my tunic and the family alighted from the car, once again the cameras were clicking away.

Once inside the Palace we witnessed what must be one of the finest staged - managed events but taken in its stride by the hardworking and knowledgeable team at the home of the Queen. This was our first time inside the Palace and seeing it for the first time, the sight is awe-inspiring. We then walked along the red carpet. The family went to the ballroom to seats arranged to face Her Majesty. In a gallery in the ballroom, the band of the Guards played a selection of music. I went off in another direction to be checked off at least six times on the official lists. I entered a large room where all the recipients were given a briefing on protocol when we met Her Majesty. A couple of notable recipients were Delia Smith and Joanna Lumley. There were a couple of Chief Constables and Deputy Chief Constables. Others included surgeons, scientists, dinner ladies and tea-ladies.

My turn came to be invested by Her Majesty. As I reached the Queen, my name was whispered to her. One of the questions she asked me was, did I look after the Royal Train when it was in North Wales. I replied that I did, and she thanked me for the service that the force gave. She then pinned the medal of the MBE onto a suitable hook on my tunic. She is such a fine-looking lady, very few photographs capture the softness of her eyes, the smile that plays around the corner of her mouth, the texture of her skin and the pleasure she seems to exude from doing a job, if not tiresome, must be repetitive.

After the Investiture I was escorted to the ballroom. As the last recipient received the award, Big Ben struck the hour of twelve, we rose from our seats. Her Majesty smiled a radiant smile at all of us, then departed. I re-joined the family and had photographs taken with them at the Quadrangle inside the Palace grounds and also on the road opposite the Palace by a photographer provided by the force. Colin De'ath then took us back to the Bonnington Hotel for lunch and then conveyed us to Euston station for the train home.

Figure 23 Bill and family outside Buckingham Palace on the occasion of his investiture with the MBE

Figure 24 Bill outside Buckingham Palace on the occasion of his investiture with the MBE

I travelled to a hotel near to Carlisle railway station on Wednesday 12 May 1995 for a two-day Area Management Team meeting. The following day Thursday 13 May 1995, Desmond O'Brien the then Chief Constable called into the hotel we were attending, on his way back from Scotland to present me with a miniature MBE medal.

The Empire Hotel in Llandudno was the ideal location on Tuesday 16 May 1995 to address the Welsh Rail Users Consultative Committee annual conference on the work of the force in North Wales. The force allowed me to stay overnight at the hotel, after an enjoyable dinner with the committee members.

More football duties on Saturday 20 May 1995. I escorted Irish and North Wales based Manchester United football supporters on an early morning Holyhead to London Euston passenger train for the fiftieth FA Cup Final being played at Wembley since the Second World War, in which Everton played Manchester United. Everton won the game 1 - 0. I returned to Holyhead with a late evening service. Many of the fans were well behaved as they were subdued following their loss. However, I had to issue a couple of friendly words of guidance to some of the fans.

At the beginning of June 1995, I received further requests for rail safety talks at schools leading up to the summer holidays.

Friday 2 June 1995, I attended an emergency services safety day, with participants from the local police, Fire Brigade, and the RNLI, in the events arena in Rhyl, which was attended by local school children. It was a good vehicle for the force to promote railway safety to the local community.

Over the years British Rail and its predecessors ran dedicated trains to connect with the ships to and from Ireland. One such train was the overnight 'Irish Mail' which used to depart from Holyhead at around 01.50 hours for London Euston. The departure of the train was always subject to the punctual arrival of the ship from Ireland and there was always a footnote in the timetable to this effect. The train would have limited stops to London.

With the privatisation of the railways, the practice of holding the train for the ship was frowned upon by the railway authorities. I believe it was in 1995 the train itself was retimed to depart Holyhead at around 03.50 hours and would call additionally at Rugby, where it would pick up commuters for London who were mainly first-class season ticket holders. At the busy times on departure from Holyhead, the train would be full and sometimes there was standing room only. By the time the train arrived in Rugby most of the passengers were fast asleep on the seats or on the floor of the carriages, including the first class. Some were lying in their own vomit, excrement, and urine if it had been a particularly rough crossing and from excess duty-free spirits and beer. It was not a very pleasant situation. There were numerous complaints from the Rugby commuters. BTP officers were repeatedly called to the train at Rugby. The railway authorities even wanted the BTP to escort the train from Holyhead to London on a regular basis to make sure that the first class was kept clear. Due to the lack of manpower in those days, it was impossible to accede to the request. Instead, I came up with a quite simple solution that I had used at Holyhead a few years previously and this was to lock the first class 'out of use' at Holyhead and only let genuine passengers in at the stops. Simple, it worked a treat.

In the late spring of 1995, one thousand special audio cassettes were distributed throughout Wales, including my patch, to farmers, urging them to take greater care when using railway crossings.

The dangers of misusing automatic level crossings were highlighted by the National Farmers Union after the BTP revealed that two hundred and sixty three people were killed or injured in the UK between 1990 and 1994 - most of the incidents occurring at automatic and open crossings found in rural areas.

As dawn broke over North Wales one Saturday morning in July 1995 the driver of an early morning Holyhead to Cardiff train had a shock just after he went through Abergele and Pensarn Station, he saw the body of a male hanging from a footbridge. I was called out from home. On examination of the body, I found a suicide note. The body was removed from the bridge into a hearse which was on the beach, ready to go to the local mortuary. As the hearse set off, it got stuck in some wet sand, so myself, the lugubrious undertaker and his assistant spent the next few minutes digging it out. Then it was off to the Mortuary at Ysbyty Glan Clwyd with the body.

The Annual General Meeting of the North Wales Victim Support Scheme was held on Wednesday July 12, 1995, and in my absence, I was elected as Vice-Chairman of the scheme.

Friday 14 July 1995 saw a rail strike by the staff, and pickets were out at key locations on the North Wales Coast. It was impossible to staff all the locations with a police officer, so they were covered by myself and a PC on a mobile patrol. No problems were encountered.

The following day, Saturday 15 July 1995, rail services began to return to normal on the North Wales Coast as Bangor played Chester in a friendly football match at Farrar Road, Bangor. Despite several fans travelling by train from Chester, myself and my officers ensured that all was quiet.

I was on duty on the North Wales Coast on Sunday 16 July 1995 in connection with a steam-hauled special train, which attracted the usual number of spectators from far and wide. A couple of persons were reported for trespass.

On Sunday 23 July 1995 I was on duty at Rhyl railway station in connection with a Royal Visit to Rhyl. I believe it was His Royal Highness Prince Charles, Prince of Wales, who came to officially re-open the refurbished Rhyl station.

A friendly football match took place on the evening of Tuesday 25 July 1995 at Farrar Road Bangor between Bangor and Tranmere Rovers. Hardly any fans travelled from the Wirral, but a few local fans travelled from Holyhead. The evening passed off quietly.

A European football match between Bangor City and Widzew Lodz during the evening of Tuesday 8 August 1995 drew several local fans and a handful from Poland. As there is a large Polish population in Wrexham and Pwllheli amongst other places in North Wales, several North Wales based Polish fans attended as well. All passed off very peacefully due to some robust policing from myself and my officers.

Sunday 13 August 1995 I was on duty as a standby escort officer in connection with the 1995 FA Charity Shield (also known as the Littlewoods Pools FA Charity Shield for sponsorship reasons). This was an annual football match played between the winners of the previous season's Premier League and FA Cup competitions at Wembley Stadium.

This year was the seventy third FA Charity Shield, and was contested by Blackburn Rovers, who had won the Premier League, and FA Cup winners Everton. It was Blackburn Rovers second successive Charity Shield appearance, while Everton were appearing in their eleventh and their first since 1987. Everton won the match 1–0 with a goal from Vinny Samways.

A local football derby Bangor v Rhyl a contender for potential trouble, was played at Farrar Road, Bangor on Saturday 19 August 1995. I, and a couple of officers monitored the fans travelling from Rhyl. There was no trouble before or after the match.

Monday 9 October 1995, I received a letter from a concerned resident of a house that overlooked the railway station at Bangor, complaining about the state of the wall near to Belmont Tunnel. He stated that the coping stones on side at the Holyhead end of the tunnel were loose, and one was already missing; he also highlighted cracks in the walls. He was concerned that vandals could dislodge a coping stone and throw it onto a passing train. He had reported the matter to the railway authorities in early September and nothing had been done. He was asking if I could do anything to assist. I wrote back to him and stated that I would speak to the local Area Works Supervisor and had requested that my officers pay attention to the location.

Within a few days all the necessary repairs had been carried out and I informed the gentleman. I received a further letter from him thanking me for my excellent service and support. Another satisfied customer.

The evening of Monday 6 November 1995 saw me addressing members of the Betws - y - Coed Community Council on the work of the force and the work we carried out on the Conwy Valley Railway Line.

Saturday 18 November 1995 was a sad day as we said farewell to PC Doug Worster after around twenty-seven years with the force which were all spent at Holyhead and Bangor, as he retired from the force. We gave him a good send off a week later at the railway club in Holyhead.

Doug was replaced by PC Gordon Millar who transferred from the London Underground Area.

At the beginning of December 1995 all the 'Officers in Charge' within the Force were informed that they had to attend four modules to qualify for a Certificate in Management, being run in connection with the Institute of Management, at Tadworth during 1996. The modules were Managing People assignment – *Motivation at Work* and Managing People - *Discipline and Related issues,* (Covered over one module). Managing Operations assignment - *Customer Focus*, Managing Information assignment - *Communication Audit* and Managing Financial Resources assignment - *Planning, Communication Audit and Budgeting.*

Each Module had to be followed up by a written assignment overseen by a mentor from the force. The written work would then be marked by an independent assessor from the Institute of Management. Four trips to Tadworth!! As if I did not have enough work to do.

Between Tuesday 12 December 1995 and Thursday 14 December 1995, myself and other officers from the area were on duty at Holyhead railway station monitoring Irish football supporters travelling in connection with an Eire v Holland Football International match at Liverpool's Anfield ground. One or two supporters were dealt with for various offences.

The afternoon of Saturday 23 December 1995 saw Rhyl play Bangor at Rhyl's Vale Road ground. The few fans who travelled from Bangor were escorted to and from Rhyl by myself and officers from Bangor. No problems were encountered, on this particular day.

After an eventful start to 1995, 1996 started off fairly quietly. I began booking more rail safety visits with the local schools, Brownies and Girl Guides up until May.

Sunday 28 January 1996 saw me travelling to Tadworth for the first of my Certificate in Management modules. During the week, I met up with some old colleagues and new ones. We were all different ranks ranging from Sergeant to Chief Inspector. We had one thing in common, we were all 'Officers in Charge' of police stations and classed as equal. Therefore, we were all on first name terms. On my return I had an assignment to write up.

Saturday 17 February 1996 saw me on duty for the Wales v Scotland five nations rugby union match at Cardiff Arms Park. Very few supporters travelled by train, probably due to the cost. A few years previously the railway authorities used to charge ten pounds return, to travel on the 'Rugby Special'. But nowadays the cost was that of the ordinary fare, which was beyond the pockets of most people.

Ireland played Wales in a five nations rugby match on Saturday 2 March 1996. I was on duty with other officers from Friday 1 March 1996, St David's Day to Sunday 3 March 1996 monitoring the Welsh fans travelling to and from Holyhead by train. Although the Welsh fans on their return had been drinking heavily on the ship, there were no problems from them.

During the second week of March 1996, I had to step up patrols to Conwy railway station due to a recent outbreak of criminal damage. Large chunks of plaster were ripped from the walls of the waiting shelters on both platforms and thrown onto the tracks. A resident of the flats overlooking the station gave us some valuable information as to the identity of the culprits.

Saturday 16 March 1996 was fairly busy as Wales were playing France in a five nations rugby union match at Cardiff Arms Park and England were playing Ireland in the same competition at Twickenham. We had both Welsh and Irish rugby supporters travelling on our patch. All went smoothly.

Sunday March 21, 1996 saw me returning to Tadworth for the second of my four Certificate of Management Modules. On this module there were some familiar faces from the first one and some new ones. Again, on my return I had an assignment to write up.

The fifty first FA Cup final since The Second World War was played at Wembley on Saturday 11 May 1996 between Liverpool and Manchester United, which Manchester united won 1 - 0.

I escorted Irish and North Wales based Manchester United fans to London Euston on an early morning train from Holyhead and returned with them on a late evening service. The fans were in high spirits on the return and one or two of them had to be given words of guidance about their conduct.

Wednesday 3 April 1996 was a busy day for me. It started off with Shirley and I travelling to Liverpool for my railway long service award, for which I had chosen a Barometer. On returning to Bangor, I went to the Seiont Manor Hotel, in the shadow of Mount Snowdon, near Caernarfon for the AGM of Môn / Gwynedd Victim Support Scheme.

Figure 25 Bill being presented with his railway long service award by Chief Superintendent Geoff Griffiths

A trip to Crewe on Monday 15 April 1996 saw me putting in a full day at the Crewe police station for a planning exercise in conjunction with the forthcoming 'Euro 96' football Championship matches.

In May 1996 we were issued with new side handled batons and speed cuffs and had to undergo a two-day training course in Bangor on Monday 20 May 1996 and Tuesday 21 May 1996.

I was paired up with Sean Braithwaite for the training and whilst I was in the process of handcuffing Sean, I accidentally hit him in his left eye, causing some bruising to it. The only snag was, that Sean was due to be married on the following Saturday. Fortunately, the bruising had subsided in time for the big day.

I booked on duty at 07.30 hours on Monday 3 June 1996, after a weekend off. I dealt with the paperwork and reports that had found their way into my in tray. At about 10.35 hours I received a telephone call informing me that there had been a fatality near to Pen y Clip tunnel, near Penmaenmawr. On arrival I found the body of a young student teacher from a village near to Bangor. Apparently, he joined the 10.23 hours Bangor to Crewe train at Bangor, which was formed of a class 37 diesel locomotive and four carriages, known as 'slam door', stock. As it was exiting the tunnel at a speed of seventy five mph, witnesses saw him fall from a door of the front carriage of the moving train. Passengers looked hopelessly and horrified as the body flew by the carriages they were in. A passenger pulled the communication cord and the train was halted.

On arrival at the scene, I arranged for the train to be taken out of service at Llandudno Junction for a thorough examination of the carriages and the one from where the man fell from. Details of all the witnesses were obtained. The body was covered over and later removed to the Mortuary at Ysbyty Gwynedd, Bangor. The line was reopened to rail traffic after eighty minutes.

A subsequent examination of the carriages found no faults whatsoever. At the subsequent inquest, a verdict of suicide was returned.

Tuesday 9 July 1996 saw me on duty in Valley sidings in connection with the overnight stabling of the Royal Train there. I was able to go from home straight to the sidings.

The following day Wednesday 10 July 1996 saw me on duty at Bangor railway station in connection with a visit by HRH The Prince of Wales to the city.

Following reports of trespass and anti-social behaviour at Llanrwst station, on Friday 12 July 1996 I spoke to the year nine pupils at Ysgol Dyffryn Conwy, (Llanrwst High School), Llanrwst, re the dangers of the railway. Shortly after this visit I received a very complementary letter from the school Industry Links Coordinator. The incidents of trespass were drastically reduced after my visit.

I was looking forward to a well-earned rest day on Saturday 13 July. The ring of the telephone at 08.00 hours soon put a stop to that. I was informed by Area Control that a man who had travelled on a train from Llandudno Junction was seen to jump through a window as it approached Bangor Tunnel. I immediately went to Bangor.

On arrival I ascertained that a man from a village in the Conwy Valley and who was suffering from depression was seen to board a Manchester Victoria to Holyhead Sprinter Train at Llandudno Junction. During the journey to Bangor he went to the rear cab, which was being used by the conductor, but who at the time was in the train collecting fares. Once in the cab the man managed to open the window and jump through it as the train was passing the Maesgeirchen housing estate on the outskirts of Bangor.

A teenager from the housing estate heard some shouting coming from the railway track and went to investigate. He saw the man on the track, throwing stones at the lines trying to attract attention. The youth rendered first aid to the man and arranged for the emergency services to be called. He was taken by Ambulance to Ysbyty Gwynedd and later transferred to the North Staffordshire Hospital with multiple injuries. The rest of the day was taken up with the examination of the train and taking witness statements. Following advice from the Crown Prosecution Service, the man later received an official caution for the offences disclosed.

It was not only children and youths responsible for trespass on the track. I had a problem with golfers hunting for lost golf balls on the line from Llandudno to Llandudno Junction, just on the outskirts of Llandudno where the railway line runs alongside the Maes Du Golf Course. Not only were they setting a bad example to children, but they were putting themselves in danger. We mounted an education programme with the club's secretary. One or two golfers were prosecuted to set an example.

During the summer of 1996, the North Wales Police introduced a 'plastic bubble' into the rear of their cars. The rear seats were removed, and a reinforced secure plastic bubble was installed to convey prisoners in. PC Gordon Millar produced a paper stating that this would be a good idea for Bangor, where much of the time the officers worked alone. The paper was duly submitted to Force Headquarters.

Between Tuesday 23 July 1996 and Thursday 25 July 1996, I attended a Health and Safety course at Tadworth. On arrival back at Bangor I had another assignment to write up to qualify for a Health and Safety Certificate.

Figure 26 A caricature of Bill drawn at Tadworth

We were allowed to travel on the London Underground trains, for free, whilst on duty on production of our warrant cards, provided that we attended an incident should the need arise. I travelled on my warrant card from Euston to Charing Cross on the Northern Line, on my way to Tadworth in connection with the above course.

On alighting at Charing Cross tube station, I heard a tannoy broadcast for a member of the British Transport Police to attend the supervisor's office. I duly complied with this request. On arrival I introduced myself as Sergeant Rogerson from Bangor. The Station Supervisor looked somewhat surprised and said in a Cockney accent to his assistant, "Banger, Banger, where the bleeding hell is Banger, is it on the 'effing' District Line. Blimey Guv where did you say you were from, you got here before the local lads Guv". I told him that Bangor was in North Wales and as I heard his request, I dived out of the office into a telephone kiosk and changed into my 'bat suit' and flew down. We both had a good laugh. He informed me that my services were no longer required. Apparently, it was a busker who had been causing some problems but had left.

It was off to Tadworth on Sunday 4 August 1996 for the third of my Certificate in Management modules. On the Wednesday afternoon as part of the module we visited the Surrey Police Headquarters. One of the departments we visited was the firearms section. The officer in charge of the shooting range asked if I'd ever fired a gun before and I told him of my exploits in Amsterdam. He gave me a loaded pistol with six rounds in it. I fired them at the target and to my surprise I had hit the target five times, goodness knows where the sixth one went. He said that I had redeemed myself after Amsterdam. On arrival back in Bangor on Thursday 8 August 1996 I had another assignment to write up .

I had to put my assignment to one side on Sunday 11 August 1996 as I with other officers escorted North Wales based Manchester United fans to and from Watford Junction, (The line between Watford Junction and London was closed due to a derailment of a passenger train on 8 August 1996), in connection with the Charity Shield football match which was being played at Wembley between Manchester United and Newcastle United, a game which Manchester United won 4 - 0. There was no trouble on the journeys.

Figure 27 Bill on patrol on a London Euston to Holyhead train which was conveying North Wales based Manchester United football supporters from Wembley

North Wales Police held a 999 display with local emergency services attending in Rhyl on Sunday 18 August 1996. I was in attendance with a rail safety display which was seen by many children who were local and on holiday.

I travelled to Tadworth on Sunday 1 September 1996 for my last module of the Certificate in Management. On returning on Wednesday 4 September, I had another assignment to write up and submit.

The Magistrates at Llandudno Magistrates' Court, on Wednesday 11 September 1996 heard all about a man from Rhyl whom I'd reported for trespass at Llandudno Junction station earlier in the year. They fined him £40 with £30 costs. Back at Bangor more school safety visits were arranged until the end of the year.

Between 21.45 hours and 22.00 hours on Friday 1 November 1996 whilst on Platform One of Rhyl railway station a sixteen-year-old youth from near Prestatyn approached a fifteen-year-old youth from the Rhyl area and began punching and kicking him. The younger boy fell to the ground, where the older youth repeatedly kicked him in the head and upper body. The boy was taken to Ysbyty Glan Clwyd at Bodelwyddan near Rhyl, where he remained with severe facial injuries for four days. I commenced enquiries into this cowardly attack and shortly afterwards the sixteen-year old year was arrested and charged. He subsequently appeared at the local youth court.

During November 1996 I learned that I had successfully passed all my Certificate of Management modules and the Health and Safety course.

Following a paper submitted by PC Gordon Millar earlier in the year, I travelled to Tadworth on Friday 6 December 1996 to pick up a Peugeot people carrier for a trial basis, as the force were thinking of introducing a dual-purpose van for patrols and conveying prisoners at various locations throughout the force. I returned with the vehicle on the 7 December 1996.

As 1996 was drawing rapidly to a close the railway system closed down on Christmas Day and Boxing Day. However, at about 06.00 hours on Friday 27 December the early turn booking clerk at Rhyl railway station had a shock when she discovered the body of a male person lying on the track adjacent to Platform One. It appeared that the male had been struck by one of the last trains on Christmas Eve, but none of the train drivers reported it. The body was removed to the Mortuary at Ysbyty Glan Clwyd, Bodelwyddan, near Rhyl. I commenced enquiries, and it was established that the death was not suspicious.

Overall, with one thing and another, various meetings including Victim Support Scheme, seminars, courses, rugby traffic, football traffic, fatalities, and school visits, 1996 proved to be a very exhausting year for me. I wondered what 1997 would bring.

CHAPTER 23

THE BANGOR YEARS JANUARY 1997 – DECEMBER 1998

Confusing the Prince of Wales

January 1997 started off on an incredibly sad note. On the evening of New Year's Day, a young twenty-year-old woman, with a five-month-old baby, from Colwyn Bay and who suffered from Post-Traumatic Stress Syndrome and mild schizophrenia went to Colwyn Bay station and was struck by a train and killed instantly.

The morning of Friday 3 January 1997 I attended the mortuary at Ysbyty Glan Clwyd for the post-mortem of the young woman. Later that day at 14.00 hours I had to attend the Coroner's office, in Ruthin to formally open the inquest into her death.

It was off to Tadworth on Monday 6 January 1997, the people carrier that we had on trial at Bangor since the beginning of December 1996 was being transferred to Tadworth. On arrival at Tadworth I was allowed to use the Instructor's lounge for afternoon tea. An overnight stay in Tadworth saw me visiting some local hostelries in the area.

Tragedy struck again on the 9 January 1997, the day of the young woman's funeral, who was killed earlier in the month. A male friend of hers, five hours after the funeral, went to the location where she was killed and he himself was struck and killed by a train. Another post-mortem to attend and another inquest to open.

Wales played Ireland in the five nations rugby on Saturday 1 February 1997. I and my officers were kept busy over the weekend monitoring the Irish and Welsh supporters who were travelling to Cardiff. All in good spirits and singing their hearts out.

Following receipt of an invitation I was invited to address the members of Aberconwy council on Monday 3 February 1997 on the work of the force. The usual barrage of questions were fired at me, including 'what were the British Transport Police doing about crime and disorder on the railways in the county'. I was able to bat these off like Sir Garfield Sobers at the crease.

Although retirement was over four years away, Shirley and I travelled down to London on Tuesday 4 February 1997 for a retirement seminar organised by the BT Police Federation on Wednesday 5 February 1997.

Following the successful completion of the 'Officer in Charge' modules, the force paid for me to join the Chartered Institute of Management, meaning I had some more letters after my name, and I was eligible to join the local North Wales branch of the Institute.

More safety talks were booked in with the local schools, Brownies and Beaver groups.

Thursday 6 March 1997 saw me at the BBC Bryn Merion Studios in Bangor for an interview on the BBC Radio Wales Breakfast Show in connection with trespass and vandalism and anti-social behaviour on the railways in North Wales.

Following the interview, I enjoyed a nice, cooked breakfast in the canteen there.

A talk on the work of the force was the order of the day, to the North Wales Railway Circle, Prestatyn branch on the evening of Friday 7 March 1997.

Another Public Forum was held in Rhyl on Monday 10 March 1997 and was well attended by the community. They came armed with questions, concerns and observations about crime on the railway. I was able to pacify them.

Having joined the local branch of the Chartered Institute of Management at Bangor I attended my first meeting on the evening of Wednesday 19 March 1997, which was a presentation by the local Coroner, which included a couple of my cases. I was welcomed by all the members, which included two senior police officers from the North Wales Police, who I knew very well.

Shirley and I celebrated our silver wedding anniversary on the 22 April 1997. On Saturday 26 April 1997 we held a party at the Valley Hotel with family and friends. One of the guests was Paul De-Vette from the Nederlands Spoorweg Polite, who I'd met a few years previously. I had invited Paul and his wife Sonya, who had family in the Holyhead area. Unfortunately, Sonya was unable to attend. However, Paul came to Great Britain with three motorcycle colleagues from the Blue Knights (An international law enforcement motorcycle club) for a short break. I invited his colleagues to the party as well. These colleagues were tall, had beards, long hair and were well built, and when in their leathers, they looked very intimidating. The party was also attended by PC Sean Morgan who was on duty at Bangor the following morning.

Paul and his colleagues arranged to meet Sean for a visit at the police station for a coffee at around 10.00 hours. Sean like myself was a bit of a joker and he decided to 'set up' the duty Rail Operator, Andy Locke. At around 09.45 hours Sean went to Andy's office and informed him that he had just received information from the North Wales Police that there were four armed and dangerous Dutchmen on motorcycles in the area and under no circumstances should they be tackled. But it was highly unlikely that they would come to the railway station as they would most probably head for the wilds of Snowdonia. Paul and his colleagues rode into the car park at around 10.00 hours which was witnessed by Andy Locke. Andy ran to the police station and having a job to get his words out, he informed Sean that 'the suspects' had arrived at the station and Sean invited him in to catch his breath. The next thing there was a knock at the door and as Sean opened it there was a look of sheer panic on Andy's face. The tension was broken when Paul said, "Hiya Sean". Andy then realised that he had been set up. I will not repeat here what was said by him. But he was mighty relieved.

A regular tabletop train crash exercise was held in Crewe on Friday 13 June 1997. This exercise was to test our reactions to a real-life train crash should the need arise. It was attended by the various agencies.

On the evening of Tuesday 24 June 1997, I attended the Neptune theatre in Liverpool for a play entitled *'I dare you'* in which youths from the Liverpool area were invited to see this play all about railway safety. It was performed by a group from Huddersfield.

The afternoon of Monday 30 June 1997 saw me at Holyhead High School delivering safety lectures to some of the pupils, as we had received information about their conduct at the station.

On the evening of the same day. I was invited to address the Isle of Anglesey County Council Police Liaison Committee on the work of the force. This particular meeting was normally attended by the North Wales Police Chief Constable or the Superintendent in charge of the Anglesey Division, but they decided on a change. Two days later I received a letter from the committee thanking me for my presence and the excellent address on the background and duties of the British Transport Police. The members found it most enjoyable and informative and stated there was a great deal more which I could have said, had the time allowed. Even though we had left Holyhead in February 1989 the members expressed sadness that the force was no longer based at Holyhead.

The afternoon of Tuesday 1 July 1997 saw me back at Holyhead High School delivering more safety lectures to the pupils appertaining to their behaviour.

The play 'I dare you' had two performances at Theatre Colwyn, Colwyn Bay, on Friday 4 July 1997 and both performances were well attended by pupils from local schools. I was on hand to distribute safety goody bags provided by the force.

I attended the children's outpatient's department at Ysbyty Glan Clwyd, Bodelwyddan, on the morning of Monday 21 July. It was the start of their safety themed week. I had a rail safety exhibition in the department.

Just after 17.00 hours on Tuesday 29 July 1997, at the start of the school holidays, the driver of a train saw three children on Ty Gwyn level crossing near Abergele, playing 'chicken'. They ran across the crossing in front of the train and then jumped out of the way at the last minute. Following this incident, I contacted all the local newspapers and issued a general safety warning for the school holidays which were just beginning. The BTP schools liaison officers from Crewe came to assist me, visiting the numerous caravan and chalet parks in the area talking to the children and parents.

Even though we had left the Port of Holyhead in 1989 we still had jurisdiction and involvement there, so I was always invited to the port security meetings. One such meeting took place on Friday 22 August 1997.

I travelled to Tadworth on Friday 29 August 1997 for an 'Officers in Charge' Dinner where our Certificates in Management were formally presented by Desmond O'Brien the Chief Constable. I returned to Bangor on Saturday 30 August 1997.

Betty Williams, the MP for Conwy, became a personal friend of the family when I first met her as a local Councillor back in 1986. Betty was the guest speaker at the Institute of Management meeting on Wednesday 10 September 1997 at which I attended.

In September of 1997 I received a complaint from Valley Community Council to the effect that youths were causing anti-social behaviour problems on the village railway station during the late evenings. Following high profile patrols to the station the youths were suitably dealt with.

I later received a letter of thanks from the Community Council for our efforts. Further unannounced visits were made to the station.

I made a presentation on the work of the force to the members of The Llandudno and Conwy Valley Railway Society during the evening of Thursday 10 October 1997, following which I received a nice letter of thanks.

Keith Roberts, one of my PC's, had his retirement function at the Trearddur Bay Hotel, Trearddur Bay, on Friday 7 November 1997. He had just retired after around twenty-five years with the force at Holyhead and Bangor.

The Institute of Management's meeting on Wednesday 12 November 1997 saw Chris Leah from the railway industry as the guest speaker.

Saturday 22 November 1997 saw a local football derby between Fflint and Bangor. Very few Bangor supporters travelled by train.

Figure 28 Bill outside the Bangor Police Station

Another Port of Holyhead Security meeting took place on the morning of Wednesday 26 November 1997.

Since the early 1980's British Rail ran a special train from Holyhead to Cardiff in connection with the rugby fixtures at Cardiff Arms Park and the new Millennium Stadium. The train usually consisted of between ten and twelve coaches. British Rail charged a flat fare of ten pounds. The trains were very well supported and were usually full by the time we left Abergavenny.

With privatisation moving at a fast pace the special trains still ran, albeit at a much higher price, the normal train fare. There was a relief train from Crewe to Cardiff which consisted of a two-coach diesel multiple unit (DMU) and would pick up supporters between Crewe and Abergavenny leaving the main train to run non-stop from Wrexham.

Looking to save costs the train operating company used the two coach DMU to run from Holyhead to Cardiff and the locomotive hauled train to run from Crewe. Both sets of stock would travel empty from Cardiff the day before of the match. This did not work at all, as there was potential for disorder. The DMU on departure from Llandudno Junction was vastly overcrowded and the relief special from Crewe ran virtually empty. I wrote to the railway management at Swindon pointing this out and offered a solution as to how they could swop the trains around. I received a very curt reply informing me to mind my own business and stick to policing the railways. In reply I informed them that was exactly what I was doing, preventing disorder. I never received a reply, but the next time the trains ran the 'Status Quo' had resumed.

Wales played The 'All Blacks' at Cardiff Arms Park in a rugby match on the afternoon of Saturday 29 November 1997. An early morning tour of duty saw me with my officers monitoring the local North Wales fans travelling to the game.

During the early hours of Wednesday 3 December 1997 local farmers demonstrated at Holyhead Port against the cheap imports of beef from Ireland. To vent their anger, they threw several boxes of beef burgers into the harbour. Although the North Wales Police were responsible for policing the port, they called on our assistance as we still held jurisdiction there under the British Transport Commission Act of 1949. I and two of my constables were called out from home to assist. (I always kept a spare uniform at home) Later in the day assistance was afforded from a Mobile Support Unit from Liverpool.

In early December 1997 I visited Holyhead High School, along with other safety critical organisations, for a safety day. This had been sponsored by Barclays New Futures, where several children from the local primary schools attended the unusual safety presentation. A puppeteer from Menai Bridge used his puppet character 'Kevin' to illustrate the dangers of succumbing to peer pressures and joining in acts of vandalism and the heartache caused to victims. I provided safety goody bags for the children from the force.

As in previous years there was a plethora of prosecution files and cautions to be dealt with, as well as attending routine meetings with the force, railway managers, and the local police, along with outside agencies.

1998 started off fairly quietly from me. The New Year is already into its eighth day - Thursday 8 January 1998. It seems like only yesterday that it was Wednesday 7 January 1998! Today, saw me out in the evening doing a presentation on the work of the force to the Colwyn Bay Women's Guild.

As usual I began to contact the local schools and youth groups to book rail safety talks up to Easter.

Saturday 17 January 1998 Bangor played Rhyl in a local football derby at Farrar Road, Bangor. Duty was performed with my officers but fortunately no trouble.

Wylfa Power Station, on the Isle of Anglesey, was the location on Wednesday 28 January 1998 for a tabletop Nuclear Flask exercise, the scenario involved a nuclear flask train crashing with a passenger train on the main railway line on the Isle of Anglesey.

A Saturday morning duty was performed on 21 February 1998 in connection with the England v Wales rugby five nations match at Twickenham. Several Welsh supporters travelled from North Wales, but they were all well behaved.

A local football derby took place in Rhyl between Rhyl and Bangor, on Saturday 28 February 1998. Trains were monitored and the fans on the whole were well behaved. Friendly warnings were issued to a couple of them.

Wednesday 11 March 1998 saw me attending the local branch meeting of the Institute of Management and I was persuaded to join the committee.

The following Wednesday 18 March 1998 I attended a meeting at the Stena line offices, Holyhead, in connection with a forthcoming Ireland v Wales rugby union five nations match on Saturday 21 March 1998. An exceptionally large number of Welsh supporters travelled over to Ireland on Friday 20 March and Saturday 21 March.

Between the evening of Saturday 21 March and the early hours of Monday 23 March 1998 whilst it was closed, someone smashed a window and broke into the Signalbox at Deganwy, on the Llandudno Junction to Llandudno railway line and stole a pack of twelve detonators. In the wrong hands these detonators had the potential to kill someone. I handed the enquiry over to the CID from Crewe.

I was on duty with other officers at Holyhead on Sunday 22 March 1998 for the return of the rugby supporters. Although they were high in spirits from the famous black Irish stout, they caused no real problems. One or two of them had to have a friendly warning. They were then escorted on trains from Holyhead.

Sir Trefor Morris, Her Majesty's Chief Inspector of Constabulary, paid a visit to our Crewe police station in late March as part of a formal inspection, and I was one of the officers on hand to meet him. He spoke to me about the duties we performed in North Wales.

Sunday 5 April 1998 saw the Wales football team play France at Wembley and I was required to work on this day to monitor fans travelling to London. All passed off peacefully.

At around 23.30 hours on Friday 15 May 1998 a young woman who had been to a night club in Llandudno was dropped off in a taxi at Llandudno Junction railway station to catch a late-night train to Bangor. As she was walking to the station entrance in semi darkness a male person, whom she did not get a good look at, came up behind her and indecently assaulted her. The attacker fled when a car drove up.

Following the indecent assault on the female at Llandudno Junction, I met the team from Crimestoppers Wales for a reconstruction of the incident. I played the part of the sex attacker and my daughter played the part of the victim. The reconstruction was shown on the television after the local Welsh news each night for a week. One morning I answered the telephone at Bangor. It was the Crimestoppers office in Cardiff. The voice on the other end said, "Guess what Sarge, we've got a suspect for you... it's you!"

A lady rang in and said, I'm sure that the man you are after is Sergeant Rogerson, the man on the television looks just like him" We had a good laugh.

As our resources throughout the force were stretched, I underwent some basic Scenes of Crimes training on Wednesday 24 June 1998, so that I could deal with minor incidents rather than call the Scenes of Crimes officer (SOCO) all the way from Manchester.

The town centre of Holyhead was suffering an unusually high proportion of anti-social behaviour at the end of June 1998. On Wednesday 1 July 1998 I attended a meeting with the North Wales Police at Holyhead to devise a strategy to combat it. After all, once it was sorted out, I did not want the youths coming down to the railway station causing mayhem, we had had enough of them over the years.

In early July 1998, the Signalbox nameboard was stolen from Llandudno Signalbox, where it had been for around one hundred years. The sign was to be removed and donated to the Llandudno Museum. Local enquiries proved negative. However, it turned up a few weeks later in a Cardiff auction house and my colleagues from Cardiff recovered the sign and it was then handed to the museum.

Early in the evening of Friday 24 July 1998 I was on duty in the sidings at Valley for the arrival of the Royal Train conveying HRH Prince of Wales which was to be stabled overnight prior to his Royal Highness visiting RAF Valley on Saturday 25 July to present the 'Wings' to the personnel passing out and to attend a family's day. I completed my tour of duty at around Midnight, as I had to be back on duty at Holyhead railway station at 06.00 hours the next day for the arrival of the train.

Saturday 25 July 1998 I and other officers under the command of the late Superintendent Tom Baker, booked on duty at Holyhead at 06.00 hours to await the arrival of the Royal Train. The Royal Train duly arrived at Platform One, at around 09.30 hours and HRH Prince of Wales alighted and walked to his official car. On the way he stopped to say "Good morning" to me, as I was on duty by the exit gate. He then went up to the RAF base.

Figure 29 Bill briefing PC Steff Buck at Holyhead on the occasion of the arrival of HRH Prince of Wales

Myself and all the other officers were stood down and we adjourned to the Crown Restaurant in the town centre for a well-earned sumptuous cooked breakfast.

At around 11.00 hours I booked off duty and went home to change into my best suit, after which I went up to the RAF base to work on the lifeboat stall. The RNLI had been invited to take an inflatable lifeboat and a souvenir stall at the family's day.

In the meantime, my daughter, Alison, who was a civil servant working at the base, and a member of the Trearddur Bay lifeboat crew was invited to have lunch with HRH Prince of Wales. After the lunch finished, she left and changed into her lifeboat crew attire.

HRH Prince of Wales came to the lifeboat stall. He then approached my daughter and said to her "We have just had lunch together". To which she said "Yes". He then approached me and said, with a smile, "Have we met before?" To which I informed him that we had, and that I was the Sergeant on duty at Holyhead railway station earlier in the day. He then asked all about the lifeboat to which I was able to furnish him with the information. Via his personal protection officer, he made a donation.

Figure 30 Bill explaining the workings of a 'D' class Lifeboat to HRH Prince of Wales at RAF Valley on 15th July 1998

Friday 31 July 1998 saw festivities along the North Wales Coast to celebrate 150 years of the 'Irish Mail' train running between Holyhead and London. The train first ran between London Euston and Holyhead on the 1 August 1848. Myself and my officers paid attention to the stations where a special train stopped.

The force experimented with stab resistant vests at selected stations. Due to the officers working by themselves most of the time at Bangor, I applied for two to be allocated to Bangor. My request was refused.

A couple of weeks later PC Sean Braithwaite went out on patrol on the 09.06 hours Holyhead to London Euston passenger train. During the journey between Bangor and Llandudno Junction, Sean came across a man who was acting suspiciously. Sean began to question him, and the man pulled out a knife with a six-inch blade and pointed it at Sean. After a few tense seconds, the man turned the knife around and handed the knife to Sean. He was arrested and charged. On arrival back at the office, Sean put a report into the Area Commander about the incident, which I countersigned with my comments. Two days later, two stab resistant vests arrived. Body armour is now worn as personal protection equipment for officers throughout the force.

The first round of the Cup Winners cup was played at Bangor's Farrar Road ground between Bangor and Haka of Finland on Thursday 13 August 1998 with a 19.30 hours kick off. I and other officers were on duty at Bangor to monitor supporters travelling along the coast. Just a handful of supporters travelled by train and caused no problems.

I accompanied Superintendent Tony Thompson of the force when he attended the North Wales Police Headquarters in Colwyn Bay as the guest speaker at the media officers conference on Friday 9 October 1998.

Conwy County Council were thinking of introducing new byelaws appertaining to consuming alcohol in public places and I was invited to a meeting on Wednesday 28 October 1998 to give an input re the application to railway premises within the county.

Saturday November 14, 1998 saw Wales play South Africa in an International Rugby match at Wembley. I was on hand to monitor supporters travelling to London. All were very well behaved.

The force had recently re-introduced Special Constables, and on Monday 16 November 1998 I attended our police station at Crewe to interview potential candidates for Bangor.

Overall, 1998 was a fairly busy year with routine matters requiring my attention.

CHAPTER 24

THE BANGOR YEARS JANUARY 1999 – JULY 2000

Going Dutch again

The New Year of 1999 was barely forty minutes old when tragedy struck at Gaerwen on the Isle of Anglesey. Unlike Christmas Day and Boxing Day when trains didn't run, they ran on New Year's Day.

At around 00.40 hours after celebrating in a nearby pub, a young man walking along the railway lines in the direction of Bangor, near to Gaerwen level crossing was hit by an empty stock train travelling at around seventy miles per hour from Llandudno Junction to Holyhead. Paramedics attended but he was sadly declared dead at the scene. The driver of the train was treated for shock. Following the incident, I made an appeal in the local papers for people to be aware of the dangers of the railway.

Most of January 1999 was taken up with routine meetings, including a Stena Line security meeting at Holyhead, internal force meetings, local council meetings, rail industry meetings. I also held interviews in Bangor for Special Constables. Unfortunately, there were no suitable candidates. I undertook several cautions of offenders.

Monday 1 February 1999 saw me travel to Liverpool to be measured for new body armour, which was to be issued to all front-line officers.

The force, being a statutory body had to, by law, introduce a Welsh Language policy. On Tuesday 9 February 1999 I travelled on the early morning train from Holyhead to London Euston to attend Force Headquarters for a meeting with senior officers from the force to discuss the policy.

During the month of February 1999 my attention was drawn to a group of people who were purchasing high value rail tickets with fraudulent cheques at the booking offices throughout the North West and on the North Wales Coast, to various parts of the country.

Myself and Detective Sergeant Mike Walsom from Crewe, and a couple of other CID officers commenced enquiries and the culprits were arrested and charged with various offences.

On appearing at court, they pleaded guilty. Following the court appearance, I received a letter of appreciation from the Banking and Treasury department of First North Western Trains in Manchester, who had been the main target of the fraud.

Several routine meetings were held throughout February 1999 as well as a couple of rugby matches in which the supporters needed monitoring on the trains along the North Wales Coast Line.

March 1999 was another busy month for me with meetings, school visits, cautions, public forums and steam trains running along the North Wales Coast.

I addressed the Chester and North Wales Rail Users' Association Annual General Meeting in Llandudno on Saturday 10 April 1999, on the work of the force. Following the meeting I received a letter of thanks from the Chairman.

"Thank you very much for your valuable input to last Saturday's meeting. Several of those who were present have been in touch to say how useful they found the whole event; your little talk was an eye-opener to those who were previously unaware of the existence of the British Transport Police.

Thank you for all your work towards improving the safety of rail users in North Wales".

The following day Sunday 11 April, saw Wales play England in a rugby match at Wembley and there was a steam train excursion along the coast, so it was a busy day monitoring rugby fans and railway enthusiasts.

On the morning of Wednesday 28 April 1999, I accompanied DC Down from Force Headquarters to a guest house in Llanberis to make enquiries with the owners into alleged offences concerning fraud and corruption in the London area, involving the railway industry. Several documents were seized as part of the investigation.

Later that day I had an anti-social behaviour meeting with the Bangor City Centre Partnership

The Rotary Club of Holyhead held a services day at Holyhead High School on Friday 21 May 1999. Attendees were from the high school and local primary schools. The service participants included myself with a rail safety display. A thank you letter was received from the Headteacher.

"Thank you very much for your participation in last Friday's Services Day. It was obviously a huge success, and this was mainly due to the efforts of people like yourself who gave up the whole day to demonstrate the work done by your service.

The comments made by the Primary School children and staff illustrated the enjoyment given, as well as the information imparted".

June 1999 was taken up with official cautions, meetings, train patrols and duty in connection with the steam train excursions.

Figure 31 Bill in pensive reflection whilst on duty at Llandudno Junction in connection with a steam train excursion. 'Merchant Navy' locomotive 30005 'Canadian Pacific' in view

His Royal Highness Prince Charles was invested as the Prince of Wales at Caernarfon Castle on July 1, 1969. On the eve of the Investiture, two local men, it is believed, intended to blow up the main Chester to Holyhead railway line at Abergele and Pensarn with a bomb made by a third person. The bomb exploded prematurely killing the two men and they were later dubbed the 'Abergele Martyrs'. After being caught, the bomb maker, then a sergeant with the Army, pleaded guilty to eight charges and was jailed for ten years.

Following the incident, rallies were held each year in Abergele between 1970 and 1999 but were stopped after the daughter of one of the men complained that some people got drunk at her father's graveside and others were seen urinating near the graveyard.

A discrete British Transport Police presence was maintained at Abergele and Pensarn railway station each year. During my tenure at Bangor I covered most of the rallies. A much higher police presence was maintained in the town centre and at the Church by the North Wales Police.

Just eleven sympathisers turned up for the march in 1999. A spokesperson for the rally said: "We want to remember the two men on the thirtieth anniversary of their deaths and remember what they did. It will be a black flag parade of remembrance not a celebration of nationalist culture". There was no trouble, the rally passed off peacefully.

On Friday 9 July 1999 I went to Ysgol Dyffryn Conwy (Llanrwst High School) Llanrwst, to talk to the pupils about the dangers of the railway, as the summer holidays were rapidly approaching, and we had been experiencing trespass on the tracks there.

The School/Industry Links Co-ordinator sent me the following letter.

"Thank you for coming to talk to our pupils last Friday. They found your presentation very interesting and informative. I hope that it has also helped them to see possible dangers on and around railways and encouraged them to have a more responsible attitude".

The Charity Shield football match was played between Arsenal and Manchester United at Wembley on Sunday 1 August 1999, in which Arsenal won 2 - 1. I was on duty on the North Wales Coast to monitor fans and escort them travelling to Wembley.

The majority of August 1999 was taken up with trespass and vandalism patrols along the North Wales Coast and with cautions to juvenile offenders.

Figure 32 Bill at a rail safety exhibition

The Millennium was on the horizon. At 09.30 hours on Friday 27 August 1999, I attended a press conference at the North Wales Police Headquarters in Colwyn Bay to announce our proposed plans for policing the Millennium.

It is always pleasing to receive letters of appreciation. Straight after the above press conference I went to Llandudno to assist PCs Morgan and Braithwaite with an arrest of a couple of people for theft on the railway in Llandudno. After processing them at the town's custody suite we were requested by the North Wales Police to assist them with a suspect device incident at a bank, in the town centre. The incident, which was declared as a major police operation, involved the evacuation of a large part of the town centre and lasted for many hours. We assisted with the manning of the cordons. A few days later we received a letter of appreciation from Chief Superintendent Larry Davies, the Divisional Commander for Llandudno.

I hosted a crime prevention display on the 4 September 1999 at Bangor railway station with the late Sergeant Mick Owen and PC Geoff Davies, the Area Crime Prevention Officers.

Wales played Switzerland in an international football match at Wrexham on Saturday 9 September 1999. A handful of supporters travelled from Bangor and other stations to Wrexham. All passed off peacefully.

I think it was in September 1999, during the early hours of a Monday morning for two consecutive weeks, a five-barred metal farm gate was placed onto main Holyhead to Chester Railway Line at a place called Star, approximately one mile to the west of Llanfairpwllgwyngyllgogerychwyrndrobwllllantysiliogogoch, known locally as Llanfair P.G. or Llanfairpwll, on the beautiful Isle of Anglesey. Observations were set up by myself and Detective Sergeant Mike Walsom, from Crewe, on the railway embankment, near to the scene of the crimes. On one Sunday evening / Monday morning both of us wore separate large green dustbin liners to blend in with the grass and foliage. Previously it was agreed that we would call on the assistance of a dog handler from the Liverpool sub-division to assist us. The plan was for him to be parked up in a lay-by on the nearby main road so that he could have easy access to the scene if required.

After carefully giving him directions, we arranged to meet him in the station car park at the said Llanfairpwllgwyngyllgogerychwyrndrobwllllantysiliogogoch, at 23.45 hours on this particular Sunday evening, for a briefing. Well, 23.45 hours came and went and still no sign of the dog and handler. We contacted him via the radio via Liverpool Control. (No mobiles in those days). He assured us that he was in the car park and was awaiting our arrival. We told him that we were there, and we could not see him. He was adamant that he was there and that we were in the wrong location. After a bit of detective work, I established that he was in fact at Llanfairfechan station some twelve miles to the east of us. He quickly joined us, and we settled down to our observations which proved negative. However, we eventually caught the culprit, who was a farmer's daughter, who suffered from mental health problems.

Access to the mainland side of Robert Stephenson's famous Britannia Bridge which connects the mainland with the Isle of Anglesey is via a railway owned narrow lane, leading from the main road in the Treborth area of Bangor. The area of land immediately underneath the bridge is railway owned as well. Due to its isolated location, it attracted a lot of anti-social behaviour, such as fly tipping, courting couples and illegal raves etc.

Due to my limited resources at Bangor and the vast area I had to cover it was virtually impossible to give the area the attention it deserved.

However, Phil Gerard a North Wales Police general purpose dog handler, for their Western Division, covering the Isle of Anglesey and Gwynedd, and myself, came up with a cunning plan to thwart the culprits. Phil and his family had recently moved into a cottage in the lane. He asked if it would be possible to park his dog van in the lane thus preventing vehicle and pedestrian access to the bridge. In return, he would patrol the area with his faithful companion, a German Shepherd, as part of his exercise. The plan was cleared with the local railway management and the anti-social behaviour ceased almost overnight.

October 1999 began with a couple of days visiting Holyhead High School to present railway safety talks, a Port security meeting at Holyhead and cautions of trespassers caught during August.

During October 1999 I had more police-orientated meetings to attend along with safety talks to the local Brownies.

During the evening of Thursday 21 October 1999, I made a presentation to some of the North Wales Police officers at their Force Headquarters in Colwyn Bay on the work of the British Transport Police.

The month of October culminated with yet more meetings, planning for the Millennium, and cautions of offenders who had committed various offences which didn't warrant court proceedings.

The month of November 1999 began exactly the same as October with a couple of days visiting Holyhead High School to present railway safety talks, a Port security meeting at Holyhead and a couple of cautions in Bangor

Monday 15 November 1999 saw me attend a meeting of the Denbighshire Towns Safe Committee in Rhyl. The rest of the week was taken up with cautions for trespass and other offences.

The last month of the twentieth century had arrived, December 1999. I was busy preparing for New Year's Eve. The prophets of doom had predicted that the world would end, computers would crash, electricity systems would fail, trains would stop running due to the signals not working etc. Area Headquarters had sent me manual telephone pads, self-heating meals, bottles of mineral water and orange juice.

The rest of the month was taken up with routine meetings and cautions. I also had to find out which fuel stations would be open on New Year's Eve and to ensure that the police car was filled up on that morning.

Friday 31 December the last day of the twentieth century had finally arrived. I was rostered to work 19.00 hours to 07.00 hours (I had been originally rostered to work 11.00 hours to 19.00 hours) along with PC Mike Rhodes and PC Sean Morgan. I duly booked on at 19.00 hours and discovered that PC Sean Braithwaite, who had been covering the day shift had experienced a relatively quiet day.

The night progressed quietly, and finally midnight arrived; this was what we had all been waiting for. Would the world end as the prophets of doom had predicted? The three of us went out onto Platform One at Bangor railway station to wish each other a Happy New Year and Millennium etc. and watch the fireworks over the City of Bangor.

We then returned to the office to find that nothing had changed, the dates on the computers changed to 1 January 2000, and the crime reporting numbers reverted back to zero, the trains were still running, the electric supply was normal. In fact, it was quieter than a normal New Year's Eve.

At around 00.35 hours on 1 January 2000 a train driver reported seeing some trespassers at Llanfairfechan. We all went down there and reported eight people who were on a camping holiday in the area, for trespass. A good start for my figures.

It was so quiet for the rest of the night that the duty Inspector in the Area Control room told me to book off duty at 03.00 hours which I did.

The brand-new January of the brand-new Millennium was fairly quiet with routine meetings, a public forum in Bangor and cautions for various offences.

The first rugby sporting fixture of the new Millennium for me, took place between Wales and France at Cardiff on Saturday 5 February 2000 in the new six nations rugby union match. This was the first year that Italy had joined, hence its new title. Not as many fans as we expected travelled by train.

The North Wales Police were introducing a new system of dealing with youth offenders. It was based on the football red card system. The Inspector responsible for this new procedure came to my office on Thursday 10 February 2000 to discuss it, as we were to be involved in the pilot scheme.

Saturday 19 February 2000 saw Wales play Italy in a six nations rugby union match at Cardiff. All was quiet from the fans.

Saturday 4 March 2000 was a busy day for me and my officers. England played Wales at Twickenham in a six nations rugby union match. I and other officers were on hand to monitor the supporters travelling to London. Quite a number Welsh fans travelled down to London, on the whole they behaved themselves. One or two of the younger element had to be given some fatherly advice from me.

An unusual event took place on Saturday 18 March 2000, the Britannia Bridge which connects the mainland to the Isle of Anglesey was to celebrate its sesquicentenary, as the bridge opened to rail traffic on 6 March 1850. As 6 March 2000 fell on a Monday this year the celebrations for the event were held over until Saturday 18 March 2000. The event attracted a large number of visitors and dignitaries to the area and to Bangor railway station where the official celebrations took place. One of the dignitaries was Michael Argent QPM, Chief Constable of North Wales. We had our photographs taken together on the platform and he remarked, "Two Chief Constables together". It was policed successfully by myself, PCs Sean Morgan, and Braithwaite.

Figure 33 Bill and PC Sean Morgan on duty at Bangor in connection with the sesquicentenary anniversary celebrations of the opening of the Britannia Bridge

Following the event, I received a complimentary letter from the organiser of the event, a gentleman from Chester.

'Many thanks indeed for the support of the British Transport Police for the celebration of the Britannia Bridge last Saturday. It certainly was a splendid occasion which had a tremendous party atmosphere and one which was enjoyed by everyone present – and we were blessed with good weather. The whole programme came together very well, and I have heard nothing but praise from every quarter for those who contributed to the event. Everyone comments on how wonderfully intense the day was, with so many things to do, see and read. Many people were impressed with the amount of preparation which had been put into the programme by the various organisations involved. It will certainly be a very hard act to follow, and one which put the coast of North Wales on the map for the day.

I very much appreciate all of the efforts that were put in by yourself and all of the police officers both prior to the event and on the day itself. This certainly helped for the smooth running of the celebration, and could you please pass on my thanks for the very cheerful, enthusiastic, and polite manner in which everything was done. The high profile of the uniformed officers added colour and character to the whole scene. I just hope that things aren't too humdrum in the aftermath!"

Once again, many thanks for your contribution which helped to make for an unforgettable day'.

Figure 34 Bill on duty at Bangor in connection with the sesquicentenary anniversary celebrations of the opening of the Britannia Bridge

Figure 35 Bill and Larry Davies at Bangor in connection with the sesquicentenary anniversary celebrations of the opening of the Britannia Bridge

Also, on Saturday 18 March 2000, Wales played Scotland in a six nations rugby union match in Edinburgh. Hardly any supporters travelled by train.

Jack Straw, the then Home Secretary arrived by train at Llandudno Junction on Friday 24 March 2000 for a meeting in Llandudno. I was on hand at the Junction for his arrival and departure. He did have the courtesy to stop and have a chat with me about my duties.

A six nations rugby union match between Ireland and Wales on Saturday 1 April 2000 necessitated a police presence on the trains to monitor the behaviour of the Welsh fans travelling to and from Ireland. On the whole they were all well behaved. As usual some of them had to be told about the error of their ways.

I was required to work on Sunday 2 April 2000 to deal with the fans returning from Ireland. A majority of them, around seven hundred, arrived back on the late afternoon ferry from Dun Laoghaire. Fortunately, we had a train large enough to accommodate them for their forward journey from Holyhead. During the week, First North Western Trains ran trains consisting of a diesel locomotive and six carriages along the coast to and from Birmingham as part of their normal timetable. Each Sunday, for the evening departure, two of the trains were doubled up, therefore the 18.30 hours departure to Crewe, was formed of two class 37 diesel locomotives and twelve carriages.

Today, was no exception. However, the train would only wait for five minutes if the ferry was late, unlike the days of British Rail when the train would be held until the ferry arrived. I received word that the ferry was running late, and it was touch and go if it made the train connection. I managed to get a hold of ten minutes on the train, but this was looking doubtful. The next train from Holyhead would be at around 20.40 hours and would be a two-coach train, not adequate to accommodate the fans. The ferry arrived just as the ten-minute deadline approached. I just happened to see 'some smoke' coming from the second locomotive and pointed this out to the driver and that he probably required the assistance of a fitter. By the time the fitter had examined the train, the fans were all on board and the train departed with a police escort around twenty minutes late. The funny thing is that the train arrived in Crewe on time. Everybody was happy.

The next morning Monday 3 April 2000, I received a telephone call from one of the railway managers who said "Nice try, Bill. Your devious plan worked". I put the phone down, sat back in my chair with a bright smile and gave myself a mental pat on the back.

This train also saw hen and stag parties returning from riotous weekends in Dublin. By the time they had joined the train they were exhausted after their exploits in the Emerald Isle. However, on one occasion one 'stag' member still had the energy to run up and down the train to the annoyance of other passengers dressed only in cling film. He was suitably dealt with.

Most of April was taken up with meetings, search awareness training, anti - trespass patrols, train patrols and cautions mainly involving juveniles who had been behaving in a disorderly manner.

Once again, it is always pleasing to receive letters of appreciation for assisting our colleagues. At 09.18 hours on Thursday 27 April 2000, the day before I was to go on annual leave to Italy, the emergency services were summoned to the Ty Newydd Bail Hostel at Llandegai, near Bangor, following a report of a resident having collapsed and died. It was suspected that the deceased had died from a drug overdose.

Staff at the hostel suspected the deceased had been given drugs by another resident, as the suspect resident, had also been seen coming out of a third resident's room shortly before the death.

As a result, the suspect and the occupier of the other room were arrested by the North Wales Police on suspicion of being concerned in the supplying of controlled drugs.

The first officers on the scene had managed to gather all remaining residents into one communal lounge and secure access to all accommodation. It was then necessary to carry out a systematic search of each room in the presence of their occupiers, to satisfy the North Wales Police, that there was no evidence relating to the death, or any other evidence of drug abuse on the premises. The number of North Wales Police officers on duty at Bangor were clearly insufficient, as there were some twenty rooms to be searched. Overhearing the incident on the North Wales Police radio, I realised that they had a mammoth task, so I offered my assistance along with the late PC Dave Tucker and PC Sean Braithwaite who were on duty with me. This offer was readily accepted by the Inspector on the scene. We attended the hostel where we assisted and remained until all the searching was completed. Indeed, I had the task of assisting in the removal of the deceased. The Chief Superintendent (Operations) North Wales Police commented in a letter to Paul Nicholas Assistant Chief Constable (Operations) British Transport Police, that the task would have taken considerably longer if I hadn't offered our services, which was typical of the invaluable assistance we provide to the North Wales Police on many occasions, much of it clearly outside our remit.

The disused Platform Three shopping complex at Colwyn Bay railway station, which had become a regular meeting place for local youths since it closed and had been the bane of my life, was finally demolished in April 2000.

A wave of vandalism in late April 2000, saw thousands of pounds worth of damage caused at sites within the jurisdiction of the North Wales Police, in Colwyn Bay, Mochdre and Conwy areas. In the most serious incident damage estimated at around thirty thousand pounds was caused to a property in Station Road, Colwyn Bay. The town's railway station did not escape either, with around a dozen windows on the overbridge damaged by stone throwing. Also, a clock on one of the platforms was damaged. The vandals also targeted a lift used by elderly and disabled passengers. A joint investigation resulted in the prosecution of some local youths.

On Tuesday 9 May 2000 and Wednesday 10 May 2000, I attended the annual conference of the Wales Rail Users Consultative Committee, in Llandudno where I gave a presentation on the work of the force. I was afforded an overnight stay with a delicious meal and after-dinner drinks at the town's Empire Hotel where the conference was held.

Week commencing Monday 22 May 2000 was a particularly busy week with community safety meetings in Llandudno, Bangor, and Crewe.

Figure 36 Bill on duty at Valley sidings by 'Jubilee' locomotive 45596 'Bahamas'

The Lifeboat 'Her Majesty the Queen' that I helped raised funds for in the 1991 Police Lifeboat Appeal was taken out of the RNLI's relief fleet and put on permanent service at Lytham St Annes. I received an invite to the handing over ceremony on Sunday 4 June 2000, which was a low-key affair compared to when she entered service and was named by Her Majesty the Queen.

The rest of June was taken up with the usual round of meetings and cautions throughout North Wales. Annual leave was also taken.

Another trip to Amsterdam came along. A few years earlier, as previously alluded to, I had befriended a police officer from the Nederlands Spoorweg Polite, (Dutch Transport Police) Paul De-Vette. The force was to undergo a massive reorganisation and their Federation were not too happy about it. They put an appeal out within the organisation requesting to know if any officer had contacts with the British Transport Police Federation. Paul immediately contacted me to see if I could assist. I put him in contact with Phil White (General Secretary of the Federation). I knew Phil very well, as Phil and I had worked together at Holyhead a few years earlier. A few weeks later I received an invite from Phil to accompany him and some other officials of the Federation to Amsterdam to meet with the Federation Officials from the Spoorweg Polite. We spent a couple of days as guests of the Federation.

Again, July 2000 was taken up with meetings, cautions, anti-trespass patrols. On Saturday 22 July and Sunday 23 July 2000 I attended a model railway exhibition in Colwyn Bay with a rail safety stand which was attended by a number of interested people.

CHAPTER 25

THE BANGOR YEARS AUGUST 2000 – SEPTEMBER 2001

Dealing with the man who lost his home-made toffee

The seventy eighth Charity Shield football final was played on Sunday 13 August 2000 between Chelsea and Manchester United, a game which Chelsea won 2 - 0. I was on hand to monitor North Wales based Manchester United supporters travelling to London.

In mid-August 2000 I was contacted by Force Headquarters, requesting me to pay a welfare visit to retired Sergeant Bob Jones who was living by himself in Rhos on Sea. Bob was now a widower, in his eighties and sadly his health was deteriorating. He was looked after by a carer. Bob was a native of Mold, North Wales and had begun his career at Mold Junction in the 1940s. He then moved to Birkenhead where he met his wife. He was then promoted from there to uniform sergeant in Dublin when we had a police presence there. When he was made redundant from Dublin, he was posted to London Kings' Cross and Stratford Freightliner depot. He told me that it was like going from the frying pan into the fire. A total contrast. He retired to North Wales. I paid him a couple more visits before he sadly died.

Rhyl played Bangor in a local football derby at Vale Road, Rhyl on Tuesday 19 September 2000. I and other officers were on duty to escort Bangor fans to and from Rhyl. No trouble was experienced.

Tuesday 26 September 2000 saw me speaking to the new year seven intake at Holyhead High School on the subject of rail safety.

October 2000 started off busy for me. I had a safety meeting in Crewe on the morning of Monday 2 October 2000, then it was straight up to Holyhead High School to address more pupils on railway safety.

During the afternoon of Tuesday 3 October 2000, I was invited to Gwalchmai Primary School, Isle of Anglesey, to talk to the pupils about railway safety, prior to a visit to Holyhead railway station that I had arranged for them and a visit to the National Railway Museum at York.

The morning of Thursday 5 October 2000 saw me at Pen-Cae Primary School Penmaenmawr addressing the children on railway safety.

The afternoons of Monday 9 October 2000 and Tuesday 10 October 2000 saw me back once again at Holyhead High School addressing yet more pupils about railway safety.

The railway arches underneath a road / rail bridge, known locally as the 'H' bridge, to the west of Rhyl railway station, were a haven for rubbish to accumulate and for youths to gather. On Wednesday 11 October 2000 I met on site with a representative of the Railtrack Property Board to discuss securing them.

Week commencing 16 October 2000, was again taken up with meetings with Denbighshire County Council and the Victim Support Scheme and with cautions and reprimands.

Around the middle of October 2000, I was called to a fatality at a level crossing in Porthmadog. Although the whole of the Cambrian Coast Line was now the responsibility of the Shrewsbury Police Station, I was the nearest officer. The driver of a car from Rhyl was crossing the railway line and failed to see the red light at the ungated crossing, due to the sun being in his eyes. On arrival at the scene, I liaised with my colleagues from the North Wales Police and commenced enquiries until Sergeant Derek Cheetham and a colleague arrived from Shrewsbury.

During the week commencing 6 November 2000 I had baton and personal protection refresher training and meetings in Rhyl.

The rest of the days leading up to 23 November 2000 were taken up with train patrols, meetings, reprimands, and cautions of juveniles who had been misbehaving along the North Wales Coast.

Figure 37 Bill on a train at Bangor station discussing a suspect ticket with Conductor Ross McAlister

The force had decided to re-introduce Clerical Officers to the smaller police stations to assist the 'Officer in Charge'. A lot of my work was administrative, and I always said that I was the highest paid clerical officer in the force since Alison Jones had been made redundant a couple or so years earlier. On Thursday 23 November 2000 I along with Graham Smart the Chief Clerk at Area Headquarters, interviewed three possible candidates at Bangor. We chose one, Mrs. Carys Ainscough, who later became a Police Community Support Officer (PCSO) and eventually left the force. She was worth her weight in gold. I was able to concentrate more on police work out in the community.

With retirement less than twelve months away I attended a pre - retirement seminar in Newton St Loe, near Bath, between Monday 27 November 2000 and Wednesday 29 November 2000, which had been arranged by the force in conjunction with an Insurance company.

At the beginning of December 2000, a boy aged around thirteen was on Colwyn Bay railway station, when he was approached by two youths who made violent threats and robbed him of his bike. I took him and his mother to Llandudno police station for a photographic identity parade, whereby he was shown photographs of likely suspects. As he was looking through the albums, he kept on picking out members of his own family, which became embarrassing for his mother. He eventually picked out two suspects (who were not members of his family). The suspects were eventually arrested and appeared at Caernarfon Crown Court where they received custodial sentences.

The majority of December 2000 was taken up with routine police work. On Thursday 21 December 2000 I attended a meeting in Cardiff with senior officers and members of a firm called 'SERCO' who were applying for the Wales rail franchise. Sadly, 'SERCO' were unsuccessful in their bid.

The end of the 2000 saw me complete my last full year as an operational officer and I was wondering what 2001 would bring.

The New Year of 2001 was barely forty minutes old when tragedy struck at Gaerwen on the Isle of Anglesey. Unlike Christmas Day and Boxing Day when trains didn't run, they ran on New Year's Day. At around 00.40 hours after celebrating in a nearby pub, two young men were walking along the railway lines in the direction of Bangor, near to Gaerwen level crossing when one of them was hit by an empty stock train travelling at around seventy miles per hour from Llandudno Junction to Holyhead. Paramedics treated the youth, who had suffered serious head and leg injuries, at the scene before being transferred to Ysbyty Gwynedd, Bangor, on arrival he was rushed to the operating theatre, but sadly died three hours later whilst in the theatre. The train driver was treated for shock. Following the incident, I made an appeal in the local papers for people to be aware of the dangers of the railway. A similar incident occurred on the same day at almost the same time in 1999 in Gaerwen involving the same train.

Again, on New Year's Day in 2001, the driver of the 09.20 hours Bangor to London Euston Inter-City train discovered a local man lying by the trackside at Llandegai tunnel, near Bangor. It was believed that he jumped from the top of the tunnel between 06.00 hours and 09.00 hours. He was still alive and taken to Ysbyty Gwynedd, Bangor, where he received medical treatment and later made a full recovery. It transpired that he was suffering from a mental illness. No further action was taken against him.

It was to be my last operational year with the British Transport Police. The terrible foot and mouth outbreak began this year. Also, Carys the new Clerical Officer commenced duty.

Figure 38 Bill at his desk in the Bangor Police Station

Tuesday 9 January 2001, I attended Rhyl police station to carry out a photo identification on some youths that had assaulted a local youth. The culprits were picked out and later arrested.

The evening of Tuesday 16 January 2001 saw me addressing the local branch of the North Wales Railway Circle on the work of the force. Overall, over the years I had a very good relationship with the members, who assisted me in being the eyes and ears in respect of offenders on the railway.

Wednesday 17 January 2001 I was in Rhyl for a Crime and Disorder meeting and then in Llangefni, Isle of Anglesey, in the afternoon for a crime reduction meeting.

On the morning of Wednesday January 24, 2001, I attended a Stena Port security meeting in Holyhead. This was handy for me as I could book on duty at Holyhead.

Friday 26 January 2001 saw me travelling to Area Headquarters in Manchester for Performance Training. This was a new initiative by the force, which they had hired consultants to run the initiative.

January concluded with me attending Friars High School, Bangor to deliver rail safety talks on the morning of Wednesday 31 January 2001. The afternoon was taken up with a meeting of the Bangor City Partnership at the city hall.

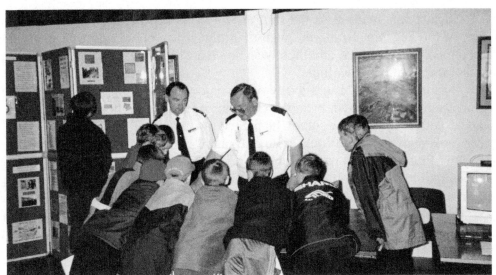
Figure 39 Bill and PC Dave Tucker at a rail safety exhibition

Saturday 3 February 2001 saw Wales play England in a six nations rugby match at Cardiff. I was on duty at Bangor to monitor the fans who travelled and were very well behaved.

On Monday 5 February 2001, Carys, the Clerical Officer, received a call from a firm of Solicitors desperate to cancel a witness travelling from Stratford upon Avon to Bangor Magistrates' Court to give evidence in a two-day trial. The case was adjourned at 09.45 hours, after the witness had set off. The solicitors tried the British Transport Police at Birmingham, Wolverhampton, and Shrewsbury in vain, to contact him via tannoy systems at the respective stations all to no avail. I worked out the route of the witness and his expected time of arrival in Bangor. Carys and I intercepted him as he arrived at Bangor. I took him to the police station and made him a cup of tea after which he returned to his home.

The firm of Solicitors from Manchester wrote a letter of appreciation direct to the Chief Constable, David J. Williams, thanking us for our valued assistance.

One Friday morning in early February 2001, I cannot remember the exact date, I was on duty in my office at Bangor railway station. It was a beautiful sunny morning. The warm February sunshine had placed me in a good mood, after dealing with the mound of paperwork that had been sent from Area Headquarters. It was the usual stuff, the Chief Superintendent wanted everything doing by last week. I was looking forward to a weekend off.

I went to the booking office with an enquiry and as I was going across the car park, I came across a man who was having an asthma attack. He had just arrived by train from Liverpool. The attack was bad one and I called an Ambulance to take him to hospital. Once the Ambulance arrived and he was stabilised, the man informed me that his bag was on the train, by now it was on its way to Holyhead. I assured him that I would make the necessary enquiries to recover it whilst he was at Ysbyty Gwynedd. I obtained his full details.

Contact was made with the staff at Holyhead railway station and there was no sign of the bag. So, I rang the man's family in Liverpool and told them about him being taken to hospital and there was no sign of his bag. They thanked me and said that they would contact him.

A short time later, I was in my office enjoying a cup of coffee when an off-duty rail operator from down the coast came in. He had been shopping with his wife in Bangor and on leaving the station he picked up a package, which he had found in the car park and which he took around Bangor with him. On the way back, he decided to bring it to me to have a look at.

Unlike the television detectives, I did not open a small corner of it and put some on my finger and have a taste. I had a gut feeling of what it was.

Bingo! it contained a rather large amount of heroin amounting to what I later learned was thirty thousand pounds worth. A call was immediately made to the North Wales Police drugs squad who quickly turned up. I mentioned about the man with the asthma attack.

I had hit the jackpot, a Bell Fruit Gum! The North Wales Police were interested in this man and they came to the BTP station. A call to Ysbyty Gwynedd was made and he was due to be released any time. Sure, enough he arrived back at the station and along with PC Sean Braithwaite, we watched him via the station's CCTV system. He was retracing his footsteps from the train, he was frantic, and I thought he was going to have another attack.

He then came to the BTP station enquiring if his bag, containing some special toffee, which had been home made by his elderly aunt, had been found, after he dropped it in the car park. Desperately trying to keep a straight face, at his description of the contents of the package, Sean and I made an excuse to speak to him on the platform, where he would be picked up by the CCTV playback system. I gleaned some more information from him and advised him that I would get one of my officers on the case straight away. He must have thought the British Transport Police were naive, but in fact we were well ahead of the game. To see his actions, unfold on the CCTV was like watching a comedy programme.

He was allowed to go back to Liverpool so that the National Crime Squad could make further enquiries about him.

It transpired that he was a courier for a gang in Liverpool and was carrying drugs to North Wales. He was later arrested and charged. At a subsequent hearing at Caernarfon Crown Court he pleaded 'Not guilty', however, after reading the evidence, the defence Barrister on the advice of the presiding Judge, persuaded him to change his plea. He received four years imprisonment. Following further arrests in Liverpool a substantial amount of heroin and crack cocaine was recovered.

Sean and I received a nice letter of appreciation from the North Wales Police for our involvement in the case.

Like anywhere else in the country, North Wales suffered from its fair share of graffiti on the railway, especially at Holyhead, Bangor, Llanfairfechan, Colwyn Bay, Llandudno Junction, Rhyl and Fflint. At Llannerch Road West, in Rhos on Sea, vandals had painted a thirty-foot abstract mural on a wall opposite to the railway line.

So bad was the graffiti in places the North Wales Daily Post newspaper ran a nearly a full-page article on the problem in their edition dated February 15, 2001. Following this, our anti-graffiti squad from Manchester came and gave me some valuable assistance in locating the culprits.

19 February 2001 the countryside's worst nightmare begins with a routine inspection at Cheale Meats abattoir in Little Warley, south of Brentwood, Essex, that finds "highly suspicious" signs of foot-and-mouth disease in twenty-seven pigs.

20 February 2001 the then Ministry of Agriculture, Fisheries and Food (now the Department of Environment, Food and Rural Affairs) confirmed the outbreak. The abattoir and two farms that supplied the suspect pigs have a five-mile (eight-kilometre) animal exclusion zone put round them. Tests at a farm next door to the abattoir, and owned by the same family, confirm the presence of foot-and-mouth there too.

Due to this several sporting fixtures were put in doubt especially where fans were required to travel to and from Ireland.

Saturday 24 February 2001 saw me booking on duty at 05.30 hours to escort North Wales based Liverpool supporters to Cardiff. The 2001 Football League Cup Final was played between Liverpool and Birmingham City on 25 February 2001 at the Millennium Stadium, Cardiff.

Fortunately, robberies on the railway system in North Wales were rare. In early February, a robbery took place on Rhyl station, when a couple of youths robbed a youth. Another photo identification to identify the suspects in this case saw me at Rhyl police station on the evening of Tuesday 27 February 2001. The victim managed to pick out both offenders who were later arrested and charged with robbery.

Wednesday 28 February 2001 saw me travelling to Crewe for a meeting with the Deputy Chief Constable and other Officers in Charge re force objectives to reduce crime on the railway network.

Carys, the Clerical Officer was settling into her new role and this allowed me to get out and about more on the patch instead of being tied up with paperwork.

Despite the foot and mouth disease the Wales v Ireland rugby six nations match went ahead on Saturday 3 March 2001. I was required to book on duty at 16.00 hours and travel to Chester to escort both Irish and Welsh fans returning from Cardiff. All was quiet. All the foodstuffs brought into the country by the Irish fans was confiscated at Holyhead Port.

The following day Sunday 4 March 2001 I worked from 15.00 hours to 02.00 escorting Irish and Welsh rugby fans along the coast and then public order duty at Holyhead railway station. Both sets of fans were in fine voice especially the Welsh singing songs of their homeland.

Chief Superintendent Geoff Holmes, the Area Commander paid me a routine two-day visit on Thursday 8 March 2001 and Friday 9 March 2001. We took some senior officers from the North Wales Police out to dinner as a thank you for their assistance towards us.

I had to reprimand some pupils for stone throwing on Tuesday 13 March 2001, at Ysgol Coed Menai, (a semi -secure school), Menai Bridge, which was situated near to the railway, for pupils with learning and behavioural difficulties.

On the afternoon of Wednesday 14 March 2001, I was back in the Council offices in Llangefni for a Crime and Disorder meeting. It was then to Holyhead police station to administer reprimands to local youths for trespass.

The early afternoon of Thursday 15 March 2001 saw me visit the primary school in Llandudno Junction. Following this I had a meeting with the local rail manager, Ben Davies. It was then to the Labour Club at Llandudno Junction for an evening Public Forum, which was well attended by the local community who aired their usual grievances about trespass and disorder on the railway.

An early start on Friday 16 March 2001 saw me at Rhyl High School to address around eleven hundred pupils at their assembly on the dangers of the railway, following reports of trespass and vandalism.

Monday 19 March 2001, I had a meeting with the local rail union representative at Holyhead following concerns of behaviour on the late-night trains into Holyhead. I was able to secure additional resources from Liverpool to deal with the problems.

March culminated with me attending Rhyl police station on Saturday 31 March 2001 to administer some reprimands to the local miscreants. Whilst I was there, the duty Inspector asked me to accompany him to the town centre to carry out a couple of street identities of suspects for thefts in the Rhyl area.

Week commencing 2 April 2001 was taken up with meetings and reprimands in Liverpool, Rhyl, and Bangor.

Personal protection refresher training was undertaken on Tuesday 10 April 2001 at Bangor.

More reprimands were administered at Holyhead police station on Thursday 12 April 2001 to local youths for trespass and disorderly conduct.

A trip to the Royal Air Force base at Valley on Tuesday 24 April 2001 saw me attending a meeting with the RAF Police regarding the forthcoming RAF Air Show at the base. After this meeting it was straight up to Holyhead police station to administer a reprimand to a local youth for disorderly conduct.

On Friday 11 May 2001 I visited the high school in Blaenau Ffestiniog to speak to two hundred pupils. On arrival I was greeted by the headteacher who offered me a cup of coffee. I was then looked after by the deputy headteacher, who apologised that due to exams, the assembly hall was unavailable, but the gymnasium was set up for my talk.

We went to the Gymnasium where the forms were set out in a 'herringbone format', with the vaulting horse being used for my television. As we were discussing the layout, one of the gym mats, in the middle window of the gym, slipped to the floor. We walked over to pick it up. The deputy said to me "They are there for two reasons, one to block the light out for your television and the other to stop you getting shot!" I stopped and looked at him. He said, "You heard me correctly, to stop you getting shot!", He then explained that in one of the houses opposite the school lived a pupil who had recently been expelled for bad behaviour and retaliated by taking shots at the school with an air gun. He went onto explain that the pupil might decide to take a pot shot at me as I was in uniform shirt - sleeve order.

He went onto say, "Look on the bright side, the Ambulance station is only just across the road and if you are shot and providing that they are in they can take you to the Hospital in Bangor". I thought 'talk about the wild west'. All passed off peacefully.

In 2001, when Wembley Stadium was being rebuilt, the FA Cup was played in Cardiff between Arsenal and Liverpool on Saturday 12 May 2001 with Liverpool winning 2 -1. I escorted a train from Holyhead to Cardiff and return with North Wales based football supporters. There was no trouble.

The Wales Rail Users Consultative Committee held their annual conference in Wrexham on Tuesday 15 May 2001 and Wednesday 16 May 2001. The late Superintendent Tom Baker and I were guest speakers at the conference. All I remember of the Tuesday evening is that Tom and I boosted the profits of the brewery.

Week commencing 21 May 2001 was mostly taken up with meetings, reprimands, and a safety talk to the local Beaver's group in Bangor, along with a Victim Support Annual General Meeting.

The afternoon of Wednesday 4 July 2001 was taken up with a meeting of the Bangor City Partnership. However, the meeting was not in the usual City Council Chamber, but in the Banana House of the University gardens at Menai Bridge. This was a very unusual location to hold a meeting to say the least. It was very warm in the green house despite the shade from the trees. Fortunately, it was a short meeting.

In early July 2001 at around 02.30 hours, I was awoken in the early hours of the morning by the telephone ringing at home. I answered it and I was informed that there was a person with a gun on a train at Bangor railway station and that an Armed Response Unit from the North Wales Police were in attendance. I went immediately to Bangor. I parked my car in the official staff car park for the British Transport Police. As I was about to ascend the stairs to my office, an armed response officer from the North Wales Police suddenly appeared out of the darkness and pointed a fully loaded police revolver at me. 'Good job I had my brown underpants on at the time'. I quickly identified myself and went to my office to change into uniform. I liaised with the sergeant in charge of the Armed Response Unit (ARU).

It transpired that two Irish brothers had travelled over from Ireland on the overnight ferry to Holyhead and began drinking heavily. On arrival at Holyhead, they joined the 01.50 hours Holyhead to Birmingham boat train. During the journey to Bangor the two brothers began arguing with each other. One of the brothers, who lived in Northamptonshire, stated that he was going to shoot the other with a gun and pointed to a bulge in his left-hand side jacket pocket. The brother who had been threatened, believed that his brother was capable of such an act, as a few years previously, during an argument, he had been slashed across the face with a knife by his brother, scarring his face for life. The conductor of the train was informed, and he informed the police of the circumstances.

Myself and the Sergeant from the ARU put on railway high visibility vests over our uniforms.

We arranged for the conductor of the train to announce to the passengers that the train was being delayed due to a technical fault on the train (A reasonable excuse because the trains, 175 units, had recently been introduced to the North Wales Coast and were prone to technical problems) and we purported to be railway fitters, checking for faults. We boarded the train and found the alleged offender fast asleep. He was handcuffed and arrested without any resistance. During a subsequent search, no firearm was found. It transpired that 'it was the drink that was talking'. He was conveyed to the custody suite at Bangor police station for questioning by our CID from Crewe. In the meantime, Superintendent Tom Baker from Area Headquarters in Manchester had arrived. These new trains were the first on the North Wales Coast to be fitted with CCTV cameras and this was the first occasion that we had to use them in a criminal case. The train eventually departed Bangor some three hours late. The offender was bailed for further enquiries.

Before returning to Manchester, Tom Baker took me to the Little Chef on the A55 at Bangor for a breakfast. On returning to the office at Bangor I had to deal with the usual barrage of press enquiries relating to the incident.

Thursday 5 July 2001, I attended a table-top rail crash exercise in the Gymnasium of RAF Valley. This was to test the reaction of the emergency services should a real-life train crash occur. The RAF looked after us very well indeed with their hospitality.

Friday 6 July 2001, I visited Kingsland Primary School, Holyhead which is located right next to the railway line. There I delivered rail safety talks to the pupils.

I attended an Anti-Social Behaviour conference in Llandudno on Wednesday 11 July 2001, hosted by the North Wales Police and the local council.

Saturday 21 July 2001 Colwyn Bay played Stockport in a pre-season friendly football match at Colwyn Bay. There was no trouble. Also, on this day I attended the local model railway exhibition with a rail safety stand. I was back in Colwyn Bay on Sunday 22 July 2001 at the model railway exhibition with my rail safety display.

As I was now due to retire in September, I started taking Lieu days, time owing to me from overtime worked and annual leave. Retirement was well and truly on the horizon.

I was back at the RAF base at Valley on Thursday 2 August 2001 to attend another exercise, whereby an aircraft crashes onto a train as it is landing. The main Chester to Holyhead railway line runs through the middle of the base. There are a set of emergency signals on the railway line which are controlled by the personnel in the control tower of the base.

A community safety day was held in the events arena at Rhyl on Tuesday 7 August 2001. I was there with a rail safety display, which was well attended by local children and those on holiday.

The FA Charity Shield was played between Liverpool and Manchester United at the Millennium stadium Cardiff, on Sunday 12 August 2001, whilst Wembley was being rebuilt, Liverpool beat Manchester United 2 – 1. I escorted a train to Cardiff and return. This was to be my last football duty, as I was shortly going to retire and would be taking more annual leave.

On the return leg there was a fan who was an absolute nuisance. He was dealt with for disorderly conduct and ejected at Hereford. On the station platform he told me that he would be reporting me and said that he would have my job. I had great pleasure in informing him that he could have it as I was retiring shortly. That shut him up.

The RAF Open Day was being held at RAF Valley on Saturday 18 August 2001 and I was on duty at the base to patrol the railway line with PC Sean Braithwaite. An MSU was on duty at Rhosneigr railway station, where passenger trains made additional stops conveying the people attending the open day.

September was mainly taken up with annual leave prior to my retirement. Ged Hindley who was to take over from me came to visit me for a handover meeting. The last week of my career started with an appearance at Chester Crown Court to give evidence in a robbery that had taken place in Rhyl earlier in the year. The offenders pleaded 'Not Guilty'. However, the Judge called the prosecuting and defence Barristers into his chambers for a conference, after which a guilty plea was entered by the defendants.

My last duty was a Victim Support Meeting in Caernarfon on Thursday 20 September 2001.

I cleared my desk on Friday 21 September 2001 and booked off duty for the last time at 16.00 hours. Little did I know that I was to return to the force in a few years' time.

My final day in the force was Saturday 22 September 2001, the day of my fiftieth birthday and was taken as a rest day. Sunday 23 September 2001 dawned; I was now a civilian.

During the timeline of the previous three chapters I have dealt with many arrests, fatalities and reporting people for summons, attending meetings etc. It has been impossible to record all of my incidents. The following are just a few which I can remember vividly being involved in but not put a date to.

I was on duty at Bangor in the downstairs general office, which was very small, by myself one particular day and at around 12 noon I made a pot of tea intending to have it with my sandwiches, when I received a call to attend the London train that had just arrived at Platform Two. On arrival I spoke to the conductor who had a youth with him, whom he suspected of dodging his train fare. As it was a particularly cold day, I invited the youth, as a voluntary attender to the office. On arrival I obtained his name and address and poured myself a cup of tea, offering one to the alleged offender, which he accepted. I gave him his rights, one of which, 'he was free to leave at any time'. He said to me "Did I hear you right, I can leave at any time?" I replied, "That is correct, you may leave if you wish, it will be less paperwork for me.". He said, "I don't like the police, I never tell 'em anything, but you seem a decent copper, so I'll tell you what you want to know". He was true to his word. He had travelled from Crewe without a ticket and had offered his fare from Llandudno Junction. He was reported and later fined.

Another incident involving the same train, I was on Platform Two when my attention was drawn by the conductor to a young man who had alighted from the train. The conductor suspected him of evading his fare.

I invited him to the office as a voluntary attender, which he agreed to. As normal procedure, I obtained his details and carried out a Police National Computer (PNC) check on him. The operator asked me if I had him handcuffed. I told him that I had not, as he was a compliant person. The operator advised me to handcuff him immediately, as he was wanted by the Metropolitan Police for two armed robberies in London, about four years previously. I handcuffed him and called on the North Wales Police for assistance in conveying him to the custody suite at Bangor police station. He was documented. A few hours later two officers from the Metropolitan Police arrived and conveyed him back to London. I received a nice letter of thanks from the Met. He was caught just because he was trying to save a couple of pounds on his train fare.

The third incident involving this train. I was on duty again by myself preparing a prosecution file and I was called to the train at Platform Two, to a suspected fare evader. He was a young lad. As I was talking to him on the platform, he made a run for it from the station. I gave chase after him and eventually caught him hiding in the Bible garden of the city's Cathedral over, a mile away. I was exhausted. I arrested him and with the assistance of the North Wales Police I conveyed him to the custody suite at Bangor police station, where he was documented. He had travelled all the way from London without paying his fare. On arrival back at my office, my two constables' PCs Morgan and Millar had returned from their patrols of the North Wales Coast and on hearing about my escapade started dropping hints that I should enter the London marathon or at least the Menai Bridge half-marathon! I was known as 'Sergeant Christie' for a couple of months.

During the currency of the timetables this train would either terminate at Bangor or go through to Holyhead. We were called to this train two or three times a week, usually because of somebody evading their fare. Some days the Revenue Inspectors would mount a revenue protection operation at Bangor station on the footbridge leading from Platform Two. Invariably this train was always late. I remember one Friday being on duty with the Revenue Inspectors and the train rolled in about seven minutes late. I said rather dryly "That's the earliest it's been late this week". They just collapsed in fits of uncontrollable laughter.

A suicidal man was seen walking along the railway lines and climbing onto a signal gantry about forty feet from the ground approximately two hundred yards from Llandudno Junction railway station and threatening to throw himself off. He was coaxed down to safety. His actions caused around an hour's delay to train services. Due to his mental state no proceedings were brought against him.

A man from Llandudno was remanded in custody charged with interfering with signalling apparatus near Rhyl railway station and Endangering the Safety of Persons on the Railway.

One Sunday afternoon four youths from the Liverpool area, who had travelled from Blaenau Ffestiniog to Llandudno Junction on a bus replacement service, caused a disturbance during the journey. They then boarded a London bound train at Llandudno Junction. Before the train departed one of them produced an air gun. The station staff called the Police. North Wales Police were first on the scene and attended with an armed response unit. We attended from Bangor.

A Gatt air pistol, which was not loaded, was recovered during the incident which lasted for about an hour. A sixteen-year-old youth was arrested and taken to Llandudno police station and later charged with a firearms offence. He was then bailed to appear before a youth court later.

A man from the North Wales area who was on probation for two indecent assaults, indecently assaulted a woman in broad daylight whilst she was on Conwy railway station, by lifting her skirt and putting his hands between her legs. He was eventually arrested at Llandudno Junction railway station. At a subsequent court appearance, he was given a six-month jail sentence which was suspended for two years, and was ordered to pay £15 costs.

In rural areas, particularly in North Wales, a common offence was that of 'Omitting to Shut a Level Crossing Gate'. I dealt with several offences at the occupational crossings between Llanfairfechan and Abergwyngregyn on the North Wales Coast Line. Failure to close these gates could lead to cattle or sheep straying onto the lines and causing death to themselves or the derailment of a train. So, each report was treated seriously. One summer, I received a report from a farmer in the Abergwyngregyn area stating that the gate at a crossing connecting two of his fields was constantly being left open. The only snag was that it was at around 05.00 hours in the morning. So, it was up before the dawn chorus. I went to the scene arriving there at about 04.30 hours. A short while later a resident of Bangor came across the crossing and failed to shut both gates. I reported him for the offences. It transpired that he was using the crossing to go to the seashore to pick cockles. After I had reported him and sent him on his way the farmer very kindly provided me with a welcoming mug of tea and toast. The offender was heavily fined at Bangor Magistrates' Court.

A train conductor based at Llandudno Junction was suspected of stealing money from the booking office at Llandudno Junction railway station. Sean Braithwaite and I made enquiries into the incidents. On one day the booking clerk left a specific amount of money on a table. It had been counted before and after each staff member had entered the office, and the amount had been correct. Our suspect entered the office for a new cash float. He then walked over to the table to count the float and then left. The booking clerk then counted the money and found twenty pounds to be missing. We arrested our suspect on suspicion of theft. A specially marked twenty-pound note was recovered from him and he made a full and frank admission of that and previous thefts. He was charged. On appearing at Llandudno Magistrates' Court, he was fined two hundred pounds after pleading guilty. He stated that he had been experiencing money problems and resigned after the incident.

Around the time of the aforementioned incidents another theft of monies took place in the booking office at Llandudno. The rail operator there was allegedly pocketing money from excess fares which had been paid to him by passengers who were alighting at the station without previously purchasing a ticket. The CID became involved and a number of 'test purchases' were undertaken. He was arrested and charged. On appearance at court he was acquitted of the offences.

I was on duty one Saturday evening on a train patrol of an old two coach DMU between Llandudno Junction and Rhyl. The train stopped at Abergele and Pensarn station and a youth boarded the train. The conductor went to him and asked him for his ticket, and he could not produce one. He was then asked to pay his fare, which he refused to do, and he became abusive to the conductor. At this point I was in the brake van situated in the middle of the train and could hear and see what was taking place. The conductor said to the youth who had his back to me, "I'll call the police". To which the youth replied, sarcastically, "Where are you going to get a f*****g copper from?" By this time I had left the brake van. I tapped the youth on the shoulder and said, "As you were saying". The look on his face was an absolute picture. He paid his fare to Rhyl and was reported for using abusive language.

We had all rehearsed on a regular basis for it and hoped that it would never happen – the derailment of a nuclear flask train. Early one afternoon I was on duty in my office at Bangor railway station when I received a telephone call from the station supervisor at Llandudno Junction advising me that a nuclear flask en route from Trawsfynydd to Sellafield had derailed in the sidings. My heart went into my mouth. PC Sean Morgan was out on patrol, so I managed to contact him and direct him to the scene. I caught the first available train and met up with Sean. The flask was upright, and it was just the front bogie that had derailed. Apparently, the track points were faulty and as the flask was going over, the points split causing the derailment. Everything else was intact, no damage. There was no need for the cavalry. In fact, I hadn't heard from them, which was unusual! They were conspicuous by their absence. As in these cases the driver, guard and shunter needed to be breathalysed under the Transport and Works Act. Gwynfor the station supervisor had reported the incident to his control room, who in turn requested the services of the private company they used to breathalyse staff. Gwynfor informed me that it would be at least 18.00 hours before they arrived and asked me if we could breathalyse the crew so that the railway could continue to function. I agreed to this request and PC Morgan and myself undertook the task with our breathalyser equipment. The test proved negative. The staff had a cup of tea and were back at work.

Myself and my officers were repeatedly called upon to escort the evening and late-night trains along the North Wales Coast in connection with the pundits returning from Chester horse races. Excessive alcohol consumption was always the main problem.

During my career I was lucky enough to work with some fantastic officers who were the cream of the force. I have detailed in the previous chapters some of the incidents I have been involved in at the places where I was stationed at. However, so as not to identity a couple of cases or individuals I will mention the recollections here.

One senior officer who I worked with was so pedantic that you had a better chance of getting prosecution cases past a scrap-yard Alsatian dog than you did past him.

On one occasion, I was trying to explain to a senior officer about a case. He clearly did not believe me and said, after listening to the facts. "I'm not a complete idiot", to which I replied, "What part of you is missing?" He went up like a bottle of pop.

One of my Constables came into the office and stated that the car had been filled up with petrol instead of diesel. He blamed it onto the attendant at the fuel station. I asked if he had been to the regular one and he confirmed this. I stated that I may look green and I do get out of the office occasionally and fill the car up and stated that the service station was self-service. He sheepishly admitted to the mistake.

Just before going into a suspect, I said to a CID officer, "He's as deaf as a door post, you'll have to shout at him". I said to the suspect "The officer who is going to interview you is as deaf as a door post, you'll have to shout at him". It was amusing listening to the interview.

One afternoon a CID officer had spilled some tea on his chair. A little later in the evening as it was drying the cleaner came into the office. I said with a straight face "He couldn't get to the toilet in time". Her face was an absolute picture.

On another occasion the same officer had been using some very strong glue to mend something and had put the remainder of the tube in the litter bin. The cleaner came in and she said, "That's a strong smell". I said "Yes, the officer has been glue-sniffing, it's a habit he's got". I don't know what she thought of the officer concerned. It was all good old-fashioned harmless fun.

I went to speak to a group of women in late November, which was particularly mild weather wise. Whilst I was waiting for the members of the audience to settle in I was talking to the organiser and remarked that I had been in the garden earlier in the day and had been trimming my fuchsias, a task which I normally carry out in October. The lady who reminded me of Ada, the character played by the late Les Dawson said to me "Yes, I had to trim my bush last week it was getting very straggly". I had a job to keep a straight face.

I worked with a detective. He was good, he could detect and find anything – except his wallet when it was his round.

I went to a briefing held by a senior officer of a provincial police force. His linguistic phrases were the source of great amusement. As he was sorting through his papers he said, "I have an itinerant here somewhere", instead of saying "I have an itinerary somewhere". One of the officers at the briefing told me that he once came out with an absolute classic. He was describing the porch over his front door which was covered in a clematis plant. What he actually said was "I have a clitoris around my front porch".

I worked with a female officer who was very uncouth. Before the start of a shift she would regale us with details of her recent sexual activities. Not for the faint-hearted.

CHAPTER 26

THE RETIREMENT YEARS 2001 – 2005

Appearing before the Magistrates

Sunday 23 September 2001 arrived. I was now a civilian. No pager, no phone calls during the night. No more wrestling with drunks and druggies in the toilets at Rhyl railway station on a cold winter's night. It seemed very strange not having a warrant card. I had no alternative employment to go to. Shirley and I just planned to relax for the next twelve months, in fact we booked a holiday each month, to England, Ireland and Europe.

The night of Friday 28 September 2001, I held my retirement party at the Valley Hotel, which was organised by Carys Ainscough the clerical officer at Bangor and PC Sean Braithwaite. Over one hundred and thirty guests attended from far and wide. I received quite a few presents from my colleagues including the North Wales Police. Betty Williams MP, who attended, gave a lovely speech in my honour. It was a great night. Some of the guests had decided to stay the night at the hotel. Others had travelled by train. The only snag being that the last train from Valley was 19.40 hours just as the party was beginning. However, the hierarchy of the railways arranged for a special stop for the 01.50 hours Holyhead to Crewe train at Valley.

When I arrived home, there was another surprise waiting for me. My old office reclining chair was in the front room. I had spent many an hour in this chair mulling over files and discussing cases with people.

I joined the National Association of Retired British Transport Police Officers (NARBTPO) and the National Association of Retired Police Officers. (NARPO).

However, I was still going to be involved with the Institute of Management and the local Victim Support Scheme, which still gave me contact with the British Transport Police at Bangor. I still visited the office at Bangor to assist Ged Hindley with one or two matters that had cropped up, nothing too serious, I hasten to add. I was now Vice Chair of the Institute of Management Bangor branch and Vice Chair of the Môn Gwynedd Victim Support Scheme. For the first few months of my retirement, it just seemed as if I was on extended annual leave.

During the evening of Thursday 4 October 2001 and with the ink still wet on my pension application form, I delivered a talk on the work of the force, on behalf of the force, in Abergele to a gentlemen's group.

Saturday 13 October 2001 was a great day. Wales were playing Ireland in a rearranged rugby match. No police duties! instead, it was to the local church in Valley to attend my son's wedding. It seemed very strange not working on a Saturday for a sporting fixture.

I became a volunteer driver for the local Hospice conveying the patients from their homes to the day care centre in Holyhead or the hospital in Bangor.

The rest of the year was taken up with work in connection with the local Victim Support Scheme and of course, attending the Bangor police station Christmas dinner.

Thursday January 10 2002 saw me attending my first BTP retired officers lunch in Liverpool. It was great to see so many of my ex-colleagues from around the North West and other areas.

It was off to Birmingham on Tuesday 12 March 2002, to attend my first meeting of the Annual General Meeting of the National Association of Retired British Transport Police Officers.

Again, on behalf of the force, during the evening of Wednesday 3 April 2002 I was in Abergele to make a presentation to a ladies group on the work of the force.

The rest of the year was taken up mainly with voluntary work at the Trearddur Bay lifeboat station of the Royal National Lifeboat Institution, holidays, attending retirement parties for my colleagues who had reached retirement age, retired officers' lunches in Liverpool and Birmingham and meetings with the Victim Support Scheme. Planning holidays for 2003 was very much in the forefront of my mind.

On Monday 16 September 2002 Shirley and I went on a twelve-day coach tour of Northern Ireland and the Republic of Ireland. Our first night was spent at a recently refurbished hotel in the delightful city of Newry near to the border between the two countries. There was still evidence of the troubles in the area. The army were still flying helicopters in the area. After dinner, Shirley and I went out for a walk into the city centre. On returning we spent some time in the bar with our fellow passengers before retiring to bed. We were rudely awakened at around 01.30 hours by the fire alarm. I looked through the door security spy hole to see two youths running along the corridor. We both made our way down to the fire assembly point, where we met the coach driver, Fred. At the assembly point the duty manager informed us that two youths had conned their way into the hotel, by using false hotel room cards. They went to a conference room where they damaged brand new tables and chairs, and set off the fire extinguishers, causing the activation of the fire alarm.

Fred and I spotted the culprits and my old instincts came to the fore and we made a citizen's arrest. We then requested that the manager called the police. After a few minutes he assured us that the police were on their way. Time went on and the two youths were becoming more and more agitated. The manager admitted that he had not called the police, so we had to release the two youths. He stated that the police would not turn out for a trivial matter. The following morning the general manager apologised profusely. On the way to Belfast our guide informed Fred and myself that he and the hotel management knew who the culprits were and that they would be dealt with appropriately. I didn't ask, but I could guess. It was estimated that the damage caused ran into several thousands of pounds.

2003 started off fairly quietly with holidays being taken. In March one of the Court Ushers at Holyhead Magistrates' Court was due to retire and he asked if I would like to apply for his vacancy. Following a successful interview, I was appointed as a part time Court Usher at Holyhead Magistrates' Court.

I was also responsible for providing cover in the courts at Llangefni, Bangor, Caernarfon, Pwllheli and Dolgellau. This work brought me back into direct contact with members of the public who had unfortunately found themselves on the wrong side of the law, Solicitors, police colleagues from the British Transport Police and the North Wales Police.

The work was both serious and amusing. I was to remain with the Court Service until Friday 16 September 2005.

Friday 22 August 2003 myself and two other retired officers went to the retirement party of a senior officer in Manchester. To save money on overnight accommodation at a hotel in the city centre we booked a family room which had three separate beds in it. On returning from the social evening, we continued drinking in the bar of the hotel, oblivious to the other guests. On retiring to the room, I went to the reception to obtain the key which was duly handed to me by the night porter. He then enquired if the other two gentlemen would require their keys. I informed him that we were all in the same room. He then tapped the side of his nose with his finger, pointed it at me and winked. It was only the next morning that we found out that there had been a gay conference on in Manchester and a lot of the delegates were at our hotel.

At Holyhead court I became known as 'The Stationmaster'. One day I was in the foyer of the court talking to the Front of House Manager, Steve, yes that's what we were classed as, 'Front of House staff'. I was approached by a defendant who asked which court he was in. Consulting my list, I saw that he was listed for court number two. I said to him "Go up the stairs, turn left and you'll find Platform Two in front of you". There was much rapturous laughter from Steve. I was also known around the courts as a bit of a joker.

Once a month, usually on a Thursday, was the fines court in number one court at Holyhead. This particular Thursday, I was the duty usher and there were three females on the bench, assisted by a female clerk. Downstairs in the main office was located the fines officer from Denbigh. The clerk asked me to bring up a female who had failed to pay her fine for non-payment of a television licence. I escorted her into the court and presented her to the Magistrates. This female was young and extremely attractive. Her excuse was that she had moved from the area and claimed that she did not receive any correspondence relating to the original fine. The Magistrates enquired about her current circumstances. She revealed that she now had a hairdressing and beauty salon business, in the North West of England, and that she was able to pay any monies and fines due, immediately. After deliberating for a few minutes, the Magistrates fined her. They instructed me to take her to the fines officer. Also, the Magistrates instructed me to bring up the next defendant.

As I was exiting the court, the chair of the bench called me back. I sent the young lady downstairs. I returned to the bench and the Chair said, with a mischievous wink, "If you are not back within twenty minutes, we'll come looking for you". I bowed to them, with a smile and left the court. I caught up with the young lady and arranged for her to pay the fine. I returned to the court some five minutes later without the defendant I had been requested to bring back with me as they had failed to turn up.

As I entered the court, the Chair said to me, "Did you sort out the fine for the young lady?" I replied. "I certainly did ma'am". After checking that there was no one else in the courtroom apart from the Magistrates and the Clerk, I went onto to say, "Whilst I was talking to her downstairs, she asked me if I would like anything for the weekend". All three Magistrates drew in a sharp intake of breath, and the Clerk put her head in her hands and shook it from side to side wondering what I was going to say next. I said, "Yes please, and she said come to the salon, collect the paint and brushes and paint the salon for me". The Magistrates burst out into fits of laughter. The Clerk suggested that this would be an ideal opportunity to have a well-earned coffee break.

One of the senior Magistrates came to me one day and said that I had set the court back at least fifty years. I was perplexed by this remark. Thinking that I had done something drastically wrong. He informed me that the Magistrates were impressed by my attitude as I brought the defendants in. He went onto say that I had restored some discipline and respect to the court, by making the defendants spit out their toffees or chewing gum into the bin, making sure their mobile phones were off, hands out of their pockets and that they stood up straight, etc.

All defendants were listed to attend court at 10.00 hours, although it was impossible for all of them to be heard at that time. Those who had been bailed by the police or at a previous court would technically be in breach of their bail if they did not appear at 10.00 hours and would be liable to a fine.

One day I was at Caernarfon Magistrates' Court and took details of the defendants who entered the building. I then gave the details to the Clerk of the Court. At about 11.15 hours one defendant, sauntered in as if he was on a fortnight's holiday at a nearby holiday camp. I informed him, rather sternly, that he should have been at Court at 10.00 hours. To which he replied, "It's a waste of time I'm never on before eleven thirty". I booked him in with the Clerk and mentioned that he had an attitude problem.

I returned to the foyer where he was. He was now sat next to another defendant and in a voice, so that I could hear, he said, "I hope he's not the f******g judge, he'll send me down". When he appeared in court, he got the dressing down of a lifetime from both the Clerk and the Chair of the bench.

One afternoon, there was a special court at Holyhead convened to hear a private prosecution brought by a government department. The trial was heard in front of the District Judge. After hearing all the evidence from the prosecution and the defence, the District Judge adjourned the case whilst he deliberated. He intimated that we would have time for a cup of tea.

Whilst we were waiting for the District Judge to return, the defence solicitor asked me what life was like in the British Transport Police. I regaled him and his client of some of the more amusing incidents I had been involved in. His client said, "You must be the Fred Dibnah of the Courts, it was worth coming here today just to listen to you!".

Dolgellau Magistrates' Court now sadly closed, was also used as a Crown Court on an as required basis. One day I was rostered to go to a sitting of a sexual offences trial in Dolgellau court which was sitting as a Crown Court.

I arrived at the court and was informed that the main witness would be using the newly installed video link equipment to present her evidence. This equipment had only been installed a couple of weeks previously and this was the first time it would be used live. Luckily, a similar system had been in use at Holyhead for a few months previously, so I was confident in its use. However, like any good Usher I decided to give the equipment a run through before the actual trial. Good job I did, as myself and the security officer discovered that it had been wired incorrectly, therefore it was not working as it should have done. It went without saying that the judge was not best pleased. There were red faces in our main office at Caernarfon. The problem was quickly fixed, and the trial went ahead a few weeks later, only for the defendant to plead guilty after the jury had been sworn in.

One day I was on duty at Llangefni Magistrates' Court, Isle of Anglesey. This court is now sadly closed. It was a small court with just one courtroom. The foyer was about fourteen-foot square with a small waiting room leading off. From the main office the whole foyer could be seen. One day whilst I was on duty there, the court business, involving a couple or so guilty pleas had been concluded, apart from one defendant from Aberystwyth who was in custody in the cells at the adjacent police station and we were awaiting the arrival of his solicitor from that town. As time was getting on there was no sign of the solicitor so I rang his office to be assured that he was on his way. A short time later I received a telephone call from the solicitor to say that he was in the court building and that the staff had no knowledge of his client. I assured him that I too was in the building and I asked where he was in the building. He stated that he was in the foyer. I told him that there was no one in the foyer as I had an interrupted view of the area. He categorically stated that he was in the building. After further questioning, I ascertained that he was in fact in Llanelli Magistrates' Court some, one hundred and fifty miles away. His client was released on bail and we all went home for an early lunch.

At the courts I used to sit in on a number of trials. I would despair at how unprepared some police officers were, when presenting their evidence. Then they wondered why the case had been dismissed or why they were criticised by the bench. When I was a serving police officer I used to go through the evidence of my officers with them in the event of a 'Not guilty' plea. I used to say to some of the officers before they gave their evidence, "Fingers crossed, and buttocks clenched".

I much preferred it when the District Judge presided over trials as he could make decisions a lot quicker than the Magistrates who could be long-winded. One such case, where they were particularly long-winded was in the case of several juveniles, who after being found guilty and had reports prepared by the Probation Service, were being sentenced for a case of serious disorder in Holyhead. The case started at 10.30 hours and lasted until 20.30 hours. A District Judge would have had it completed it by lunch time.

I was on duty in the youth court at Holyhead when the Crown Prosecution Service (CPS) Solicitor drew my attention to a file. He said, "You were a police officer, what do you think of this remark", pointing to a 'post it note'? The file related to a local juvenile.

The CPS had sent it back to the Criminal Justice Department of the North Wales Police requesting further information from the officer in the case and asking for his availability for a court attendance to give evidence. The letter was on top of the file. The Inspector in the Criminal Justice Department had turned up the bottom right hand corner had had written 'PC Jones (Not his real name) please comply'. The officer had placed a 'post-it note' on top of the letter which read 'Sir, additional information attached. I didn't realise it was my job to go to court to give evidence'. I just shook my head in disbelief.

Over the years of visiting courts, I was aware that the Solicitors, particularly the defence solicitors, and more recently the Crown Prosecution Solicitors, did not have too much knowledge of the workings of the railway and the railway law. Whilst working in the courts the CPS Solicitors would often ask me about the railway law. In 1980, I purchased a book entitled *The Law of the Railway'* by Leslie James BA, LLB, FCIT. He was a Barrister-at-Law of Grays Inn and at one time had been a regional Chief Officer of the British Transport Police. Whenever there was a complex British Transport Police prosecution, I was often asked to lend this book to the CPS. It came in very handy for some of the case law.

In April 2005 the Court Service underwent a reorganisation and we became Civil Servants. The paperwork just tripled.

In June 2005 whilst I was working at the court in Holyhead, I became aware that the British Transport Police were looking to recruit a Community Partnership Coordinator for North and Mid Wales based at Rhyl. I applied for the position and was successful. My starting date was Monday 3 October. 2005 So, it was goodbye to the courts and to prepare to re-join the BTP.

CHAPTER 27

THE CIVILIAN YEARS 2005 – 2006

Back with the force and coming face to face with 'The Beast'

Monday 3 October 2005 at 09.00 hours, I reported to my old office at Bangor for my first day back with the force as a civilian employee attached to the Operations Department, which initially was for a two-year, full-time contract. It felt quite strange going back. I met up with Sergeant Andy Hemmings and later in the morning with Inspector Alan Radford who was the Operations Inspector for the Western Area of the force. Although I was officially based at Rhyl, I was able to work from the Bangor police station. I was given a uniform of a force issue polo shirt with the force crest, black trousers, and a force issue fleece from the dog section. One thing was missing, a vehicle to transport me to the areas I had to cover.

I was one of three Community Partnership Coordinators that had been recruited to the Wales and Western Area of the force. Pete Conway, an ex-West Midlands police officer was based at Birmingham to cover the Midlands, and his post was funded by a Midlands partnership agreement. Andy Evans an ex-South Wales police officer was based at Cardiff to cover South Wales and myself for North and Mid Wales. Mine and Andy's posts were funded by the Welsh Assembly.

My responsibilities were to deliver rail safety talks to the schools in the six counties of North Wales, the Isle of Anglesey, Gwynedd, Conwy, Denbighshire, Flintshire and Wrexham and along with those in the county of Ceredigion and the county of Powys, which stretched right down to Ystradgynlais, some one hundred and fifty six miles away from Bangor. The force's police station at Swansea was only fourteen miles away from the end of my patch. Also, I had to liaise with the Crime and Disorder Partnerships and other crime reduction agencies that had been set up in the counties, this would mean closer collaboration between the BTP and the other agencies involved, including the North Wales Police and the Dyfed Powys Police.

I had a large area to cover but had no vehicle and the force did not have a spare one. It was agreed that I could use my own vehicle and claim the mileage until such time a vehicle became available.

My first task was to arrange to attend the Crucial Crew events that were being held in the high schools on the Isle of Anglesey later in the month.

Crucial Crew, is a group of organisations consisting of members such as Fire and Rescue Services, British Transport Police, Food Standards Agency Wales, Network Rail, RNLI, electricity suppliers, Women's Aid, Barnardo's, The Samaritans, The Dogs Trust, British Red Cross, NSPCC, local Road Safety Units, various drug and alcohol support charities, local trading standards departments, local waste awareness departments and some local police forces.

The representatives of the agencies deliver essential and life-saving safety and PSHE messages to year six and seven children throughout Wales at the Crucial Crew events.

The presentations and workshops are delivered by professionals. They are designed to be relevant, engaging, curriculum linked advice, involving real life situations.

Usually no more than six agencies attend a school at any one time for a day. We take over a classroom and the children come to us for their talks, which last around thirty minutes. In North Wales, year seven pupils, which are the first-year pupils in the high schools, are targeted. We had a set pattern each year for visiting the high schools. The ones in Wrexham would be visited in January; Denbighshire, in March / April, May / June; Conwy, Gwynedd; June / July; October, Isle of Anglesey and November, Flintshire. The North Wales Crucial Crew events were organised by the education department of the North Wales Fire and Rescue Service in collaboration with the North Wales Police Schools Liaison Officers (SLOs).

Basically, my task at the Crucial Crew events and other schools was to talk to the pupils openly and frankly about the dangers of spending time near the railway lines, embankments, railway stations and level crossings etc., as well as drawing attention to the importance of the prominent signs and symbols warning of danger. I also had a set of films to show, some with an unhappy ending.

I had left school at the age of fifteen, as I hated every moment of it, not realising that years later I would be working full time in schools and enjoying being in the schools. Schools nowadays are vastly different to when I was at school. But the basic ingredient is still there, to educate children.

Another establishment I was expected to liaise closely with was Dangerpoint at Talacre near Prestatyn. This is an award-winning interactive visitor centre, open during the school term time for schools and organised groups and during the school holidays for a fantastic family day out. The centre offers visitors the opportunity to learn about safety. Designed like a film set, visitors journey from the home to the beach, countryside, playground, farm, a railway, and other settings. Visitors learn about risks and how to keep safe, whilst most importantly, having fun.

Most of the first week was taken up with making contacts with agencies in the various counties. However, on Wednesday 5 October 2005 I went to Dangerpoint to introduce myself to the staff and the Rangers. (These are the people who take the visitors around). When the force was establishing my post, they were looking at basing the postholder at Dangerpoint.

The morning of Monday 10 October 2005 saw me attending my first high school in my new role, for a Crucial Crew event, Ysgol David Hughes (David Hughes High School) Menai Bridge. Although, I had not delivered a rail safety talk for some four years it was surprising how quick it came back to me and it felt only like the previous week that I had delivered a talk.

I travelled a few miles on Thursday 13 October 2005 to Holyhead High School to participate in a Crucial Crew event. Later that day I was to meet up with Inspector Derek Cheetham at Bangor, who was based in Shrewsbury and whom I had known for a number of years, to discuss anti-social behaviour at the Cambrian Coast Line stations.

After an early rise on Friday 14 October 2005, I travelled to Area Headquarters in Birmingham for a formal induction to the force.

Most of October and November were taken up with Crucial Crew events and partnership meetings in North Wales establishing contacts with the various agencies.

At one of the schools I attended I used their television to play my film which was on a VHS tape. The television was a very old colour one, in a brown wooden surround with push buttons for the various functions. I think it was one of the first colour televisions to be used in a school. About halfway through the film the horizontal hold went on the television, and I walked over to adjust it. As I was doing so, I said to the pupils "You are very lucky to have a colour television. When I was at school, we did not have one and the only thing we had was a slate and chalk for some of our lessons". One lad put his hand up and said, "Did you go to school with Fred Flintstone mister?" I could see the teacher drawing a sharp intake of breath. I was quick and said "No, I went to school with Barney Rubble, because we are older than Fred" That shut him up. I thought I'll go back to my cave and gnaw on a mammoth bone!

One of the many partnership meetings I attended was that of the North Wales branch of the Weston Spirit, a charity set up by Simon Weston MBE CBE, who was severely burned in the Falklands conflict. The charity was set up to help young people with training and education. Sadly, this charity is no longer in existence. My role was to involve the youngsters from the charity in painting murals depicting local scenes, such as ice creams, sandcastles, deck chairs, fish and chips etc., for display at Llandudno railway station.

Most of January 2006 was taken up visiting the ten high schools in Wrexham for Crucial Crew events.

After an early breakfast on Wednesday 1 February 2006, I travelled to Cardiff to meet in person my counterparts, Pete Conway from Birmingham, and Andy Evans from Cardiff.

An early start on Wednesday 8 February 2006 saw me in Hope, Flintshire, meeting with the Wrexham to Bidston Rail Line Community Partnership Officer. Then it was off to the local high school for a rail safety talk, to the whole school. Following this I went to the Welsh medium school in Wrexham to talk to the members of their railway club, during the lunch break.

A charity organisation called 'Making Tracks' had recently been formed and had its base on Colwyn Bay railway station. The purpose of the organisation was to involve local youngsters in gardening projects at the local railway stations, towns and villages. On Thursday 9 February 2006 I attended my first meeting of the organisation at the local offices of the Youth Offending Team. Prior to my appointment members of the team had prepared murals, depicting local scenes from the Colwyn Bay area, and were displayed on the town's railway station.

Tuesday 28 February 2006 was a memorable day for me. I had the great honour to be invited to the Houses of Parliament by my local Member of Parliament for Ynys Môn, Albert Owen. Firstly, I attended a service at 12 noon to mark St David's Day, Patron Saint of Wales, circa 601, in The Chapel of St Mary Undercroft, Palace of Westminster, below the Houses of Parliament. At 15.00 hours I was invited into the public gallery to watch some debates taking place.

Then at 16.00 hours in a committee room, I had the honour of addressing the North Wales Members of Parliament, on my work with the force and that of the force in general.

I joined the Transport and Salaried Staff Association (TSSA). This was the first time in my life I had joined a trade union.

My little car was getting worn out with all the excessive mileage, so at long last I was allocated a vehicle. St David's Day, 1 March 2006 saw me travelling to Shrewsbury to collect it from the railway sidings. It was a ten-year-old LDV van, call sign 'Echo 98', with four blue lights on the roof, blue lights on the radiator grill and 'British Transport Police' decals on the side panels, along with the force crest on the front and rear doors.

I got into this vehicle, started it up and it immediately began belching plumes of evil smelling black and blue smoke from the exhaust and other orifices on the van. The Platters song *'Smoke gets in your eyes'* immediately sprung to mind. The Shunter came running out of his cabin thinking that someone was starting up a nearby Class 37 diesel locomotive. To say it was a 'shed' would be an understatement.

I headed back off to Bangor, slamming it into first gear, then it slowly crept into second gear and nearly into third as I negotiated the picturesque streets of Shrewsbury. As I gathered up speed after leaving the outskirts of Shrewsbury, I managed to get it into top gear and rattled along the A5 and A483 roads. Once on the A55 dual-carriageway it rocked from side to side, as it rattled along. I very quickly gave it the nickname of 'The Beast'. Driving it along the roads, reminded of the song sung by Bill Hayley and his Comets *"Shake, rattle and roll"* and *"Shakin' all over"* by Johnny Kidd and the Pirates. You certainly would not drive along to Pat Boone singing *'Speedy Gonzales'*. The title of the Anthony Newley song *"Why"* came to my mind as I was heading back for Bangor. Ah well, at least it was a set of wheels for me.

Being convinced that the spare parts were genuine antiques. I assumed that the logbook was written in Latin. I think it was insured for fire, theft, and Viking raids! As I drove along, I wondered if the BBC were filming an episode of the *'Antiques Road Show'* along my route. It certainly was an incongruous vehicle.

There is much hypocrisy written and spoken by politicians and others about the air pollution in our country and elsewhere in the world. There is much criticism of diesel-guzzling and smoke belching from vehicles, as one of the major contributions to air pollution. 'The 'Beast' was certainly no exception. My body was still shaking at the end of the day.

Parking this contraption at Bangor railway station was almost impossible due to the layout of the car park. When required, the force allowed me to take 'The Beast' home every night and permission was granted for me to park it at the village police station which was adjacent to the main A5 trunk road and near to the commencement of a 30-mph restriction. I parked it in such a position that the rear doors were facing traffic coming from the direction of Holyhead. The amount of people who thought it was an 'Arrive Alive' (Now, 'Go-Safe') vehicle was unbelievable, but it had the desired effect in slowing motorists down coming from a 60-mph restriction.

To recover from the previous day's encounter with 'The Beast' a train journey on Thursday 2 March 2006 saw Sergeant Andy Hemmings and I travelling to Chester for a meeting of the local Train Operating Companies. (TOCs). This gave me some more useful contacts.

The evening of Monday 13 March 2006 saw me attending a meeting of the station adopters in the village hall at Llwyngwril on the Cambrian Coast. I went over in 'The Beast'. North Wales as you are probably aware is a very mountainous area and we have some very steep hills on roads to negotiate. One hill in particular is between Maentwrog and Gellilydan, near Trawsfynydd on the A470. I took a good run at the hill, but 'The Beast' was slowly going slower and slower. It went at a pace of a receding Swiss glacier. It clearly did not like steep hills. I glanced in my rear-view mirrors and could see a line of traffic behind me. Fortunately, there was a layby halfway up the hill. I pulled in and counted at least fifteen cars passing the layby. I continued towards Dolgellau and the village of Llwyngwril, mainly on the level.

On Friday 17 March 2006 I met with Eleanor Burnham the local Assembly Member for the Wrexham area in her office at Rossett near Wrexham. Eleanor was a very useful contact as she could bring up any of our concerns to the Assembly members.

The majority of April was taken up with the usual school visits and meetings with the various organisations in the locality. On one of the days I had a 'tail wind' behind me on the A55, which helped the 'The Beast' along. One of the schools I attended a little boy said to me during the questions session at the end of my presentation, "My brother was killed on the railway last week and when he came home, I said it was a dangerous place!"

It was the end of an era today, Friday 26 May 2006. As I have previously mentioned I did my initial recruit training at the number one Home Office District Training Centre at Bruche near Warrington in 1971. Some months earlier it was announced that Bruche was to close on Friday May 26 2006. I received an invite to attend the final passing out parade at the centre, which I duly accepted. It was very well attended, and it was nice to visit some of the old haunts there. During the final parade it poured down, a sad end to a fine institution.

The rest of the month was taken up with visiting schools to promulgate the all-important rail safety message to the pupils before they broke up for the spring holidays.

At one school in June 2006 during the question session a little girl desperately trying to attract my attention kept putting her hands up alternatively. When I asked what her question was, she said. "I had my hands cut off by a train last week".

One of the schools I visited was Ysgol Ardudwy, Harlech. (Harlech High School), which lies in the shadow of the beautiful Harlech Castle. As I was driving along the road to Harlech, the magnificent castle came into view, and I could imagine Ivor Emmanuel up on the ramparts singing *'Men of Harlech'*.

October 3, 2006 arrived I had now been back with the force for a year. It had gone quick with all the school visits and partnership meetings.

I left 'The Beast' at Bangor on Thursday 5 October 2006 as I travelled by train to visit the police station and for an overnight stay in a guest house in Shrewsbury, prior to attending a meeting the next day. On Friday 6 October 2006 after breakfast I changed into my suit. Whilst I was checking out, the proprietor of the guest house made a great fuss of me. I could see that he was trying to extract certain information from me about my employment and where I had been and where I was going. It turned out that he thought I was the AA inspector and had to come to inspect the premises for his grading. Off I went to my Wrexham safety group meeting in Ruabon, chuckling to myself. I had been mistaken for different people over the years, a salesman in a supermarket, a coach driver, and a cemetery attendant, amongst others. The AA inspector was a new one.

After we were made redundant in Holyhead in 1989 the officers decided that we would meet up on a regular basis for a social evening. So, it was on the evening of Friday 6 October 2006 that a reunion of all the old Holyhead based officers at the Trearddur Bay Hotel was held.

At one of the schools I visited in October 2006 a little lad was going to ask me if you could be prosecuted for going onto the railway, but what came out was, "Can you be prostituted for going onto the railway".

One of the schools I had to attend in November 2006 for a Crucial Crew event was the Argoed High School, Mynydd Isa, near Mold. Due to building works in the car park I had to park 'The Beast' in the playground. At lunchtime when I had finished, I fired up 'The Beast' and as usual, plumes of blue smoke erupted from the exhaust. The next thing I knew, was that Melfyn Hughes from the North Wales Fire and Rescue Service, who organised the Crucial Crew events, knocked on my window and said jokingly "The kids have all run inside for fear of being gassed. I'll arrange for a fire-engine to follow you in the behemoth to Bangor!" The following week I was again involved with Crucial Crew events in Flintshire.

I had a long day ahead of me on Wednesday 15 November 2006. After attending a Crucial Crew event at St Richard Gwyn Roman Catholic High School in Fflint, I had to drive 'The Beast' to Builth Road, in Mid Wales for an overnight stop. As I was driving in heavy rain and the light fading fast, on a lonely stretch of road between Newtown and Llandrindod Wells a man flagged me down and informed me of a Volvo car that had skidded off the road and had crashed into a crash barrier on a bend.

He then informed me that he had contacted the local police but as I was approaching, he rang them to cancel their attendance. I had to explain to him that I was not the local police and that he should contact them again. I used 'The Beast' to protect the scene and directed the traffic until arrival of the local traffic officers. I continued on my way soaked to the skin. On arrival at my overnight accommodation, which was an upmarket country house, I was politely advised to park 'The Beast' out of sight of the other vehicles, which were upmarket ones. It was about the only occasion I felt sorry for 'The Beast'. I could imagine it stood in the corner like a naughty schoolboy!

I had a nice room complete with a bath, which was welcome after my soaking on the road and driving 'The Beast' around some of the narrowest and hilly roads in Wales.

At dinner I ordered a soft drink as I was not allowed an alcoholic one on expenses. The waiter very kindly brought me over a nice pint of black and white 'orange juice' from Ireland.

The next morning, I attended a 'keeping Powys safe' conference at the Royal Welsh Showground in Builth Wells. As I was driving back to Bangor, through Porthmadog in the early evening, I was flagged down by a couple of residents informing me that there was a large-scale fight taking place in the locality. I went to the scene and the fight appeared to be over, fortunately the local police arrived. 'The Beast' had a lot to answer for.

Earlier in the year I had been asked by one of the South Wales based BTP Inspectors (who described me as 'a legend'), as part of a Welsh Assembly initiative, to involve local school children in designing a rail safety poster and for it to be judged by the local Station Manager. I arranged for a group of children from a primary school in Llandudno Junction to design a poster. I then contacted Venue Cymru the main theatre in Llandudno to see if the star of the forthcoming pantomime, Matt Baker, who had just left the children's programme Blue Peter, and now of Countryfile fame, would be agreeable to present the prizes which were to be donated by Arriva Trains Wales and Venue Cymru. Matt agreed to this request. On Wednesday 29 November 2006 myself, Ben Davies the local Station Manager and a couple of other people judged the posters and picked out three winning entries.

On Friday 8 December 2006 I attended a local Victim Support conference and lunch in Llandudno. Later that day I attended Holyhead Magistrates' Court to make a presentation on my work to the local Magistrates. I was quietly informed that my presence as a court usher in the courts was sorely missed.

I gave 'The Beast' a rest for my next venture, which was on the morning of Saturday 9 December 2006, which saw me travelling by train to attend Venue Cymru to meet up with Matt Baker and the winners of the posters. They were made up with their prizes. They were also elated to meet Matt Baker. The winning posters went on display at local railway stations.

On the run up to Christmas I visited a few more schools. Then took Christmas and the New Year off.

CHAPTER 28

THE CIVILIAN YEARS 2007 – 2008

Meeting the BBC Wales Weatherman

On returning to work in January 2007 I was kept busy booking school visits and partnership meetings. The first week in January 2007 began with a couple of meetings. The second week was taken up with an introduction to the Prince's Trust, (The Prince's Trust is a charity in the United Kingdom founded in 1976 by Charles, Prince of Wales, to help vulnerable young people get their lives on track. It supports 11 to 30 year olds who are unemployed and those struggling at school and at risk of exclusion). Also, a school visit, a talk to the '41' Club in Valley and partnership meetings in Colwyn Bay and Manchester.

I was up early as usual on Thursday 25 January 2007 to travel in 'The Beast' to a special needs school in Wrexham for a Crucial Crew event. At around 07.10 hours I was driving along the A55 dual carriageway at a speed of around fifty mph. I started to slow down to negotiate the roundabout at Llanfairfechan. As I began to change down the gears, nothing happened, they were not engaging, S**t! I managed to negotiate the roundabout and drove the vehicle at a reduced speed to Llandudno Junction railway station, where I arranged for the recovery of it. I then returned to the office at Bangor, cursing the vehicle. It turned out that the gear linkage had worn out due to the age of the vehicle. 'The Beast' was back on the road shortly afterwards.

Firing up 'The Beast' early on the morning of Friday 2 February I disturbed some nesting crows, who vented their anger at being woken up at such an unearthly hour by squawking their beaks off and no doubt waking the rest of the sleeping community of Valley. I then drove down to Abergele Primary School, delivering a rail safety talk. The afternoon was taken up with a meeting at Colwyn Bay railway station in the offices of the Making Tracks organisation.

The rest of February 2007 was taken up with a long planned and well-deserved holiday for three and a half weeks to New Zealand. During my time away I was informed that 'The Beast' would be replaced.

I returned to work on Wednesday 7 March 2007 after my relaxing holiday to New Zealand. On arrival in the car park at Bangor the hairs on the nape of my neck prickled. I shivered. Shock, horror, 'The Beast' was still there. I was now ready for another holiday! I was informed that there was no immediate sign of it being replaced. I now had three days of Crucial Crew events in Denbighshire.

The remaining working days in March were taken up with school visits and partnership meetings. One interesting meeting was on Thursday 29 March 2007 at Venue Cymru, Llandudno.

It was an environment conference to which the force had been invited. The participants were limited to twenty-five.

I arrived at around 09.30 hours ready for 10.00 hours start. I was the first one there. I went to the toilet, on returning to the conference room there was another participant there. No one else turned up. So, we worked through the best we could with the facilitators. At lunch time there was enough lunch on the buffet table for twenty-seven people. It was sad to see so much food wasted especially at an environmental conference.

I do not think that I am superstitious, touch wood, but today is Friday 13 April 2007. I fired up 'The Beast' for the very last time for a trip to Porthmadog for a meeting of the Cambrian Coast Railway Liaison Group. For the most part, to be fair, 'The Beast' played a key role in getting me to and from the schools.

The good news was on the afternoon of Thursday 19 April 2007 after a Crucial Crew event at a high school in Colwyn Bay, it was off to the car hire company to pick up a hire car. At long last I had said goodbye to 'The Beast'. Apparently, it was going for scrap.

Week commencing 23 April 2007 saw me involved in more Crucial Crew events in the County of Conwy and visits to two primary schools in the Wrexham area. It was sheer luxury driving around in the top of the range Volkswagen, with cruise control. After 'The Beast' it was like driving a Rolls Royce. However, the force expected me to visit local car dealers to see if one of them would sponsor me a vehicle. A local dealer had sponsored the North Wales Police Schools Liaison Officers. I visited several dealers, but I was out of luck.

One of the questions I ask during my presentation is what could happen if you throw a stone or a brick at a train. The usual answer is, 'It could smash a window and hurt or kill the driver or passengers'. Whilst I was at a primary school in May 2007, one lad, who reminded me very much of 'Brains' from the TV series Thunderbirds, disputed this. He said, "If the train is travelling at sixty-two miles an hour and the stone weighs less than a kilogram and the wind is blowing in a north-westerly direction then it wouldn't hit the window". The teacher just rolled her eyes and shook her head. I told him in no uncertain terms that it still had the potential to break a window and kill someone.

A rewarding day occurred on Friday 8 June 2007 I accompanied twenty-one special needs pupils whose ages ranged between nine and sixteen, from Ysgol Gogarth, a special needs school in Llandudno on the train to the Conwy Valley Railway Museum in Betws - y - Coed. During the journey I gave them each a 'goody bag' full of colouring books, quizzes, crayons etc. They were each given special tickets for the journey.

On arrival at the museum we had a picnic in the grounds and the owner, Colin Cartwright, very kindly opened up the tram system and the miniature railway for them. Their faces were an absolute picture of delight.

It brought great joy to me, to look after these children who were less fortunate than myself and others. I was reminded of that great tenor Josef Locke (Himself an ex police officer), singing, *'If I can help somebody'*.

Tuesday 19 June 2007 saw me travelling to Cardiff by train for my annual appraisal with Inspector Mike Edwards. I stopped overnight in Cardiff and met up with Andy Evans in a bar of a well-known pub chain. Unusually for me I bought the first round.

The bar was very crowded, so we had to stand at an upright support which had a ledge around it. After a short while, Andy then went to the bar to purchase two more pints of the black stout from over the water. I was stood there, people watching, when I was approached by a young black girl, who enquired as to what I was doing in Cardiff. Sensing that she was on the game, I played along with her and informed her that I was on business. She told me that she was also on 'business'.

At this juncture, Andy was approaching. I told her that I was here with my boyfriend, pointing to Andy, whose face was a picture and to his credit he never spilled a drop of the black neck oil. I have never seen a woman leave as quickly as she did.

The morning of Wednesday 11 July 2007 saw me at Abergele railway station meeting with people in connection with the Prince's Trust. The afternoon presented me with a new venture. I was invited to join the Wales Crimestoppers Board at their meeting at the North Wales Police Headquarters in Colwyn Bay.

Monday 16 July 2007, I travelled down to Cardiff for an overnight stay prior to a Crimestoppers meeting in the capital.

A bright summer's morning greeted me on Tuesday 17 July 2007. After a hearty Welsh breakfast at the guest house, I met up with Terry Flynn, Chairman of the Wales Crimestoppers Board for an informal meeting at the main Police Station in Cardiff where the Crimestoppers office was located. We all had a good laugh when I mentioned that I was identified as a sex attacker a few years earlier following an appeal on Crimestoppers.

Following an earlier visit to the school, Thursday 19 July 2007 saw me at Ty Croes railway station, Isle of Anglesey, meeting with a group of fifty school children from Pencarnisiog Primary School for a train trip to Bangor. On arrival at Bangor, I showed them around the station and explained the dos and don'ts of an operational railway station.

Figure 40 School children from Pencarnisiog Primary School at Ty Croes railway station on the occasion of a school trip organised by Bill to Bangor

On the way back the children were in reserved seats in a carriage of the two-coach train. As the train was en route back to Ty Croes, a man who was behind me said, "The wife and I were having a quiet journey from Birmingham until you got on"! I turned around to see that it was the late ex PC Hughie Rowlands from the BTP at Birmingham, with whom I worked. Hughie was travelling to Holyhead to meet up with his family. I realised that his remarks were in jest.

I still had the hire car, and on Thursday 26 July 2007, I attended a meeting at Area Headquarters in Birmingham, for a meeting with the Area Finance Officer to show me how to prepare a business case for a force vehicle.

Decent time was made along the Welsh roads, on Friday 27 July 2007 travelling to Machynlleth to attend an unruly behaviour meeting, with members from Network Rail, Arriva Trains Wales, the local rail unions and local council officials. On the return whilst driving between Machynlleth and Dolgellau two Hawk Jets from RAF Valley flew past me. I thought they will be home in a few minutes time. It would take me another two hours or so to reach Valley.

A day in the office at Bangor on Monday 30 July 2007 found me preparing a business case for a permanent vehicle.

I was returning to Holyhead on Friday 10 August 2007 by train from a partnership meeting in Machynlleth. After the train departed from Newtown, I was aware that the female Conductor was having problems with a couple of women from the travelling fraternity, who were refusing to pay their fare. I went to them and introduced myself as a member of the British Transport Police and showed them my identity card. They soon paid up.

On arrival at Welshpool they left the train, doubting my parentage. It transpired that they were well known to the officers at Shrewsbury.

The end of my two-year contract was on the horizon. However, the good news was that it had been extended for another two-years.

Network Rail held two-day annual events around Great Britain called 'No Messin' in towns where trespass and vandalism was a major problem. On Thursday 23 August 2007 and Friday 24 August 2007, they held an event in the Peace Centre, Warrington. As Arriva Trains Wales used Warrington Bank Quay Station and immediate areas with trains travelling from North Wales to Manchester, I was invited to assist with the rail safety stand on both days. The two days were well attended by a number of agencies to entertain the children. Even Manchester City Football Club turned out their youth team and I had a kick about on the field with some of them. The only snag was that I had to drive there and back each day, dodging the roadworks on the A55 North Wales Expressway. The Department of Transport put warning signs out about a week before any roadworks were due. With all the continuous roadworks on the A55 I suggested 'tongue in cheek' that they should put signs out informing people when the road would be clear of roadworks.

Friday lunchtime, 31 August 2007 I was dressed in my suit and was just leaving the storeroom, near to the booking office of Bangor railway station. I had been sorting out some material for the forthcoming school visits in September, when I saw sergeant Andy Hemmings in the car park with a person he had just arrested on behalf of the Cheshire Constabulary. He stated that he was waiting for the North Wales Police to convey him to the custody suite at Caernarfon Police station, but they were short of officers. I volunteered to take him in the marked police car. I collected the keys along with my briefcase containing the all-important lunch. On arrival at Caernarfon the prisoner was booked in with the civilian detention officer, who I had met when I worked in the courts, when he was working for the company who escorted the prisoners to court. He asked me who I was, and it was obvious that he had not recognised me. I said, "I am his solicitor; he doesn't travel anywhere without me". He looked very perplexed. Just then the custody sergeant came in and he recognised me and asked how I was. The penny then dropped for the civilian custody officer. I then had my lunch in the back room whilst Andy booked the prisoner in.

A jaunt along the A55 on Thursday 25 October 2007, took me to Colwyn Bay where I attended the Conwy County Council offices in the town for a North Wales Practitioners meeting at which I was elected chairman of the group. It was indeed an honour for me and the force to chair this group.

In one of the schools in November 2007 my name was changed in the matter of a few minutes. I introduced myself at the reception as Bill Rogerson. Shortly a teacher came along, and the receptionist introduced me as Bill Rogers. I then went to a classroom where I was introduced to another teacher as Bill Robertson, who in turn introduced me to the class as Bob Robinson.

At one of the Crucial Crew events in January 2008, which was a full day event, a few more agencies were in attendance, one of whom was the sex education team. It went without saying that the children were on a high after hearing about the do's and don'ts of sex. During my question session a boy put his hand up and I asked him what his question was. He said, "I know how to make babies". I said, "We will just concentrate on railway safety, today" He said, "You take off the 'y' and add 'ies'".

During the winter months snow can be a problem in North Wales on the A55 road between the summit of Rhuallt Hill and Pentre Halkyn where it is extremely high up. One morning as I left Bangor for a school in Wrexham, it was a dull day, by the time I arrived at the bottom of Rhuallt Hill on the A55 it was snowing furiously, and as I was ascending the hill, my phone burst into life. I pulled into Holywell services just further down the road. The call was from the North Wales Fire and Rescue Service to advise me that the Crucial Crew event in Wrexham had been cancelled. I had some breakfast at the services and made my way to Rhyl where I completed some paperwork.

As Andy Evans, my counterpart, was in Australia, on Wednesday 6 February 2008 I travelled from Cardiff to Pontypridd to represent the force at the unveiling of the murals there, that had been painted by the pupils from the Prince's Trust, to adorn the station. The unveiling was carried out by a local television celebrity Derek Brockway who is the BBC Wales Weatherman and a Valleys Kids Ambassador. I met Derek personally after the unveiling and had a long chat to him over a cup of coffee. A lovely man.

By March 2008 Pete Conway, my Midlands counterpart, had left the Community Safety Partnership post and had transferred to another department within the force. This left a vacancy. There was a major trespass and vandalism problem on the main line from Birmingham New Street to London Euston in the Lea Hall area on the outskirts of Birmingham.

On Tuesday 18 March 2008 I travelled to Birmingham to meet up with a Schools Liaison Officer from the West Midlands Police at Birmingham International railway station to discuss the problem.

The National Motorcycle Museum near to Birmingham International Railway Station was the location for a Railway Community Safety Forum which I attended on Wednesday 19 March 2008, to represent the Wales Western Area of the force. The forum was also attended by the Chief Constable Ian Johnson.

I attended a Crimestoppers meeting in Colwyn Bay on Wednesday 2 April 2008. At this meeting I was elected Chairman of the organisation. This was indeed a feather in my cap and one for the force as well.

In Mid-April 2008 I heard that my application for a permanent force vehicle had been successful and that it would be delivered shortly.

Over the years I had been a member and Vice Chair of the Môn / Gwynedd Victim Support Scheme and later when it became the North Wales Victim Support Scheme, following a reorganisation, I became a Trustee. On the 29 April 2008 I received a letter thanking me for my work as a Trustee and informing me that in the coming months all the local schemes would be amalgamated to form a national charity. The letter went onto say that I would be welcome to remain an ordinary member of the National Scheme. Due to my other numerous commitments, I decided to have no further involvement with them on the committee or as a Trustee. I did however receive a nice engraved glass plaque in recognition of my services for the organisation.

A brand-new Vauxhall Astra arrived on Thursday 5 June 2008. It only had 6 miles on the clock. So, it was goodbye to the hire cars.

Friday 6 June 2008 saw me attending the local Victim Support Scheme Annual General meeting in Conwy. It gave me an opportunity to say my goodbyes to the members, whom I had worked with over the years. Then it was onto a Making Tracks meeting in Colwyn Bay.

The force did not run any School Liaison Courses, so I devised one, using material that had been previously used at Tadworth. On Tuesday 10 June 2008 Andy Evans and myself travelled to Area Headquarters in Birmingham to train about fourteen Police Community Support Officers in Schools Liaison duties. The Sergeant in charge of the Neighbourhood Policing Teams (NPT) sent a letter of thanks for the input that we had put in.

A Crucial Crew event in Porthmadog was undertaken on Wednesday 18 June 2008. On this day there were six agencies in the school, two of whom were myself with my usual graphic film show and the Foods Standards Agency (FSA). Pete from the FSA shows an animated cartoon film to accompany his talk on food hygiene. One of the clips in the film shows a man sat on the toilet suffering from diarrhoea and there are associated sounds with his unfortunate condition as well. We had three presentations before the morning break and three after the break. During break time the children had obviously discussed between themselves what they have seen so far. After break, I was waiting by the classroom door for my class to come in. One of the pupils looked at me and said, "Are you the man with the diarrhoea?"

My fame had spread far and wide. The West Midlands Fire and Rescue Service had recently opened a new headquarters in Vauxhall, on the outskirts of Birmingham City Centre. There, they were setting up a visitor's centre similar to Dangerpoint, called Safeside. On Thursday 10 July 2008 I travelled to Birmingham to meet up with the manager to discuss the script for the railway scenario. I stayed overnight in Birmingham.

The following day, Friday 11 July 2008, at the invitation of the West Midlands Police, I went to the International School in Tile Cross, a suburb of Birmingham, and near to Lea Hall, where there was a lot of trespass and vandalism on the tracks.

The ink was barely dry on the morning newspapers on Tuesday 22 July 2008 when I had an early drive to Cardiff to visit the ITV Wales studios in Cardiff for a Crimestoppers Board meeting.

An overnight stay in Birmingham with Andy Evans was the order of the day for Tuesday 29 July 2008. The following day Wednesday 30 July 2008 we trained up more PCSOs in schools liaison work.

There was a distinct autumnal feel to the day on Monday 15 September 2008, my first day back after annual leave, as I drove to Oswestry for three days of Lifeline events organised by the local Rotary Club at the Showground. The Lifeline events are very similar to the Crucial Crew events but aimed at year six pupils from the primary schools.

The Lifeline events were visited by the District Governor of the Rotary Clubs, local dignitaries, such as the Chairman of the local council, and the local Mayor along with the local Vicar. Whilst I was talking to the Vicar, it became evident that he was interested in railways and stated that he would dearly love to visit the Severn Bridge Junction Signalbox at Shrewsbury. This Signalbox is Europe's largest surviving mechanical Signalbox. I told him I would see what I could do. I made a phone call later that day to the Operations Manager of Network Rail at Shrewsbury and he gladly agreed for the Vicar to visit the Signalbox. He gave me his permission to pass on his mobile number to him so that he could arrange a visit at a time and date to suit them both. Being a bit of a joker, I found out what time the Vicar's service was on a Sunday.

The next day I saw the Vicar and informed him that I had arranged for him to visit the Signalbox. A bright smile appeared on his face. I informed him that it was any Sunday at 10.00 hours. The Vicar's face dropped, and he said, "That's the time of my service". I put him out of his misery and told him to ring the Operations Manager to arrange a mutual time and date. I could hear the good Lord going, "Tut, tut" and shaking his finger at me.

Following my attendance, I received a letter of thanks from the organiser for my enthusiasm straight after my holidays. And, for setting up a link between Dangerpoint and the NSPCC which eventually delivered a first-class anti-bullying exhibit at the Lifeline event.

It was off to the International School in Tile Cross, Birmingham on Tuesday 7 October 2008 for more railway safety talks and workshops with the pupils. After the talk I received a letter of thanks from the Assistant Headteacher thanking me for the excellent work I carried out with the students.

A visit to my old CID stamping ground in Leicester was made on Wednesday 8 October 2008. This time it was for a meeting at the offices of the Prince's Trust, who were after my services to assist with a project in Derby.

Following the training of the PCSO's in school's liaison duties earlier in the year it was off to Area Headquarters on Wednesday 29 October 2008 to join Andy Evans and the Area Commander, in presenting them with their certificates.

It was an early start on Thursday 6 November 2008 to drive over to Derby to make a presentation to members of the Prince's Trust in the old roundhouse, which was an old railway building and that had been restored. I was informed prior to my visit that lunch would not be provided, but I could claim reasonable expenses if so desired. On arrival at the premises, I told the duty receptionist who I was and that I was here to make a presentation. I was directed to a room. On entering this room I was welcomed and informed to help myself to the buffet, which I did. After a short while I discovered that I was in the wrong room. I did offer to pay after explaining that I had been misdirected, but the offer was refused. I eventually found the right room.

Friday 7 November 2008 it was another Crucial Crew event this time in Mold at the Maes Garmon Welsh medium school, which is located next door to the Mold Alun High School. It was easier to park the car in the car park of the Alun school and walk through to the Maes Garmon school. As I was doing so, I noticed a group of pupils playing football on the green between the two schools. One of them kicked the ball and it headed in my direction, so instinctively I kicked it back to them. My aim was not too good, and it began heading towards a classroom window. I was stood by a notice which proclaimed, *'Anyone making a nuisance of themselves on these premises will be reported and ejected'*. I thought S**t. However, my luck was in and the ball hit the brickwork between two sets of windows. *'Talk about Maradona and the hand of God.'* The pupils all shouted, "Good on you mister!" One of them recognised me from a previous visit to the school and shouted "It's Doctor Gory. Are you going to year seven, to show some more dead bodies?" I told them that I was. With this a couple or more of them put their thumbs up. At least I had made an impression on some of them.

During the break time at a Crucial Crew event in Fflint High School on Thursday 13 November 2008 I was enjoying a well-earned cup of coffee and biscuit, when I saw a car drive into the car park at very high speed and the driver performed a hand break turn. It was like something out of a scene from the television programme *'The Sweeney'*. This incident was witnessed by members of the school staff and some of the Crucial Crew team. The North Wales Police Schools Liaison Officer had not yet arrived, so it was all eyes on me. I explained that I had no jurisdiction but would go and speak to the driver.

I went to the car and spoke to the driver who was around nineteen years old and an ex pupil. His father, a lot taller and heavier build than myself, then alighted from the passenger side and said, "You lot are always picking on our family, we've done nothing wrong". He started squaring up to me, by this time I was joined by the female Schools Liaison Officer from the North Wales Police. I pointed out to him the CCTV cameras situated around the school and this calmed him down. Both were warned as to their conduct. It transpired that both father and son were very well known to the police in Fflint.

Back in the staff room I received a round of applause and one member of the Crucial Crew team said jokingly "I would have done my bit and sent the Red Cross man out to you if things got worse!".

At one of my presentations in November 2008 I told the children that a 'Virgin' train can travel at speeds of up to one hundred and twenty-five miles an hour when it is between Crewe and London. Nine times out of ten the children try to catch me out by asking "What is a Virgin?", followed by the giggles. I calmly tell them that it is a company owned by Sir Richard Branson. Next question please?

I am always asked if I have ever picked up any body parts from fatalities to which I tell them that I have. Some come back to me and asked if I have picked up every part of the body, followed by the giggles.

The year culminated in visits to schools and partnership meetings.

CHAPTER 29

THE CIVILIAN YEARS 2009 – AUGUST 2010

Meeting the head of John The Baptist, and an arresting moment

As usual the year began filling up the diary with school visits and partnership meetings.

I set off by train on Tuesday 3 February 2009 to travel to Nottingham for an overnight stay. Andy Evans should have joined me but due to the adverse weather in South Wales he was unable to make it.

Wednesday 4 February 2009 I attended the offices of the BTP at Nottingham where I trained up some of the East Midlands based PCSOs and a couple of staff from East Midlands Trains in delivering schools liaison messages to local schools.

I was privy to an amusing telephone conversation during the morning of Wednesday 11 February 2009 when I visited St John the Baptist Primary School, Penmynydd, Flintshire, to speak to the pupils about railway safety. On arrival the Headteacher invited me into his office for a welcome cup of coffee. Whilst we were having a friendly chat, the telephone rang. He said to me, "I love answering the phone here". He picked it up and said, "Good morning, the head of John the Baptist speaking…."

It is 06.00 hours the following day and the alarm was beckoning me to rise and shine, as it was off to another old stamping ground. This time it was to Crewe to attend Mablins Lane Primary School, which is situated right next to the main West Coast Railway Line. There I delivered safety talks to the pupils. At the end of my presentation there was the usual barrage of questions and observations from the pupils. One lad said to me "I electrocute my brother when he annoys me" The teachers looked on in amazement and absolute horror. I imagined that he had a piece of cable with bare wire at both ends which he stuck into the mains and gave the other end to his brother. I said, "How do you do that?" He said, "I drag him to the trampoline and put his hand on the pole". (Trampolines are notorious for giving off static electric). I thought I'd better not to annoy him if I met him on Crewe station.

When I arranged the talk, the teacher asked if there was any charge for the visit. I stated that there was not, as it was all part of the service. However, a nice cup of coffee and chocolate biscuit would be welcome. On arrival at the school I was greeted with a cup of coffee.

At break time again I received a nice cup of coffee and was handed a tin of luxury Belgian chocolate biscuits, which had been purchased from a well-known upmarket chain store with a food outlet.

Thursday 19 March 2009 was the day of my three yearly driving assessment in Shrewsbury which I passed with flying colours. I drove around the streets of Shrewsbury, and the nearby dual carriageways and motorway with a Sergeant from Birmingham who was a qualified driving instructor. It was like taking your driving test all over again. Certainly, keeps your mind focussed and on your toes.

The following week, Tuesday 24 March 2009, I was up early to travel to Safeside at the West Midlands Fire and Rescue Service Headquarters, Duddeston, to meet up with the manager and to assist in finalising the script for the rail safety scenario there.

Bright eyed and bushy tailed, I was off early on Wednesday 27 May 2009 to a meeting in Birmingham with PC Dave Jones, whose duties now included school's liaison for the West Midlands. This took some pressure off me.

The month finished off on Friday 29 May 2009 with a day in the office at Bangor, preparing for more schools and meetings in June. On that evening I went to Tesco's superstore in Holyhead to collect money in buckets for the RNLI with Shirley between, 17.00 hours and 19.00 hours. At 18.17 hours I was stood in the foyer with my back to the exit door, when I heard the alarm at the exit sounding. I turned around and saw a young man running out with a large television, hotly pursued by the security man who was shouting "Stop that thief". Instinctively I stopped him and brought him down to the floor in an approved police hold. (I had not lost my touch).

I informed him that I was making a citizen's arrest and cautioned him. My collecting bucket had fallen out of my hand on to the floor and my coins spilled out of the bucket. The security man came to assist me with the thief, who by this time started to struggle with me. As we were restraining him, he hit the security man in the face, resulting in bruising and a black eye. By this time there was a large crowd gathered who were just stood there watching. I said, "It's not an all ticket concert, somebody ring for the police". A short time later two officers from the North Wales Police attended. The first words one of the officer's said to me was, "I thought you'd retired". As they were formally arresting him, he claimed that the money from my bucket was his, having fallen out of his pocket during the struggle.

Ten gruelling working days lay ahead of me from Monday 1 June 2009 until Friday 12 June 2009. I had been invited to take part in the North Shropshire Crucial Crew events at Nesscliff Army Camp, between Wrexham and Shrewsbury. This Crucial Crew was organised by a committee of people from the area, after a legacy had been left to fund the education of young persons in the area and from across the border in Powys. The events were targeted at year six pupils who were in their last year of primary school.

Each day the pupils were brought in by coach to see the fourteen agencies who were presenting safety messages. For my scenario I still had the model railway which had been donated to the force in 1993. I had to present fourteen, twelve-minute sessions every day, between 10.00 hours and 14.30 hours. Like most of the other agencies I operated from an army hut. A couple of agencies, such as the National Farmers Union were out in the open air.

Each day I had to drive from home to Nesscliff and back through the tranquil scenery of North Wales and Shropshire. There was no overnight accommodation on offer. It was a round trip of two hundred miles each day. At the end of the ten days I had clocked up two thousand miles. I used to set off at 06.30 hours to wrestle with the roadworks on the A55 and the rush hour traffic around Chester and Wrexham. I would arrive just after 09.00 hours.

Arriving at this time gave me time to have a relaxing cup of coffee and a chocolate bar. I would arrive home each evening at around 17.00 hours. I looked forward to the weekends. I estimated that I spoke to around one thousand six hundred and eighty children and their teachers over the ten days.

Figure 41 Bill talking to some pupils at the rail safety display in connection with a Crucial Crew event at Nesscliff Army Camp

I was visited at home on Saturday 6 June 2009 by a North Wales Police Officer, who I did not know, and who wanted a statement from me in respect of the Tesco incident. To begin with she asked for my name and no other personal details. She then asked me to describe what I had witnessed before she wrote down the account. I gave her a full description and one of the phrases I used was, "………. instinctively I looked at my watch and it was 18.17 hours……". After my verbal account. She said to me, "That's a fantastic account, I wish everybody was like you. Have you ever given a statement to the police before?" I then revealed my identity. She said to me "You could have written your own statement down".

A few days later the culprit pleaded guilty at court and I received a nice letter of thanks and a shopping voucher from Tesco in appreciation of my actions.

Ysgol Glan y Môr, High School, Pwllheli, was visited on Tuesday 16 June 2009 for a Crucial Crew event. On arrival back home, I had a routine Doctor's appointment with my GP. Whilst on the scales he looked at my weight and then looked at me and said to me with a smile on his face, "School Dinners?" To which, I sheepishly gave a positive reply.

A full day, including a school dinner, completely ignoring the Doctor's advice from the previous day, for a Crucial Crew event at Porthmadog High School was undertaken on Wednesday 17 June 2009.

A pleasant day out was enjoyed on Thursday 18 June 2009 taking a party of special needs children from Ysgol Gogarth, Llandudno by train to Betws-y-Coed. On arrival Colin Cartwright the owner of the Railway Museum at Betws-y-Coed, offered his hospitality to the children by letting them ride on the miniature railway. After which we all enjoyed a picnic. On arrival back at Llandudno the bright smiles on the faces of the children said it all for a wonderful and satisfying day out.

Wednesday 1 July 2009, my contract had been renewed for another twelve months, which was great, I could plan for the year ahead.

A bright sunny morning greeted me on Monday 13 July 2009 as I drove to Wrexham to attend the Laurel Park Primary School delivering rail safety talks to the pupils. I said to one of the teachers, "It's not long now until the school holidays" She replied "Yes, ten days, four hours, twenty eight minutes, forty two seconds and counting."

The North Wales Crucial Crew organisation held their Annual General Meeting at Rhyl Fire Station on Friday 17 July 2009. This was a very useful meeting where we debriefed the previous year's Crucial Crew events and how we could improve or rather how the schools could improve on their organisation of them.

Figure 42 Bill shares a story with Larry Davies and the late Gwyn Roberts at Dolwydellan railway station on the occasion of the 130th anniversary of the Conwy Valley railway line

My day off, Sunday 6 September 2009, had a surprise in store for me. I was at a craft fayre with the RNLI souvenir stall at the Trearddur Bay Hotel, when I met up with Viv Head an ex Detective Inspector from the force. I had known Viv for several years. Over a drink he floated the idea of starting a History Group to preserve the artefacts and documents of the force, which were quickly being disposed of.

I readily agreed to become a founding member and took on the role of Secretary and Treasurer. The Group is now going from strength to strength.

Another early morning start, on Friday 23 October 2009 and it was off to St Annes Primary School Wrexham for a delivery of rail safety talks. When booking the talks, I had asked the teacher who I was to liaise with on the day of my visit, if I could use the school's IT equipment to which she agreed. On arrival I was taken to the assembly hall which was to be my base. The teacher informed me that the laptop and the projector were not connecting to each other. I told her that I was a technophobe. She then stated that she would send in Billy the Technician. I was expecting a man about my age with a brown smock to come in. A few moments later the double doors burst open and in walked Billy, an eight-year-old pupil. "He said "Hello mister. Miss tells me that the laptop and projector are not connecting". I replied, "That's right". He looked at the equipment, and like an old man, rubbed his chin and said "Yes, we have a Panasonic laptop and an Epson projector". He looked at the keyboard on the laptop, pressed a couple of keys and the two connected together. He said, "There you are mister, both talking to each other, see you later". I just stood there in amazement. A little later it was the turn of his class to come and see me. On entering the room, he put his thumbs up and said, "Everything alright mister?" I said, "Yes thank you". I turned to the class and said to them, "Billy got the equipment working for this old dinosaur!" He stood there ten-foot tall with a bright smile on his face.

Another early start was made on Wednesday 25 November 2009 to travel to the Wrexham area to visit two primary schools. Ysgol Tan y Fron and Johnstown Junior School, to deliver rail safety talks. At one of the schools I arrived earlier than my allocated time. After a cup of coffee, the teacher said that we could make an earlier start and that I could have some extra time with the pupils. In the classroom the teacher introduced me and said, "Bill has arrived a little early, so he is going talk for a little bit longer". A young lad put his hand up and said, "Will you be finished by three, cos we go home then?" I assured him that I would be finished by lunchtime.

Like most other forces, the British Transport Police suffers a lot of sickness from their officers and police staff. As an incentive to encourage officers and staff not to go off sick a points scheme was introduced a few years ago. Every officer who completed a twelve-month period without taking any time off sick were rewarded with fifty attendance points, which could be exchanged for goods to the value of £50 from a specialist catalogue.

The previous year a Detective Constable from Bristol, decided to ask members of the Wales and Western Area to donate their points via himself for use at a Hospice in the city. This proved successful. At the beginning of 2009 nominations for a similar scheme were invited from members of the Wales and Western Area of the force. The applications went before a panel. I successfully applied for Ty Gobaith, a Children's Hospice near Conwy to be the recipients of the points. I collected some two thousand points from members of the Wales and Western Area of the force. This equated to around £2000. I then visited the fundraising office of the Hospice in Llandudno Junction, where they selected items from the catalogue for use in the Hospice.

Christmas came early for the Hospice, for it was on Wednesday 2 December 2009, that I along with Superintendent Mike Layton and Inspector Mark Shaw, attended the Hospice and presented the gifts to them, which included the state of the art digital piano, a camcorder, a 32" digital television, DAB hi-fi, plus other fantastic goodies. The gifts certainly made a difference to the children. We were then invited to a tour of the Hospice.

Figure 43 Bill with Superintendent Mike Layton and Inspector Mark Shaw presenting the gifts to the staff and a patient at Hope House Hospice on 2 December 2009

Thursday 25 March 2010 was spent in the office undergoing a Welsh Language exam which had been formulated between the force and a local college. I passed with flying colours.

A week previously, a nasty incident occurred at Ashchurch Railway station, near Tewkesbury, Gloucestershire, whereby a pupil who was on one of the platforms with a group from a nearby school jumped from the platform and into the path of an oncoming train and then back onto the platform. The driver of the oncoming train had to apply the train's emergency brake.

The offender was dealt with by the force. I was asked to go and pay the school a visit a speak to all the pupils about the dangers of the railway. This I did on Friday 26 March 2010. Following the visit, the school sent me a letter of thanks.

Friday 30 April 2010 saw me on a full day's visit to Manchester. In the morning I attended a level crossing conference in the offices of Network Rail. In the afternoon, I attended a drop-in session for civilian staff of the force. The force were proposing to change the contracts of the civilian staff and the new contracts would have enhanced benefits. I instantly signed on the dotted line.

On Wednesday 12 May 2010 it was off to Liverpool for an audition in connection with 'The Weakest Link'. More of this in the following chapter.

Tuesday 25 May 2010 saw me venturing beyond Wales for the long drive down to Clyst St Mary on the outskirts of Exeter, Devon to drop off the model railway for a safety day, the following day. It was then to the police station at Exeter St David's railway station, to meet up with ex Sergeant John Bulleyment MBE and to pick up some documents for the History Group, which were being disposed of. I then spent the night in Exeter.

The following day, Wednesday 26 May 2010, I attended the primary school at Clyst St Mary, at their safety day and throughout the day taught rail safety to the pupils. The organiser sent me a letter of appreciation along with some of the comments in respect of the agencies that attended. Some of the pupils wrote about my talk. *'Trains are interesting, but you must not get too close to railway lines'. 'I Set a good example to others when I am on a platform and tell a grown up if people are doing things wrong'. 'You should always use a proper crossing'.*

The children's rhyme goes Doctor Foster went to Gloucester, but after leaving the school at Clyst St Mary, it was not Doctor Foster going to Gloucester it was yours truly, who made an overnight night stop in Gloucester. On the way back home to North Wales on Thursday 27 May 2010 I visited Field Court Junior School, Gloucester to talk about rail safety.

I was at a primary school which shall remain nameless. As I was delivering my talk a young pupil was busy examining the interior of the right nostril with his right hand index finger. I told him that if he carried on much longer he would lose his finger. He quickly withdrew it and I noticed that he had a big bogie on the end of it, which he promptly placed in his mouth and ate it. I've seen several children over the years wipe their noses on their sleeves.

Wednesday 30 June 2010 I attended a meeting of the North Wales Practitioners at the North Wales Police Headquarters in Colwyn Bay. From there it was over to Aberaeron for an overnight stay.

I went to Aberaeron Primary School on Thursday 1 July 2010 to present rail safety talks to the pupils. Then it was off to another Celtic part of Britain, this time to the beautiful county of Cornwall for an overnight stay.

A level crossing at Carn Brea near Camborne was being plagued by children playing on the barriers. So, it was decided that I should attend the local primary school.

Cornwall is a favourite part of the country for me. When I was young, and my children were young, I used to spend my holidays in Cornwall. I was looking forward to my overnight hotel stay in Hayle, owned by a well-known chain of hotels. I had the evening planned out. Go into the nearby beautiful town of St Ives for some fish and chips and reminisce. As I was driving along the A30 the sky was very heavy. I ran into a downpour of Biblical proportions. As I was on Bodmin Moor the phone rang. I pulled over at Bolventor, near Jamaica Inn to ring the caller back. It was the hotel where I was booked in for the night. I was informed that the room that had been allocated to me had been flooded and that I had been allocated another room.

On arrival at the hotel it was still raining very heavily, in fact it was still of Biblical proportions and was set in for the night. So, my visit to St Ives was thwarted. I had to make do with the pub next door. I got soaked just walking a few yards from the hotel to the pub.

The next day Friday 2 July 2010 the rain had abated, and it was onto Roskear Primary school Camborne to speak to the pupils. After my visit it was back up the A30, the M5 and the M4 to a Brethren School in Chippenham, Wiltshire, to speak to the children who were embarking on a trip to Weston Super Mare.

Sadly, Andy Evans my counterpart in South Wales was on long term sickness, so it was off to Cwmbran for a two-night stay on Wednesday 14 July 2010. Most of the day was spent travelling down to South Wales.

A visit to Croes Ceiliog High School, Cwmbran to speak to the year eight pupils was made on Thursday 15 July 2010. Then it was off to the ITV Wales studios for a Crimestoppers Board meeting.

It was back to Croes Ceiliog High School, Cwmbran, on Friday 16 July 2010 this time to speak to the year nine pupils.

The rest of the month was spent preparing to appear on the show *'The Weakest Link'*.

CHAPTER 30

THE CIVILIAN YEARS - THE WEAKEST LINK

"Bill, goodbye you are the Weakest Link!"!

There are no lifelines, phone a friend, 50/50, ask the audience. You are the banker.

'The Weakest Link' started in August 2000 over on BBC 2. Due to my work governing the time I arrived home, I never watched it but heard about it and read about it in the papers. I first watched it in January 2002 when I was on holiday in Whitby. A couple of years later, I along with several hundred other people applied to become a contestant. The application form was duly completed and forwarded to the BBC. A couple of months later I received a telephone call inviting me to take part in an audition in Llandudno the following week. Due to other commitments I was unable to attend and was not offered an alternative venue.

It was not until January 2010 when I reapplied. The application form was duly sent off by email. In May whilst en route to visit a school in Gloucester, I pulled over into the service area on the M5 to answer a text from Shirley. She requested that I ring Sarah in *'The Weakest Link'* office in Glasgow. I called Sarah and a short interview ensued. I was offered the chance to attend an audition in Bangor the following week. Upon consulting the diary, I found that I was unable to attend, but I was offered an audition in Liverpool which I accepted. I was given the choice of three time slots, 09.00 hours, 11.00 hours, and 13.00 hours. I took the 11.00 hours slot.

On arriving back home the following day there was an email waiting for me from the BBC congratulating me on being selected to attend a *'Weakest Link'* audition.

On Wednesday 12 May 2010 I left Valley on the 06.35 hours train to Chester, changing for Liverpool. On arrival at Liverpool there was time for a coffee before I went to the Jury's Inn at the Albert Dock. The Receptionist directed me to the first floor, where I met some other potential contestants and some of those who were on the 09.00 hours audition.

At 11.00 hours we were all ushered into a meeting room, where we met two of the show's researchers, one of whom was playing the part of Anne Robinson. We stood in front of a set of chairs arranged in a half moon. Sarah, one of the researchers asked us all to complete a personal data form, as we were doing so, we had our photograph taken and we produced photographic identity, which in my case was my passport. We were also asked about dates to avoid, such as holidays, dental appointments etc.

We were informed that if we were successful at the audition, we would hear from the BBC within six weeks. If no reply, we had to assume that we had been unsuccessful. If we were successful, we could wait for well over one year before we heard if we had been selected for a show and even then, there was no guarantee of making an appearance within any set period. The whole process would have to be started all over again.

We then had to complete a written thirty question general knowledge quiz in three minutes. This duly done, we then played a game of *'The Weakest Link'* with Ross, the second researcher, playing the part of Anne Robinson. It was great fun. We had to introduce ourselves, and then Ross fired the questions at us.

After the game we were asked to leave the room and were called back individually this time to face a camera and answer personal questions asked by Sarah and to talk about our work, family, and hobbies in general. I left Liverpool with an open mind.

At the beginning of June 2010, I received a letter from *'The Weakest Link'* office in Glasgow advising me that I had been shortlisted for the show.

A couple of weeks went by and I was contacted by Ross Proudfoot, from *'The Weakest Link'* office, whom I had met in Liverpool asking if I could be available to appear as a contestant on *'The Weakest Link'* on Thursday, 19 August 2010 at 07.00 hours. I stated that I was available. Talk about being fast-tracked. Ross then made an appointment to ring me one evening to discuss my biography and he said that he would need at least three quarters of an hour. On the evening in question, he was on for well over an hour.

A couple of days later I received a contestant's pack detailing all what would happen on the recording day. There were yet more forms such as contestant release indemnity and statement of health to fill out and send back.

The week prior to travelling to Glasgow, I received an email detailing all my travel arrangements and overnight accommodation, which was to be at the Campanile Hotel, near to the BBC studios in Glasgow. We were told to take at least three choices of outfits to wear. There was no need to worry if they got creased during the journey as the one you would be wearing would be ironed, although they had to be clean as stains and marks show up easily on TV. There were restrictions on certain colours and patterns as they created a strobe effect on camera. The show I was appearing in was the first one to be recorded in High Definition (HD). Strictly no black tops as the 'Queen of Mean' was the only one allowed to wear black.

On Wednesday 18 August 2010 I travelled early morning to Birmingham for a BTP History Group Committee meeting. I then travelled up to Glasgow at no cost to the BBC as I used one of my free passes. On arrival at Glasgow, I found an Italian restaurant where I had dinner, the 'Beeb' would reimburse £12. I then took a taxi to the hotel; the fare being refunded by the 'Beeb'. I settled into the hotel.

The next morning at 05.10 hours the alarm clock was merrily dancing away on the bedside cabinet. After getting ready it was downstairs to the restaurant for breakfast at 06.00 hours, where I met my fellow contestants and two others who were standby contestants. As we had an extremely strict timetable to adhere to, we were picked up at 06.45 hours precisely by a minibus which conveyed us to the BBC studios, where we were booked in by the security staff and issued with our passes. We were then taken to a room where we were given name badges which had to be affixed to our shirts/blouses and we had to learn the names of the other contestants.

Tea and coffee along with biscuits were served. As this was being done, two ladies from the wardrobe department came along and took the three outfits we had brought along.

We were then taken individually to see another researcher who rechecked our biographies. After this it was to the makeup room where make up was applied to us. Whilst I was in the makeup room, I started talking to the makeup lady and remarked that she did not sound Scottish but Cumbrian. She confirmed that she was from the Penrith area. As the conversation developed, I discovered that she had gone to school with a cousin of mine. We then had the outfit we were wearing returned to us and it was to another room to put them on. The wardrobe department had inserted sweat pads into the shirts and blouses. We needed them under the hot studio lights.

After all this we were taken to the contestants' holding room and put into podium order (this is the room which you see in the opening titles) and given a briefing about the actual recording. The makeup ladies came in and touched up our makeup. Then one of the producers and a cameraman came in and moved us around into different positions and then filmed the opening sequence for our show. We were then able to have a group photograph taken with our own camera.

When all this had been completed, we were taken to the 'green room' for a Danish Pastry and another drink. Then it was down to the recording studio. En route we had the chance to visit the loo for the last time until after the recording.

In the studio, which was in virtual darkness, a member of the floor team showed us in with a torch. We could see the podiums with our names on, except for mine which was missing. This was brought a short while later. Microphones were attached to us A briefing was given; on not to touch the blue light around our name as this was of a high voltage, one thousand volts, to be exact. We went on to be briefed on protocol, on when to turn the name board over, how to do the walk of shame, which had to be done twice due to the camera angles. We then had a rehearsal on introducing ourselves 'NATO' was the mnemonic, name, age, town, occupation, and how to turn the board over, not as easy as you think. We had to memorise the names of all the contestants and where they were standing, the ones on my immediate right and left were difficult to see, so it was important that you got their names correct should the need arise.

At 10.30 hours precisely the music started and the 'Queen of Mean' herself walked in and it was, Lights, Camera Action!, the recording of the show had begun for real. At one end of the studio was the bank board and the clock, it was difficult to see them, without turning your body, which was frowned upon, only a very quick glance of the eyes was allowed. Introductions over, the questions were fired at us.

At the end of the first round we were then asked to write on the board who we thought was *The Weakest Link*. As we commenced to write the names down, Anne Robinson left the stage and went to a room where she picked up a couple of biographies. A researcher walked behind us and made a note of who we voted for. This information would be fed back to Anne, as she does not speak to the first 'Weakest Link', except to say "Goodbye..you are the Weakest Link." To fill in time we had to overwrite the names several times, this could take up to five minutes. Then we were told to place our boards back in the rests on the podium. A researcher came round to make sure that we had put them back correctly as there was a knack on how to do it. There was time for a breather. The makeup ladies came around touching up the makeup, as necessary. The only place to sit was on Anne's podium.

Anne returned and we were then asked to reveal who we thought was 'The Weakest Link'. On the word 'Link' we had to pick our boards up and take them to chest height. As the camera came round to us and a red light showed we had to turn our board over and say the name. After all the boards had been turned over Anne selected a couple of people to have some banter with.

This process was repeated for each round. Unfortunately, I was voted off in the second round and did not get the chance to have any banter with Anne. I believe that this was because my biography was not as juicy as some of the others. I did not have a Black Country accent, one lady who was forty-eight, was married to a man aged sixty-one. The window cleaner was divorced after an affair and was living with somebody else, a lot younger. Another lady did not have time to bother with men, and a young man from Ireland was a Sandwich Artist. Was somebody who had been married for thirty-eight years with two kids and three Grandchildren, comparatively boring or was it because Anne was afraid of me, as I had said in my interviews, I was ready to give Anne as good as I got from her and more. I will never know.

However, somebody did say that I did have a strong personality, and this showed in the auditions and that I would have given Anne a run for her money. I was asked why I did not join a proper police force. I said that I did, on the 05 April 1971....The British Transport Police. There was no answer to that from the enquirer. I was also asked what Anne would pick up on me. I said my weight and the fact that I live in North Wales. The researchers were alerted to the fact that I was ready for the 'Queen of Mean'.

The ditties that Anne says at the end of each round such as....
Who thinks a pair of Knickers are two robbers?
Who is so thick that their luggage would report them missing?
Who is a Michelin Star Moron?
Whose glass is half full and whose head is half empty?
Who is rubbish enough to be collected by the council?
Are written by a script writer for her.

After doing the walk of shame, I was taken to a small room where I was given some water and looked after by a researcher. Shortly afterwards I went to another room where I filmed the post walk of shame interview. Then it was back to the 'green room', for a sandwich lunch and to briefly meet the contestants who were filming the afternoon show. Each show takes two hours to record.

The only people that get to meet Anne Robinson are the ones in the final. It was a very memorable experience.

CHAPTER 31

THE CIVILIAN YEARS AUGUST 2010 – JULY 2011

Encountering rude drawings on the Whiteboard, having tea with Prince William and facing redundancy again

Fresh from my appearance on 'The Weakest Link' I was back at Bangor. Week commencing 23 August 2010 was occupied with partnership meetings and a service for the police vehicle.

One of the meetings was a telephone conference regarding level crossing safety. These types of conferences were becoming more and more popular within the force.

It was a dull late summer's morning on Wednesday 8 September 2010 when I travelled down to Cardiff to meet up with Andy Evans who told me that due to health issues, he would be shortly leaving the force.

I was now the only one left out of the original three Community Partnership Coordinators.

A trip over the border to Chester was made on Thursday 9 September 2010 to meet up with Gary, the new Crimestoppers Coordinator for North Wales and the North West of England.

A Crucial Crew event was held at a High School in Flintshire in early November 2010. I remarked to one of the teachers that the white projection screen was covered in white correction fluid. She informed me that it was to blank out rude slogans that the children had appended. I said to her, pointing at the screen, "Like this penis and testicles in the bottom right hand corner". She just shook her head in horror and reached for the correction fluid.

On Wednesday 1 December 2010 with a full tank of diesel, the new month saw me driving down to Bristol Temple Meads railway station to deliver schools liaison lectures based on the Tadworth model to the Neighbourhood Policing Team. It was then off to Swindon for an overnight stay.

Thursday 2 December 2010, I awoke to thick snow outside my hotel and had to dig the police vehicle out of the parking lot. Fortunately, the main roads were clear, and I was able to attend the Normarsh Junior school at Royal Wootton Bassett, where I was joined by a couple of PCSOs from Bristol, to shadow me. As I headed home the daylight was fading fast. At least the snow had stopped.

The year 2011 opened for me with a few days off in lieu of overtime (TOIL) worked in 2010. Little did I know this was to be the start of my last year with the force as a civilian.

Figure 44 Bill teaching year 7 pupils at St Joseph's High school Wrexham during a Crucial Crew event

I attended the primary school in the remote village of Clee Hill, near Ludlow, on Wednesday 9 February 2011. I used my 'Sat Nav'. On arrival in the village I was informed by the voice of the apparatus that I had arrived at my destination. No school in sight. A chat with one of the locals put me right. It seemed that I was about quarter of a mile from the school. It appeared that all the premises in the village used the same post code.

I booked Thursday 24 February 2011 off as time in lieu, as His Royal Highness Prince William and his future wife Miss Kate Middleton were attending the Lifeboat Station at Trearddur Bay to name our new Lifeboat, an Atlantic 85, *'Hereford Endeavour'* As Chaplain to the station I had a part in the ceremony by reading the Bible Lesson. It was supposed to be a low-key ceremony, but word had got out and it seemed that the whole population turned out. There were television cameras from all over the world. Prior to the naming ceremony I was walking around the outside of the station making sure that things were in place, when I was approached by a Special Branch Officer from the North Wales Police, whom I knew from my days as a warranted officer. He said to me, "Bill, once a police officer, always a police officer. Could you mingle with the crowd and see if there is anyone suspicious or you feel that isn't right?" I did as requested, but no one stood out. Following the ceremony, I met with Prince William who asked about my role with the RNLI and about my work with the BTP. I later had tea and cake with him and Miss Middleton in the crew room.

I travelled up to Carnforth on Tuesday 15 March 2011. The quondam glories of my own school days are long gone. However, in the afternoon I visited the high school in the town to deliver a rail safety talk. This visit brought back memories for me, as this was my old high school. A few things had changed.

I did not tell the liaison teacher that I was 'an old boy' of the school until I arrived. Whilst enjoying a cup of coffee in the staff room, formerly my first form room, the Headteacher came in and introduced himself to me.

He arranged for me to be taken on a tour of the school after my presentation. He asked when I was at the school, I told him the years that I was there. A few moments later he came back with a panoramic photograph of the pupils from 1964. I found myself on the photo and identified myself to him. He said with a smile "I'm glad you are there otherwise; it would have been five hundred lines in retrospect!". In my school days I ran the school's railway club and had a habit of going down to the station in the dinner break to collect the British Transport Films that we had ordered. More often than not, I was late back, sometimes arriving back by the skin of my teeth. The teachers knew where I had been, it was always extra homework.

In the evening it was to the Carnforth Station Heritage Centre to present an illustrated talk on the work of the force. I met a few people whom I had not seen for several years.

After an overnight stay in Carnforth it was off to London for an overnight stay on Wednesday 16 March 2011.

The following day, Thursday 17 March 2011, I attended the Railway Safety Standards Board Annual Conference at their offices in central London.

The start of the new week saw me travelling to Ysgol Pen y Cae Wrexham to speak to the infants and juniors on Monday 21 March 2011. On my visits it was customary to get to know the pupils a little better, so I usually ask a couple of them where they are from. I said to one pupil "Where do you live?" to which he replied "Portugal". I said, "Where in Wrexham is that?" He replied, "Its abroad mister". I said, "I bet you have to be up really early to catch the bus?" The teacher said to him "You don't live there, you live in Churchill Drive (name changed), Wrexham". He replied "Yes, I know miss, but Portugal is much nicer!"

I visited a primary school in Shrewsbury, and the headteacher invited me into her office to have a cup of tea before the lessons started. I remarked that her accent was more northern than midlands. She informed me that she was from Manchester originally but returned frequently with her husband after school on a Friday for the weekend. She went onto say that the Senior Citizens Railcard she held came in very handy. I said to her, "Madam surely, you are defrauding the railway?" She said very sternly, "I've never defrauded anyone in my life!" Then she realised that I was being polite to her and she said, "Sadly no one ever asks me for proof of age".

The working week ended on Friday 8 April 2011 on a sad note for me. I visited Aberconwy High School, Conwy for a Crucial Crew event. As I was leaving, I received a telephone call from the Area Inspector, Dai Davies, who asked me to meet him at Llandudno Junction Station. I could tell by the tone of his voice all was not well. On arrival at the Junction Station I met up with Dai and he told me that my contract was not being renewed in July and therefore I was being made redundant. The news came as a bit of a shock at first, but by the time July came around, I would have had nearly six years with the force, four more than I was originally contracted to.

The first meeting of my redundancy took place in Shrewsbury with Chief Inspector Sandra England from Cardiff and a representative of Transport and Salaried Staff Association (TSSA), who represented me to make sure that I received a fair deal. I did not expect anything less. Friday 22 July 2011 was to be my last day with the force.

With my suitcase duly packed I travelled down to Bristol on Tuesday 26 April 2011 to deliver a presentation on the work of the force to the Bristol branch of the West Somerset Railway Association. I was accompanied by retired PC Bob Edwardes and serving Sergeant Mark Harris. I gave an overview of the history of the force. Bob spoke about his career in the force and Mark gave an overview of the modern day BTP. Following this, a letter of appreciation was received from the association.

I set off reasonably early on Tuesday 10 May 2011 to travel to Nesscliff Army camp for a meeting of the forthcoming Crucial Crew event in June.

Following this visit I took time off in lieu and annual leave otherwise I would have lost it.

Returning to work on Tuesday 24 May 2011 I travelled to Shrewsbury for two redundancy meetings with Chief Inspector Sandra England and the TSSA representative.

As I had a school visit the next day I stayed overnight in Shrewsbury. The overnight accommodation was at the Prince Rupert Hotel, in the very heart of medieval Shrewsbury town centre. It is reputed to date back to the 12 century. I was allocated a very pleasant, but small room.

The next morning, Wednesday 25 May 2011 as I was checking out, the receptionist asked if everything was alright with my stay. I told her that it was and had no complaints. She again asked me, and I assured her that everything was perfect. Jokingly I said, "I was awoken at three am this morning by an irate man who was banging on my door. I told him that it was a good job that I was still up playing my bagpipes!" I said my goodbyes.

It was not until March 2015 when I was at home recovering from a left hip replacement, when I was watching 'Britain's Most Haunted' on the television, and the room I had stayed in at the Prince Rupert was featured. It was reputed to be haunted and a couple of guests were interviewed about their ghostly encounters in the room.

The week started off on Monday 20 June 2011, as I travelled to Shrewsbury for another redundancy meeting with Chief Inspector England from Cardiff.

Due to my impending redundancy, I resigned from the Crimestoppers Board, as I felt that I would not be able to continue to give them the service they deserved, post July. I received a nice letter of thanks along with a framed certificate of thanks. from the Chief Executive, Michael Laurie CBE, recognising the time and effort that I had put in, often flying a lone flag for the charity in North Wales,

On Tuesday 12 July 2011 it was off to a Crucial Crew event at Dyffryn Nantlle High School, Penygroes near Caernarfon. This was the very first time during my time in North Wales that I had been to the school and it was also my last Crucial Crew visit.

My final school was on Wednesday 13 July 2011 when I set off to Hawarden High School, Deeside, Flintshire to speak to the year seven pupils about rail safety. On the way back the words of a Frank Sinatra song came into my head *'...and now the end is near....'*

On arrival back at the office I hung up my car keys, my 'chalk and mortarboard' and said my goodbyes to the staff. For the rest of the time, I was taking time off in lieu and annual leave. I had a drink with the lads at a local pub before riding off into the sunset.

Saturday 23 July 2011 I was no longer employed by the force, but eligible for a second pension from them.

When I first re-joined the force in 2005, I was only supposed to visit the six counties of North Wales and the County of Powys. Over the years, my travels took me to South Wales, Shropshire, Worcestershire, Staffordshire, Cheshire, Warwickshire, the West Midlands, Leicestershire, Nottinghamshire, Lancashire, Derbyshire, Merseyside, Greater Manchester, Gloucestershire, Somerset, Wiltshire, London, Devon and Cornwall. I estimated that I drove around one hundred and eighty thousand miles up and down the country and travelled a few thousand more miles by train.

It was a lonely life on the road. I had the radio for company and was able to take advantage of the national and local traffic information promulgated across the airwaves. Being forewarned of traffic hold ups I was able to make use of 'rat runs'. I had driven in all types of weather, sunny, cloudy, hailstones, rain, thunder and lightning, snow blizzards, dense fog, you name it I drove in and through it.

Some of my journeys entailed early starts, some days I was up before the milkman, before Terry Wogan was in the shower and the proverbial lark was up and flying around.

I stopped in a variety of hotels and guest houses for my overnight stays. At some of the hotels I was upgraded to the executives suite. For the showers in some of the accommodation you needed a PHD in plumbing to be able to work them.

My time as a civilian with the force was extremely rewarding, visiting the schools and other education establishments. On arrival at the schools, I was always greeted with a welcome cup of coffee or tea, and on some occasions there was even a bacon sandwich on offer. At break time there was always a cup of coffee or tea on offer with a biscuit or two. At some schools there was always a copious supply of beverages throughout the day. I even managed to sample some school dinners. I must say that they have improved vastly since I was at school.

I also visited Brownies, Guides, Cubs and Scout groups. I used to tell the Scouts that I was a Scout. In those days we wore a beret and a 'Baden Powell' (very similar to what the Mounties of the Royal Canadian Mounted Police wear). We also used to carry a dagger around with us. Nobody blinked an eyelid at us, nowadays we would be locked up. Sad world.

I had a great satisfaction that I had been doing a worthwhile job educating children in rail safety. Liaising with the relevant authorities to make the railway environment safer for all who worked on it and used it.

For my efforts I was rewarded with numerous letters of appreciation from the schools, the force and the partnerships. During my six years back with the force, apart from annual leave and TOIL, I was gainfully employed visiting schools, partnership meetings and exhibitions. I am proud to have made a small but significant contribution.

Little was I to know that I was to return to the force later that year.

CHAPTER 32

THE VOLUNTARY YEARS 2011 – 2015

Returning for a third career with the force. A third visit to Buckingham Palace. Becoming an author.

This chapter deals with my early voluntary years with the force mainly visiting schools. It seemed very strange going back to the force for third career. Most of my visits were in connection with Crucial Crew events, something which I enjoy doing. I get a great deal of satisfaction from them, interacting with the pupils.

Also, I have visited a couple of primary schools when a special request has been made for me to visit the school by the Headteacher. I soon gained the nickname of *'The boomerang'*.

My first school visit as a volunteer was to Fflint High School for a Crucial Crew event on Halloween, Monday 31 October 2011. This was followed by a few more during the month of November to the high schools in Flintshire.

The New Year of 2012 started off the same as previous January's with visits to the high schools in Wrexham for Crucial Crew events. The force allowed me the use of the unmarked police vehicle at Bangor for my visits.

Due to my expertise with special needs and pupils with behavioural problems, I was persuaded to attend Y Wyddfid special needs school, Llandudno, on Thursday 2 February 2012 to speak to a group of children with behavioural problems.

Later that month on Thursday 23 February 2012 I was asked to attend a similar school near Conwy. The evening of the following day saw me in Rhyl teaching the local cubs railway safety.

In April 2012, to celebrate our Ruby Wedding anniversary, Shirley and I treated ourselves to a well-deserved trip on the Orient Express from London Victoria to Venice.

Whilst in the lounge car of the train, my police instinct came to the fore. It was great watching people pass through, I was wondering who the spy was, who could qualify as a 'murderer'. Were this couple having an illicit affair? What was the occupation of this person? Was he an accountant, if so, he could tell me about his job, which would help me get to sleep at night? Was Hercule Poirot about to appear?

Figure 45 Bill relaxing on board the Orient Express

Figure 46 Bill and Shirley ready for dinner on the Orient Express

The Member of Parliament for Ynys Môn, Albert Owen, very kindly sponsored two visits to the Houses of Parliament for members of the History Group.

I travelled down to London for the visits to meet the participants and these were undertaken on Monday 24 September 2012 and Tuesday 25 September 2012. The guide was ex BTP officer, PC Kevin Gordon.

It is surprising what you learn about your family. In May 2013 Shirley and I went on a cruise and land tour in Alaska. Prior to boarding the ship in Vancouver, we had dinner with a cousin of mine, Bob, who lives there. Over dinner we discussed the arrest of a British fugitive, in Spain, which had been featured on the news that evening. This in turn led to the mention of Ronnie Biggs from the Great Train Robbery, which was fifty years ago in 1963, and how he was at large for so long.

Bob quite casually said, "I was involved in the Great Train Robbery." After being careful not to spill my pint of Canadian beer, which I was enjoying after a long flight from Manchester, I thought, was I going to get a belated cough! After all he emigrated in 1964. What was the number of the local Mounties? Could I make a lawful arrest?

Then he quickly clarified that he was a witness for the prosecution at the subsequent court hearing. At the time of the robbery, Bob was a young bank clerk with the National and Provincial Bank in Leicester. A couple of days before the robbery he had bundled up some notes for disposal and had signed the wrappers on the bundles. These notes were part of the proceeds of the robbery found at the farmhouse. Little did he know that these notes were to be part of history.

As I was a volunteer and driving a force vehicle, I had to undergo a driving assessment on Tuesday 30 July 2013, in the Shrewsbury area, which I passed with flying colours.

In between my Crucial Crew events during the month of October I found time on Tuesday 15 October 2013 to travel over to Peterborough to deliver a talk to the local branch of the U3A on the history of the force on behalf of the History Group.

On Friday 1 November 2013 Shirley and I attended a ceremony in Birmingham where I was presented with the recognition of Community Volunteer of the Year for the Wales and Western Area in respect of the hard work I had carried out in 2012 / 2013 on behalf of the British Transport Police.

In late February 2014 I received a letter informing me that I had been nominated as a contender for Community Volunteer of the Year in the forthcoming Complimentary Policing Awards in London.

Shirley and I attended the ceremony in London during the evening of Monday 24 March 2014. The nomination citations were read after which the host said, "And the winner is......Bill Rogerson, Wales and Western Area". I was deeply humbled and honoured to receive this award.

Figure 47 Bill receiving the Volunteer of the Year award from Assistant Chief Constable Alan Pacey

A different kind of message was delivered on Wednesday 30 April 2014 where I had to attend Ysgol Dinas Bran School, Llangollen to talk about 'Careers with the British Transport Police' to the School's sixth form.

The rest of the year leading up to November was taken up with Crucial Crew events in the North Wales high schools.

2014 was the centenary year since the start of the Great War. Myself, Phil White, Glyn Thomas, Viv Head, Ed Thompson, Rob Davison and Martin Lambert, members of the History Group committee set out on Tuesday 2 December 2014 to take part in the nightly ceremony at the Menin Gate in Ypres. We were intent on laying wreaths to commemorate the one hundred and thirty-four railway and dock police officers who gave their lives in the conflict and to visit some of the memorials and battlefields in the surrounding Flemish Fields.

It was an enlightening and rewarding journey that left a mark on all of us. Inspired by the 'WIPERS TIMES' newspaper printed in the trenches. Viv Head our then Chairman, wrote the following article for the Group' 'WIPERS LINES' special newsletter.

Great Railway Journeys

We came from all parts of the country to meet at St Pancras International at 10am on Tuesday 2 of December 2014. Bill Rogerson came from Holyhead and Rob Davison from across the Irish Sea - both had set out the day before. Others began their day early to make the rendezvous on time. One, Ed Thompson, who had the shortest distance of all to travel, nearly didn't make it.

With some mechanical apparatus tearing up the track bed, his train ground to a halt on the outskirts of south-east London to go no further. But with some fortitude and a willingness to fork out £25 for a taxi fare, make it he did.

Eurostar carried us safely and swiftly to Lille International in France where a short walk brought us to Lille Flanders station for the first of our two connecting trains to Ypres in Belgium. It was cancelled. We discussed the alternatives- a bus, two taxis, hiring a car... We did the sensible thing and retired to the nearest hostelry for refreshments to await the next train in 90 minutes or so.

After that there were no further hitches and at the Regina Hotel in Ypres, we met up with Martin Lambert a serving BTP officer (and member of the History Group), who has been guiding battlefield tours for ten years. As we would soon find out, his knowledge and expertise were invaluable. We retired to a nearby restaurant to discuss tactics.

There were no cancellations on the return journey but there were one or two little blips... Our advertised departure from Ypres, just before noon, was only going to go halfway and from then on it was a bus. We retired to the station bar to await the next direct train service in an hour. It was plain sailing then all the way to Lille International. The check-in gate was not yet open and so we retired to O'Conways, the ubiquitous Irish bar, to wait.... (Do you detect a theme here?)

Three pints of Guinness and three pints of Kilkenny s'il vous plait. Oh yes and six cheeseburgers avec frites. The beer came in good time but then suddenly the air was rent by a strident alarm and an insistent recorded irritating female voice urging us to evacuate the building immediately.

Lille International is a big complex and people streamed out of every available exit. We waited in the cold on a high bridge above the station; there was not an official in sight. Soon the alarm stopped but who will say if we can return? The beer was still sitting where we had left it and the cheeseburgers turned up in time. The word according to the waitress was that it was a fire alarm test. What!!!

Menin Gate

The first thing you notice about Ypres is what a beautiful place it is with many fine buildings and cobbled streets. Even more remarkable is when you remember that the whole place was flattened in the 1914-18 war and that it has been painstakingly rebuilt with traditional methods. The cathedral and the cloth hall look as though they have been there for centuries.

There has been a service of Remembrance at the Menin Gate every night since 1st November 1929 with the exception only of four years during WW2. The Memorial Arch that is now the Menin Gate was completed in 1927 and it is a truly magnificent building, especially when lit up at night.

It was said to be a rather quiet service that evening with only a couple of hundred people gathered. It began with a reading and a profile of one of the soldiers who died on the battlefield nearby. As always, a bugler from the Ypres fire brigade sounded the last post.

One of the brigade buglers is 83 years old and has played the last post for 60 years only missing it twice. Bill Rogerson was privileged to have been selected by the Last Post Marshall to read the Exhortation, He stood in the centre of the road and his voice boomed out amongst the assembled crowd –

They shall grow not old, as we that are left grow old: Age shall not weary them, nor the years condemn. At the going down of the sun and in the morning, we will remember them.

We seven men stood beneath the gate with heads bowed as the crowd hushed for the minute's silence.

Then it was time to lay the wreaths, first were a group of four young children, perhaps eleven-year olds, from Peterhouse Primary School. And a good job they did of it too. Six of us formed two ranks of three; Bill Rogerson, Rob Davison and Phil White laid the wreath on behalf of the British Transport Police and Viv Head, Glyn Thomas and Martin Lambert laid the wreath on behalf the British Transport Police History Group. We marched across the central roadway and climbed the steps to lay the wreaths.

After the ceremony, we searched through the fifty-four thousand names listed on the panels to locate four railway police officers with no known grave. Martin Lambert had taken it upon himself to bring a number of small wooden crosses, one for each man and each bearing the force crest and inscribed with name of the individual. He placed these at the foot of the corresponding panel.

In February 2015 I was again nominated in the force complimentary policing awards as Volunteer of the Year. The citation was read to the assembled guests and read

'Bill was nominated for this award last year, and due to his outstanding contribution to BTP as a volunteer, he and his colleagues were delighted when he was successful. It is no accident that he has been nominated again this year, as his commitment has not changed, or his effort slowed down.

Bill served as a police officer with British Transport Police completing an exemplary 30 years of service, retiring on 22/09/2001. Having retired he returned to work for the organisation as a School Liaison Officer. Sadly, funding ran out for this role, but this did not deter Bill, who returned to his role as an unpaid volunteer. This is Bill's 3rd year of that voluntary work, and the passion in his work remains as strong as ever.

Bill has given up 261 hours during 2013 and is now developing others, such as PCSOs by taking them on his school visits, promoting further community contacts and introducing a new generation of BTP staff across the area. This will provide a lasting legacy to his work to ensure this continues well beyond Bill's time with BTP – although we sincerely hope he will stay with us for some time yet!'

I was not successful, but it was great to be recognised and nominated once again for my work.

At the beginning of March 2015 in the Divisional Complementary Policing awards I received a certificate thanking me for the valuable contribution I made in supporting the British Transport Police to achieve the force objectives for 2014.

On Friday 20 March 2015 I entered hospital as a patient for the first time in fifty-eight years to have a left hip replacement. This left me grounded for a couple of months.

The previous year, in Her Majesty's Birthday Honours List, it was announced that Shirley had been awarded the British Empire Medal (BEM) for services to the RNLI, local charities and the community of Valley.

On Tuesday 12 May 2015 we attended a Garden Party at Buckingham Palace to celebrate her honour.

In early June of 2015, Mike Layton an avid writer of police related books rang me with a proposition. I arranged to meet him for lunch in Birmingham on Monday 15 June 2015. He mentioned that no one had ever written a book about the history of the British Transport Police dog section and that he was seriously considering writing a book on the subject and invited me to be the co-author.

I had only ever written a couple of articles for magazines and a couple of editorials. I returned home chewing the proposition over on the train. The following day I gave him my answer, yes, I was up to the challenge and I immediately set about contacting current and ex dog handlers from the force. My research took me to Manchester, Crewe and the National Railway Museum in York. I also read many books and magazines relating to the dog section.

I was in contact with Mike virtually every day. The wonders of email. Goodness knows how we would have managed without it.

The end result was a 287-page book, *'Police Dog Heroes'*, which was published in 2016. Writing this book was certainly an eye opener. I didn't realise how much work went into writing a book. It certainly gave a me a flavour to write this book you are reading.

Little did I know that in 1971 when I first acted as a stooge for the dog section as a young Police Constable in Birmingham, that I would be doing it again some forty-four years later as a force volunteer in London playing the part of a terrorist.

At 09.00 hours on Thursday 3 September 2015 I along with four other volunteers had the privilege to join PC Will Atkinson a Dog Trainer, and PCs Rob Smith and his dog 'Bruno' a yellow Labrador, and Pete Beal and his dog 'Bobby' a black Labrador in a four-hour explosives detection training exercise on the main concourse at London St Pancras International Railway Station. As well as dealing with domestic services, in 2007 it became the London Station for the Eurostar services to Paris and Brussels and beyond.

This was an ideal location due to the importance of the station and the diverse number of people using the station to and from the continent. The exercise concluded on the concourse of the neighbouring Kings Cross Railway Station, which was thronging with people.

For security reasons I cannot divulge the full details of the exercise, except to say that under the supervision of the expert eye of PC Will Atkinson it was used to hone the skills of these two, four legged 'Sherlock Holmes's', and as part of their Home Office licensing.

Each time the dog made a successful indication he was rewarded with a tennis ball and there were plenty of tennis balls being handed out at the two stations.

Following the closure of our training school at Tadworth in 2010 a housing developer built some houses on the site. The History Group successfully applied for a Blue Plaque to be placed on the development.

On the late morning of Wednesday 28 October 2015, I along with some other members of the History Group committee attended the unveiling of the plaque, followed by a sandwich and a pint at the nearby pub, 'The Blue Ball', which used to be frequented by BTP and Met officers on a regular basis. Apart from our group there was only about three other people in the pub. The landlord informed us that since the BTP had vacated the school, business was quiet in the evenings and he only opened on selected lunch times. In fact, (tongue-in cheek) he was thinking of suing the Chief Constable for lack of business! 'The Blue Ball' could certainly tell a tale or two.

Figure 48 Bill with members of the British Transport Police History Group on the occasion of the erection of the blue plaque at the former training school Tadworth

CHAPTER 33

THE VOLUNTARY YEARS 2016 – 2020

Working with the sniffer dogs - playing the terrorist

I know it's an old cliché, they say as you get older the years come and go around very quickly 2016 came around very quickly.

During the month of January I braved the winter weather to visit a few schools in the Wrexham area for Crucial Crew events.

At the expense of the force, on Friday 4 March 2016, Shirley and I travelled to Birmingham to attend an awards ceremony on Saturday 5 March 2016, as I had again been nominated for a complimentary policing award. I was unsuccessful but received a nomination certificate and enjoyed a nice buffet provided by the force.

Figure 49 Bill receiving a volunteer nomination certificate from Chief Superintendent Peter Holden

A Social Science fair was held at Bangor University on Wednesday 16 March 2016 and the force had an information stand with a couple of representatives from Force Headquarters and I was asked to go along to assist them. It was a remarkably interesting day speaking to the students. I got a lot of enjoyment from it explaining about the force and about my careers with them.

Saturday 23 July 2016, I joined some members of the South Wales branch of the International Police Association for a trip up Mount Snowdon. The weather was typical at the top, rain and misty.

Following the successful publication of *'Police Dog Heroes'*, Mike Layton who had written a book with Alan Pacey an ex Assistant Chief Constable of the BTP - *'Tracking the Hooligans'* to which I had contributed some anecdotes and was published in early 2016, contacted me again. He wanted to write a follow up book.

I gave the project some thought and decided to assist him as I had enjoyed writing and researching *'Police Dog Heroes'*. I set about carrying out a lot of research including a visit to the National Railway Museum in York. The result was that a book entitled *'The Hooligans Are Still Among Us'* was published in 2017. This book that you are reading had to go on the back burner.

The BTP police station at Ebbsfleet, Kent was the venue for a History Group Committee meeting on Thursday 29 September 2016.

A talk to the U3A in Trearddur Bay on the history of the force, on behalf of the History Group was undertaken on Friday 18 November 2016.

I had a surprise on 1 December 2016, as I was made a British Transport Police History Group, History Writer, for my contributions to the History Group. There have been several people who have made a significant and valuable contribution towards documenting BTP history, often over a period of years. The History Group believes it appropriate to recognise these contributions by conferring on them the informal title of 'BTP History Writer'. This is intended as a simple recognition of good work done.

Thursday 5 January 2017 it was off to Liverpool for the British Transport Police North West Retired Personnel lunch. These lunches are held three times a year usually in January, April and October and are organised by retired Inspector Frank Loftus. I try and go as often as I can, and on some occasions, Frank allows me a spot after lunch to promote the History Group.

A break from the normal Crucial Crew events was the order of the day on Friday 31 March 2017. There was a proposal to run a Eurostar service from London St Pancras to Amsterdam and as such the security services from Britain and the Netherlands wanted to carry out some sniffer dog training on a train. I and other volunteers from the force, with 'suspicious items', sat on a stationary Javelin High Speed Train at St Pancras and played the part of passengers, whilst the dogs did their training under the supervision of the BTP Dog Section.

Tuesday 6 June 2017 I received a certificate for valuable contribution made to the British Transport Police which was recognised during national volunteer's week 1 June to 07 June 2017.

On Wednesday 11 October 2017, I attended the Annual General Meeting of the North Wales Branch of the International Police Association in Conwy.

I travelled to Newcastle Upon Tyne on Thursday 14 November 2017 to present an illustrated talk on the History of the force on behalf of the History Group, to the local branch of the Railway Correspondence and Travel Society (RCTS).

A History Group Committee Meeting was held at the Sub-Divisional Police Headquarters, Birmingham on Wednesday 13 December 2017.

The New Year of 2018 started off as usual with a trip in early January to Liverpool for the North West Retired Personnel lunch.

The rest of the month was taken up with Crucial Crew visits to the high schools in Wrexham. This year I decided to stay over for a few nights. This gave me the chance to go and have a pint with Pete Morris one of my retired officers from Holyhead. I also visited my son's, in laws who live in Wrexham and my cousin who lives in Ellesmere.

The History Group Annual General Meeting is always held on the last Monday or penultimate Monday of March followed the next day by a committee meeting in Birmingham. This year the AGM was held on Monday 26 March 2018 with the committee meeting being held on Tuesday 27 March 2018. We usually have two face-to-face committee meetings a year with other business being conducted by email.

I was the guest speaker at the BTP North West Retired Personnel lunch in Liverpool on Thursday 12 April 2018. Not only did I speak about the History Group, but I regaled the sixty or so members with some anecdotes from my careers with the force.

The North Wales branch of the International Police Association was in danger of closing due to the lack of committee members. To save it from closure I volunteered my services as Chairman and was accepted. A couple more members came forward and we were able to form an executive committee to save the branch of the IPA from extinction.

For more years than I care to remember I was always invited to Pendorlan Primary School in Colwyn Bay to deliver rail safety talks as part of the healthy schools week. Wednesday 27 June 2018 saw me attending my annual visit to the school. It is a friendly school and I always receive a warm welcome and this year was no exception.

In April 2018 Denis Hunt Secretary of No 4 Region Wales and acting secretary of the North Wales IPA Branch received an International Police Association Travel Form from Ghiora Szabo a retired police officer from Israel, stating that in late July and early August he would be on a round Britain cruise on the *'Brilliance of the Seas'* which was due to dock in Holyhead on Friday 3 August 2018. He requested that the only assistance he required was for him and his wife Miriam to visit the town of Holyhead.

The form was forwarded to myself, in my capacity as branch chair of the North Wales section and I agreed to contact Ghiora prior to his visit to Holyhead and kept in regular contact with him until the ship docked at Holyhead.

Friday 3 August 2018, following weeks of glorious sunshine in Holyhead, it was a typical Welsh rainy day when we met. The first stop was a local cafe for a coffee and an exchange of IPA and British Transport Police memorabilia along with typical souvenirs from our respective countries.

I discovered that Ghiora who was now approaching 80 years young and Miriam are both from Romania but left the country in 1965 when Ghiora was 26, due to the troubles in that country. They moved to Israel where Ghiora joined the police force.

Obviously, Ghiora spoke Romanian, and Hebrew. He also spoke Hungarian and Spanish, fluently. He had a broken command of the English language, French and German.

Communication was difficult, there was no doubting that, but with the aid of a translation app on my mobile phone, the language barrier was broken down a little. Ghiora stated that he had served for thirty years as a police officer in Israel, which he said was remarkable as the life expectancy for a police officer was a lot less than that. It transpired that he was a rank equivalent of our Inspector and he also served as a firearms instructor. He served for most of his career in the city of Karmiel about fifty-four kilometres north-west of the port of Haifa.

He joined the IPA Israel Section on the 1 January 1969 and has been a continuous member ever since. He travels widely around the world and wherever he goes he contacts IPA members. His hobby is artistic photography.

After the meet and greet I showed them around the port town of Holyhead and St Cybi's Church. Lunch was taken in a local café after which I took them to my house for tea and biscuits and to meet Shirley and my two granddaughters. Sadly, it was time for Ghiora and Miriam to return to ship and I took them back to Holyhead via a scenic route taking in Trearddur Bay and South Stack. On arrival back in Holyhead it was time for one last look at St Cybi's Church and finally back to the town's railway station where they caught the shuttle bus back to the ship.

It was indeed a memorable day of international friendship and one to be remembered for a long time to come.

Earlier in the year on behalf of the History Group, I had been invited to be the guest speaker on the history of the force, at the Chipping Norton Railway Society meeting in the beautiful Cotswolds on the evening of Tuesday 4 September 2018. As it was such a long way, Shirley and I decided to make a week's holiday in the area.

After several years, I resurrected the ex-Holyhead Officers reunion at the Trearddur Bay Hotel, and we all met on the afternoon and evening of Friday 12 October 2018. This year colleagues from the North Wales Police were invited. A convivial time was had by all. In typical police style I was the first to arrive and the last to leave.

The evening of Wednesday 16 January 2019 I chaired the Annual General meeting of the North Wales branch of the International Police Association. I was re-elected as Chairman.

A trip to London to meet up with Glyn Thomas was the order of the day on Monday 28 January 2019 for an afternoon meeting with the interim Chief Executive of the British Transport Police Authority to discuss the History Group. The meeting was very productive.

The new month of February 2019 began for me on the evening of Friday 1 February 2019 with me as guest speaker for the History Group on the history of the force, at the Lakes and Lune branch of the Railway Correspondence and Travel Society (RCTS) meeting at the Royal Station Hotel, Carnforth.

Sunday 24 March 2019 I was in Aberystwyth Police station for a regional meeting of the International Police Association. After this meeting it was straight to Birmingham for an overnight stay, prior to the History Group Annual General meeting on Monday 25 March 2019 and a committee meeting on Tuesday 26 March 2019.

Carl Foulkes the new Chief Constable of the North Wales Police and an ex British Transport Police officer agreed to be the Patron of the North Wales Branch of the International Police Association. On Friday 24 May 2019 along with David Moore the branch treasurer, I attended the North Wales Police Headquarters to present him with his patron's certificate and other memorabilia.

Due to the indisposition of the Wales Regional Chair of the International Police Association I was invited to represent the region along with Denis Hunt the Regional Secretary at the Annual National Council Meeting at Coombe Abbey, near Coventry, between Friday 7 June 2019 and Sunday 9 June 2019. It was pleasing to see that Martin Turner a BTP Inspector from Milton Keynes was elected at the meeting as a Vice President of the Association.

The rest of the year was taken up with History Group activities along with the publication of History Lines and school visits.

In January and February 2020 my usual visits to some of the Wrexham schools for Crucial Crew were undertaken. On Friday 28 February 2020, I visited Ruabon High School for a Crucial Crew event. When I left in the snow, I was unaware it would be my last such outing for some time. Before my next booked visit in March 2020, the school visits were brought to an abrupt halt by the restrictions imposed by the terrible COVID-19 (Coronavirus) outbreak.

However, I was able to continue my History Group work from my desk in my study. The Annual General Meeting and subsequent committee meeting scheduled for March were cancelled, although we were able to conduct essential business via email.

I have got to the stage where I have been teaching the grandchildren of the children that I taught years ago. Some of the police officers I have worked with recently were not even born when I joined.

I have often been asked what I fear. Two things spring to mind, snakes and school dinner ladies. Over the years I have visited many schools indeed and have encountered some very formidable school dinner ladies. I was in one primary school for a late morning slot and as I was in the hall for the lesson the teacher asked me to finish my lesson at 11.57 hours come what may. I thought this is a funny time. She explained that the hall doubles up as the school dining room and the dinner ladies come in at 11.58 hours precisely to set up the chairs and tables for the pupils and woe betide if you are a second over your time. Sure, enough as I was finishing at 11.55 hours to be on the safe side, I saw two of them by the door like members of the All Blacks Rugby team ready to perform the haka before a match.

Another question I was repeatedly asked by children was if I have ever shot anyone, to which I tell them that I have not, but have used a gun on the police firing ranges in Amsterdam and Surrey.

I am often asked, when did I join the British Transport Police and I tell them that it was in 1971. You can see their brains working overtime to work out how old I am. One lad said to me "You must be very old mister".

I have estimated that since I began teaching railway safety to children in 1979, I have spoken to over one million young persons. It was all very worthwhile.

I do hope that you have enjoyed the book. It would be appreciated if you could leave a review good or bad on Amazon. Many thanks indeed.

Bill Rogerson 2021

ACKNOWLEDGEMENTS

Members of the British Transport Police History Group
Serving and retired colleagues from the British Transport Police
Serving and retired colleagues from the provincial police forces.
Serving and retired colleagues from the railway industry
Members of the Royal National Lifeboat Institution
Retired officers of the Metropolitan Police
Michael Layton QPM retired Chief Superintendent, for his guidance and encouragement
Gareth Huws retired schoolteacher for assisting with the part of the proof reading
Shirley Rogerson BEM for assisting with the proof reading
Joan Stockdale retired journalist
First North Western Trains
Arriva Trains Wales
Larry Davies retired Chief Superintendent North Wales Police and Community Rail Officer Conwy County Council
Trefor Edwards retired Superintendent North Wales Police
The late Gwyn Roberts photographer
Kevin Gordon retired British Transport Police Officer
Steve Burrows for the publishing work and advice

ABBREVIATIONS

AA	Automobile Association
AGM	Annual General Meeting
AHQ	Area Headquarters
ARU	Armed Response Unit
ASAP	As soon as possible
ASLEF	The Associated Society of Locomotive Engineers and Firemen
BBC	British Broadcasting Corporation
BEM	British Empire Medal
BRSA	British Railways Staff Association Club
BTP	British Transport Police
CBE	Commander of the Order of the British Empire
CBIM	Companion of British Institute of Management
CCTV	Close Circuit Television
CIA	Central Intelligence Agency (America)
CID	Criminal Investigation Department
CND	Campaign for Nuclear Disarmament
COC1	A department within New Scotland Yard
CPS	Crown Prosecution Service
DC	Detective Constable
DCI	Detective Chief Inspector
DHQ	Divisional Headquarters
DI	Detective Inspector
DMU	Diesel Multiple Unit
Dr.	Doctor
DS	Detective Sergeant
EBD	Ethylene Dibromide
FA	Football Association
FHQ	Force Headquarters
FSA	Food Standards Agency
GP	General Practitioner
HALF BLUES	Wearing a civilian jacket over the police uniform
HGV	Heavy Goods Vehicle
IPA	International Police Association
IRA	Irish Republican Army
IT	Information Technology
ITV	Independent Television
JAG	Joint Objectives Group
KC	King's Counsel
KGB	Komitet Gosudarstvennoy Bezopasnosti, Committee for State Security

MASH	Mobile Army Surgical Hospital
MBE	Member of the Order of the British Empire
MP	Member of Parliament
MSU	Mobile Support Unit
MV	Motor Vessel
NARBTPO	National Association of Retired British Transport Police Officers
NARPO	National Association of Retired Police Officers
NATO	Name, Age, Town, Occupation
NPT	Neighbourhood Policing Team
NSPCC	National society for the Prevention of Cruelty to Children
OIC	Officer in Charge
PACE	Police and Criminal Evidence Act 1984
PC	Police Constable
PCSO	Police Community Support Officer
PhD	Doctor of Philosophy
PINS	Police Information System.
PNC	Police National Computer
PSHE	Personal, Social and Health Education
QPM	Queen's Police Medal
RAF	Royal Air Force
RCTS	Railway Correspondence and Travel Society
RMT	The National Union of Rail, Maritime and Transport Workers
RNLI	Royal National Lifeboat Institution
RUCC	Rail Users Consultative Committee
SLO	Schools Liaison Officer
SOCO	Scenes of Crimes Officer
TOC	Train Operating Company
TOIL	Time of in Lieu
TPO	Travelling Post Office
TSSA	Transport Salaried Staff Association
TUC	Trades Union Congress
TUCC	Travel Users Consultative Committee
UEFA	Union of European Football Associations
USA	United States of America
USSR	Union of Soviet Socialist Republics
VHS	Video Home System
VSS	Victim Support Scheme
WAAF	Women's Auxiliary Air Force
WACSO	Wales Association of Community Support Officers
YMCA	Young Men's Christian Association
YOTS	Youth Offending Team

BIBLIOGRAPHY

Westmorland County Records
Cumbria County Council Records Office, Kendal
Mallerstang – A Westmorland Dale by Mary M. Thompson
British Transport Police Journals
The Blue Line
The London Police Pensioner magazine
Level Crossings, by Stanley Hall and Peter Van Der Mark
British Transport Police Wipers Lines edited by Viv Head
The Archives of the Metropolitan Policewomen's Association.
Wikipedia – various articles
Police Dog Heroes by Michael Layton and Bill Rogerson
The Hooligans are still among us by Michael Layton and Bill Rogerson
Holyhead and Anglesey Mail
Daily Post (North Wales) edition
Bangor and Anglesey Chronicle
Focus North West
Wipers Lines
Murder in Mind from the Marshall Cavendish Reference Collection
A Regional History of the Railways of Great Britain. Volume 11 North and Mid
Wales by Peter E Baughan. Published by David St John Thomas
The British Transport Police History Group website
Chester and Holyhead Railway published by David and Charles
The House of Lords Records Office
The Public Records Office Kew

PHOTOGRAPH ACKNOWLEDGEMENTS

Author: Figs 1,5,9,10,11,12,17,18,19,22,30,32,39,40,41,44,45,46,48
British Transport Police: Figs 3,4,20,23,24,25,47,49
The late Gwyn Roberts: Figs 28,35,36,37,38
Larry Davies: Figs 13,31,33,34
First North Western Trains: Figs 14,15,16
Home Office: Fig 2
John Cave: Fig 6
Norman Kneal: Fig 7 (& Cover photo)
Railtrack: Fig 21
Tanis Morrey: Fig 27 (& Cover Photo)
Hope House: Fig 43
Member of Tadworth Civilian Staff: Fig 26
Unknown: Fig 8 (& Cover Photo), 29,42